C000257281

THI

Julia Copus has published four collections of poetry, including *The World's Two Smallest Humans* (2012), shortlisted for the T. S. Eliot Prize and the Costa Poetry Award, and *Girlhood* (2019), winner of the inaugural Derek Walcott Prize for Poetry.

Charlotte Mew (1869–1928) was an English poet and short-story writer. Born in Bloomsbury into a middle-class Victorian family, her work was published and admired in both the UK and America. The first and only book of poems to appear in her lifetime, *The Farmer's Bride*, came out in 1916 when she was in her mid-forties. On the strength of it, Mew was awarded a Civil List pension, with recommendations from three of her most ardent admirers: John Masefield, Walter de la Mare and Thomas Hardy.

This Rare Spirit
A Life of Charlotte Mew

JULIA COPUS

faber

First published in 2021
by Faber & Faber Ltd
Bloomsbury House
74–77 Great Russell Street
London WC1B 3DA

This paperback edition first published in 2022

Typeset by Faber & Faber Ltd
Printed and bound by CPI Group (UK) Ltd, Croydon, CR0 4YY

A CIP record for this book
is available from the British Library

ISBN 978–0–571–31354–9

2 4 6 8 10 9 7 5 3 1

for my parents
and i.m. Val Warner (1946–2020)

I think that my soul is red
Like the soul of a sword or a scarlet flower

(from 'The Quiet House')

Contents

CONTENTS

Illustrations

With thanks to copyright-holders for permission to reproduce images in this book. The illustrations list uses the following abbreviations:

Harry Ransom Humanities Research Center, the University of Texas at Austin (HRC)

Kislak Center for Special Collections, Rare Books and Manuscripts, University of Pennsylvania (KCSC)

Mary C. Davidow collection of research materials on the life and career of Charlotte Mew (1869–1928), Special Collections Department, Bryn Mawr College Library (BMCL)

The Poetry Collection of the University Libraries, the University at Buffalo, the State University of New York (Buffalo)

UCL Press (UCLP)

Illustrations in order of appearance:

The Bugle Hotel in Newport, Isle of Wight – *public domain*
W. B. Mew, Langton & Co. signage – *public domain*
Mew's Ales & Minerals beer mat – *courtesy of the author*
Anna Maria Kendall, May 1863 – *BMCL*
Frederick Mew, April 1863 – *BMCL*
Charlotte and Anne Mew, January 1878 – *BMCL*
30 Doughty Street – © *Susan Murray, 2020*
Henry Mew, January 1880 – *BMCL*
Charlotte's parrot, Wek – *Buffalo*
Charlotte with six of the seven Chick sisters in the garden of the Chicks' home, Ealing, 1889 – © *Chick family private collection*

Lucy Harrison – *public domain*

Charlotte Mew in her twenties – © *Chick family private collection*

Cover of Volume I of *The Yellow Book* – *courtesy of the British Library*

Aerial view of University College London, taken *c.*1920 – *UCLP* (Department of Physics, UCL, from *The World of UCL*, Harte N., North J. & Brewis G. London: UCL Press, 2018)

Calendar made by Charlotte Mew – © *Chick family private collection*

Embroidery worked by Charlotte Mew – *courtesy of the author*

Anne Mew, 1897 – *BMCL*

Freda Mew, August 1896 – *BMCL*

Whitecroft Hospital, the county asylum on the outskirts of Newport, Isle of Wight – © *Mary Evans / Peter Higginbotham Collection*

Catherine Dawson Scott – *HRC*

May Sinclair *c.*1910 – *KCSC*

Front cover of *The Farmer's Bride* – *courtesy of the author*

Sketch by CMM of pipe-smoking man – *Buffalo*

Harold Monro – *Historic Collection / Alamy Stock Photo*

Sydney Cockerell in 1917 – © *Walter Stoneham / National Portrait Gallery, London*

Sketch by CMM of boarding house dining table – *Buffalo*

Charlotte in 1921 – *Buffalo*

Charlotte in pinstripe jacket and silk tie, *c.*1922 – *Buffalo*

Hogarth Studios, Charlotte Street – *courtesy of the author*

The gravestone of Charlotte and Anne Mew in Fortune Green Cemetery, Hampstead – © *Keiren Phelan, 2020*

Watercolour of Charlotte Mew in 1926 by her friend Dorothy Hawksley – © *Dorothy Hawksley / National Portrait Gallery, London*

Family Trees

The Mew Family Tree

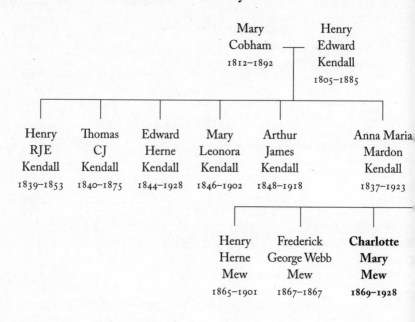

Mary Cobham 1812–1892 — Henry Edward Kendall 1805–1885

Henry RJE Kendall 1839–1853

Thomas CJ Kendall 1840–1875

Edward Herne Kendall 1844–1928

Mary Leonora Kendall 1846–1902

Arthur James Kendall 1848–1918

Anna Maria Mardon Kendall 1837–1923

Henry Herne Mew 1865–1901

Frederick George Webb Mew 1867–1867

Charlotte Mary Mew 1869–1928

The Isle of Wight Cousins

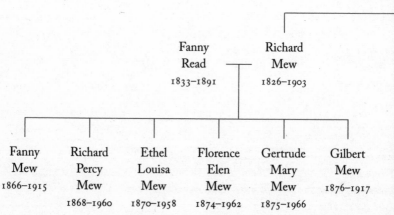

Ann Norris 1796–1878

Fanny Read 1833–1891 — Richard Mew 1826–1903

Fanny Mew 1866–1915

Richard Percy Mew 1868–1960

Ethel Louisa Mew 1870–1958

Florence Elen Mew 1874–1962

Gertrude Mary Mew 1875–1966

Gilbert Mew 1876–1917

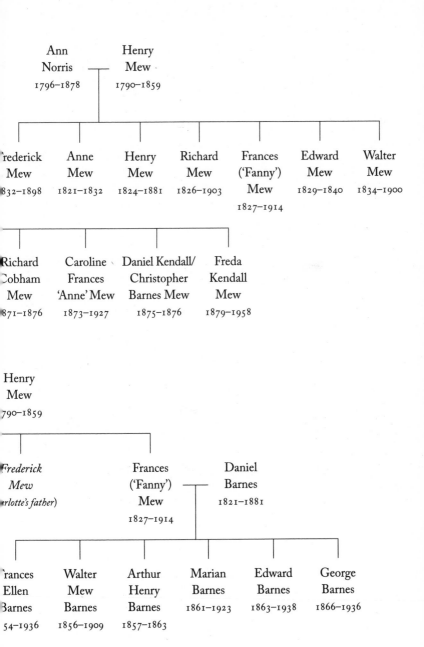

Ann
Norris
1796–1878

Henry
Mew
1790–1859

Frederick
Mew
1832–1898

Anne
Mew
1821–1832

Henry
Mew
1824–1881

Richard
Mew
1826–1903

Frances
('Fanny')
Mew
1827–1914

Edward
Mew
1829–1840

Walter
Mew
1834–1900

Richard
Cobham
Mew
1871–1876

Caroline
Frances
'Anne' Mew
1873–1927

Daniel Kendall/
Christopher
Barnes Mew
1875–1876

Freda
Kendall
Mew
1879–1958

Henry
Mew
1790–1859

Frederick
Mew
(Charlotte's father)

Frances
('Fanny')
Mew
1827–1914

Daniel
Barnes
1821–1881

Frances
Ellen
Barnes
1854–1936

Walter
Mew
Barnes
1856–1909

Arthur
Henry
Barnes
1857–1863

Marian
Barnes
1861–1923

Edward
Barnes
1863–1938

George
Barnes
1866–1936

1897 map by Edward Stanford showing the location of Charlotte Mew's
first two addresses, in Doughty Street (A) and Gordon Street (B).
Mew lived in this small area of London nearly all her life, moving just west
of the Bloomsbury district in her last decade.

Introduction

The Charlotte Mew I have come to know during the course of writing this book is quite different from the evanescent image I had in mind when I started, formed from a medley of information from the articles, websites, book chapters and theses I had read about her, as well as from two previous biographical accounts. One of these accounts is contained in an unpublished PhD thesis from 1960, by the American scholar Mary Davidow; the other – by far the more widely influential – is Penelope Fitzgerald's affectionate and absorbing portrait *Charlotte Mew and Her Friends*, first published in 1984. As I got deeper into my own research, I found a number of the preconceptions I had about Mew's character and work altering out of all recognition.

Mew is perhaps best known for two things: she is the author of the much-anthologised poem 'The Farmer's Bride', and she committed suicide while living alone in a single room in a street crowded with near-identical nursing homes. That much is true, and the gruesome manner of the death has continued to skew notions of who she was and how she lived her life, a distortion compounded by the fact that death itself is a recurrent motif in her poems and stories. It was the untimely loss to cancer of her beloved sister Anne that set the wheels in motion for the sad final weeks of Mew's story. But in essence, her personality was rather different from that of the mythical tortured poet – as her friend Alida Monro was at pains to point out when she introduced the first complete collection of Mew's poems in 1953:

It must not be thought, as has been supposed by many who judge from Charlotte's own writings, that she was always in a state of depression. This was far from the truth. She was a great teller of stories and always had new ones, never failed to see the humour in any situation, and never went on a visit anywhere without coming back with a riotous account of what had taken place.[1]

Even so, the end – and the means of that end – was no surprise to Mew's friends when it came. Anne had been closer to her than anyone: they shared not only a particularly close sibling bond but the burden of safeguarding various family secrets and the experience of being clever and ambitious women (Anne was a painter) at a time when it wasn't seemly for women of their social class to be either. The author of Mew's obituary in *The Times*, Sydney Cockerell, remarked that the pair 'had more than a little in them of what made another Charlotte and Anne, and their sister Emily, what they were'.[2] That assessment would have pleased Charlotte Mew. In her 1904 essay 'The Poems of Emily Brontë', she made a host of perspicacious comments about Emily's life and character that so closely mirror her own she appears at times to be describing herself – specifically the more guarded version of her self that emerged in later years, shaped by the many sorrows she had weathered. Emily was, in Mew's words, 'one of nature's outcasts – a self-determined outlaw', who lived with the sadness of an 'ever-unsatisfied desire' and looked out upon the world 'with a curious indifference and mistrust', and yet her disposition – in spite, or perhaps because, of these personal torments – was 'more than human in its compassionate gentleness for the doomed and erring'.[3] The same could be said a hundredfold of Charlotte Mew, who displays in her work an unsettling facility for inhabiting the minds and voices of others. In her dramatic monologues, she not only speaks out for but through the mouths of the disappointed, the deranged and the desolate – a conjuring act so well executed that at least one contemporary newspaper reviewer seemed to think Mew possessed supernatural powers, crediting her with 'an eerie ability to get beneath the skin of her broken men and women'.[4]

Mew's literary output was modest: a dozen stories and essays appeared in magazines, and twenty-eight poems were published in two editions of *The Farmer's Bride* – the only book to appear during her lifetime; a further thirty-two poems make up *The Rambling Sailor*, the collection that was issued a year after her death. In his obituary, Sydney Cockerell suggested many more poems had been written that had fallen prey to house moves, spells of depression and an over-zealous editorial eye: 'There can be no doubt that her fastidious self-criticism proved fatal to much work that was really good, and that the printed poems are far less than a tithe of what she composed.'[5] Whether or not that is true, Alida Monro added weight to the supposition by recounting some years later an occasion when she'd visited Mew for tea and watched her making paper spills to light her endless cigarettes or to give to her parrot, Wek, to chew on. Noticing some writing on the spills, Alida asked if Mew was using up old letters that way, and was told, 'I'm burning up my work. I don't know what else to do with it.'[6] Anne was also present on that occasion, and it is an indication of Mew's playful, and often inscrutable, nature that neither Anne nor Alida could decide whether the comment was made in jest, or if Mew really was destroying original work.

Charlotte Mew once commented on just how much of a person remains hidden even from one's nearest and dearest: 'So little do we people who spend our days together know each other!'[7] It follows that still less may be discerned by those who are not so near, and in Mew's case, our vision is further obscured by the fact that she set particular store by her privacy. She was a woman who did not wish to be scrutinised or summed up – as several anthologists seeking biographical details learned to their cost. But in spite of these obstacles, a great deal comes to light, and the more we discover about this extraordinary writer, the more readily we understand her guardedness. She never married, and if she had lovers, she would certainly not have wanted posterity to know about them; but the strong seam of sensuality running through her work makes us more than usually curious about who

3

the real-life recipient of such passion might have been. We are used to knowing such things: in the case of many other writers of Mew's era, the beloved's identity was either known at the time or was quickly brought to light by the most cursory biographical research. The emotional entanglements of T. S. Eliot, Thomas Hardy, D. H. Lawrence, W. B. Yeats and Oscar Wilde, for instance, are all well documented. In Mew's case, no trace survives (if it ever existed) of any romances in her life – let alone of sexual encounters – and nothing that could be described as a love letter, either to or from her, has been found.

There was one rumour in circulation during her lifetime that hints at an early taste of romance, and that was retold by her avowed 'favourite' cousin, Gertrude, to doctoral student Mary Davidow in the late 1950s. Gertrude revealed that there had been some sort of 'mutual attraction' between Charlotte Mew and Sam Chick, the elder brother of the Chick sisters whom Charlotte knew from school.[8] Still, it is possible that, despite the passion of her poetry, she was a virtual stranger to romance, though not to the romantic impulse. Her work is full of shared kisses, sea breezes, the intoxicating scent of hair, the 'wandering passion' of lovers' eyes and hands, and so on. She writes in the voices of male and female lovers alike. But the swarm of narratives that has amassed to fill the silence surrounding her romantic life and sexual preferences is almost wholly based on conjecture. The best known are those that recount Mew's romantic attachments to three specific women, as outlined in Fitzgerald's *Charlotte Mew and Her Friends*, but they are unsubstantiated and of doubtful origin. In the case of her friendship with short-story writer Ella D'Arcy, I have included a note at the foot of the main text at the point where my account differs most significantly from that given by Fitzgerald.

It is curious that, despite a dearth of information on the subject, the question of Mew's sexuality has become so closely linked both with her identity and with her work, and the idea that she was unarguably lesbian has stuck. In Chapter 7 I consider how and why that idea first surfaced. Mew may have been attracted to women, or to men – or indeed to both;

whatever the truth about that, no clues have been left to suggest that her feelings ever found an outlet. Perhaps the most likely possibility is that she sublimated her sexual and romantic impulses into her work. It is chastening to consider what Mew herself might have made of such enquiries. To judge from her writings, she would have found it difficult to see how an insight into her sexual preferences could be relevant to her work. As she wrote of Emily Brontë, 'It is said that her genius was masculine, but surely it was purely spiritual, strangely and exquisitely severed from embodiment and freed from any accident of sex.'[9]

What is certain is that the difficult circumstances of Mew's life meant there were many matters she prioritised over finding a sexual partner – chief among which was the decision, according to Alida Monro, not to have children because she didn't want to pass on the family's strain of insanity. In nineteenth-century Britain, that decision would have made good sense: eugenics, and the idea of a responsibility to future generations, was at its height in the 1880s and '90s, just as Mew was coming into womanhood. The other choice she made was to put the wellbeing of her increasingly vulnerable family unit ahead of other considerations at every juncture. She was still in her twenties when, upon the death of her father, she effectively took on the mantle of head of the household, and her letters suggest that, from that time on, she was with the family for most hours of most days. Her daily life was filled with running the house, caring for her needy mother and her siblings, and arranging the family's legal and business affairs. If the desire for a sexual relationship did play a part in Mew's life, it was a facet that she barely allowed to see the light, if at all.

When *The Farmer's Bride* was published, in May 1916, critic Gerald Gould told readers that if they followed his recommendation and bought Mew's book for themselves, they could not possibly 'fail to recognise the new and true note of genius'.[10] Gould was well regarded (he would go on to become fiction editor of the *Observer*) and he was not the only person to enthuse about the collection. Mew's work attracted strings of superlatives from those critics and writers who took note of it: Thomas Hardy said she was 'the greatest poetess' he knew of;[11] Siegfried Sassoon that she was 'the only poet who can give me a lump in my throat';[12] and American poet Hilda Doolittle that she was one of just three poets then living to have succeeded in the difficult form of the dramatic monologue.[13] The problem was that, despite the high profile of these admirers, their number remained relatively small and their enthusiasm failed to spark a wider interest. Though sales gently gathered pace over the years, the book never sold in large numbers.

It cannot have helped that Mew had, from the outset, an extreme antipathy towards self-promotion – an antipathy that stemmed from a deep desire for privacy that did her work no favours. She refused time and again to supply biographical information to editors of the anthologies and magazines in which her poems appeared. Nor was she willing to play the game of literary preferment: Lady Ottoline Morrell (an influential patron of the arts) tried in vain to befriend her on more than one occasion. Timing was against her too: the middle of the First World War was not the best time for a book like hers to appear. The reading public was hungry for poetry that was either written from the trenches or that offered some sort of bucolic escape from the madness of battle – of the kind produced by the so-called Georgian poets. Mew's work, with its unusually long lines, mixed metres and emotionally challenging subject matter, was too startling for editors of a traditional bent. When *A Book of Women's Verse* appeared in 1921, Hardy wrote to its rather conservative editor, J. C. Squire, with the comment that he was 'disappointed to find you had omitted Charlotte Mew'.[14]

Mew was a very different type of writer from most of the Georgians – as witness the fact that she was excluded from all five volumes of Edward Marsh's influential *Georgian Poetry*. The fact that she was a woman may have contributed to that particular omission: the series's opening volumes contained no female poets at all, while the final anthology included only the aristocratic, and well-connected, Vita Sackville-West. Mew, by contrast, was an inveterate outsider: except for a brief association, in her mid-twenties, with the crowd that attached itself to *The Yellow Book* quarterly, she kept herself apart from literary groups and cliques – in spite of living for three years on the next street from Virginia Woolf and her siblings. Edith Sitwell (who had her own literary circle) complained that she had tried to persuade Mew to visit, 'but she is a hermit [. . .] and though she was very nice to me, she wouldn't come.'[15] Mew's stance was that literary renown ought to have nothing to do with personal celebrity. But while she had no interest in fame for herself, she was far from indifferent to the fate of her work: she was hurt by the lack of critical attention paid to *The Farmer's Bride* and wrote to her publisher that, having heard all sorts of wonderful things in private from a number of potential reviewers, 'it is clear that a privately & publicly expressed opinion are two different things'.[16]

Mew's notion that the writing should be able to speak for itself has, in the end, proved prophetic. Since her death in 1928, her work has attracted enough support to keep it – in particular, the poetry – from fading into obscurity. In 1973, Philip Larkin devoted five pages to Mew's poetry in the *Oxford Book of Twentieth Century English Verse*, a volume for which he had always intended, he said, to select good poems rather than defer to the big names.[17] Larkin's view was that a whole cohort of poets from Mew's period was in danger of being forgotten: 'I am interested in the Georgians,' he told his editor, Dan Davin, 'and how far they represented an "English tradition" that was submerged by the double impact of the Great War and the Irish-American-continental properties of Yeats and Eliot.'[18] Partly because of her omission from Edward Marsh's anthology series, Mew was never much associated with the Georgian school (and given their subsequent decline in reputation it might be argued that she had a lucky break), but nor was she striving for the same effect as Yeats or Eliot. It has been suggested that her approach was diametrically opposed to Eliot's description of poetry as 'an escape from emotion'; she believed, on the contrary, that 'the quality of emotion' was 'the first requirement of poetry'.[19] But Eliot made a crucial qualification to his statement: 'of course, only those who have personality and emotions know what it means to want to escape from these things', and in reality, the approaches of the two poets were not so very far apart. Mew was continually exposing the basic stuff of her lived experience – what Eliot called 'the present moment of the past' – to the pressure of her own instinctive world of metaphors, and in so doing she forged precisely the sort of 'new art emotion' that Eliot extolled.[20] In 1981, Val Warner's seminal edition of Mew's *Collected Poems and Prose* generated a fresh appetite for the work in literary and academic circles, and three years later, Penelope Fitzgerald's book brought Mew to the attention of a more general readership. Poets Ian Hamilton and Eavan Boland have both edited selections of her poetry, with Boland describing *The Farmer's Bride* as 'one of the most remarkable poetry publications of the first half of the twentieth century'.[21] John Newton, editor of Penguin's more recent *Complete Poems* (2000), has also spoken out eloquently about Mew's rightful place in the canon, describing her work as 'powerfully direct, passionate, and charged in the simplest and purest English language'.[22] Some of her stories, too, have continued to be printed in anthologies; when Elaine Showalter included Mew's 'A White Night' in her *Daughters of Decadence*, she referred to it, memorably, as 'a feminist counterpart of Conrad's apocalyptic *Heart of Darkness*'.[23]

It's not difficult to see why Mew's work has continued to find such devoted supporters. Hers is an instantly recognisable voice, speaking clearly above the babble of many of her contemporaries. The poems are full of strangeness and half-glimpsed narrative. Where did such a voice – as confident as it is startling – come from? 'Mew's are the kind of poems', Ian Hamilton has said, 'that force readers to want to know about the author's life and personality.' Charlotte Mew – part respectable Victorian, part New Woman – is an absorbing subject. Her life is full of the kind of tragedy, derangement and intrigue that she conjured for her own, rather gothic, short fiction. It is set against a complex backdrop of unrest and rapid change, as one century tilted into the next. Mew shows us what it was like to live through such a time as an outsider – from literary Bloomsbury, from the world of intimate relationships, from marriage and motherhood, and ultimately from the world at large because of the secrets she had to keep from it.

It is partly because of the energy Mew put into keeping those secrets safe that half-truths and fictions about her have become commonplace in the years since her death. If her story is to be told, it ought to be told here as fully as possible and without embellishment. My approach has therefore been to take in the full span of her life and return to original sources: to her letters (many previously unexamined), her life-writing, her family's household and medical records, and the diaries and testimonies of friends. In some instances even Mew's poems may be called as witnesses to the narrative of her life – though so far there has been surprisingly little examination of the points of contact between her life and work. Of course, we should never assume that biographical particulars can be inferred from a writer's fictional works, but there are suggestions that Mew was the kind of writer who took such a connection as read; she was certainly that kind of reader. In her essay on Emily Brontë she offers specific phrases from the poems as evidence of Brontë's own character traits. She even goes so far as to claim that 'the true – the one original likeness – Emily herself has sketched: it is outlined in these slim pages of neglected verse. The eyes that watched unweariedly to find "how very far the morning lies away"; the "chainless soul", the "quenchless will", the "savage heart", and the "resentful mood" are mirrored here.'[24] If nothing else, it is an invaluable insight into how we might read Mew's own work for clues.

And it is the work itself for which Mew should be remembered; my hope is that this life will lead readers back to that work. She herself believed in it so strongly that she insisted *The Farmer's Bride* be printed in such a way that all its long lines might remain unbroken on the page, just as she had written them; she knew that their full effect would be lost if they were allowed to run over. Her insistence meant that the book had to be published in an unfamiliar shape, described by Alida Monro, of the Poetry Bookshop, as 'a rather ugly quarto page'.[25] In spite of such displays of apparent surety, Mew's was a fragile kind of self-belief, easily shaken by the response of the outside world. Like many writers, she was more affected by a general inattention to her work than she was by the plaudits it attracted. In the final account, her disappointment was justified: her achievements continue to be insufficiently recognised despite the work's extraordinary sensuality, its intimate, forthright tone and distinctly modern idiom. Besides an uncanny gift for ventriloquism, the poems demonstrate a masterful orchestration of sonic drama – sudden shifts in dynamics springing partly from the blow-by-blow accounts of the moments Mew describes, and partly from the music of her words.

This Rare Spirit is a record of my quest to refind Charlotte Mew; my hope is that it might play its part in helping to restore her to her rightful place in our literary heritage. Above all, it is perhaps Mew's skill at painting pictures that makes it most likely her work will prove, in the end, indelible. Once read, it is hard to dismiss from one's mind the image of the villagers racing over the dark fields with their lanterns, in pursuit of the 'Farmer's Bride'; harder still to look away from the direct gaze of the institutionalised 'Ken' whose eyes meet ours reprovingly, 'as two red, wounded stars might do'; or to forget the speaker of 'The Quiet House' as she hurries to answer the doorbell, opens the door onto an empty, lamplit street and concludes 'I think it is myself I go to meet.' By tuning in to Mew's own words with the sort of alertness that allowed her to hear 'the whole world whispering', I hope that we too may manage, across time, to meet something of that self.

JULIA COPUS,
Somerset, 2020

Prologue

DECEMBER 1876

If Lotti craned her head right, to look out of the attic window of her nursery, she could see through the peeling, freckled green-grey trunks of the London planes into the locked gardens of Mecklenburgh Square. Four paths extended in an X shape from a cluster of central trees out to each corner. The trees were bare at this time of year, but in warmer months, when the yellow jasmine was in flower, the gardens would fill with croquet players and children and flocks of sparrows, chirruping loudly and feasting on the orange-scarlet hips of the sweet briar. Beyond the gardens was the Foundling Hospital, opened in 1741 by sea captain Thomas Coram in response to the alarming number of infants left abandoned on the streets of London. Sometimes on Sundays, her father would put on his top hat and walk with her and her two brothers, Harry and Richard, to hear the renowned hospital choir singing in the chapel. After the services, they would visit the dining hall to chat with the foundling children who ate their Sunday roast at long refectory tables. Her little sister, Anne, was only three and remained at home on these occasions, being considered too young to sit quietly through the length of a sermon.

In the other direction, she could just see, a mile in the distance, the imposing steeple of St George's Church, where her parents had married during the stormy winter of 1863, a week before Christmas. The church's white, tiered pyramid, topped with a statue of King George I in classical dress, would remain a part of her psychological landscape all through adulthood, a symbol of religious obedience and piety which the child narrator of her poem 'The Changeling' would one day dismiss with a gleeful defiance: 'But the King who sits on your high church steeple / Has nothing to do with us fairy people!'[1]

The house faced west; on bright afternoons the sun poured in through the tall windows of the lower floors and the high, small windows of the attic. It stood at the north end of a salubrious Bloomsbury street, a fifteen-minute walk from King's Cross station, which had been designed by Lewis Cubitt, the husband of Lotti's great-aunt Sophia; their daughter, Ada, had been a witness at her parents' wedding. Number 30 was positioned at the point where Doughty Street joined Mecklenburgh Square, and was laid out – like many others in the street – over five storeys. There was a kitchen in the basement and a day and night nursery in the attic, where Lotti passed most of her time, right at the top of the house, with her siblings and her much-loved nurse, Elizabeth Goodman. Elizabeth was in fact more of a second mother than a nurse. One day Lotti would publish a short memoir about her, saying as much.[2] A Lincolnshire woman, fifty years of age, strict but fair, with an upright gait and dark, intelligent eyes, she was a strict disciplinarian, and more than once lately she had beaten Lotti for her naughtiness, with a calm crescendo between the spanks of 'Will you? *Will you??* WILL YOU?'[3] In spite of her sternness, she had a youthful sense of fun, and the children loved her. She planned treats for them and dreamed up grand careers, and sometimes she invited them down into the kitchen, taking as much delight as they did in watching a lump of sugar in a spoon melt into dark 'pig's blood' over the gas.[4]

Lotti never stayed in trouble with Elizabeth for long, and for the most part her days were full of magic, in spite of their set routine. Each morning began with a plunge in the bath, which, for the tiny Lotti, was 'cruelly cold in winter'.[5] There was breakfast at eight, dinner at noon and tea at six. She ate her meals with her siblings at the round table in the day nursery, where Elizabeth also taught them their first lessons in reading and writing. Except on Sundays, the children were free to choose their own reading material, although reading purely for pleasure was an activity that Elizabeth tolerated rather than encouraged. Very likely the children had copies on their shelves of the ever-popular *Robinson Crusoe*, *Alice's Adventures in Wonderland*, *The Water Babies* and Hans Christian Andersen's *Tales*. There was poetry too. Lotti was particularly fond of Thomas Hood and Felicia Hemans – those 'friends of my innocent childhood', as she would later call them.[6]

But there was one book that Elizabeth insisted on her charges reading every day. *The Believer's Daily Remembrancer* was the work of a Baptist minister, James Smith, and comprised a series of page-long devotional readings, one for each day of the year.[7] Many of the teachings were sobering, and some – for a small child – were probably downright disturbing. But the book had an unexpected compensation: beneath each day's reflection was a short verse, nearly always in regular iambic tetrameter, occasionally in ballad metre, like the lines of a hymn:

> O may thy counsels, mighty God,
> My roving feet command;
> Nor I forsake the happy road,
> That leads to thy right hand.[8]

With its emphasis on humankind's unworthiness in the presence of an all-seeing God, the book must have made for daunting reading for Lotti and her siblings.

Of all of those siblings, it was her brother Richard with whom Lotti spent most of her playtime; he was closest to her in age, and co-conspirator in her schemes and games of make-believe. As it turned out, there was plenty of time for both: between meals and lessons, the children were broadly left to their own devices. If the weather was fine, they could play out in Mecklenburgh Square (as local residents, the family held a key), but they had at all times to keep in mind that outside the house they were on public display. In insisting on such standards, the Mew family was simply following the mores of the day. One anxious house-hunter, hoping to move his family into London around this time, wrote that a 'garden attached to the house is preferable to a *detached* garden (like Gordon Square), as in Gordon Square children have to be dressed and nurse-maided regally, aristocratically'.[9]

On bad-weather days, the nursery table, with its heavy, fringed cloth, served as a private cave; adults were forbidden entry. The children could help themselves to books from the nursery shelves and toys from the toy-chest. There was paper to draw and write on, and coloured chalks. There was a rocking horse, and a beautiful doll's house with a fashionable bay window, built especially for Lotti and Anne by their father Fred, a talented architect. Best of all, there was a Noah's ark, with painted wooden figurines. Along with a small troop of battered soldiers, these 'unzoological animals', as the adult Charlotte would describe them, became the heroes and villains of the children's made-up stories.

The nursery had been unnervingly quiet lately – a world away from the commotion of the previous winter, when another baby had joined them just days after Lotti's sixth birthday.[10] Most of Elizabeth's energy had been taken up then with caring for the new arrival, and that was no bad thing as far as Lotti was concerned: while the baby was with them, she had enjoyed a period of unprecedented freedom. But baby Daniel – who had seemed healthy enough – died after only a few months. For a long while afterwards Lotti's mother, Anna Maria, had been more than usually short-tempered; Fred retreated into his study, and Lotti made sure to tiptoe past it whenever she came downstairs. In the midst of this disquieting atmosphere, the children turned to Elizabeth for reassurance. She slept near them in the attic, but that didn't stop Lotti lying awake for hours sometimes, worrying about Elizabeth's eventual demise and 'doing sums on the knots of the counterpane to prove that she could live on for years and years and was not really so very old'.[11] Most of the time, though, Elizabeth seemed to the children 'as fixed a part of the universe' as their daily bath.[12] She was tutor, nurse and confidante to them. Occasionally at bedtime, before pulling down the blinds in the night nursery, she would take Lotti's finger and point to stars through the high window, naming them as she went. Lotti thought the stars were God's angels and that Elizabeth was reciting a litany of their Christian names: *Venus, Arcturus, Capella . . .*[13]

Looking back in later years, Charlotte would remark that her nurse had occupied 'the place of chief friend and adviser, and, when trouble came to the house, of consoler'.[14] But Elizabeth's steady presence was no protection against the harsh realities of life. Not even a year had passed since baby Daniel's death when Lotti's brother Richard caught scarlet fever, for which everybody knew there was no cure. He was quickly removed to another room, which Harry, Lotti and Anne were forbidden to enter. Elizabeth looked after Richard with her usual fastidious care, but he died anyway, and the household was plunged into deep mourning for the second time in nine months, the rooms hushed, the mirrors covered in black crêpe. When Richard was with the rest of the children, they had been allowed downstairs in the evenings, to spend a short time with their parents and join them for pudding – blancmange or a piece of pie or steamed pudding with custard.[15] Now everything had changed.

Lotti may or may not have seen Richard laid out in death; children were sometimes excused from viewing the body if there was thought to be a risk of infection. But if she did, the sight of the lifeless five-year-old boy must have left a lasting impression: Lotti herself had only just turned seven. Did she feel, as children often do with such things, that she was in some way to blame for the death? The lines she found in her *Daily Remembrancer* that particular bedtime – 9 December 1876 – would have offered little solace, and if she paid attention to them, we can only hope she knew better than to take them at face value:

> May I from every act abstain
> That hurts or gives my brother pain:
> Nay, every secret wish suppress,
> That would abridge his happiness;
> And thus may I Thy follower prove,
> Great Prince of peace, great God of love.[16]

Whether or not she was taken to view the corpse, the shock of Richard's death was to stay with her for life, and it seems a likely source for a late poem. 'To a Child in Death' (1922) is addressed directly to the absent child. In it, the speaker describes the sheer force of the protectiveness felt towards a loved one, as well as the ultimate powerlessness of that love in the face of death. By the time of its composition, unexpected imagery had become one of Mew's hallmarks, and in the opening lines of this poem, she fixes on a characteristically startling simile to embody the protective effort: 'Love made us feel, or so it was with me, like some great bird / Trying to hold and shelter you in its strong wing.' A painful bewilderment about the purpose of a world that no longer contains the loved child pours from the closing lines of the first stanza:

> What shall we do with this strange summer, meant for you, –
> > Dear, if we see the winter through
> > What shall be done with spring?
> This, this is the victory of the Grave; here is death's sting,
> That it is not strong enough, our strongest wing.

But bewildering as it may have seemed, the world did continue, and Lotti did her level best to keep in step. Richard's death was the first major trauma she encountered, and it set a pattern for life. Loss – and the deep and lasting grief it provoked in her – would also be a pervasive theme in her writing. By the age of seven, she had witnessed two deaths in the family, and was already learning to find solace in the world of words. Night after night she went to sleep with the rhythm of one of the *Daily Remembrancer* verses in her head. In years to come, the imaginative powers she had fostered in her make-believe games with Richard would help form the remarkable poetry of her adult years, as she searched for ever more compelling ways of telling her story. Her evolution as a poet had begun in the nursery.

The absences that occurred in Charlotte's life – caused sometimes by death, sometimes by other, less clearly defined events – would, in time, result in her growing detachment from the world. And if that detachment was sometimes judged as aloofness, it was one born always of a deep protective instinct rather than any sense of superiority. As the years passed, her family would become increasingly reliant on her, and Charlotte responded by turning inwards – withdrawing both to the privacy of the family unit and to her own inner world. The strange turns and reversals of the Mew family's life, and the painful secrets they would feel it necessary to keep, bound Charlotte so tightly to them that at times she would be in danger of suffocating. To those on the outside, the defiant, fun-loving child appeared to grow into an adult whom Edith Sitwell felt at liberty to describe (in 1919) as 'a grey tragic woman [. . .] sucked dry of blood [. . .] a hermit, inhabited by a terrible bitterness'.[17]

She was never this to her friends, for whom 'no one could be more warm-hearted and witty in her talk and in her friendship'.[18] One friend thought her 'the most sincere person one could meet'; another (who had known her since her schooldays) described her as 'deeply affectionate', and a third as someone who possessed a 'peculiarly sweet' nature.[19] However sweet her nature, the delicate balancing act she sustained between her professional and private lives put Charlotte under a pressure that, more than once, proved all but impossible to bear. At the same time, it was precisely that pressure which (to paraphrase Auden) hurt her into poetry in the first place and helped shape the extraordinary writer she was to become.

Good Five-O'Clock People

PRE-1869

Anna Maria Kendall reportedly believed that in marrying Fred Mew she had 'lowered her social rank'.[1] In an age when such things mattered, the social standing of their respective families was not, in fact, so very different, but while Fred had been brought up amid the cut and thrust of his family's two businesses, for Anna Maria even the business of housekeeping was, as Mary Davidow has suggested, 'looked upon with disdain': she 'had never been taught how to manage the household finances; domestic tasks were regarded by her as the sole responsibility of hired help'.[2] To make matters worse, Fred was employed in the architectural firm owned and run by Anna Maria's father.

Anna Maria's misgivings would have puzzled anyone acquainted with the Mews in their native Isle of Wight. Frederick Mew had been born into a highly respected family there, to Henry and Ann Mew (née Norris) on 14 March 1832, amid the noise and bustle of the Bugle Hotel, a busy coaching inn that stood in the middle of the high street in the ancient market town of Newport. With white stone pilasters either side of a corniced entrance, the inn was one of the oldest on the island and had been in the family since 1816. It served as the community's main posthouse and the principal departure point for coaches to all regions of the island, the rattle of wheels and tramp of hooves a constant backdrop to proceedings. It ran its own services along several of the routes, and at the back of the property there were stables, watering facilities, fodder stores and harness rooms.[3] In Isle of Wight dialect, a 'bugle' is a young bull (from the Latin for a steer, *buculus*), and when Henry Mew took over as licensee in 1829, he brought with him a family of bullish young sons. Once the family was complete, Fred Mew would be the second youngest of four boys who survived beyond childhood. There was also one girl, Frances (known from the start as Fanny). To Henry and Ann's lasting sorrow, another daughter, Anne, had died at the age of eleven, just two months before Fred was born.

Henry Mew was a grafter. As well as managing the day-to-day running of the inn and stables, he hosted numerous dinners for the island's many events, and quickly established a reputation for the warmth of his hospitality and the quality of his cooking. Just a fortnight after Fred's birth (and not yet three months after his young daughter's death), he was busy serving up a lavish supper to the Crockford Union pack of harriers after their final hunt of the season.[4] The island's papers marvelled at meals 'served up in Mew's surpassing style of excellence' at which 'every delicacy of the season' could be found.[5]

The festivities on these occasions were undoubtedly helped along by liberal supplies of alcohol. The Mews had long been a family of brewers, maltsters and spirit merchants; in 1814, Henry's uncle, Benjamin Mew, had set up his own brewery. The company was passed on to Henry's cousin, Walter Baron Mew, who made such a success of things that in 1873, Walter Langton of Lambeth injected £20,000 capital into the business, and the company became W. B. Mew, Langton & Co. The firm received a further boost in 1850 when it was granted a Royal Warrant to supply Queen Victoria whenever she was in residence at her home on the island, Osborne House.

The Mews' other family concern was nearby New Fairlee Farm, which provided extra quarters for the Bugle's horses and pasture for the younger horses who were not yet working, as well as fresh produce for meals served up at the inn. The farm lay on the outskirts of the town, at the far end of a track leading from Staplers Road, looking out over the lively waters of the Solent.[6] (The track, not officially named in Henry's day, is now called Mews Lane.) It was here at the farm, rather than the inn, that Fred spent the majority of his childhood. The 1841 census shows him, aged nine, living at New Fairlee with his elder brother Richard (then fifteen) and younger brother Walter (seven), under the supervision of a Mr and Mrs Croad, while the farm itself operated under the stewardship of a young bailiff. It was a half-hour walk between farm and inn, and the boys went freely back and forth between the two, the journey on foot only tedious in wet weather when the lanes filled with mud.

As Fred and his brothers approached school age, they were each enrolled in turn at Mr Wotton's School for Young Gentlemen on the Old Kent Road in London.[7] Whatever their individual ambitions, the assumption was that at least some of them would go on to run the family businesses. In due course, Henry junior took on the running of the inn, investing as much energy in the enterprise as his father had done before him, and in 1865, not long after his fortieth birthday, he was rewarded for his efforts by being elected Mayor of Newport. He responded by throwing a lavish ball at the Bugle, which was attended by around two hundred guests who 'partook of a most liberal spread' and danced until morning. 'We feel convinced that the kindness and great liberality of his Worship and the Lady Mayoress will not soon be forgotten,' gushed the *Isle of Wight Observer*.[8] The farming business was managed at various times by both Walter (the youngest) and Richard, who would remain at New Fairlee Farm for the rest of his life, eventually raising a large family of his own there.

Meanwhile, Fred had developed a taste for city living and, finding he had a talent for numbers and drawing, he set his sights on a career in architecture. By the age of nineteen, he had already completed his apprenticeship, was working on his first commissions and had taken lodgings in Sidmouth Street – just a short walk from his future home in Doughty Street. In 1859, the year of his father's death, he received a significant pat on the back when the renowned architect Henry Edward Kendall junior proposed him for membership of the Royal Institute of British Architects. By the following year, he had joined Kendall as junior partner and exhibited a design (an impressive but ultimately unsuccessful proposal for the new Assize Courts in

Manchester) at the Royal Academy of Arts. Hard at work in the firm's office at 33 Brunswick Square, he had ample opportunity to observe his boss's pretty and dainty eldest daughter, Anna Maria.[9]

While Fred was a newcomer to the profession, the Kendalls' architectural pedigree stretched a long way back. They had played an important role in shaping the landscape of Brighton during the early 1800s. The Kemp Town esplanades beneath the cliffs were built to their designs – complete with sloping sea walls, steps down to the beach and a tunnel under the road leading to the private, landscaped gardens of Sussex Square. Lewis Carroll spent many of his summers in Sussex Square in the 1870s and '80s, and it is thought that the Kendalls' tunnel from the gardens to the sea (heavily clad in ivy by the time Carroll knew it) was the inspiration for the rabbit hole in *Alice in Wonderland*.

The Kendalls were respectable in the way that counted highly in late Georgian and Victorian society; their family tomb in Kensal Green Cemetery was an elegant and imposing monument built in white stone and decorated with encaustic tiles. But beneath this veneer of propriety, there lay at least one scandal that seems never to have been alluded to in public: the subject of Henry Kendall junior's parentage. His birth certificate is missing from the records, but such evidence as can be gleaned from censuses and other documents suggests that Charlotte Mew's maternal grandfather was illegitimate. His own obituary in *The Builder* states simply that he was 'born in London',[10] while Colvin's *Biographical Dictionary of British Architects* informs us that his father, Henry Kendall senior, was 'described as a man of "gentlemanly manners, noble and generous in disposition, tall and handsome in person." He married twice, and had a son and two daughters.'[11] If Kendall senior did indeed marry only twice, then Kendall junior – already seventeen by the time of his father's first documented marriage, to twenty-eight-year-old Anne Lyon – was born out of wedlock. He was nonetheless brought up by his father in some style – and if that behaviour was unconventional, it was not perhaps out of keeping for a man who would go on, at the age of ninety-four and unhappy with the condition of widowhood, to marry a woman sixty years younger than him.[12]

Illegitimacy carried a major stigma in nineteenth-century England, despite the fact that it occurred in all levels of society. If it was present in the Kendall family's background, it might go some way towards explaining, on the one hand, the extreme guardedness with which Anna Maria approached life and, on the other, her preoccupation with appearances and tendency to hauteur. All these traits would eventually manifest, to varying degrees, in Charlotte herself. One friend who met the poet in her later years wrote of her 'defiant reserve' – although the same friend was also keen to point out that 'as she got accustomed to a person this defiance vanished completely'.[13] And among the many accounts testifying to Charlotte's kind-heartedness, there is at least one report of her perceived snobbery: after visiting for tea, the American poet Sara Teasdale apparently left feeling slighted, and wrote to her husband afterwards, 'It rather bothers me to be considered a vulgarian, but they all secretly consider us as such – that is, her type do.'[14] By 'her type', she presumably meant to imply a societal group that had hung on to a certain brand of Victorian Englishness whose behaviour was inherently condescending. The truth behind Charlotte's reserve was more complex: while she may have sympathised with the importance her mother placed on outward show, she was all too aware of its shallowness. In an early poem, 'Afternoon Tea', an exasperated speaker makes it clear how little time she has for gossip and small talk:

> Please you, excuse me, good five-o'clock people,
>> I've lost my last hatful of words,
> And my heart's in the wood up above the church steeple,
>> I'd rather have tea with – the birds.

The writer of such a poem is unlikely to have shared the superior attitude of what Sara Teasdale branded 'her type', even if she did go along with the usual five-o'clock rituals. Close friends knew that Charlotte was no snob, but Anna Maria's pretensions undoubtedly left their mark on her daughter. It would have been something of a miracle if they had not: Charlotte shared a house for over fifty years with this tiny but domineering woman whose death would one day leave her feeling, she wrote, as useless as a 'weed', rooted out of the earth and tossed aside.[15]

Whatever the truth of Henry Edward Kendall junior's parentage, he was raised as a legitimate member of the Kendall family. His father not only gave him his exact name, in full, but employed him as a pupil in his practice. It wasn't long before the son was making his own mark, and moving in distinguished circles. His influential *Designs for Schools and School Houses* (1847) is dedicated to Samuel Wilberforce, Bishop of Oxford and fierce opponent of Charles Darwin – an indication, perhaps, of the climate in which his own children were raised. Charlotte's mother, Anna Maria, was the eldest of those children, four of whom survived into adulthood. Charlotte knew best her aunt, Mary Leonora, who remained at her parents' home until her death, and an uncle, Edward Herne. Anna Maria's youngest brother, Arthur, signed up for the merchant navy at the age of sixteen, developed a taste for liquor and soon found himself banned from the family home. At the age of twenty-two, he forced his way back into the family's new house in Burlington Road, Paddington, during the early hours of the morning and burgled the wine cellar, making off with fifty bottles of wine (valued at £12) and a cameo shell and opera-glass (£8 8s). The local papers reported the subsequent court proceedings in colourful detail:

A policeman named Beeby stated that on the morning of May 4, at two o'clock, he saw the prisoner, who was accompanied by four other young men, go up the steps of Mr Kendall's house and knock violently at the door. [. . .] At half-past three he saw the prisoner and two of his companions nearly opposite the house. The parlour window was thrown open and a person was opening the door from the inside. The prisoner and another walked up the steps and went in. The door was then closed. It was afterwards found that the door of the wine cellar had been forced open with a poker and a small butcher's cleaver.[16]

Charlotte's grandfather, Henry Kendall junior, told the court that his wayward son had caused him 'great grief and anxiety by his bad conduct'[17] – and not for the first time: it emerged that Arthur had stolen from him on three previous occasions. On the other side of London, in Doughty Street, Anna Maria was no doubt as sickened as her father at the disgrace her brother had brought on the Kendalls' good name.

By that time, she was Anna Maria Mew, a married woman, busy forging a new branch of the family and struggling to adjust to life in a less prosperous house than the one in which she'd been raised. Delicate, pretty and overly concerned with appearances, she was described by those who knew her as 'not at all what one might call an intellectual'.[18] She was conservative by nature – opposed to change because change made her nervous – but her strong inclination towards preserving the status quo would find itself increasingly challenged as time went by. Her children were born into a country that was near the height of its global power and poised for social change: workers' rights were being formalised, the franchise was slowly being extended, and women were making a stand for their right to be educated. Liberal prime minister William Gladstone had been in office for almost a year when Charlotte was born. He was not a favourite with the fifty-one-year-old monarch, who would go on to describe him as 'that half-mad firebrand'. But for the time being, Queen Victoria herself was largely absent from the scene: her beloved Albert had been dead for eight years and she was rarely seen in public. (She would eventually emerge from her seclusion when baby Lotti was not yet two.)

Fred and Anna Maria were six years into their marriage by the time of Charlotte's birth on 15 November 1869; the conflict of their thirty-five-year union would play out in her psyche for her entire life. Her mother's overriding need to keep up appearances was forever at odds with her father's instinctive sense of fun and devil-may-care approach to life. Charlotte's own nature would take in all of this; and out of the warring components there would emerge a rare and generous spirit that – in spite of the fact that she was cherished by her friends – seemed never entirely at ease in the world, never entirely trusting. Two accounts left by friends who knew the poet in her forties attest to the complexity of her personality; indeed, they might almost have been written about two different people. In 1913, Catherine Dawson Scott noted in her diary that Mew had 'a wonderful young soul – neither quite boy nor quite girl', and concluded some months later that 'Under the curious husk is a peculiarly sweet, humble nature.'[19] It was a shrewd but partial assessment and, of course, gave no indication of how Charlotte herself might be feeling.

A second friend, Alida Monro, was asked to write a biographical portrait for a posthumous edition of Mew's *Collected Poems*. She recalled the poet's 'square shoulders' and 'tiny hands and feet'; her 'fine white hair' and eyes 'bright with black lashes and highly arched eyebrows'. The distinctive eyebrows and curly hair were her father's, the small hands and feet from her mother; but the path Charlotte chose to carve out for herself was entirely her own. That path was difficult at the best of times; on occasions it seemed impassable. And perhaps it would have been had she not inherited one more, invaluable, trait from her father's side. It was a trait that had enabled her ancestors to set up and grow two flourishing family businesses, and that belied her frail constitution and diminutive stature: an aptitude for sheer hard graft. Nobody could know, of course, how Charlotte perceived her surroundings from inside that 'curious husk', but a further detail from Monro's biographical sketch provides us with a clue. Almost in passing, she adds that Charlotte 'usually carried a horn-handled umbrella, unrolled, under her arm, as if it were psychologically necessary to her, a weapon against the world'.[20]

2

Bad Milk
1876–1879

At the start of 1876, Lotti's father was spending most of his waking hours in his study. Now in his mid-forties, he was on the plump side, with a round face, high forehead and slightly hooded eyes. His curly dark hair had receded far back at the crown but was fuller at the sides, and more than compensated for by a thick moustache, sideburns and a greying chinstrap beard. He was by this time firmly established as junior partner in his father-in-law's architecture firm – now renamed, accordingly, Kendall & Mew. When Fred and Anna Maria were first married, the firm's registered address had been just a short walk away from them in Brunswick Square, where Grandpa Kendall and his family then lived, but by the time Lotti was born, the Kendalls had moved to Paddington. A few years earlier, the extra distance might have presented more of a problem, but the Metropolitan Underground Railway now ran regular services between Paddington and the city: glossy wooden carriages, gas-lit and hauled by steam locomotives. If Fred needed to meet with Mr Kendall in person, he had only to walk to nearby King's Cross station to make the short train journey. For the most part, though, he worked out of his own office at home. He was not unusual in this: of the sixty-two houses on Doughty Street, seven were occupied by architects, and only one of those practised from a different address. There were also two solicitors, a surgeon and a mathematical instrument maker on the street, all running businesses from their homes.[1] Only some of them had young families, as Fred did, however, and if Mew's 'The Quiet House' has any basis in reality, the atmosphere must at times have tested him to the limit:

When we were children old Nurse used to say,
The house was like an auction or a fair
Until the lot of us were safe in bed.

These days Fred seemed hardly present in the house at all, and if his withdrawal derived in part from a desire to escape the chaos of his domestic situation, it was also driven by the pressure of a new and important deadline. At the start of the year, the Hampstead Vestry Committee had invited fifteen selected architects to send in designs for a purpose-built hall. Meetings were currently held in one of the dining halls at the local workhouse, a room that was 'ill-ventilated and inconvenient, and not at all times available'.[2] A small neighbouring house was rented in addition for the offices of the clerk, surveyor and others, but the cramped space was something of a fire hazard and generally 'ill-adapted for its purpose'.[3] The vestrymen's wish list for the new building included airy offices, storerooms, a meeting hall and a larger, public hall that they could hire out for lectures, concerts and so on. Designs were to be submitted to the committee by the start of April and labelled, as was the custom, with mottos in place of the architects' names. So it was that Fred spent the first three months of 1876 gathering more detailed information about the vestrymen's requirements, making sketches, eventually settling on a plan, and refining his preliminary schematic drawings into a finished design. It would have been more than enough work for two men, but now that Mr Kendall was seventy-one and had begun to slow down, the lion's share had fallen to Fred. He threw his full weight behind it, his determination to secure the commission fuelled by the need to provide for his still-growing family.

While Fred was immersed in this challenging project, Anna Maria had her own preoccupations. At thirty-nine, her tiny physique was beginning to look bony, rather than dainty, in growing contrast to the oil painting that hung on the wall in the parlour reminding everyone of her glory days. Alida Monro, seeing the painting many years later, concluded that in her youth Anna Maria had been 'very pretty and bright, like a little bird'.[4] The painting is now lost, but Charlotte would go on to memorialise it in some detail in her longest poem, 'Madeleine in Church' (1916):

> There is a portrait of my mother, at nineteen,
>   With the black spaniel, standing by the garden seat,
>   The dainty head held high against the painted green
> And throwing out the youngest smile, shy, but half haughty and
>   half sweet.
>   Her picture then: but simply Youth, or simply Spring
>   To me to-day: a radiance on the wall,
>   So exquisite, so heart-breaking a thing
>   Beside the mask that I remember, shrunk and small,
>   Sapless and lined like a dead leaf,
> All that was left of oh! the loveliest face, by time and grief!

Anna Maria's face, in middle age, was not yet 'sapless and lined like a dead leaf', but neither was she young, and she had just carried her sixth pregnancy to full term. Fred's emotional support would no doubt have been welcome, but he was pouring all his energies into his work. The vestry hall competition could not have come at a worse time. A month before the final designs were due in, an odd decision was made. The couple's new baby had been named Daniel Kendall Mew at birth, but four months later, on 2 March 1876, both fore-names were formally changed at his baptism to Christopher Barnes (Barnes was a name from Fred's side of the family). Whatever the reasons for the name change, the conclusion that all was not well at 30 Doughty Street is hard to avoid.

It turned out to be a timely baptism. On 21 March, just as Fred was pulling out all the stops to make his deadline, the baby died without warning, of convulsions. He had lived for only four months. The couple announced their loss in the *London Daily News* the following week.

The death of a baby was not nearly so uncommon as it is today: infant mortality rates in Britain were growing in the second half of the nineteenth century, in spite of steady improvements in diet and sanitation. In 1860, the rate in England and Wales for deaths that occurred before a baby's first birthday was 148 per thousand live births; in 1880, it was 153.[5] The figures compare starkly with the current rate of around four deaths per thousand live births, but the relative prevalence in Victorian times did not, of course, make the experience less distressing for those involved.[6] Heart-breaking accounts of such losses abound in letters and diaries of the period: 'a sight full of agony' is how one mother describes the vigil she kept at the bedside of her one-year-old daughter in 1856; 'a peep into a gulf I had not looked down before,' writes another, after the sudden death of her baby son: 'I almost dread losing the sound of God's voice.'[7]

What must Lotti have made of her baby brother's death? At the age of six, she was probably more unsettled than comforted by what she read in her *Believer's Daily Remembrancer* on the day of his passing. 'There is no rest for the Christian in the world. There will be always something to disturb, perplex, or distress him: it is an enemy's land. But Jesus says, "I will give you rest."'[8] As soon as children were old enough, they were expected to take part in the grieving and mourning process, which included viewing the corpse after it had been washed and dressed, often in a white nightgown, with hands folded over the chest.[9] If the aim was to give the impression of sleep, it's hard to imagine who might be taken in, as Mew herself was to comment decades later in 'Beside the Bed':

> Someone has shut the shining eyes, straightened and folded
>   The wandering hands quietly covering the unquiet breast:
> So, smoothed and silenced you lie, like a child, not again to be
>   questioned or scolded;
>   But, for you, not one of us believes that this is rest.

The atmosphere in the house now went from bad to worse. Babies' deaths from convulsions, though not uncommon, were thought to be largely preventable. A contemporary household guide advises, with a plainly accusatory tone, that seizures might be occasioned by 'some fault in the food of the child':

> The food may be unfitted to the tender wants of the infant. It may be artificial milk instead of maternal; or it may be bad milk instead of good. And even in the case of a child fed with its own mother's milk it may happen that a sudden derangement of the mother's milk – as, for example, by a fright – will occasion a convulsion in the child.[10]

It's not known whether Anna Maria fed baby Daniel/Christopher by breast or by bottle, but either way it must have been difficult for her to avoid feeling that she had somehow failed in her duties. If she did breastfeed, it's possible she blamed the work-obsessed Fred for the stress that had caused her milk to become 'deranged'.

At the time of the baby's death, Fred had still not heard if his bid for the Hampstead Vestry Hall had been successful. The design he'd submitted, titled – as all his previous designs had been – Cavendo Tutus (the Latin meaning 'safety through caution'), was Italianate in style, and was to be faced with red bricks and dressed with creamy Portland stone. At the start of April, the *Building News and Engineering Journal* ran a piece commenting on each of the submissions, and concluded that Cavendo Tutus was of all of them 'the most symmetrical and dignified'.[11] In the second week of April, Fred got the news he'd been hoping for: the vestry committee had voted to adopt his plans.[12]

Much of Fred's summer would now be given to settling the details and selecting suppliers for the many tenders that had been received for the building work. But for six-year-old Lotti and her siblings, the start of summer meant only one thing: a trip to the Isle of Wight to visit their father's family – a trip that almost always went ahead, whether Fred was able to join them or not. Uncle Richard, who had grown up with Fred at New Fairlee, now lived on the farm with a family of his own: Lotti's Aunt Fanny and her five Mew cousins – Fanny (the eldest), Ethel Louisa,[13] Florence Elen, Gertrude Mary ('Gertie') and little Gilbert. Gertrude Mary was Lotti's favourite,[14] in spite of being six years her junior, and it was she who recalled in later years an incident that took place at the start of one of the summer visits. Gertie had set out one warm afternoon with her mother to the Newport railroad station in a fly to collect Lotti and her siblings, who that year had come alone with their nurse, Elizabeth Goodman. After the greetings were over, Lotti climbed up into the seat beside the driver so that she could enjoy an unimpeded view of the countryside as they rode home. When Elizabeth gave her a sharp thwack with a parasol and told her to take her proper place in the back, Lotti was so enraged that she grabbed the parasol, snapped it in two, threw it aside 'with an air of complete defiance'[15] and then refused to budge. It was an early display of an aversion to authority that would remain with her for life.

Lotti treasured the time she spent at New Fairlee, where even the routines remained exciting for her. On Sunday evenings, the group would make its way down the long lane that led from the farm and then head west along Staplers Road to St Paul's, a neat, grey stone neo-Norman church in the village of Barton, on the banks of the River Medina. The church still houses a stone tablet commemorating Charlotte's cousin Fanny for her loyal services to the parish. The walk took around twenty minutes and along the way they passed the characters she would reanimate years later in her semi-autobiographical essay, 'The Country Sunday' (1905). It's here that we read about 'a strapping maiden from the rope factory' who sang in the choir, a talkative blind man who informed her that Sunday was a 'day of eyes', and a woman rumoured to be the married vicar's sweetheart: 'a slim, white-frocked personage, with wandering blue eyes, which led in their time, and not unwittingly, more than one honest soul astray'.[16] Charlotte later heard that this young woman, in her virginal white Sunday dress, had brought about the vicar's downfall.

Such observations, such curiosity about the strangers she encountered on the fringes of her life, suggest that in childhood, she already had one of the most valuable habits a writer can cultivate: she was a watcher – or 'whacher', to use the habitual spelling of a writer whose work she would come to admire greatly, Emily Brontë. In her essay on Brontë's poems, she would describe her idol's own steady gaze: 'The eyes that watched unweariedly.'[17] But at the same time as Lotti was doing her observing, she had the strongest sensation also of *being* watched, by something – or someone – unseen, so that she never felt quite private or alone. The blind man's remark about Sunday being a 'day of eyes' apparently made perfect sense to her: 'In the Sunday of my fancy,' she wrote at a distance of some thirty years, 'the sky hangs like a gigantic curtain, veiling the Face which, watching us invisibly, we somehow fail to see. It judged in those old days my scamped and ill-done tasks. It viewed my childish cruelties and still, with wider range, it views and judges now.'[18]

Perhaps she linked this 'Face' – all-seeing and ever-present – with the statue of King George I that looked out with unblinking eyes across her London neighbourhood from the steeple of St George's Church. 'The eyes of the Lord are always upon us,' she read in *The Believer's Daily Remembrancer*; 'may our eyes be ever towards the Lord.'[19] It comes as no surprise to learn that the impression of being observed – and answerable to the observer – is a key theme in Mew's work. Her poetry is crowded with images of eyes. Most of the time, they are human eyes – windows onto a wide range of emotions. Besides the passion and wantonness implied by the wandering blue eyes of the vicar's temptress, they express, at various times, fear, calmness, fickleness or suffering – and occasionally an *absence* of feeling, as witness the 'lightless' and 'frozen' eyes of the old couple in 'The Road to Kérity', for instance, their expression glazed and unreadable. Now and then in the poems, we encounter eyes of a different kind. Distinctly ethereal, these eyes stand for a scrutiny of the most inva-sive kind: 'To-morrow I will tell you about the eyes of the Crystal Palace train / Looking down on us,' says the half-mad narrator of 'In Nunhead Cemetery' to his recently buried sweetheart, refusing to acknowledge her death. The image suggests not only the flat eyes of the train windows shining in the sunlight, but the scores of hidden, watchful eyes behind them. Here, as she would do so often, Mew took particulars from her lived experience and refashioned them for an invented scenario. The train line that was built to ferry the crowds to the Crystal Palace, after it had moved to Sydenham Hill, did indeed run directly past the cemetery at Nunhead, where she would one day have occasion of her own to stand and grieve.

Watching and being watched were one thing, but they require the participation of only one party. When it came to issues of faith, Charlotte expressed, in both her letters and poems, a need for the gaze to be reciprocal. It's not entirely clear when the idea first occurred to her, but as she grew older she began to feel that if she was to commit to faith in a divine being, then the onus was on that being to make itself manifest – which meant that she had to be able to see its eyes. How otherwise was she to really believe? Through the voice of the male adolescent speaker in 'The Fête', she voices the dilemma plainly:

Mother of Christ, no one has seen your eyes: how can men pray
Even unto you?

Charlotte would fret over the question of religious faith for most of her adult life. It's an anxiety that's explored at some length in the extraordinary 'Madeleine in Church', in which the protagonist confesses that she feels more comfortable kneeling in a dark corner, directing her gaze at a small plaster saint positioned in a low niche,

than 'over there, in open day / Where Christ is hanging'. The problem
for Madeleine is that she would 'rather pray / To something more like
my own clay', and she surmises that the experiences of the little effigy
– who perhaps 'Before he got his niche and crown / Had one short
stroll about the town' – must surely be closer to her own than those
of the flawless Christ figure hanging so far above her. Even if Christ
were watching her, that is not to say that she would be truly *seen*. At
the height of her agitation, Madeleine addresses Him directly: no one
can deny, she says, that He suffers too –

> But, up there, from your still, star-lighted tree
> What can You know, what can You really see
> Of this dark ditch, the soul of me!

All this doubting might have surprised the Mews' old nanny, who
had done her utmost to instil in her young charges a proper sense
of religious awe. Evangelical fervour was past its peak by then, but
its influence lingered in the mid-Victorian nursery, and Elizabeth
Goodman was a particular devotee. She followed the teachings of
the evangelical John Wesley, and worshipped at a Wesleyan chapel
in Great Queen Street, where she evidently paid close attention to
proceedings: according to Charlotte's 1913 account of her old nurse,
'From Sunday to Sunday, she could repeat the sermon almost word
for word.'[20] Evangelicalism assumes the essentially corrupt nature
of mankind, but also of each individual; and it places great impor-
tance on the individual's personal relationship with God. Like many
nannies of the period, Elizabeth insisted on daily prayers at bedtime,
but for the Mew children, there was an added sting to proceedings:
when they reached the phrase 'Forgive us our trespasses' in the Lord's
Prayer, they were required to specify what those trespasses were. Each
night, just beyond the parish of St George Bloomsbury, Lotti knelt by
her bed and listed her sins out loud under the stone king's censorious
and far-reaching gaze.

This particular part of the bedtime routine may have a lot to answer for. At some point, anyway, the notion of paying the price for excessive joy (and not just sin) became entrenched in Charlotte's moral code. And if there is any biographical basis in the 222 long lines that make up 'Madeleine in Church', it was a lesson she had learned in childhood. Even a joy as innocuous as watching shadows cross the lawn could arouse a sharp pang of guilt in her:

> We are what we are: when I was half a child I could not sit
> Watching black shadows on green lawns and red carnations
>   burning in the sun,
>   Without paying so heavily for it
>   That joy and pain, like any mother and her unborn child were
>   almost one.

Towards the end of 1876, on Saturday 9 December, the Mew household was plunged into mourning once again, when five-year-old Richard succumbed to scarlet fever. The disease was rife during this period, and children between the ages of four and eight were particularly susceptible.[21] Elizabeth Goodman would no doubt have known the signs: a sore throat that progresses quickly to a red, sunburn-like rash, accompanied by chills, headache, body aches, nausea and vomiting. There were no cures, and treatments were alarmingly primitive. A popular medical guide from 1871 noted that 'in severe cases, when the brain suffers, some apply leeches, others take blood from the arm, and a few blister. From two to six leeches applied behind or below the ears, on each side, relieve the head symptoms, and are serviceable; but the lancet and blisters I would dissuade, having never been convinced of their benefit.'[22]

One autumnal afternoon, not long after Richard's death, it appears that it fell to Lotti to break the news to the family's 'unflinchingly agnostic' needlewoman, Miss Bolt.[23] Charlotte's satirical description of this childhood figure, who was as important to her in her way as the God-fearing Elizabeth Goodman, is typically evocative:

> To outsiders she was simply an unusually incompetent little needle-woman; but our estimate of her personality found no adequate expression. We called her affectionately 'Bolty', and enthroned her silently in our hearts. Twice a week and on occasions of domestic pressure or festivity, she used to mount the creaky stairs. She sat by the window in a favourite corner making pinafores and darning socks, for which she received a weekly salary, and generously loading our minds with priceless experiences, less marketable, alas! than the labours of her failing eyes and unskilful hands.
>
> Her appearance was unprepossessing. In age she was about sixty; and in height not much over five feet. Two pale blue eyes guarded a nose, technically speaking broken, but practically almost extinct. A small allowance of faded drab hair was parted sparsely on her forehead and gathered into a net behind. Her mouth was only significant as a vehicle of speech. In describing her hastily from memory, one would be tempted to forget it altogether, but for reminders in the shape of a couple of very prominent front teeth.[24]

Charlotte assembled her reminiscence of Miss Bolt some twenty-five years later, and it may never have been intended as straight memoir, but it is striking that, while she uses the needlewoman's real name, the names of family members have been altered. Charlotte herself becomes 'Miss Mary' (her middle name), while her brother Richard is 'Charlie'. Her elder brother, eleven-year-old Henry, is absent altogether, though he would surely have been around at the time, and most likely in the nursery itself. As the years rolled by, she would have increasingly good reason to protect her family's privacy, and in particular in regard to Henry.

On the afternoon on which Mary communicates the news of Charlie's death, she is sitting beside a flickering fire, with her little sister on her knee. The weather is fittingly restive: through the window, leaves can be seen swirling along the pavements, 'blown from the dead heaps in the square'. When Miss Bolt enters and enquires after the missing boy, Mary conveys the news as quickly as she can, taking care to avoid the word 'dead' so as not to alarm her little sister, but Miss Bolt sees no need for such delicacy:

'Dead, dead, Miss Mary! Well, 'e's 'appier where 'e is!'
'What is "dead"?' lisped my little maid softly. I bent and kissed the word away. But Miss Bolt answered the question solemnly, her eyes fixed on the low fire. 'It jest means as you go out like the candle or the fire or a noo piece at the theater wot 'asn't took. It don't matter much to anybody but them as wants the fire to warm 'em, and 'im wot perduced the play. That's it, ain't it, Miss Mary?' she said, turning a dim gaze on me.[25]

However factually accurate 'Miss Bolt' may be, the essay contains important clues about the sort of child Lotti was, or would remember herself to be. In the fictionalised account, 'Miss Mary's' primary concern in relating her brother's death is to protect the 'little maid' on her knee: her beloved younger sister. Anne was only three at the time of Richard's death, and over the years the roles adopted by the two sisters in this short memoir piece – the one guardian, the other ward – would help establish a strong and lasting sibling dynamic.

Richard's death would leave a deep mark on Charlotte's psyche. The Christmas of 1876, coming as it did just two weeks after the tragedy, was doubtless marked by it too. Ordinarily, this was Lotti's favourite season, a time when reality gave way to the enchantment of a world where, as she later wrote, 'red lights gleamed from Manor House windows; ostlers bandied jests in the court-yards of lonely inns; the crack of whips and the hoofs of post-horses drowned the wheels of the crawling cab and the bell of the muffin-man ting-tinging down our long, dull street'.[26] It's hard to imagine the usual preparations going ahead with the customary giddy excitement: the cooking of mincemeat, plum pudding and cakes; the posting of cards; the buying and wrapping of presents. That year, Christmas at 30 Doughty Street must have been an altogether more subdued affair.

As the new year stuttered into life in the wake of the family's loss, Fred discovered that building work on the Hampstead Vestry Hall was progressing less smoothly than he would have liked. It became clear that the completion date he'd had carved into the foundation stone (1877) was wildly optimistic. By March 1878, the committee members were growing impatient: when, one of them demanded to know, was the builder's 'horrible hoarding' going to be removed?[27] With a final, concerted push, the building was finished and ready for use in June; the vestrymen held their first meeting there at the start of July, and on a windy evening in November, a grand opening concert was given in the spacious hall on the top floor.[28] The public reaction to the lofty new building was largely positive. Substantially built, from red Bracknell bricks, the hall stands on the corner of Belsize Avenue and Haverstock Hill.[29] Its long and varied history is fittingly colourful: in 1913, suffragette Emmeline Pankhurst declared to a packed audience there that 'The Government must introduce and carry through a Government measure giving votes to women next session, otherwise the Government must go.'[30] But the hall is perhaps best known as a venue for weddings, including that of T. S. Eliot to his first wife, Vivienne Haigh-Wood, in 1915; two on-screen ceremonies have also been filmed there, for *Georgy Girl* (1966) and *Four Weddings and a Funeral* (1994).

The spring of 1879 brought with it a new distraction, and a potential new ally for Lotti. Freda Kendall Mew was born on 10 March, an event proudly announced in the *Morning Post* the following

Saturday. Anna Maria would turn forty-two later that month, but things had gone more smoothly than with her previous birth and the new baby flourished. Freda would grow up to be as 'remarkable' as her sisters; according to a family friend, she was 'like a flame'.[31] With mother and baby doing well, Fred felt able to return to the Isle of Wight the following month to celebrate the completion of his latest project, the Bible Christian New Chapel in Newport. The opening ceremony was hosted by his brother Henry (who had been running the Bugle Hotel for some twenty years now), with Fred proposing the toast – for 'Prosperity to the Borough of Newport': he flattered himself, he said, that the new building would prove 'a very attractive feature' and hoped it might be taken as an indication of the town's ever-improving fortunes.[32]

That autumn of 1879, Randolph Caldecott's illustrated version of *The Babes in the Wood* appeared and was widely advertised in the papers. To celebrate the event, a special edition box set of Caldecott's picture books, in brightly coloured bindings, was brought out in time for Freda's first Christmas. It may have been at this point that the title was added to the Mew children's bookshelf and made such a lasting impression on Lotti. She was enthralled by the story of two orphaned children who, on the instruction of their wicked uncle, are abandoned in a wood by a pair of crooks and left for dead; in 1923, she referred to it in the middle of three stanzas of 'Fin de Fête', a poem so admired by Thomas Hardy that he copied it out by hand from the pages of *The Sphere*:

Good-night and good dreams to you, —
　　Do you remember the picture-book thieves
Who left two children sleeping in a wood the long night through,
　　And how the birds came down and covered them with leaves?

Despite the traumas it contained, Charlotte would look back on her early life as a time of enchantment, joy and carefree extravagance. The fabric of her childhood may have been shot through with grief, but what remained with her, above all, were its 'dazzling lights and colours'.[33] She raced about the gardens of Mecklenburgh Square, woke up excited on her birthdays ('The sparrows in the square always seemed to chirp louder on such mornings'[34]), made up stories and acted them out, and looked forward to long summer holidays with her Isle of Wight cousins. Under the low ceiling of her nursery, she learned, with her nurse's help, to read and write, threaded needles for Miss Bolt and soaked up the anecdotes the old woman told as she mended pinafores or darned socks. As a writer, the idea of childhood was tremendously important to her. The words 'child' or 'children' appear no fewer than twenty-nine times in the twenty-eight poems that make up *The Farmer's Bride*. Childhood was transitory, and therefore to be treasured. Once it had gone, it could never be re-encountered; and neither could the artfully mythologised figures who populated it. The kind-hearted Bolty disappeared from Lotti's life one autumn evening, apparently without saying goodbye. This awkward little needlewoman was, for Charlotte, the 'last relic [. . .] of life's most exquisite possession – youth'. She also embodied a quality that seemed to Charlotte to belong expressly to the province of childhood, 'the spirit of goodness': 'Poorly and comically clad, it greeted me in the person of that sad, neutral-tinted little workwoman, who left me, like the childhood in which I knew her, mysteriously and without farewell.'[35]

3

A Rosebud Set with Little Wilful Thorns
1880–1883

The 1881 census shows four children living at the Mews' narrow house in Doughty Street: Henry (fifteen), Charlotte (eleven), Anne (seven) and Freda (two). Henry and Charlotte are both listed as 'scholars', and it's likely that Lotti had been at her small private day school in Gower Street for a year already. Many girls from middle-class families like hers attended such schools from around the age of ten, for five or six years, though the education they received varied widely, according to the priorities and experience of the head teacher.

Lotti loved school. She was bright, sociable and popular, and had a knack for lightening the mood; she told funny stories purely for the joy of making people laugh. She was well turned out, but she dressed simply: a black-and-white checked dress for weekdays and a plain brown one for Sunday best. Her exceptionally curly hair was cut short (it was neater that way, and easier to manage) and there was a bounce and eagerness to her movements. Her quick, alert mind made her a rewarding student to teach, and the fact that she had a natural musical gift and was clever with her hands meant that she also excelled in the 'drawing room' accomplishments considered so crucial for girls of her class. Perhaps surprisingly, for a child as strong-willed and free-thinking as Lotti, she found she actually enjoyed acquiring the artistic skills that were intended to make a lady of her: in time, she became a skilful pianist, and could turn out intricate pieces of embroidery executed to her own designs.

But the institution she attended, at 80 Gower Street, was no mere school of manners. The Gower Street School for Girls was a successor to Bedford College School, a girls' preparatory day school that was attached to the college and therefore used to high academic standards. The school was housed, like other proprietary establishments of its kind, in a private residence. Its headmistress, Lucy Harrison, was in her thirties and lived on site with a younger teacher, Ellen Mathews, and three female domestic helpers.

Among the visiting staff was the professor of modern history, Samuel Gardiner, a family friend of the Harrisons who is still acknowledged as one of the foremost authorities on the Puritan revolution and English Civil War. The geography teacher, Miss Chessar (who also taught at the highly regarded Laleham School, to the west of the city), wrote to Miss Harrison to enthuse about the standard at Gower Street and the cleverness of the pupils, concluding that 'I only know that in your school I find the greatest pleasure in teaching the children, who respond so well.'[1]

The academic opportunities the Gower Street School offered its girls were not the normal fare. In 1876, just a few years before Charlotte started there, the Schools' Inquiry Commission observed that while boys' education equipped them for the wider world, girls were being prepared only for life in the home.[2] Needlework and cookery were among the core subjects for female students, and most commentators – women included – saw them as essential training for the girls' futures as housewives. From a physiological standpoint, the level of mental stimulation required for serious academic study was generally considered harmful for girls – a view that Lord Hatherley expressed, although couched in somewhat guarded terms, in a speech he made at the opening of the new Leeds High School for Girls. His words were reported in the *Journal of the Women's Education Union*:

> He did not wish to say anything offensive, but medical men said
> there was not the same physical power and strength in the fibres
> of the brain as would enable the majority of girls to compete
> with each other in the high branches of mathematics and other
> subjects of that kind requiring great mental power and attention.

There were cases of persons having become seriously unwell in consequence of having their studies pushed too far in that direction.[3]

Quite how the medical men reached their conclusions is unclear, but in any case Lucy Harrison had no apparent concerns about the delicacy of the fibres in her pupils' female brains. Alongside the science-based courses offered at her school, she herself taught English, Latin and Natural History. She had grown up surrounded by books and book lovers – most notably her aunt, the poet Mary Howitt, whose admirers included Queen Victoria. Mary and her husband, William, also a writer, moved in elevated circles, mixing with prominent literary figures of the day, including Charles Dickens, Elizabeth Gaskell and Elizabeth Barrett Browning. In 1837, the couple had stayed with William and Dorothy Wordsworth during a tour of the north of England. From her earliest childhood, then, writers had been more to Lucy than names on the spines of books; but her lifelong passion was for the words themselves. Her lessons were inspiring because her enthusiasm for books, and for poetry in particular, was so clearly heartfelt. One former pupil recalls 'the zest of anticipation' with which she and her classmates looked forward to literature lessons:

I remember just how it felt when Miss Harrison came into the room, bringing with her, as she always did, a serene sense of freshness and space and of august things. And how swiftly we fell to work, fired by that noble earnestness, and under the unfailing impression that the poets she read with us were her own personal friends – as indeed they were. She had the power not only of imparting knowledge but of communicating atmosphere and beauty, with the result that she made many good lovers of poetry, eager to read and glad to learn by heart. I think that was one of the greatest things she did for us. One learnt how profoundly poetry counts, or should count, in life.[4]

Born in Birkenhead, Lucy Harrison was from an old Yorkshire Quaker family, and the youngest of eight children. She was in her thirties when Lotti started at the school. She wore her curly hair short – just as Lotti did – and had a warm smile, clear blue eyes and a steady gaze. By contrast with Lotti's mother – now in her mid-forties, bad-tempered and wearied by childbirth and ill health – the elegant Miss Harrison moved about the school with purposefulness and grace: she was, as one acquaintance put it, 'illuminate with strength and gentleness and merriment'.[5] She also did her bit outside the school, not least in support of the social reformer Octavia Hill, later founder of the National Trust. It was at Hill's request that Harrison supervised weekly baths for children in the Marylebone slums. For all her affability and compassion, she was no pushover. There were few formal rules at the school, but the respect she commanded 'made talk about rules unnecessary'; they were simply kept.[6] She didn't suffer fools gladly and had no time for know-it-alls and socialites. But if pupils were willing to conform to a simple code of conduct, there was nothing Miss Harrison would not do for them. She wrote plays tailored to their strengths, and offered extra lessons to the older girls as needed.[7] Teaching, for her, was a vocation, and her pupils adored her.

Like most of the women who staffed the new schools and colleges for girls, Miss Harrison was unmarried. Full-time, paid employment was still taboo for middle-class women after marriage: it would have been an unthinkable slight on the capabilities of the wage-earning husband.[8] But Miss Harrison had additional reasons for wishing to remain single. Not only did she treasure her independence too much to think of marrying, her romantic feelings were for women rather than men, as would soon become apparent.

Miss Harrison's sexual orientation did not preclude men from being attracted to *her*, of course. In the 1860s, she had helped out at the Working Women's College in Queen Square, Bloomsbury, where at least one of her male colleagues took an interest in her 'finely proportioned figure'. Arthur Munby taught Latin at the college, had an eye for the ladies and confessed his libidinous thoughts in his diaries. He was nearly forty when he first made mention of the twenty-two-year-old Lucy Harrison: 'Found Miss Harrison, the pretty superintendent, at her desk, with rose-coloured ribbon in her hair; and student girls lounging in the saloon-like coffee room.' He was as taken by Miss Harrison's boldness as he was by her looks: at a college function in March 1866 he had noted that she '*whistled* an elaborate accompaniment of a song which her sister sang and played', adding that he had never heard a lady whistle before. He admired, too, her 'buxom' physique: she looked, he mused, 'like a more intelligent dairymaid'.[9]

Good-natured, attractive, inspiring and in the prime of life, it would be surprising if Miss Harrison hadn't been a romantic focus for some of her pupils over the years, especially given the increased prevalence of same-sex crushes in same-sex schools. Novelist and suffragist Evelyn Sharp, one of the writers into whose circle Charlotte would later be drawn, revealed in her memoirs that she had regularly fallen in love with 'Olympian goddesses' in the years above her at school.[10] Whatever the nature of Lotti's feelings for her teacher (and she may well have been unclear about this herself), we know that she was deeply attached to her. It's impossible to overestimate the importance of the connection. Recent studies have shown just how fundamentally the support supplied by a close teacher–pupil relationship can affect a child's mental health, particularly if that child is emotionally vulnerable.[11] No matter what happened at home, Miss Harrison was a constant and unchanging presence in Lotti's life; she had become, like Elizabeth Goodman, a 'fixed part' of her 'universe'. Such lodestars would remain crucial to her throughout her life. Luckily, whether by fortune or design, she would rarely find herself without one.

We might picture Lotti in one of her English lessons, straight-backed, her small face tilted upwards as Miss Harrison held forth on the nefarious representation of women in certain Middle English texts – a subject on which the teacher would later publish her thoughts:

'In the Middle Ages when monkish ideals prevailed, women were regarded as the evil *par excellence*; they of all creatures were to be avoided if a man would save his soul alive.'[12] The trope of the purportedly 'evil' woman was one of Lucy Harrison's bêtes noires, and it's one that Charlotte would explore in several of her poems, most extensively in 'Madeleine in Church', in which the narrator comments of her namesake, Mary Magdalene, 'She was a sinner, we are what we are: the spirit afterwards, but first, the touch.'

If Charlotte was also influenced by her teacher's literary preferences, it was a solid foundation for her later life as a poet. Miss Harrison particularly enjoyed giving lessons on Early and Middle English literature, from *Beowulf* to Shakespeare, but her tastes were far broader than that. She was a voracious and inquisitive reader, as witness the many books mentioned in her diaries during her years at the school. The works of Spenser, Shakespeare, Dickens and George Eliot nestled on her shelves alongside the histories of Carlyle and Macaulay.[13] Her favourite poets included Dante, Coleridge and Wordsworth (especially the *Lyrical Ballads* and *The Prelude*), Emily Brontë, Tennyson and Browning, whose poems she found 'a great delight and refreshment'.[14] Miss Harrison believed that a poem could provide the reader with a fresh access to reality – a belief she expounded on in a school-leavers' address, in which she advised the girls to look again at the poems of Alice Meynell:

> Read her sonnet 'To a Daisy'. There I think you will find something about the daisy that you have never thought of before, though you have loved it from babyhood, have gathered it, drawn it, thought of it, and have known it in almost all its aspects. She will tell you something not only about the daisy but about your own mind and about the universe.[15]

In the sonnet in question, the flower serves as a symbol for the mysteries of creation. The daisy hides secrets that will only be revealed when the speaker is part of eternity, looking back out at the world

47

through the daisy itself 'from God's side'. What is it like to view the world from this fixed, flower-sized perspective? Or indeed from any perspective other than one's own? The poem suggests that we cannot properly know – or not, at least, in this life. But we can try. Harrison was urging her pupils, as they went out into the world, not just to *read* poetry but to apply the insights they learned there to their daily lives. In later years she would write to a friend, 'What a happy world it would be if more people really took poetry to help them to live. I am more and more struck as I grow older in noticing how very few people regard poetry seriously or ever think of applying it to their lives, and all the while it is the supreme essence of life.'[16]

The poetry Mew wrote in her adult years suggests that Miss Harrison's early lesson on perspective had gone deep. Time and again in her poems she imagines her way into the heart of another life and gives it voice. Sometimes the being with which she identifies is human; other times, as in Meynell's 'To a Daisy', it is not. But Mew being Mew, she went a stage further than her predecessor: in her work, the identification is so intense – so absolute – that the resulting poetry sounds less like an act of ventriloquism than an instance of possession, even when the poem is delivered in the third person. John Keats once described in a letter to a friend how 'if a sparrow come before my window, I take part in its existence and pick about the gravel'.[17] Mew had the same ability. Towards the end of her life, some of the magnificent old London plane trees (just like those overlooked by her nursery window) were cleared from Endsleigh Gardens, on the south side of Euston Square, to make room for new buildings. Mew's response, 'The Trees are Down' (first published in 1923), recounts how the trees had stood in all weathers, feeling the winds that blew in over the rooftops from the sea; and how her own heart had flinched with every stroke of the axe. The lines themselves are sonically and emotionally resonant, but the sentiment itself, throughout most of the poem, is nothing exceptional. Then, in the final five lines, she does something that lifts the poem beyond mere reflection: with an eerie sense of theatre, she cuts out all background noise

– the gales and the incessant blows of the axe – and locates us inside the felled trees themselves as they lie dying in the grass, so that we hear *with* them 'a quiet rain', 'the sparrows flying' and 'the small creeping creatures in the earth where they were lying'.

It would be simplistic to overemphasise the contribution Lotti's school years made to her ability to write lines like these, but certainly she flourished under Miss Harrison's tutelage. In literature lessons, her early love of words was applauded and nurtured – just as well, perhaps, since the 'making of verses' wasn't countenanced at home, where Elizabeth Goodman was in the habit of sweeping densely covered sheets of manuscripts, over which Lotti had laboured 'pathetically', into her dustpan with a gesture of 'indiscriminate disgust'. The habit of writing poetry, so Nurse Goodman told Lotti and her siblings, with some disdain, was no better than that of smoking. Both vices were unquestionably 'injurious to the brain'.[18]

As important as Miss Harrison was, Lotti also needed company of her own age, and the Gower Street School had plenty to offer. Other girls were drawn to her natural exuberance and sense of fun; Lotti herself, it seems, was looking for something more profound. She took her friendships seriously and went to some lengths to maintain them, making an effort to get to know her best friends' families and writing long, chatty letters in the vacations, which she peppered with little ink-drawn sketches to illustrate some joke or other. Her efforts were evidently appreciated: several of the relationships begun at Gower Street survived into adulthood, including a few made with older girls, like Margaret ('Maggie') Robinson, who was six years her senior. The daughter of a prosperous draper, Maggie went on to study at Newnham College, Cambridge, became a gifted zoologist and married the renowned marine biologist Edward Browne. The couple would provide valuable support for Mew during stormy times ahead.

Also at school with Lotti were Edith, Mary and Harriette Chick.[19] The Chick family were successful lace-makers from Honiton in

Devon, who had recently moved into London, just north of Oxford Street. When the family was complete, there would be seven girls and three boys. A photograph from 1886 shows the adolescent Lotti, arms crossed and looking suitably sullen, with six of the Chick sisters clustered round her. (Dorothy, the youngest, was not yet born.) The Chicks, too, were to play an important role in Charlotte's adulthood. The eldest girl, Edith, was almost exactly Lotti's age, and the two became close friends, but it wasn't long before Lotti grew attached to the whole family.[20] She visited them often throughout her teenage years and early twenties, and at Christmas she never failed to send gifts: linen handkerchiefs initialled by hand, meticulously made pieces of embroidery and, every year, without fail, a handmade pocket-sized calendar for the father, Samuel, illustrated with intricate pen-and-ink drawings, little figures brought to life with skilful cross-hatch shading.[21]

One of these calendars, for the year 1890, survives. It depicts a rural scene at harvest time. In the top left corner, a young woman is emptying the sheaves she has gathered in her apron into a wicker basket, while in the opposite corner a second woman stands upright, resting her back. In the centre foreground, a brawny man with his sleeves rolled to the elbows is embracing another woman from behind. The woman looks down and away, with a coy tilt of her head. He carries a pitchfork in his free hand; she, a rake, which she has balanced nonchalantly against her shoulder while the man leans in towards her, as if whispering sweet nothings in her ear. The detail in these drawings is extraordinary, given that each figure is no more than two inches high. Anne was the sister who would go on to specialise in art, but Lotti was clearly gifted in this area too.

Besides the Chick clan and Maggie Robinson, Lotti's closest school friend was a quiet, self-possessed girl called Ethel Oliver. From North Country Quaker stock, Ethel had dark eyes, sharp, chiselled features and a reputation for integrity and reliability. There was a hint of the North Country in her speech, as well as the occasional 'thee' and 'thou'.[22] She lived with her family in the Keeper's House next to the main entrance of the Royal Botanic Gardens at Kew, where her father, Daniel, was Keeper of the Herbarium. He was also Professor of Botany at University College, London, a stone's throw away from Miss Harrison's school, and since the Oliver family was – like Lucy Harrison – Quaker, the Gower Street School seemed a sensible choice for Ethel. The only problem was that Kew was some nine miles from Gower Street and the trains were infrequent. When Daniel had first taken on the professorship in 1860, he'd known that in order to make time for both his jobs, he would need to deliver his lectures at eight o'clock in the morning. Ethel's great-nephew, Sir Stephen Oliver, has pointed out that the only railway station serving the district in those days was Kew Bridge, and no train left from there early enough to get Daniel to his lectures on time. The solution he settled on added an extra leg to the journey, but it ran like clockwork:

> [Daniel] was woken each morning at 5 o'clock by the Gardens' night-constable tapping with a pole on the bedroom window until an answering hand appeared – varied on Fridays by the hand releasing an agreed gratuity of 2s. 6d. for the week's service. At 6 a.m. a cab arrived to take Daniel to Hammersmith, from where the journey was completed on the Metropolitan Railway.[23]

We can only hope that by the time Ethel started at Gower Street, the train service from Kew had improved and she was spared this gruelling journey before the start of the school day. Either way, it's likely that she would have accepted her circumstances with a quiet forbearance. She was not given to making a fuss. Indeed, compared with her outgoing elder sister, Winifred, she was distinctly taciturn; Miss Harrison's niece, Amice Macdonell, a fellow pupil at the school, remembers her as a 'stiff, silent girl',[24] though Amice was six years younger than Ethel, and formed this impression at an age when composure might easily be taken for stiffness. Above all, Ethel was a carer – kind-hearted, non-judgemental and fiercely loyal. Over the years Charlotte grew to appreciate more and more what she saw as her friend's 'Quakerly' quietness.[25] The two were almost exactly a year apart in age (Lotti was the younger) and they had many things in common. They both became accomplished pianists while still at school, and were passionate about art and litera- ture, and they both had older brothers who had begun to follow their fathers' career paths. After leaving school, Henry Mew was articled to Fred as an architectural student, while Frank Oliver studied his father's subject, botany, at University College, London and then Cambridge.[26] Lotti's and Ethel's sisters, Anne Mew and Winifred Oliver, also had parallel interests: both were talented painters who would go on to study at art college (Anne at the Female School of Art in Queen Square, and Winifred at the Slade).[27]

But while the outward facts of family connections corresponded, the atmosphere in the Mew and Oliver households could not have been more different. While Lotti's father retreated to his office to work on his architectural projects, Ethel's parents typically spent their evenings 'sitting together under the light of an old colza lamp with a Turner Liber print propped up between them; the mother at her needlework, and their father reading some art book'.[28] Professor Oliver – a talented draughtsman and painter in his own right – was lifelong friends with John Ruskin, a frequent visitor to the house on Kew Green.[29] Among his other friends were painters Alfred William Hunt and Arthur Hughes, whose daughter also attended Miss Harrison's school in Gower Street. Not surprisingly, the Olivers owned a number of original paintings. True, the walls of the Mews' home were hung with paintings too, but they were nearly all of the technical type – architectural drawings and paintings of buildings that Fred or his father-in-law had worked on.

As for the mothers of the two families, Mrs Mew was a proud and needy woman who went to considerable lengths to keep her private life private – sometimes at great cost to those around her. As a result, first- hand accounts of her are thin on the ground, but here and there we catch a glimpse. Lotti's school friends saw her occasionally when she brought little Freda Mew to dance classes at the school. One of these friends remembers her as 'certainly silly' and 'all decked out in blue boas'.[30] Ethel's mother, Hannah, on the other hand, was deadly serious and moved in altogether more cultivated circles. She was a close friend of the poets Dora Greenwell and Jean Ingelow, who in turn counted Tennyson and Christina Rossetti among her own friends.[31]

Here was a family whose sensibilities were close to Lotti's own, but if she dreamed of being welcomed into its fold, then, for the time being at least, she was to be disappointed. In spite of the Olivers' artistic leanings, attitudes at the Keeper's House were far from permissive. Hannah was rather remote and disapproving – 'a bit of a sourpuss', in the words of one of her grandsons.[32] The family anecdote that she insisted all money coming into the house should be washed suggests that she was also rather neurotic – if not an out-and-out snob. She wasn't keen on her daughter's excitable friend, though the reasons are unknown. In her early teens, Lotti went through a High Church phase; she wore a small cross around her neck, silver on weekdays and a gold one 'for best'.[33] Stephen Oliver has suggested that, as a confirmed Quaker, Hannah may have worried about the influence Lotti was having on Ethel's thoughts on religion. Or perhaps Lotti was simply a little too lively for her tastes. Either way, it made no odds: Ethel was self-assured enough to listen to her own judgement on the matter, and she stuck loyally to her friend.

Lotti was by no means the only target for Hannah's disapproval. When Winifred Oliver brought back her carefully worked drawings from a life class, her mother demanded that she bury them in the garden – in order, she said, to avoid corrupting the servants.[34] To twenty-first-century sensibilities her reaction is pitiful – not to mention cruel; at the time it would have been less surprising. Nudity aside, in certain quarters of society it was still thought inappropriate for women to express themselves publicly, through paint, print or any other means; nor were they considered quite up to it. So it was that Winifred and Lotti stood by as their early artistic efforts were swept out of sight. The ignorance surrounding such responses to women's creative efforts seemed ignorant even of its own existence. There were names for the type of girl who disregarded the usual constraints placed on her gender; author and phrenologist Amy Barnard described her as 'a rosebud set with little wilful thorns' – an epithet that particularly applied, she said, to those girls who displayed 'bookish' tendencies, as Lotti did.[35] For the time being, there was very little Lotti could do about the situation. But she was not about to abandon her passion. If the products of her imagination were destroyed for now, the imagination itself remained very much intact.

4

What You're Made, That You'll Be
1883–1886

As Lotti grew into adolescence she gained very little in height – settling at around four feet, ten inches – but her face lengthened slightly into a fine oval and her figure softened in the usual way. There was never any danger of her being plump, but when she began developing her first curves, the family's needlewoman (the no-nonsense Miss Bolt) saw fit to offer some timely advice on dieting. She warned Lotti about a young lady she knew who, in an effort to stay slim, had taken to sucking lemons and drinking vinegar by the saucerful – and had died soon afterwards. 'If you should ever feel yourself spreading,' she cautioned Lotti, 'don't you be tempted to foller 'er; for what you're made, that you'll be.'[1] Lotti still had her hair cut short in early adolescence, the tight curls clustered high on her forehead. The arch of her brows became a little more pronounced, lending her an earnest, slightly quizzical look, but she had lost none of her playful energy. A fellow pupil at the Gower Street School remembers her from around this time: 'There was something piquante about her; she had bright eyes, was light and small-boned; had a way of turning round as she talked, sort of pirouetting on her feet; hands and feet were small. I recall often laughing with her.'[2]

In the company of her elder brother and affectionate younger sisters at home, surrounded by good friends at school and thriving under the tutelage of Miss Harrison, thirteen-year-old Lotti appeared to have everything to look forward to. But it was during the long, hot summer of 1883 that certain strands in her life began to unravel. Towards the end of the academic year, it became clear that all was not well with Lucy Harrison. She had been teaching at Gower Street for nearly twenty years, and running the school for eight of those. Besides the inevitable fatigue, a tendency to depression was now brought to a head by two unwelcome milestones in her personal life. In the spring of the previous year, her mother had died. With her father already dead, and no children or partner to turn to, she had only a sister to mourn with. In the midst of her grief, the approach of a landmark birthday – her fortieth – may have prompted some self-reflection. Devoted as she was to her pupils, was she to live out the rest of her days in the noisy, crowded capital as a spinster teacher?

Living, working and sleeping in the same building was adding considerably to the strain, and as a first step, she arranged to move her living quarters from the school site to a house on Haverstock Hill in Hampstead – the same road, by coincidence, where Kendall & Mew's Vestry Hall had been completed five years earlier. She placed adverts in *The Times* and other papers announcing that a school boarding house would be opening in Hampstead in September. Now that she had two lots of rent to pay, she needed the extra income, though there was only room in the new house to accommodate three girls at the most. The advertised fees for tuition at Gower Street that year ranged from three to five guineas a term, depending on the age of the pupil. The rates for boarding, including tuition fees, were to be between £75 and £85 per annum[3] – a not inconsiderable outlay given that the average annual salary for a clerical worker in 1880 was around £90.[4]

The move would help, but Lucy doubted it would be enough to chase away her demons. Now, a long-standing dream began to resurface: since childhood she had fantasised about building a house in the Yorkshire Dales, where generations of Harrisons had lived. The rolling hills, moorland, river valleys and sweeping upland pastures were a world away from the clatter and sprawl of London, and she resolved to travel up that summer to look for a plot of land. She would be accompanied by her concerned elder sister, Agnes (mother of Lotti's schoolmate, Amice).

Lotti, meanwhile, felt the long vacation at home in Doughty Street stretching out ahead of her. For a lively, inquisitive girl on the brink of womanhood, it was not the most inspiring of districts. In 1917, D. H. Lawrence would stay a few yards from the Mews' house, on Mecklenburgh Square, in the house of fellow poet Hilda Doolittle. While there he began to write his novel *Aaron's Rod*, at one point in which we are given a glimpse of what the protagonist can see as he crouches on a seat in the garden square in a rainstorm:

> Beyond the tall shrubs and the high, heavy railings the wet street gleamed silently. The houses of the Square rose like a cliff on this inner dark sea, dimly lighted at occasional windows. Boughs swayed and sang. [. . .] He was frightened, it all seemed so sinister, this dark, bristling heart of London. Wind boomed and tore like waves ripping a shingle beach.[5]

The area may not normally have been quite so frightening, but Lotti certainly found it boring – 'our long, dull street', she would later call it.[6] A Doughty Street neighbour remembers stuffy summer Sunday afternoons in the street, when 'the always dull houses would look infinitely duller with their blinds down, and no sound would fall upon the ear save the distant hum of the cabs in Holborn'.[7]

But if the prospect of spending the vacation at home filled her with dismay, she would soon discover that there were worse things to bear than tedium. Miss Harrison, it turned out, was not the only one showing signs of strain that summer. Since leaving school, Lotti's brother Henry had been learning the architectural business, under his father's direction: he was to follow in the footsteps of his father, grandfather and great-grandfather before him. Henry was quick to learn, and when he began his training, his future – and the financial security of the whole family – looked assured. But more recently he had been finding it difficult to sleep through the night, and in the daytime was too exhausted to concentrate on his studies; worse, he seemed to have lost all interest in them. His eyes took on a vacant expression, and when questioned he said he was sure he was being secretly drugged, although he couldn't think who might be doing the drugging. He took to talking portentously, and with real urgency, about the end of the world, explaining that it was his duty to let people know such a time was coming – and coming soon. Fred's efforts at reassuring him only made him more agitated. He began quoting passages from scripture: *But of that day and hour knoweth no man, no, not the angels of heaven, but my Father only.*[8] Fred, alarmed, resolved to cut down Henry's workload.[9]

By the end of the summer, Lucy Harrison's mood was greatly improved. After much searching and several false leads, a suitable building plot had been found two miles north of Countersett, in the village of Bainbridge; to mark the occasion, she had had some trees planted on the newly acquired land. When she returned to London she was – if not entirely cured of her depression – in a far healthier state of mind, ready to face the new school year, though less inclined now to devote quite so much energy to her charges. From this time on, she would spend any free hours she had planning her private rural idyll.

Lotti, now nearly fourteen, was one of three student-boarders to take up residence at Lucy Harrison's house in Hampstead that autumn of 1883. Ethel Oliver was another, and Edith Scull, a dark-haired, 'rather stout' girl (and daughter of an American professor), made up the trio.[10] Also resident was twenty-seven-year-old fellow teacher Ellen Mathews, the daughter of a Shropshire accountant, who had moved with Miss Harrison from the Gower Street site.[11] With the Oliver family living in Kew and the Scull family in Hounslow (nine and thirteen miles, respectively, from Gower Street), it made good sense for Ethel and Edith to board. But the school was virtually on the Mews' doorstep – a twenty-minute walk away, at the outside. No doubt Fred and Anna Maria believed their high-spirited daughter would benefit generally from Miss Harrison's steadying influence, but that hardly seems enough to justify such an expense. A more likely explanation is that they were worried about the effect Henry's eccentric behaviour might be having on Lotti's own state of mind. His recent over-fondness for masturbating had not gone unnoticed, but Henry said he was unable to stop himself. Or perhaps the worry was that Lotti's excitable temperament made her particularly susceptible to Henry's rantings about an imminent apocalypse – the most likely, that is, to end up ill herself.

Boarding was Lotti's first, modest taste of independence, and she revelled in it. The usually monotonous details of domestic life became something to cherish. She now enjoyed her evening meal and breakfast in the company of Ethel, her closest friend, and Miss Harrison, her idol. Each morning, the two teachers and three students climbed into the stuffy, velvet-lined interior of a hackney carriage. Along the way, they picked up Miss Harrison's young niece, Amice Macdonell. The journey to Gower Street was neither comfortable nor quiet: hackney cabs were known as 'growlers', on account of the noise they made – the horses' hooves, the rattling windows and the juddering wheels all contributing a distinctive note to the general din as the carriage lurched over the stone-paved streets. If not entirely relaxing, it was, at least, a comparatively speedy option. At the end of lessons, the all-female party went home on foot, walking two abreast down Gower Street, then on through Camden Town to Haverstock Hill. Miss Harrison and Miss Mathews led the way; Ethel and Edith, both a year older than Lotti, went directly behind the teachers, and Lotti and Amice (five years Lotti's junior) brought up the rear. In all, the journey took about an hour. 'We walked a long way back,' Amice remembers, 'partly through noisy roads and dreary, but I walked with C. M. Mew and her talk made the way seem pleasant.'[12]

The streets they passed through in Camden on these daily walks were crowded with noisy markets, the air filled with cries of 'One penny – the lady's tormenter – all one penny,' and 'Vi'lets – sweet vi'lets.'[13] Lotti, ever the 'whacher', took it all in. Years later, she would bring just such a scene magically to life in the title poem of her American collection, *Saturday Market*:

In Saturday's Market there's eggs a 'plenty
    And dead-alive ducks with their legs tied down,
Grey old gaffers and boys of twenty –
    Girls and the women of the town –
Pitchers and sugar-sticks, ribbons and laces,
    Posies and whips and dicky-birds' seed,
Silver pieces and smiling faces,
    In Saturday Market they've all they need.

Lotti and her sisters were probably spared the more disturbing details of Henry's deteriorating condition, but the reality was that by June 1884, he was experiencing full-blown delusions. He told his father that women were entering his bedroom at night, after they were sure the rest of the household was asleep, and forcing him to have sex. It was a bizarre assertion, but it was clear he wasn't making it for effect. The distraught Fred, who had already lost three sons to illness (the first before Lotti was born),[14] set up a makeshift bed in Henry's room and slept there with the door locked, in the hope of discovering the cause of his distress. The fact that no mysterious demons visited Henry on the nights when his father was with him was easy enough to explain: why *would* they visit when they knew Fred was in the room? Henry still believed he was being drugged, and his warnings about the end of the world had become more frequent. He was speaking more quickly than ever and sometimes took to shouting at the top of his voice.[15] Fred and Anna Maria were at their wits' end; Henry had not been right for some nine months now, and – no matter how much they tried to convince themselves otherwise – he was getting worse.

The Mews almost certainly believed that Henry's frequent masturbating was a key factor in his rapid deterioration. One influential book of the day, Dr William Acton's *The Functions and Disorders of the Reproductive Organs*, had plenty to say on the subject. A chapter headed 'Insanity Arising from Masturbation' began, 'That insanity is a consequence of this habit is now beyond a doubt. [. . .] The pale complexion, the emaciated form, the slouching gait, the clammy palm, the glassy or leaden eye, and the averted gaze, indicate the lunatic victim to this vice.'[16] Another doctor, at Hanwell Asylum, thought the habit could effectively be stamped out if only its 'victims' could be warned of its disastrous long-term effects:

Would that I could take its melancholy victims with me in my daily rounds, and could point out to them the awful consequences which they do but little suspect to be the result of its indulgence. I could show them those gifted by nature with high talents, and fitted to be an ornament and a benefit to society, sunk into such a state of physical and moral degradation as wrings the heart to witness.[17]

British psychiatry at this time was dominated by the views of one uncompromisingly outspoken physician: Henry Maudsley. Maudsley had been influenced by the eugenics theories of Francis Galton (a half-cousin of Charles Darwin), whose *Hereditary Genius* had been published in the year of Charlotte's birth. The book is an investigation into the link between ability and genes,[18] and its impact on the world of psychiatry was profound.[19] Taking his cue from Galton's evolutionist views, Maudsley, too, believed in the hereditary origins of mental weakness, but he went a stage further than Galton. If insanity was hereditary, he argued, it was as unavoidable as any physical disease: 'There is a destiny made for each one by his inheritance,' Maudsley wrote; 'he is the necessary organic consequent of certain organic antecedents; and it is impossible he should escape the tyranny of his organisation.'[20]

Maudsley's views would be challenged, but for the time being they were widely accepted. How, then, must Lotti – an 'organic consequent' of an increasingly unstable antecedent – have felt when on Saturday 14 June 1884 Henry Herne Mew was admitted to London's most notorious asylum? New Bethlem Hospital was located south of the River Thames, in St George's Fields, Southwark. By the 1880s, it was a far cry from the 'Bedlam' of nightmares portrayed in films and horror stories, where chained, drooling, half-naked patients filled the shadow-filled galleries; or indeed from Hogarth's 1734 depiction in the final scene of *A Rake's Progress*. In 1857, a decision had been made to stop admitting 'parish' patients and to give preference to poor patients from the middle classes, and a few years later the last of the criminal patients were removed to Broadmoor. In 1882, a small number of paying patients were admitted for the first time.[21]

By the time nineteen-year-old Henry entered the asylum, the patients slept in rooms that opened onto long, comfortably furnished galleries, whose windows had been enlarged to let in more light. Plants and paintings hung along the length of the galleries; books and music were introduced, a recreation hall was built and provisions made for the patients' entertainment – tennis and dances and plays in the newly constructed theatre.[22] A visitor to the hospital, around the time of Henry's admission, recorded his impressions:

On entering the grand hall, the eye of the visitor is immediately attracted by the spacious staircase, which ascends from the ground floor to the council chamber above. On either side passages run laterally through the building, the one to the right leading to the male, the other to the female wards. [. . .] Amongst the men there seems but little conversation, and not much fellowship. Smoking is indulged in by such as care for it, and the general aspect of the patients is that of contentment; excepting, of course, those labouring under particular delusions. [. . .] Each of the sleeping-rooms contains a low truckle bedstead, with chair and table, light and air being admitted through a small barred window at the top. [. . .] Each door opens to the gallery, affording a promenade

250 feet in length, where the patients can walk about when the weather proves unfavourable for outdoor exercise.[23]

The examining doctor at Henry's assessment was Edwin Thomas Watkins, who settled on a diagnosis of 'acute mania with excitement & impulsiveness'. The admission form is filled out in black ink, in a hurried-looking script, and makes for unhappy reading. Henry's degree of education is given as 'superior'; his bodily health 'good'. This was the first attack of insanity he had experienced and it had so far lasted nine months. No relatives were similarly afflicted. Next to 'Supposed Cause of Insanity', Watkins has answered 'over study' – a professional judgement that can have done little to comfort Fred, though at least he had done the right thing in bringing his son to the asylum. While Fred attempted to describe the symptoms to Dr Watkins – the sleeplessness, the imagined incidents of night-time rape – Henry shouted a passage of scripture 'repeatedly & rapidly' and made violent attempts to escape. It took two attendants to restrain him. Each time he was returned to his seat, he resumed his preaching. *I have seen thine adulteries, and thy neighings, the lewdness of thy whoredom, and thine abominations on the hills in the fields. Woe unto thee, O Jerusalem! Wilt thou not be made clean? When shall it once be?*[24] 'Delusions that the end of the world is coming,' wrote the doctor, before making a brief note of two additional delusions: 'that he is the son of the P. of Wales – that he is raped at night by women'. Watkins had seen enough. When he indicated that the assessment was over, Henry began to pray, at the same rapid tempo, for the doctor's 'conversion from whoredom', and then kissed him twice before he left.

Over the coming months, Henry's troubling, and often bizarre, behaviour showed no signs of abating. The entry in his casebook notes for 19 October 1884 is typical:

Still convinced that he is the Son of the Prince of Wales. Talks to himself. Sometimes shouts aloud in airing court. Keeps much to himself. Has several times lately asked O'Savage to allow him to have a woman – the other day was more amatory than polite towards a female visitor to Col. Denning.

Three weeks later, it was noted that he had become 'troublesome' in the gallery, throwing things through the windows, and had been 'sent down to no. 1 to sleep'. 'No. 1' was the basement ward, with stone floors (instead of wood) and a brickwork ceiling, where problematic patients were sent from time to time. On 26 November, the doctor recorded that Henry had been walking very quickly up and down the gallery, was convinced he was an Afghan and 'wants the doctors to write to the Afghan Embassy in London'. Two days after Christmas, he was found to be 'much in the same state. Told me this morning that he had discovered he was the young Lord Beaconsfield. Very self conceited in manner & tone.'[25]

The repercussions of Henry's confinement must have shaken the whole family to its core. But, as the second-eldest sibling, Lotti may have felt, in addition, a shifting in her position. She had been raised from birth to look up to her elder brother – as future guardian of the Mew name, inheritor of the family business and guarantor of their financial security. What would happen now that his progress towards that goal had been interrupted? How long would he be gone? Was there a chance he might not recover? And if so, would Lotti be expected to take on his role in the family?

If such questions occurred to her, they no doubt paled into insignificance alongside the pain of Henry's absence. And it must have been a peculiar kind of pain – not dissimilar, perhaps, to that experienced by relatives of missing persons. From the day of his departure to Bethlem Henry *was*, in effect, missing: alive and yet fundamentally unreachable. No sense of closure was possible, as it is when someone dies. Worse still, it seems likely that the girls were forbidden to speak about their brother in public; the Mews' regard for social propriety was already working to erase Henry from the family story. No one keeps a secret so well as a child, Victor Hugo had stated in *Les Misérables*: '*personne ne garde un secret comme un enfant*'. He says nothing about the cost to the child.

If secrecy can derive from a sense of shame, the notion of what is shameful changes from generation to generation. In the late Victorian era, mental illness – 'feeble-mindedness', as it was often called then – was seen as an affliction of the lower social orders, a manifestation of bad blood. For Anna Maria Mew, the thought of admitting to such a taint within the family would have been unconscionable. It's likely that Lotti was influenced – if not cajoled – by her parents in the matter of keeping quiet about Henry. In any case, there is no mention of him in any of her surviving letters. Only one or two of her adult friends knew of his existence. Instead, his presence haunts her poetry. It could be argued that it is there in every line she wrote.

From the time of Henry's removal to the asylum, everything Lotti did was freighted with the knowledge of his illness, and with the fear that the same thing might happen to her and to her sisters. Her life away from Doughty Street – a life of friendship and scholarship and reassuring, everyday accomplishments – did much to distract and sustain her, but she knew her schooldays could not last forever, and that with them would go the effortless daily companionship of Ethel, Maggie Robinson, the Chick girls and other friends. In the autumn of 1884, near the start of the academic year, Ethel and Lotti both cele-brated birthdays: Ethel turned sixteen and Lotti fifteen. Ethel was due to leave at the end of this school year, and both girls were well aware of the fact, but it must have come as a blow to Lotti when her friend announced that she would in fact be going after the Christmas break – and not just leaving the school but moving out of London altogether. In January 1885, she was to take up a place at the Mount, a Quaker girls' school some two hundred miles away in York.

That same year, on Tuesday 9 June, Lotti's maternal grandfather, Henry Edward Kendall, died at home in Paddington of 'senectus' – plain old age. He was seventy-nine. The family's cook, Ann Perkin, had been present at the death, and she registered it two days later. Grandpa

Kendall's will was meticulously drafted. He had left everything – including the many medals awarded to him for his architectural drawings, his 'jewellery, trinkets and personal ornaments', as well as 'household furniture, plate, linen, china, books, wines, pictures, ornaments' and other household effects – to his wife, Mary, whom he had made joint executor with Lotti's father, Fred.[26] He left instructions that on Mary's death, everything was to be divided in equal parts between his children. Mr Kendall's practice had won a number of impressive assignments, including (ironically enough) three county lunatic asylums – in Essex, Sussex and Dorset. His personal estate was valued at £616 10s, a figure that seems modest given his professional standing. The page of the National Probate Calendar on which his record appears also shows the amounts left that same week by a timber merchant from Leeds (£742) and a harness maker from Ipswich (£438). Could it be that there were additional demands on his income? One of his sons, Edward Herne Kendall, disappears from the censuses after 1851, aged seven, but can be traced via electoral registers, living on at the family home into his forties. When his mother, Mary, died, she left £500 in trust for his use. It's feasible that – as Penelope Fitzgerald has suggested – those needs included private nursing.[27]

On Wednesday 15 July 1885, little over a month after Grandpa Kendall's death, Henry was discharged from Bethlem. The final entry in his medical notes states simply that he was 'uncured'. He had made no progress while at the asylum – if anything, he had got worse – and Fred had recently heard of a new institution that was being opened 'for the succour of persons of the middle-class afflicted with mental disease'. There was reason to hope that the staff at the new asylum might be better suited for Henry's care: it had been specifically devised 'with the kind purpose of affording weary if not worn-out brain-workers the opportunity of recovering their faculties'.[28] All the doctors agreed that 'over study' was the primary cause of Henry's illness. At the end of August, he became the thirtieth patient to enter the brand-new Holloway Sanatorium. The building, overlooking sweeping lawns, was handsomely decorated throughout; the grey marble interior was enriched with 'plentiful gilding' and hung with paintings, the patients' rooms elegantly furnished. The fees depended on the amount of accommodation required: private sitting rooms were available for wealthier patients, while for some of the less well-off inmates the costs were subsidised. The founder, benefactor Thomas Holloway – 'of pill and ointment fame' – had specified that only patients from the professional middle classes should be admitted to his asylum, reasoning that 'rich people so unfortunate as to suffer from mental disease need no monetary assistance; and the poor in a similar mental condition are already cared for in public asylums'. He wanted, he said, to help professionals whose work could not, 'like an ordinary business, be carried on by deputy', and who needed, therefore, to get back to it as soon as possible.[29] Henry's own working life had barely begun. He was twenty.

It was Amice Macdonell's little sister, Margaret, who brought Lotti the news of Lucy Harrison's decision to leave the school. The house in Yorkshire was ready and, barring one or two faults which 'I might have avoided if I had been here while it was building',[30] Harrison had pronounced herself happy with it. She would be moving up in the spring of 1885, handing the school over to her friend and fellow teacher, Amy Greener, with whom she was to fall deeply in love. After some time at Gower Street, Miss Greener would also move up to the Bainbridge house, where the two women lived out their lives together in domestic harmony. Miss Harrison would ultimately become headmistress at the Mount School – the very school Ethel Oliver had graduated to. But all that was in the future. Lotti was seated at the piano, practising, when Margaret came running in with the news of Miss Harrison's departure. When Lotti grasped what was being said she was struck by a grief so intense that she jumped up from the piano and began banging her head against a wall.[31]

She was not yet sixteen years old. Within a short space of time, she had lost the camaraderie of a brother and a best friend. With so much of what she had once assumed to be solid and enduring crumbling away around her, it was Miss Harrison who had provided the main source of stability in her life. Now she too was leaving. Lotti's instinct was to turn back to the shelter of her family; throughout her life she would remain strongly bound to them by the business of security and survival. But the chaos of her domestic situation at this present moment forced her now to look for additional coping strategies, beyond the scaffold of familial support. Under the pressure of that task, her life was dividing into three quite separate worlds. There was the world of friendship, with its attendant sanctuaries – the friends' houses where she could be carefree and amusing, and where she was loved for who she was; there was the world of words, which offered another kind of refuge – one that was thrillingly private; and there was the world of home, with its rapidly shrinking cast of occupants, and standing sentinel to a secret that was not to be carried outside its walls at any cost.

5

Marks Upon the Snow
1890–1893

30 Doughty Street had served as the backdrop for Lotti's youth –
for, as she would put it later, childhood's 'visions, its brilliant pictures
and poignant sensations'.[1] But it had not been a lucky house. In all,
it had witnessed the deaths of three children, plus another child's
removal to an asylum. However well or otherwise the family felt they
had coped with these unhappy events, moving on to somewhere new
must have been an attractive prospect. At the start of 1890, Fred Mew
secured the lease for 9 Gordon Street, in the northwestern corner of
Bloomsbury. Charlotte (as she was now more often called) had just
turned twenty.

Despite the aura of faded gentility (or what one contemporary
guidebook termed its 'tone of obsolete respectability'[2]), the area
surrounding Gordon Street was decidedly less isolated than that of
Doughty Street, largely because of its proximity to University College,
London. The Mews' new home stood in a row of tall, narrow-looking
Regency terraced houses put up in the 1820s by celebrated master
builder Thomas Cubitt on land owned by the Duke of Bedford. The
houses' long, thin gardens backed onto the university's bustling cam-
pus. The buildings at the Mews' end of the street were flattened by a
German bomb in September 1940, but a contemporary plan of the
university and its environs shows that number 9 stood roughly in the
centre of the row, almost in line with the elegant dome in the portico
of the main quadrangle. From the upstairs rooms at the back of the
house, Charlotte could see the constant traffic of students as they
hurried to and from lectures. The house was also close to three major
railway termini – Euston, St Pancras and King's Cross – and Gower

Street tube station (renamed Euston Square in 1909) was closer still, no more than a two-minute walk away.

Today, at the corner of Gordon Street and Gordon Square there stands an elegant cast-iron lamp post, the last of its design remaining in London. It was installed in the 1890s, the same decade Charlotte moved into the street, and burned for nearly a century, fuelled first by gas, then electricity, until, in 1976, it petered out once and for all. But the lamp post remains, its base decorated with a spray of acanthus leaves – symbols of enduring life – and standing sentinel to ghosts of Regency terraces long since demolished. The streetscape is dominated now by James Cubitt's brutalist Bloomsbury Theatre, where students meet for coffee in the ground-floor café that overlooks the street. In the Middle Ages, this area was known as 'Otefield', a sixteen-acre field of oats bordered, just south of where the busy Euston Road crosses the top of the street, by a brook teeming with salmon, trout and perch.

Our cities, towns and villages are threaded through with the ghosts of streets and byways, streams and underground culverts, but also with the memory trails of our past. Charlotte Mew knew this. The word 'ghost', and its cognates, appears in six of the sixteen poems in her first collection; her poetry is thronged with living ghosts, as well as lanes and waysides that knit together present, past and future. In a Mew poem the lamp post at the corner of Gordon Street might still be burning long after its final extinction, its glass bowl cradling the customary carbon arc lamp that created at nightfall a buzzing sound and a perpetual flickering on countless evenings when Charlotte returned to her house, stepping from a pool of darkness into the lamp's light.

At the southern end, Gordon Street joins the northwest corner of Gordon Square, where, from 1904 to 1907, Virginia Stephen (later Woolf) would live with her three siblings, Vanessa, Thoby and Adrian. Moving here from the sedate surroundings of South Kensington, the Stephens would be enthralled by the neighbourhood's constant bustle. Traffic rattled by most hours of the day, as deliveries were made to basement kitchens – the fishmonger with his ice-laden cart, the greengrocer, the milkman, the baker, the muffin man. Gordon Street itself retained an air of refinement. When the Mews moved there in 1890, ornate wrought-iron gates manned by uniformed gatekeepers still stood at one end. They had been installed to keep out the nuisances of public vehicles, animals being driven to market, tramps, street musicians and other undesirables; but they were not to remain in place for long. In the same year as the Mews' move, the London Streets (Removal of Gates) Act was passed, and by 1893 the gates had finally gone.[3]

Fred had bought the lease for 9 Gordon Street from the son of the previous occupant, Anne Powell, a barrister's widow. On 24 February 1890, silk merchant Ellison Powell wrote to his solicitor instructing him to note the exchange and to forward the notices for the Ground Rent to Mr Mew.[4] In March, Charlotte, her parents, her two younger sisters, Anne and Freda, and three female domestics – including, of course, the children's 'second mother' Elizabeth Goodman (now sixty-four but as vigorous as ever) – all made the move to the address that was to be home to the Mew family for the next thirty-two years.[5] Hoping they had left the family ghosts behind at Doughty Street, they quickly set about making the house their own, filling the rooms with their heavy, dark-grained furniture – among which were the circular, gate-legged oak table, six 'Adams chairs' and several valuable mirrors that would accompany Mew throughout her life.[6] They decorated the walls with the same architectural drawings and plans of Fred's that had hung in Doughty Street. With four storeys and a sizeable basement, the house was decently spacious, and presented an elegant facade to the street: the ground-floor level was dressed with white stucco and girded by black iron railings; above it, a further iron balcony fringed a *piano nobile*, with its characteristic taller windows. But, for all its size, 9 Gordon Street was notably dark and stuffy. The house faced almost due east and was brightest at the start of the day; even then the light was compromised by the proximity of the equally tall houses across the street. One visitor to the property – an artist friend of Anne's – referred to it as 'a very lovely old house in one of the fashionable London squares'.[7] But Charlotte's friend Alida Monro found it 'tall and narrow, dark and gaunt inside'.[8]

Though the move was only a short distance, it had great symbolic significance for Mew. We know that houses, and the rooms within houses, were important to her; they feature time and again in her poems and short fiction. The interest is not surprising in the daughter of an architect – except that the houses in Mew's writing are more than mere constructions. She plainly came to believe – along with her contemporary, the French philosopher Gaston Bachelard – that there is a dynamic interplay between the mind and its surroundings; that each is shaped by, and responds to, the other. In 'Rooms', published a year after her death, the exchange between house and human is explicit: 'I remember rooms that have had their part / In the steady slowing down of the heart,' the speaker remarks, looking back at the course her life has taken, and implying that if we live inside our houses, they also live inside us. Even when the occupants are absent, Mew's poetic houses are imbued with a human-like life-force. 'The Sunlit House' (1921) is in the middle of a feverish and uneasy sleep when the poet comes upon it in the opening lines: 'White, through the gate it gleamed and slept / In shuttered sunshine'. In the four brief lines of the wonderfully sinister 'Domus Caedet Arborem' (meaning 'the house murders the tree'), the city's houses metamorphose by night into devious killers: 'dark houses watching the trees from dark windows [. . .] simply biding their time'. *Caedet* – which might be translated as both 'murders' and 'cuts down' – is the perfect verb to choose here: there is no English word that quite captures the same, dual meaning.

At the time of the Mews' house move, Charlotte had recently celebrated her twentieth birthday. Gordon Street would be her home for most of the rest of her life. It was here that she would write the majority of her poems, stories and essays; she had published nothing before moving into the house and would see only eight pieces go into print after she left it. It was also the largest property she lived in. As time went by, she would inhabit progressively smaller quarters, ending her days in a single, rented room.

Charlotte Mew's family was never so well off that they could forget about money altogether, but Fred's services had been much in demand in the years preceding the move to Gordon Street, and the commissions he won must have afforded the family a degree of financial security. Indeed, the fees for two major recent projects may have planted the possibility of moving in his – or, more likely, Anna Maria's – head in the first place. At the start of 1887, he was busy finishing a commission for a convalescent children's home – the first of three that he would design, and that were run by the same order of Anglican nuns, the Community of the Sisters of the Church. St Mary's Home in Broadstairs was finally completed in July 1887, a month after the pageant and hullabaloo of the Queen's Golden Jubilee. It was a large and imposing structure, built in the Gothic style on the cliffs between Broadstairs Church and the North Foreland, for children suffering from 'extreme poverty and sickness'.[9] The finished building could accommodate three hundred children when full, and had been five years in the making.

The location of the Home had a particular resonance for Fred. In the early autumn of 1867, just four years into their marriage, he and Anna Maria had shut up Doughty Street for a holiday in Broadstairs. With them were Henry (or Harry, as he was known at the time), then aged two, their new baby, Frederick George Webb, and the children's nurse, Elizabeth Goodman. Broadstairs was a favourite destination for well-to-do Victorians seeking a rest from life in the city. Charles Dickens had been a regular visitor a few decades earlier, and by the time the Mews visited, the place had not changed much from the impressionistic snapshot Dickens has left us:

Sky, sea, beach, and village, lie as still before us as if they were sitting for the picture. It is dead low-water. A ripple plays among the ripening corn upon the cliff, as if it were faintly trying from recollection to imitate the sea [. . .] In the afternoons, you see no end of salt and sandy little boots drying on upper window-sills. At bathing-time in the morning, the little bay re-echoes with every shrill variety of shriek and splash – after which, if the weather be at all fresh, the sands teem with small blue mottled legs.[10]

Perhaps two-year-old Harry was among those playing bare-legged in the sand, patting a sandcastle into shape under Elizabeth Goodman's watchful eye, when his baby brother fell suddenly ill. Within the space of two days, he was dead.[11] Whether the diarrhoea noted on Frederick George's death certificate was brought on by a virus or some other infection picked up at the boarding house or on the beach, the young family returned to London without him. Fred must have felt a peculiar sense of destiny when, almost twenty years on, he won the commission for a children's home, to be erected in the very town of his baby son's death. Unsurprisingly, the building was designed with meticulous attention to detail.

The nuns were sufficiently impressed by Fred's work to recommend his services soon after for a second, very similar project in St Anne's-on-the-Sea, five miles south of Blackpool. The resulting Abraham Ormerod Convalescent Home was completed within months of the family's move to Gordon Street, and just three years after St Mary's of Broadstairs opened the doors to its first patients. Again in the Gothic style, the second home was finished with red Ruabon bricks and a green slate roof with large, white-painted gables. The building stood for almost a hundred years. It was finally demolished in 1984 to make way for new houses.

During all this time, Charlotte had been assiduous about keeping in touch with her old school friends – the Chick sisters, Maggie

Robinson, and Ethel and Winifred Oliver – and her move to Gordon Street now made it easier to continue seeing them on a regular basis, as one by one they enrolled for degree courses at University College, London. The first to do so, Maggie Robinson, had recently finished her degree in zoology when the Mews arrived at their new home, but Edith Chick was in the early stages of her course, also science-based. Edith had left the Gower Street School in 1886, at the age of sixteen. Her father, Samuel, had assumed that his eldest daughter would join the family's lace business at that stage, but Edith had other ideas. She had a passion and talent for learning, and to his great credit, Samuel acquiesced to her request to be allowed to stay on in education; a decision that may have been influenced by a concerted campaign in the second part of the nineteenth century to bring further education opportunities for young women in line with those of men. He made arrangements for Edith to continue her schooling at Notting Hill, where the teaching was exceptional – much of it delivered by the first generation of young female graduates from Oxford, Cambridge and London. Algebra and science featured strongly on the school's curriculum, and Edith took to the subjects immediately.[12] In the autumn of 1889, she won a place at University College to study physics, mathematics and botany; by the time the Mews moved to Gordon Street, she was halfway through her second term and deeply immersed in college life. In due course, five of Edith's six sisters would follow in her footsteps and begin their own studies at the university.

Charlotte saw the Chicks outside of term-time too. The 1891 census (taken on 5 April, a week after Easter Sunday) lists her as a visitor to the Chick family, who had moved out of their cramped quarters in Newman Street, off Oxford Street, shortly after the youngest child, Dorothy, was born, in 1887. Their new house, 'Chesterfield', was right in the middle of Ealing, on high ground looking out across cornfields towards central London.[13] In the late nineteenth century, the town was populated mainly by middle-class families and their servants. A stylish 1890s publicity booklet, in pale green covers with gilt title lettering, boasts of Ealing's elegance and spaciousness: there were, it gloats, 'absolutely no poor streets at all' and 'the thoroughfares being very wide and well lit, they form agreeable promenades either by day-light or in the evening'.[14]

Samuel Chick and his wife Emma often travelled to the continent to acquire unusual pieces of lace for the family business, and they appear to have been abroad at the time of the 1891 census, but nine of their ten children were at home. The only Chick sibling not present during Charlotte's stay that Easter of 1891 was twenty-three-year-old Sam, the eldest son, who by that time was working in Sheffield as a type founder's clerk. Sam plays a curious – and frustratingly enig-matic – bit part in the narrative of Charlotte Mew's life. Not much is known about him, but according to his niece Margaret Tomlinson, he was something of 'a black sheep in the family' and 'quite irresponsible, both about women and [. . .] about money'.[15] He is of interest because of a snippet of information that was given to Mary Davidow, who interviewed several of Charlotte's friends and relatives first hand for her 1960 PhD thesis. Mew's 'favourite' cousin, Gertrude Mary, told Davidow that there had been some sort of romance between Sam and Charlotte.[16] Davidow speculated that the romance may have accounted for the close bond that existed between Charlotte and the Chick family in the early 1890s, though that seems unlikely, given the fact that Charlotte saw the girls so often without Sam. Still, the comment remains an intriguing lead. Gertrude appears to have had no ulterior motive in making it, and she and Charlotte remained fond of each other throughout their lives.

1886 had marked the end of Charlotte's formal education, but she continued to read and to study and copy out passages from her favour-ite books, and would go on doing so for many years. Her attendance at the university's public lectures was part of a continual process of self-education; towards the end of 1891 she took another important step in that process. On Saturday 5 December, a few weeks after she turned twenty-two, she visited the British Museum to register for a ticket to the Reading Room. Membership was open to anyone over twenty-one years of age, so long as they could find a sponsor to vouch for their good character and behaviour – preferably someone in a position of responsibility, such as a teacher, governess or business owner. Perhaps Charlotte's old teacher Lucy Harrison provided a letter of support for her former pupil: Miss Harrison had been a regular user of the Reading Room during her time at the Gower Street School, and even after she moved away to Yorkshire, she visited whenever she was in London.[17]

The early part of December was exceptionally rainy that year,[18] and it's easy to picture Charlotte's small, slim figure hurrying beneath an umbrella through the grey streets to the museum's entrance (in later years she would be known for a distinctive horn-handled umbrella she carried with her everywhere[19]), the occasional omnibus splashing past her as she went. She was to make this journey many times over the years – turning right out of her front door, left at the southern corner of Gordon Square, then immediately right along Woburn Square, Thornhaugh Street, Russell Square and Montague Street, before a final right into Great Russell Street. The museum stood on the corner there, its entrance – up wide steps to the imposing neo-Grecian portico with its vast Ionic columns – just a few paces further, on the right-hand side.

The circular Reading Room at the museum's centre had a domed ceiling and a clerestory comprising twenty arched windows, through which the light streamed during daytime hours. The desks (which could seat up to 460 people between them) ran in straight lines like spokes from a hub where the superintendent and attendants sat. Two years before Charlotte was issued with her ticket, the Anglo-Jewish writer Amy Levy described the room's 'book-lined walls, its radiating rows of seats, and its characteristic, suggestive scent of leather bindings'. She brings to life for us the particular ambience of 'those hours of the afternoon or evening when the lavender-white light of the electric lamps shines somewhat fitfully through the thick atmosphere'.[20] For many women who visited, the Reading Room provided a welcome refuge from domestic duties – as it undoubtedly did for Charlotte. For some male readers, the presence of women in the room was an unwelcome distraction. In 1886, a short piece in the *Saturday Review* entitled 'Ladies in Libraries' complained that 'woman makes the Reading Room a place where study is impossible . . . woman talks and whispers and giggles beneath the stately dome . . . she flirts, and eats strawberries behind folios, in the society of some happy student of the opposite sex'.[21]

Charlotte's visits to the Reading Room were to become a lifelong habit; it was here that she would research, make notes and write drafts for many of her published pieces. Though not yet a published writer herself, as she entered the room for the first time, clammy from the rain, perhaps she felt (as many others had done) the ghostly presence of past writers who had worked under its famous dome: writers like George Eliot, Charles Dickens, Robert Browning and Christina Rossetti, all of whom Charlotte enthused about or quoted from liberally in her letters to friends. In March 1888, another Reading Room habitué, Thomas Hardy – an idol of Charlotte's – had looked up from his work and experienced the odd sensation that the room's inhabitants were embodied spirits walking among the spirits of the dead; something akin to ghosts-in-waiting. 'Souls are gliding about here in a sort of dream,' he noted in his diary: 'In the great circle of the library Time is looking into Space. Coughs are floating in the same great vault, mixing with the rustle of book-leaves risen from the dead, and the touches of footsteps on the floor.'[22]

The ticket Charlotte applied for that winter of 1891 was issued for the standard six months. Over the years, she would allow her membership to lapse for varying intervals, but in the last few years of her life, she took to renewing it on a more regular basis, in spite – or perhaps in part because – of increasingly trying circumstances. Her final ticket expired a month before she died.

Following the death of Charlotte's maternal grandfather in 1885, Grandma Kendall had moved down to Brighton for good, along with her youngest daughter, Mary Leonora, who had never married, and the family's cook and general servant, Ann Perkin. Mrs Kendall lived on in Brighton as a widow for seven years, and in the early summer of 1892, she died at home, aged eighty. Anna Maria (now in her mid-fifties) was by her side.[23] The certified cause, 'Senile Decay', meant something more specific in the late nineteenth century than a general decline due to old age: it referred specifically to the cognitive deterioration that today would be classed as Alzheimer's disease or vascular dementia. With what now looked like commendable foresight, Mrs Kendall had made a will several years earlier, in which she confirmed that her assets should be divided between her three surviving children (Anna Maria, Mary Leonora and Edward Herne), just as her husband had stipulated in his own will. After legacy duty and costs, Anna Maria's share amounted to £1,263 14s 8d.[24] The death also triggered bequests from other relatives: a one-off gift of £500 from a great-aunt, a small annuity from a great-uncle and a sizeable endowment of £2,266 12s 3d that passed to Anna Maria from her grandfather, Thomas Cobham, on Mrs Kendall's death.[25] Most of the money was held in trust and paid out in quarterly dividends – a complicated business, but, happily, one of Fred's nephews, Walter Mew Barnes, was an Oxford-educated barrister-at-law. He was more than capable of dealing with the legal details regarding Anna Maria's various inheritances, and Fred wrote him several grateful letters, signing off with 'Your affectionate uncle, Fred Mew'.[26]

In the normal run of things, the windfalls that came to Anna Maria during late 1892 and 1893 would have secured the family's finances; if Henry had been earning, the Mews might have been positively wealthy. But Henry was not earning, and what no one outside the family knew was how much of their capital was being chipped away by his medical fees. The Mews had all the usual expenses of a household of their size and social standing: besides the basics of food, clothes, laundry bills, fuel, rent and rates, there were Freda's school fees to pay, and wages for the live-in servants, which were paid out on the first of every month.[27] As a cook–housekeeper, Elizabeth Goodman would have received around £35 per year, while the 'long succession of raw girls from the country' whom she trained and sent away 'tamed and sweetened' could expect around £10 each.[28] The 1891 census lists two such 'girls', who, of course, also needed to be housed and fed: Emma Barker (then twenty) and Emily Sayer (seventeen). On top of these routine overheads, money for Henry's care had somehow to be found.

The weekly tariff for Holloway Sanatorium ran on a two-tier system: 'first-class' and 'second-class' patients.[29] We do not know which bracket Henry fell into, but we do know his care meant an extra outlay of between £65 and £109 per year – a considerable sum, given that the average wage in Britain at this time was around £225.[30] Instead of bringing in much-needed extra income, the Mews' only son, now twenty-seven, had become a steady drain on the family coffers. As if to add insult to injury, his condition had shown no improvement during his seven years at Holloway, though his behaviour had certainly become less challenging. The days he had spent walking 'rapidly up & down the gallery' at Bethlem, 'throwing things through the windows' and 'constantly gesticulating & talking to himself', were a distant memory.[31] Dr Thomas Harper now recorded that, while Henry was 'not suicidal or dangerous', he was nonetheless 'demented, dull and passive', as well as 'solitary in habits and eccentric in his actions', and he had withdrawn so far into himself that he rarely spoke.[32] This begs the question of just how much good his treatments – which included gym exercises, massage and sleep-inducing doses of bromides and chloral – were doing him. Holloway was also known for its administration of the infamous 'dry-pack' treatment, for which patients were restrained in an apparatus that 'completely enveloped' them 'by a blanket and webbing secured by five straps, the blanket then being sewn back around his nose and mouth to permit breathing'; they were only let out to defecate and urinate.[33] In 1894, twenty-one-year-old Thomas Weir, one of Henry's fellow patients at Holloway, would die after being confined for four days in the device. Henry's currently unresponsive state at least spared him from that horror, but he was clearly not well enough to be looked after at home. Anna Maria's dividends were unlikely to be frittered away on luxuries.

According to Charlotte, it had always been Elizabeth Goodman's wish to 'die in harness', and on 3 March 1893 that wish was granted.[34] As things turned out, Charlotte's careful childhood calculations – her sleepless hours spent 'doing sums on the knots of the counterpane to prove that [Elizabeth] could live on for years and years' – had come to nothing: Elizabeth did not in the end die from old age but from septicaemia caused by a freak accident that occurred as she went about her household duties. Four days later, the famous London coroner George Danford Thomas held an inquest into the death; he would investigate many suspicious and mysterious deaths during his long years of office, including the notorious Dr Crippen murder. Elizabeth Goodman's death was not suspicious, but it was memorably odd.

In all likelihood, Elizabeth had been in Gordon Street's basement kitchen when the injury happened. The septicaemia was triggered by a puncture wound in her hand made – as the death certificate notes – by a 'wooden skewer'. Skewers made of wood (as opposed to the daintier metal variety kept for serving) were generally used in the preparation and cooking of fish, and to secure rolls of beef steak and other meats. It seems a tragically improbable death, given the more immediate hazards that existed in the hot, damp, windowless space of the Victorian kitchen: the closed range oven attached to a boiler that was perpetually at risk of exploding; the arrays of caustic chemicals and poisons; the disease-bearing cockroaches that, if left unchecked (or so one 1889 household guide warned), were forever on the brink of multiplying beyond control 'until the kitchen at night palpitates with a living carpet'.[35]

Now the family stood by helplessly as Elizabeth's immune system went into overdrive to fight the infection, and her body responded with the telltale signs of rapid breathing, a racing heartbeat, fever, chills and shivering. Today, the condition is easily treated with antibiotics, provided it is caught in time. As it was, on 7 March, Danford Thomas recorded a verdict of accidental death – one more tragic domestic accident of the kind that was common in Victorian Britain. Shortly after the body had been laid out, Charlotte and her family looked on with distaste as Elizabeth's 'other' family descended on the house to clear her room and to claim their pickings from among the modest possessions, which included a rose-decorated tea caddy that had belonged to Elizabeth's mother, a battered but well-polished mahogany workbox and a china teapot commemorating Queen Victoria's Golden Jubilee. These items and the occasion of the family's visit made such an impression on Charlotte that she was able to write about them in detail some twenty years later in an affectionate memoir of Elizabeth, published in the *New Statesman* in 1913:

[A] few hours after the blinds were drawn in the quiet room upstairs all these and other things had been collected, packed, and removed in a four-wheeled cab, and the funeral in every detail loudly discussed and, not without some bitterness, arranged by a band of newly arrived relations; among them the plausible greasy sister-in-law who was always taking expensive medicines and borrowing railway fares, and the heavily scented niece with the rather sunken, bold dark eyes and a willowy figure, who had once 'sat to Sant',[36] and when not sitting to someone or other was said to be nursing an invalid gentleman at Boulogne or Worthing or Ostend. With a great display of black-bordered pocket handkerchief, they overran the house, and their moral and physical odour seemed to cling about it long after they had left it; for nearly a week they were in possession, ransacking boxes, turning out drawers, eating interminable meals, and in audible disagreement to the end about the prices and dispositions of their wreaths and crosses. I remember hoping that she couldn't see or hear them.[37]

Elizabeth Goodman had represented one possible model for a worthy life, but it was not, of course, one that Charlotte would ever have considered for herself, no matter how hard-up the family became. Victorian society had essentially narrowed the concept of 'respectable' middle-class womanhood into two categories: a woman was either a wife (preferably a wife and mother) or a self-sacrificing and necessarily celibate spinster. For women of Charlotte's class, earning money – or being *seen* to earn money – was largely anathema, except via a small number of accepted routes such as nursing, teaching or secretarial work. Some late Victorians – and Mrs Mew would certainly have been among them – believed the idea of a woman working for pay in *any* sector was déclassé.

In terms of financial security, then, marriage would have been a sensible long-term option for the Mew sisters. Freda was still in her early teens and not yet thinking about such things. Charlotte and Anne discussed the idea but at some point they resolved that the door of marriage should be closed to them: given the severity of Henry's illness, they believed it would be irresponsible to bring children of their own into the world. According to Alida Monro, the decision was made early on and never reneged upon, though it may have been regretted. Introducing her 1953 edition of the poems, Alida wrote that Charlotte 'had within herself a great and driving moral sense that kept her from deviating in any respect from the path she had chosen for herself. She and her sister had both made up their minds early in life, she told me, that they would never marry for fear of passing on the mental taint that was in their heredity.'[38]

What, then, were the options for Charlotte and Anne as they embarked upon their adult lives? The notion, to which Mrs Mew subscribed, that propriety precluded women from taking up a career left unmarried daughters in a precarious position. Once the fathers on whom they depended had died (and in the absence of wage-earning male siblings), they might find themselves completely unprovided for. One way round the problem was to earn money without being seen to earn it – ideally from some skilled craft that they could carry on within the confines of the house.

In the middle of the century, novelist Geraldine Jewsbury (who herself never married) had written to a friend, with palpable excitement:

> I believe we are touching on better days, when women will have a genuine, normal life of their own to lead. There, perhaps, will not be so many marriages, and women will be taught not to feel their destiny manqué if they remain single. They will be able to be friends and companions in a way that they cannot be now. [. . .] I regard myself as a mere faint indication, a rudiment of the idea, of certain higher qualities and possibilities that lie in women.[39]

By the late eighties and early nineties, the sense of change had burgeoned, and some of the possibilities Jewsbury had anticipated were being realised. On 7 June 1889, the first British production of Ibsen's *A Doll's House* was staged at the ornate Novelty Theatre in London. The following day, the *Pall Mall Gazette* described the closing moments of the play, when Nora leaves her husband and children and 'the street-door bangs behind her flying footsteps'. 'Will she come back?' the (male) reviewer wondered. He concluded that there was a moral responsibility to see the play, incumbent upon anyone who could get to it: 'The opportunity of a week of Ibsen at the Novelty is one that nobody who can get there (and who takes an interest in life) should miss.'[40] A number of women – including social activist Eleanor Marx and novelist Olive Schreiner – gathered in the theatre's handsome vestibule at the end of the performance to talk about what they had just seen and reflect on what it meant. The question everyone wanted answering was this: 'Was there hope or despair in the banging of that door?'[41]

At twenty-three, Charlotte was an attractive, intelligent single woman, musically gifted, clever with words and unusually dexterous; she was committed to the notion of never marrying, but clearly not content to sit at home and watch life pass her by. With Henry away, she played the role of eldest child, and almost certainly felt the need to set an example to her sisters. Whether she got to see *A Doll's House* during its run at the Novelty is not known, but one day she would write about another door that carried symbolic weight – this one of her own making. In her 1912 poem 'The Call', an unnamed (and ungendered) being calls unexpectedly on the inhabitants of a firelit room. We don't know the purpose of the creature's visit, but we could do worse than to read it as a personification of the artist's calling. The visitor has come to dislodge the room's occupants from the comfort of their 'low seat beside the fire', and is not going to take no for an answer. Now that the door has been flung wide on its hinges, the speaker understands there will be no closing it, and that they have no choice but to step outside – irrespective of what they might find:

> But suddenly it snapped the chain
> Unbarred, flung wide the door
> Which will not shut again;
> And so we cannot sit here any more.
> We must arise and go:
> The world is cold without
> And dark and hedged about
> With mystery and enmity and doubt,
> But we must go
> Though yet we do not know
> Who called, or what marks we shall leave upon the snow.

In spite of the insecurity of her domestic circumstances, Charlotte was living life to the full. She attended lectures, socialised freely and visited the British Museum's Reading Room, where she copied out page after page of writing she admired. The University at Buffalo, New York, has twenty pages of George Eliot quotations, for instance, written out in a confident hand in thick black ink with the broad-nibbed fountain pen Charlotte favoured. The notes appear to have been made in a single session; among them is the assertion – on a line of its own – that 'Art works for all whom it can touch.' The line is taken from a letter Eliot sent to Edward Burne-Jones after visiting his studio in 1873. She went on to elucidate:

> Art works for all whom it can touch. And I want in gratitude to tell you that your work makes life larger and more beautiful to me. I mean that historical life of all the world, in which our little personal share often seems a mere standing room from which we can look all round, and chiefly backward.[42]

It was a truth Charlotte knew well enough from the point of view of a reader, but it's likely she had started to consider it from another angle: from what happened next it is clear that at some point in 1893, she made the decision to try her hand as a writer.

6

A *Yellow Book* Discovery
1894

In her mid-twenties, Charlotte found herself involved with a circle of brilliant young writers and illustrators who collected around *The Yellow Book*, a magazine set up by Aubrey Beardsley and Henry Harland to express the new spirit of the age and represent its outspoken, gifted younger generation. It was the only such group she would ever be associated with. The idea of fashionable literary cliques held no attraction, but the magazine itself was enormously important to her: it would give her her first taste of publication.

The Yellow Book, and the artists surrounding it, was part of a larger mood of change in the national consciousness: the 1890s in Britain was a decade open to modernisation of all kinds, in which many new ideas took hold and many outmoded ways of thinking finally began to die away. Short-story writer Ella D'Arcy – who became the magazine's assistant editor and, for a while, a friend of Charlotte's – recalled the progressive mood in certain quarters of London at that time. It was characterised, she jibed, by an excess of catchphrases: '*Fin de siècle*. The "new" everything. "The New Woman," "The New Morality," "The New Paganism," to take a few examples.'[1] Three decades earlier, Charles Baudelaire, presiding spirit of *The Yellow Book*, had coined the word *modernité* to describe a similar era of change in 1860s Paris. *The Yellow Book*'s editor, Henry Harland, a dynamic American, had moved to London from Paris in 1884 and had been deeply influenced by Baudelaire and the French Décadent movement in general.

Harland liked to present himself as an outgoing New Yorker. His physique was on the bony side; his shoulders sloped and he was in the habit of wrapping one leg around the other while seated. At times he was clean-shaven; at others he sported a thin moustache and scrubby goatee beard; always he had an abundant mop of hair, dark eyebrows and a pair of round pince-nez, which he waved habitually on the end of a cord while he talked. He was a generous host, regularly opening up his house in Kensington's Cromwell Road for Saturday-evening literary gatherings, or 'At Homes', which Charlotte often attended.[2] Several *Yellow Book* authors have left first-hand accounts of Harland. Most, it seems, liked him well enough, and many of the women in the group found him charming, even when they were aware they were being toadied to. Ella D'Arcy describes him as 'the most brilliant, witty and amusing of talkers' and recalls how he would re-fix his eye-glasses on his nose, 'while assuring some "dear beautiful lady!" or other how much he admired her writing, or her painting, her frock, or the colour of her hair'.[3] Novelist Netta Syrett remembers best Harland's 'excited talk – he was like a boy in his enthusiasms'.[4] But author and photographer Frederick Rolfe (alias the eccentric Baron Corvo) was less flattering: he believed Harland's louche exterior was a sham. For the waspish Rolfe (who seems not to have had a kind word to say about anyone), Harland was a man who, 'despite his attempts at unconventionality – [. . .] the stories composed in dressing gown and pyjamas – was at heart a conventional bourgeois, shocked to the core by the least suggestion of irregularity or real vice'.[5] Everyone agreed, at least, that Harland was a fastidious editor, more than capable of making a shrewd judgement when it was required of him. He could, in the words of another *Yellow Book* author, Evelyn Sharp, 'be serious when seriousness mattered, and that was what lent the more effect to his freakish humour and often such wisdom to his wit, making him one of the most lovable creatures in the story of modern letters'.[6]

As far as exposure goes, Charlotte's work could hardly have landed in a better place. There are several versions of the birth of this short-lived but highly influential magazine. In Harland's own rather baroque account, the idea was first conceived by himself and art nouveau illustrator Aubrey Beardsley on New Year's Day 1894, beside a cosy fire in

Harland's drawing room 'one fearful afternoon in one of the densest and soupiest and yellowest of all London's infernalest yellow fogs':

> Aubrey Beardsley and I sat together the whole afternoon before a beautiful glowing open coal fire and I assure you we could scarcely see our hands before our faces, with all the candles lighted, for the fog, you know. [. . .] We declared each to each that we thought it quite a pity and a shame that London publishers should feel themselves longer under obligation to refuse any more of our good manuscripts. [. . .]
>
> 'Tis monstrous, Aubrey,' said I.
>
> 'Tis a public scandal,' said he. And then and there we decided to have a magazine of our own. As the sole editorial staff we would feel free and welcome to publish any and all of ourselves that nobody else could be hired to print.[7]

Harland and Beardsley proposed the idea to publisher John Lane (whom Frederick Rolfe described as a 'tubby little pot-bellied man'[8]) at the Hogarth Club on Dover Street in February 1894, where the group had repaired after a banquet hosted by Mr Waldorf Astor (later Lord Astor).[9] In 1887, Lane and his friend Elkin Mathews had set up The Bodley Head, an antiquarian bookshop and publishing house based in Vigo Street.[10] In the seven years of its existence, The Bodley Head had established a reputation for sophistication and boldness; many of the imprint's books found major American publishers. Lane was excited by the proposition of a new, upmarket quarterly and readily agreed to publish *The Yellow Book*, with Harland as literary editor and Beardsley as art editor.

With a publisher in place, assembly of the magazine proceeded quickly, and on 16 April 1894 – just three months after the idea was first mooted – Volume One appeared on newsstands and in bookshops on both sides of the Atlantic, decked out in handsome daffodil-yellow cloth boards. The cover sported a black ink drawing by Beardsley of a plump woman wearing an elaborate wig and carnival mask and smiling inanely; at her shoulder there lurks a devilish-looking man, also masked, with chiselled features and an altogether more knowing smile on his lips. At 272 pages, the publication was about an inch thick and looked more like a book than a magazine – which was, in fact, the point. It was a clear statement that this new hybrid periodical would be something substantially more than the normal magazine fare: more erudite, more enterprising and, crucially, more enduring. The separately published prospectus that heralded the first volume – in which the word 'book' or 'books' appears no fewer than twelve times in a single sentence – set out the editors' intentions with emphatic clarity:

> The aim [. . .] of *The Yellow Book* is to depart as far as may be from the bad old traditions of periodical literature, and to provide an Illustrated Magazine which shall be beautiful as a piece of bookmaking. [. . .] It will be charming, it will be daring, it will be distinguished. It will be a book – a book to be read, and placed upon one's shelves, and read again; a book in form, a book in substance, a book beautiful to see and convenient to handle; a book with style, a book with finish; a book that every book-lover will love at first sight; a book that will make book-lovers of many who are now indifferent to books.[11]

The Yellow Book would go on to publish pieces by many of the most eminent writers of the day – W. B. Yeats, for instance, and Kenneth Grahame. The first volume featured work by rising stars, including Walter Sickert and Max Beerbohm, alongside more established figures like Henry James and Edmund Gosse. There were also three female contributors to that first issue, although only one of these, the magazine's sub-editor Ella D'Arcy, went under her own name, the other two opting for male pseudonyms: George Egerton (Mary Chavelita Dunne Bright) and John Oliver Hobbes (Pearl Craigie).

The quota of women had increased slightly by the second issue, in which Charlotte Mew appeared – and this time there were no male pen names. They made for a colourful group. Scottish journalist, and occasional poet, Katharine de Mattos was the cousin of Robert Louis Stevenson, and dedicatee of *The Strange Case of Dr Jekyll and Mr Hyde*. By the time she was published in *The Yellow Book*, she had divorced her husband for infidelities and was living as a single mother, supporting herself and two children by working as a journalist. English poet Dollie Radford was a friend of Eleanor Marx. Outspoken novelist Netta Syrett was unashamedly prolific: she was to publish over sixty books in her lifetime, including novels, volumes of short stories and children's books. Ella D'Arcy and Charlotte Mew made up this impressive group.

The Yellow Book quickly became the most talked-about periodical of the day, and initial reactions were almost universally caustic. *The Times* observed that the tone was 'a combination of English rowdyism with French lubricity', while the *Westminster Gazette* pronounced Beerbohm's essay in the opening number, 'A Defence of Cosmetics', 'triumphantly silly' and wondered 'how any editor came to print such pernicious nonsense'.[12] A critic in the *St James's Gazette* agreed, finding it 'detestable in matter and unreadable in style'.[13] But the most damning of all responses came from an anonymous notice in *The Speaker*, a weekly round-up of politics, literature, science and the arts: 'We can picture Mathews and Lane calling round them the band of Bodley Head disciples, and saying [. . .] to all of them, "Be mystic, be weird, be precious, be advanced, be without value".'[14]

In 1913, writing with the benefit of hindsight, the journalist Holbrook Jackson offered a more considered view:

Nothing like *The Yellow Book* had been seen before. It was newness *in excelsis*, novelty naked and unashamed. People were puzzled and shocked and delighted, and yellow became the colour of the hour, the symbol of the time-spirit. It was associated with all that was *bizarre* and queer in art and life, with all that was outrageously modern.[15]

Charlotte must surely have been aware of initial reactions to the magazine when, in the last week of April 1894, she posted off to its editor a short story called 'Passed'. On Sunday 29 April, Harland wrote to Lane about his excitement on receiving the story: 'By post, from an entirely unknown person, a Miss Mew, I have received one of the most remarkable MSS I have ever read. A story most subtle and imaginative, and done in a wonderful original style. A new Y. B. discovery – fully as remarkable as Ella D'Arcy, though in a totally different way.'[16]

On the same day, he wrote to the twenty-four-year-old Charlotte directly, informing her that he thought her story 'in many ways a highly remarkable piece of literature' and adding that he would be happy to publish it, 'provided your price for it be within our income; and provided also you will agree to make one or two very trifling changes in the text'.[17] His letter suggests that Charlotte had raised the question of money right from the start. Harland asked her to call on him at Cromwell Road at around three the following afternoon.

This was the first time Charlotte had had her writing accepted for publication, and one might have expected her to be so elated by the success that she would view payment as a bonus. But a further letter from Harland, dated 2 May, makes it clearer still that her efforts to place the story – and probably also to write it – were motivated by money. 'I'm afraid', Harland explains to her, 'our mode of payment is like that of all the other magazines – we pay on publication, not on acceptance.' We can almost hear him thinking as he adds, 'That is our rule – to pay on publication; but if you are especially desirous to be paid now, I will speak to Mr. Lane (the publisher) on the subject and see what can be done.'[18] That Charlotte – a young, inexperienced and unpublished writer – had been forward enough to ask for her fee upfront is possibly evidence of her naïvety, but it also suggests a pressing financial need.

What did she need the money for? The ninth anniversary of Henry's admission to Holloway Sanatorium was fast approaching, and in August, the annual fees would be due. Nobody was pretending any more that he might one day recover. His medical notes from this time record that while he was in good bodily health, his mental condition remained unaltered: he was 'demented and solitary'.[19] It was almost certainly Fred who made the decision to keep him at this exclusive institution whose fees appeared to put the family's finances under such strain. Later events suggest in fact that he forced the issue, as it was surely his right to do. If anyone deserved the final say on the matter, it was Fred, whose business had – at least up till now – been shouldering the burden.

Fred's most recent projects of any financial significance were the two convalescent children's homes he'd built at different ends of the country, at Broadstairs and St Anne's-on-the-Sea, which had been completed in 1887 and 1890. There was to be one last major commission after this – another convalescent home – but it was on a much smaller scale, and wouldn't be completed until 1895. At the time of Charlotte's submission to *The Yellow Book* that spring of 1894, Fred had recently turned sixty-two, and it's possible he was already experiencing the first symptoms of the stomach cancer that, in just four more years, would kill him. If so, he may have been suffering from indigestion, nausea, bloating – perhaps even difficulty in swallowing. Whether he had stopped prospecting for commissions because of ill health, or whether offers had begun to dry up for other reasons, his architectural glory days were all but over. In the absence of a functioning son and heir, the pressure on Charlotte to start contributing to the family income herself must have been acute.

All the signs suggest that she would have done so willingly. In her 1904 essay on the poems of Emily Brontë – a writer whose life and character mirrored her own in certain specifics and with whom she identified on a personal level – she noted poignantly of Emily's

reprobate brother, Branwell, that it was Emily 'who to the last pro-
tected and forgave the sorry wreck who, once the pride, had come to
be the terror of their home'.[20]

Harland did not, in the end, go cap in hand to Lane on Charlotte's
behalf. His offer to do so that April of 1894 seems at best blithely
optimistic, and at worst insincere, since he knew that John 'Petticoat'
Lane had a reputation for dragging his heels when it came to paying
his authors, even after publication. Harland's most likely intention was
to strike a supportive note, while hoping that Charlotte wouldn't want
to pursue the matter. In the event, by June, he was wondering if he had
sufficient funds to pay all the authors he had signed up to appear in this
second volume. He wrote a long and detailed letter to Lane, listing each
writer in turn, along with a summary of the word counts of their pieces
and the fees he had agreed to pay for them; the £200 Lane had offered
to cover their fees *and* those of the illustrators was not going to be
nearly enough. The letter provides an interesting insight into Harland's
opinion of the financial worth of the various *Yellow Book* authors. At
one end of the scale, he proposes a fee of £75 for Henry James's 'The
Coxon Fund' (twenty-two thousand words long), while pointing out
that at James's usual price they would have had to pay £220 for it. At the
opposite end, Netta Syrett is allocated £5 5s for her short story (eight
thousand words). Charlotte's rate came somewhere in the middle: at
seven thousand words long, 'Passed' was deemed to be worth £10, which
was an above-average fee by *Yellow Book* standards – not at all bad for
someone Harland had recently described as an 'entirely unknown per-
son'.[21] Many years later, Ella D'Arcy would confirm that Harland had 'a
great opinion' of Charlotte's story: '"It has a real organ-note!" he would
say admiringly, his own note being that of the lightest of magic flutes.'[22]

The story, whose narrative certainly fitted the magazine's demand
for newness, centres on a young, middle-class narrator who leaves

her sewing and the comfort of her fireside one frosty December evening to explore the city, and finds herself straying into one of its seedier quarters. In a quiet church she encounters a distressed young woman, who pulls her back out into the noise of the street and leads her to a dilapidated house and up to a room where a second young woman lies motionless on a bed beside the torn fragments of a letter. In the brightness of the room, the narrator notices for the first time her abductor's 'spotless person and well-tended hands' and concludes that 'these deserted beings must have first fronted the world from a sumptuous stage' – a stage, or class, not so different from her own.[23] Whatever has occasioned their subsequent fall from grace, the social divide between these two destitute young women and our heroine would clearly be impassable under normal circumstances. But grief does not recognise class divisions, and the bereaved sister, no longer able to hold back her tears, collapses in the narrator's arms and clings to her. There follows an unexpected, and distinctly erotic, moment of intimacy: 'Her dark hair had come unfastened and fell about my shoulder. [. . .] I remember noticing, as it was swept with her involuntary motions across my face, a faint fragrance which kept recurring like a subtle and seductive sprite, hiding itself with fairy cunning in the tangled maze.' Telling the story in hindsight, the narrator claims she was 'repelled' by the proximity, but she nonetheless continues to hold the sobbing girl in her arms until her breathing quietens; even then, she goes to some lengths to avoid disturbing her distraught charge: 'I wondered if she slept, and dared not stir, though I was by this time cramped and chilled.' After agonising over whether to stay or go, she eventually returns to the safety of her own home. Months later, she encounters the girl again, decked out in crimson and vermilion (the colours of prostitutes), and on the arm of a gentleman whom we understand to be the dead sister's lover. When the narrator holds out her hands to the girl, 'craving mercy', she finds her gesture met with a 'void incorporate stare'. The moment for helping has passed.

Sociologist Andrew Roberts has suggested that the streets of Clerkenwell, in the borough of Islington, are the source for the setting of 'Passed'.[24] On close inspection, it seems likely. Walking at an average pace it would take Charlotte around half an hour to reach the district from her house in Gordon Street. 'The heavy walls of a partially demolished prison' described in the story certainly sound like those of the Clerkenwell House of Detention, whose demolition, begun in 1890, was never fully completed.[25] Other topographical features also correspond: a street near to the story's prison identified as 'bearing a name that quickens life within one, by the vision it summons of a most peaceful country, where the broad roads are but pathways through green meadows' may be Saffron Hill, which originally boasted purple fields of saffron crocuses. A Victorian handbook of London describes the street as just the sort of 'squalid neighbourhood' depicted in the story.[26] In fact, its citation had an important literary precedent – and if this was indeed the model for Mew's fictional street, it's a precedent she may even have hoped her readers would pick up on. In *Oliver Twist*, the Artful Dodger leads Oliver down this very street to get to Fagin's den, situated at its southern end. As the boy follows, he reflects that he has never seen a 'dirtier or more wretched place'. As for the story's 'unsightly church', its description closely matches that of the nearby Holy Redeemer (only recently built in Charlotte's time), which a contemporary local architect described, rather ungenerously, as a 'hideous structure'.[27] Both fictional and physical versions of the church share a 'low gateway' and a 'little gallery', and the story's 'grey-clad sister of mercy' may well have been one of the Sisters of Bethany, whose order had official links with the church and whose convent was close by in Lloyd Square.

Whatever the setting, the central action of Charlotte's story would have been instantly recognisable to readers of *The Yellow Book*. Free exploration of the city was no longer the preserve of the male *flâneur* – that practised spectator and connoisseur of street life for whom, as Baudelaire had observed, 'the crowd is his domain, just as the air is the bird's, and water that of the fish'.[28] Now, in the name of philanthropy, middle- and upper-class women could also walk without fear of judgement through the unfamiliar spaces inhabited by the urban poor, and the activity offered an appealing escape from the idleness that was otherwise imposed on them. Some worked as volunteers or as paid professionals (nurses, teachers and so on); others visited the districts independently, as artists, journalists or social chroniclers. Charlotte herself had known about such work since her schooldays, and had recently volunteered for Mary Paget's Girls' Club in St Pancras. The club was one of many similar establishments that sprang up in the 1880s and '90s with the aim of providing the country's thousands of flower girls, laundry workers, dressmakers and factory workers with some specialist educational instruction, offered according to the interests and talents of the volunteer teachers.[29] It was work that, according to a friend, Charlotte 'enjoyed enormously'.[30]

But there is an important difference between the era's typical female urban explorer and the narrator of 'Passed', who is compelled to respond to her charge's distress on an emotional level. 'She clung to me,' we are told. 'Her heart throbbed painfully close to mine.'[31] The woman philanthropist was confined to observing from a distance the situations she encountered – like a female counterpart to Baudelaire's *flâneur*, who was able 'to see the world, to be at the very centre of the world, and yet to be unseen by the world'.[32] As such it was up to *her* to define the rules of engagement. So long as she maintained the requisite social (and emotional) distance, she could retain a sense of her moral superiority – and the poor could be kept safely at arm's length. Charlotte's story does away with all that.

On the afternoon of Monday 30 April 1894, under a thin drizzle of rain, Charlotte Mew made the journey from Gordon Street to Cromwell Road, and climbed the six wide steps to Harland's front door. She had never before met with anyone from the publishing world; and perhaps Harland was surprised by the neatly dressed, inexperienced and rather small young woman he opened the door to. Certainly he saw fit, after that first meeting, to offer her some carefully worded advice on her prose style; a few days later, he wrote again, providing notes on how the story might be improved, this time suggesting something more radical than the 'one or two very trifling changes' he'd mentioned in his previous letter. 'It seems to me that the author should by his style endeavour to soften, rather than to accentuate, the effect of pain. He does not need to insist, to emphasise, to raise his voice.' He picked out a few passages, by way of example, and continued: 'I look down your page and I cannot help feeling that you would lose nothing, but rather gain much by the substitution of less violent phrases [. . .] I mean, one gains so much in climactic moments by restraint, by reserve; one loses so much by making one's language superlative.'[33]

Charlotte duly removed the offending passages, but Harland's criticism remains valid – and not only in respect to 'Passed' but to her fictional prose style in general, which tended towards wordiness and hyperbole. Curiously, these were faults that confined themselves to her fiction: her essay style was beautifully clear and her poems, when she came to write them, would be masterclasses in compression and straight speaking. The second issue of *The Yellow Book* – some hundred pages fatter than the first – appeared in July, and days later, the *Glasgow Herald* delivered a considered verdict on Charlotte Mew's story. It was, the reviewer concluded, 'a queer kind of rhapsody of London life, rather spasmodic and melodramatic, and dealing in a modestly-veiled way with a difficult subject, but with a certain power of its own'.[34]

It would be another seven years before Charlotte published her first poem, but she was already rehearsing, in 'Passed', several of the ideas and motifs that would form the backbone of her poetic output. We find here, for the first time, the image of the staircase, which would appear in no fewer than eight of the seventeen poems in her first collection; the image of loose, uncovered hair, which would feature in seven of those poems; the colour red (standing in the story, as it would do in so many of the poems, for physical desire); and, of course, the figure of the fallen woman, which – though it was a common trope in Victorian literature – seems to have held a particular fascination for Charlotte. She had first learned about prostitutes at the knee of the family's needlewoman, Bolty, whose niece Fanny had been drawn to the financial rewards of working the streets. She had gone, as Bolty put it, 'where many's gone before 'er, and where many'll go after 'er'.[35] Over the years, the prostitute motif would feature again and again in Charlotte's writing. But the most important themes in 'Passed' – themes that would be central to so much of her work – are those of insurmountable distance between people, and the wrench of separation. Charlotte's enduring obsession with these ideas must surely have been rooted in the estrangements she experienced herself: the siblings she had already lost to death or madness, as well as future episodes that would steal from her a succession of other precious and familiar presences.

The fact that so many of the ideas and images in 'Passed' eventually became dominant tropes in Charlotte Mew's poems gives us a valuable insight into how she worked – endlessly turning a subject to the light, examining it from this angle and that, each time trying to capture a different or truer note. But the story also demonstrates something emblematic of her broader vision: in 'Passed', we encounter for the first time her facility for viewing both sides of a difficult situation, and for presenting them to us in such a way that simplistic notions of right and wrong become meaningless. We sympathise with the plight of the destitute and impoverished sisters, but we do not condemn the narrator for walking away from them, because we know how much that act of desertion has cost her. Here, as elsewhere, Mew is not interested in apportioning blame, but in exposing the impassable divide that exists between individuals. Her skill – and it is a rare skill – lies in rendering her characters and their predicaments with such compassion that she elicits our sympathy for both parties in equal measure, allowing the sadness of the distance between them to speak for itself. It is a conjuring act that she would one day use to brilliant effect in her most famous poem of all, about another woman who leaves her house in search of freedom – 'The Farmer's Bride'.

7

Some Glimpses of the New Woman
1894–1895

As it turned out, the journey Charlotte made to Henry Harland's flat that spring of 1894 was to be the first of many. She was soon being invited to the legendary Saturday-evening get-togethers (or 'At Homes') that the Harlands hosted specifically for *Yellow Book* authors. The magazine's assistant editor, Ella D'Arcy, described a typical evening, listing some of the artists who might be heard amid the general hubbub:

> The large drawing room, lighted by lamps and candles only – in those days electricity had not yet become general – would begin to fill up about nine o'clock. Two or three would have dined there. Others dropped in to coffee and cigarettes. One might hear Kenneth Grahame, Max Beerbohm, Hubert Crackanthorpe, Evelyn Sharp, Netta Syrett, [. . .] Charlotte Mew, [. . .] occasionally Edmund Gosse, and Henry James.[1]

What did the newly published Charlotte make of these bustling, lamplit parties and the famous guests who congregated in the pink drawing room of Henry Harland and his music-loving wife Aline? It's likely her feelings were mixed. Evelyn Sharp was keen to stress that the *Yellow Book* crowd 'did not care much what conventional society thought of us, so long as we could succeed in pleasing our editor's fastidious taste in letters'.[2] The majority may not have cared, but in all likelihood Charlotte cared very much – if only on account of her mother. One suspects that 'Ma' (as Charlotte and Anne were now in the habit of calling her) would not have thought well of her daughter's new friends; they were not what might be called 'good five-o'clock people'. But in spite – perhaps, even, because – of this, Charlotte did attend the Harlands' At Homes, and was there often enough to be remembered in Ella D'Arcy's account. Against the stifling propriety of her home life and the building weight of family secrets, the stimulating company at these Cromwell Road parties must have been a welcome diversion.

The Harlands' room contrived to be both spacious and cosy, with a sofa, an assortment of comfortable chairs and a piano. The homely setting put guests instantly at their ease, encouraging an air of breezy informality, in which confidences might be safely shared; the company of the 'young intellectuals of the 'nineties', as Evelyn Sharp pointed out, was 'rarely dull':

> At the Saturday evening At Homes, Aline Harland, a trained
> artist in the use of a lovely soprano voice, sang French songs to
> us sometimes, or what her husband called Herrickles, the lyrics
> of Herrick set to music very charmingly by Stanley Makower,
> whose delicately written contributions to the 'Yellow Book' will
> be better remembered, perhaps, than his compositions. Leonard
> Sickert sang German and Italian songs, and sometimes there
> was instrumental music; but for the most part we talked, and
> the talkers included so many wits that I do not think it is merely
> personal bias or the enchantment of time that makes their
> conversation appear in my recollection of it to have been so gay
> and so amusing.[3]

But it would be wrong to picture these events as organised evenings of intellectual chitchat, punctuated by timely musical interludes. According to one of John Lane's Bodley Head authors, critic and translator James Lewis May, Harland would sit on the floor as often as he stood, a signal to his guests that the customary formalities could be dispensed with.[4] On one occasion he apparently forgot about his guests' arrival altogether. He had invited a small group for a mid-week dinner, but when they reached the house, in full evening dress and at the appointed hour, they found him sitting down to a plate of chops with his wife. 'I must have been drunk,' he replied when the guests reminded him of the invitation.[5] At one of the Saturday-evening gatherings, a discussion about 'some obscure French poet or artist' somehow descended into a full-scale argument about the best way to make an omelette. It ended with everyone squeezing into the Harlands' tiny kitchen while Stanley Makower attempted to prepare the omelette amidst shouts from various guests offering conflicting instructions.[6]

The Harlands' parties offer a rare glimpse of the milieu in which Charlotte moved during this part of her life. And the glimpse is intriguing because her attachment to this engaging group is so at odds with anything that came after. Even during these *Yellow Book* days, it would seem that she remained at the edge of proceedings, for although she is mentioned fleetingly in Ella D'Arcy's recollections, her name doesn't appear in any of the other reminiscences left by the magazine's contributors. Perhaps she was nervous of participating as fully as she might have wanted. Refreshing as the company undoubtedly was, the vigilant eye of the ultra-respectable Ma can hardly have encouraged in her a sense of reckless abandon. In the face of that disapproval, the fact that she attended the parties at all suggests a liberal cast of mind – as well as a healthy dose of defiance.

Was the *Yellow Book* group really such a bad crowd to fall in with? Claims made in the papers that the journal's contents were 'pernicious', 'detestable' and downright 'weird' seem curiously overstated.[7] James Lewis May found it strange that the 'sticklers for propriety' should have taken such offence at the publication's harmless caprices.[8] Evelyn Sharp thought it ridiculous: 'In the "Yellow Book" itself there is not enough impropriety to cover a sixpence, and there is no indecency at all,' she scoffed.[9] Almost thirty years after the magazine's demise, in an article written for the *Manchester Guardian*, Evelyn spoke out one last time in its defence. Her words contain more than a hint of nostalgia for the exuberance of the pre-war years:

> Perhaps it is true that no one who belonged to that set can write quite impartially about it. At the risk of posing as an old fogey, one is constrained to wonder if anywhere in the young world to-day there is a literary and artistic circle so full of vitality and promise as the one, absurdly labelled decadent, that produced those thirteen volumes perfectly printed and turned out at The Bodley Head as few books, I think, are turned out in a post-war world.[10]

The magazine had been born in the wake of the French Décadent movement, but by comparison the crowd from *The Yellow Book* were rather tame. Evelyn Sharp judged that they had been no more or less interested in sex than any other young people, and that they 'fell in and out of love with and without disaster, like other people'. She added that 'the silly charge of indecency could not be maintained by a prude' – let alone, she implies, by a level-headed individual with a tolerant outlook.[11]

Charlotte was no prude. She moved freely around the London streets, and smoked her own hand-rolled cigarettes at a time when to do so was considered a small but unambiguous act of rebellion.[12] A recent column in the *Pall Mall Gazette*, entitled 'In a Ladies Club: Some Glimpses of the New Woman', made plain the widespread – largely male – contempt for the so-called 'New Woman' of this time. It was an appellation that first appeared in the papers in the mid-1890s, and from the outset it carried a strong note of disapproval. The author of this particular article contrasts 'two sweet looking maiden ladies, with an odour of good deeds in country parishes emanating from them' with the club member who had brought them along – 'a "New Woman", scraggy of aspect, shrill of voice and slatternly of dress'. As the reporter is shown around the club, he recounts a moment when his guide, 'Rosamund', declines the offer of a cigarette from another of the club's members, explaining – or so the journalist tells us – that 'While men objected to women smoking, of course I smoked, but I never liked it. It always made me so dreadfully ill.'[13] If newspapers are an accurate reflection of prevailing attitudes, the majority of men seem to have been firmly against the idea of their wives, sisters and mothers smoking at all, especially in public; many of them believed that those women who indulged in the habit did so chiefly to annoy the menfolk. According to a friend, Charlotte used tobacco 'in order to calm her nerves'.[14] She tried to give up several times over the course of her life but never with any lasting success.

It's likely that Charlotte's smoking habit, her obvious intellect and her unmarried status – along with the company she kept during her twenties – were enough to mark her out as a New Woman in the eyes of strangers, though whether she would have seen herself as such is a different matter entirely. From this time onwards, she was also absorbed in another defining occupation of New Womanhood: she was trying, in the only way she knew how, to bring money into the house.

In January 1895, Charlotte received a letter about a second story she'd submitted to *The Yellow Book*, and although it isn't named in the letter, the description suggests it was 'The China Bowl', an altogether different creature from 'Passed'. Written in a southwest dialect, it tells the story of Rachel Parris's love for her son – a love she perceives as having been damaged by the son's recent marriage: 'She had but a room now in David's house and but a room, though that a warm one, in David's heart.'[15] An emotional tussle ensues between mother and daughter-in-law that results eventually in David's death. Once again, Harland's response was exuberant: 'I cannot possibly tell you in a letter how very fine, how splendid, I think your story,' he wrote to Charlotte. 'The humour, the wit, the supreme emotion, the grasp of life, of life in its tragedy, its relentlessness, and the rich beautiful 'cello voice – these and a hundred other qualities lift it above all praise. There is no living writer of English fiction who can touch you.'[16]

Coming from an editor who had recently published Henry James and Kenneth Grahame in his magazine, this was high praise indeed. It must have come as a shock, then, when Charlotte read on to discover that – albeit on the grounds of length alone – he was turning the story down. But he ended by making an exciting suggestion: 'I am afraid the tale is too long for the Y.B., but it would make the backbone of a volume. It is partly about a volume that I wish to speak.'[17]

As far as we know, Charlotte had no other stories ready for publication at this stage. Now, perhaps spurred by the prospect of her own collection, she redoubled her efforts. By February, she had finished 'A Wedding Day', a curious story of unendurable loneliness with the aura of a fairy tale about it, whose prose style is distinctly more modern than the baroque hyperbole of 'Passed'.[18] In clipped sentences, she presents a series of scenes, many of them with the quality of a painting stirring into life. Here, for instance, is a child spilling a pail of milk on the path to the bride's house: 'a little figure, staggering under a heavy milk bucket, coming up the path. The gate swings behind it. There is a lurch, a splash, and the path is wet again. The child sets up a wail. It rises to the open casement.'

As the story opens, we learn that – just as in 'The China Bowl' – not two but 'three fires of love burn brightly' on the morning of the wedding in question.[19] The third belongs to an older woman who has looked after the bride ever since she found her abandoned on her doorstep as a baby. The model for the older woman is, unmistakably, Charlotte's nurse, Elizabeth Goodman, who had died two years earlier. In place of reading books, she spends her leisure hours polishing 'a shining row of pots and pans', which speak to her as books speak to others, and 'say more to her as the years pass'. Her other prized possession is an old wooden workbox with brass corners – very much like the battered but shiny mahogany workbox Charlotte would list among Elizabeth Goodman's real possessions in her 1913 essay 'An Old Servant'. 'A Wedding Day' is essentially an examination of the old woman's love for her adoptive daughter; the bridegroom hardly features at all.

The narrative follows the progress of the special day, from dawn to bedtime. At around the story's midpoint, the two lovers marry, and after leaving the church 'wander on in wedded silence'while the bride's guardian 'creeps, a lonely figure, homeward'. Once there, the thought of waking in the house without her young charge strikes her as inconceivable – 'incredible. Will God withhold the dawn? It seems likelier.' Finally, just at the moment when the lovers begin embracing 'in the deepening darkness' of their bedroom, the old woman dies, alone in her cottage. Unlike 'The China Bowl', this new piece was around the same length as Charlotte's first *Yellow Book* story: it would appear she'd taken on board Harland's comment about length and had written 'A Wedding Day' with magazine publication in mind – though whether she submitted it anywhere is unknown. In any case, it remained unpublished in *The Yellow Book* or anywhere else.[20]

The Yellow Book's scandalous reputation was reinforced when a photograph of Oscar Wilde appeared in the papers in April 1895, under the headline 'ARREST OF OSCAR WILDE, *YELLOW BOOK* UNDER HIS ARM'. Wilde's arrest followed his defeat in a libel suit he had brought against the Marquess of Queensberry, the father of one of his male lovers.[21] But the headline was wrong: the book Wilde had been carrying was in fact a copy of Pierre Louÿs's hugely popular novel *Aphrodite*, bound in yellow and – ironically – far more racy than anything published in Harland's magazine.[22]

A further irony was that Wilde never wrote a word for *The Yellow Book*. Around the time of the magazine's launch, Aubrey Beardsley had fallen out with him over a commission: Wilde had sniped to a friend that the illustrations Beardsley had provided for his play *Salome* were 'like the naughty scribbles a precocious boy makes on the margins of his copybooks'.[23] As a consequence, and at Beardsley's insistence,

Wilde was banned from ever contributing to the new publication. But the papers had their story, and now the truth could do very little to shake it: in the public's mind Wilde and his supposedly debauched morals were linked with the magazine for good – as, by extension, was the still shocking notion of homosexuality.

The repercussions were immediate and severe. Lane's offices in Vigo Street were pelted with stones and some of the panes in its bay windows broken. Lane responded by sacking the eccentric Beardsley as art editor and interrupting the printing of the current edition to remove all of his drawings. It is hard now for us to imagine the scale of the scandal stirred up by the Oscar Wilde trial, or to understand why it caused such shockwaves. At the time, awareness of same-sex love was very limited – even among enlightened individuals. Evelyn Sharp (who, besides being a *Yellow Book* author, was also a free-thinking New Woman) commented that, until the trial, she 'in common, I believe, with numbers of my contemporaries, was entirely ignorant' about homosexuality.[24]

That ignorance was not, of course, universal. At the start of the year, Amy Greener had moved up to Lucy Harrison's house in Yorkshire so that the pair could live together. Amy soon joined the staff of the Mount School in York, where Lucy was already headmistress, and from this time on the two women were to be 'seldom separated'.[25] There was no ambiguity about their relationship; nor, it appears, was there any embarrassment. Lucy had sent Amy a succession of impassioned letters during their nine years apart, while Amy was still in London: 'Oh! for one hour with you again,' Lucy wrote, shortly after setting up home in Yorkshire. 'I feel as if it would give me peace and faith once more. When I am with you I feel what Milton calls "a home-felt delight, a sober certainty of waking bliss". Dearest, I do not feel at home anywhere without you now.'[26]

It may even be that Charlotte was aware of her teacher's feelings for Amy Greener; but the conjectures regarding her own feelings for

Lucy Harrison can be no more than that. In the absence of evidence, any discussion about Charlotte Mew's possible romantic attachments will always be problematic. Nothing that could be described as a love letter has been found in her handwriting. She has frequently been identified as a lesbian, a suggestion that was first mooted in print in the 1930s and later escalated by a piece of literary gossip produced many years after her death (explored in detail in Chapter 14). Her earliest biographer, Mary Davidow, mentioned nothing about lesbianism but proposed, by contrast, that Charlotte had conducted an illicit affair with Thomas Hardy for most of her adult life, an idea that is as unlikely as it appears to be groundless. Such hypotheses occur when there is a vacuum surrounding a writer's private life; we do not like to accept that no evidence can be found – or indeed that there may have been no active love life at all.

But in her work, we find countless examples of passion, sexual and otherwise; and of the sexual kind there are depictions of several varieties of desire: heterosexual, homosexual and a few that might be either. In 'Passed', she had written about the erotic charge of her female narrator breathing in the scent of another woman's hair; in her poem 'Madeleine in Church' (1916), she would meditate on a passionate kiss shared with a man – the only one, says Madeleine, that she would 'care to take / Into the grave with me'. Here is how she describes the aftermath of that kiss:

> Almost as happy as the craven dead
> In some dim chancel lying head by head
> We slept with it, but face to face, the whole night through –
> One breath, one throbbing quietness, as if the thing behind our
>   lips was endless life,
>   Lost, as I woke, to hear in the strange earthly dawn, his
>   'Are you there?'
>   And lie still, listening to the wind outside, among the firs.

What her writing champions is passion itself, in all its forms; her poems speak out several times (most extensively in 'Madeleine in Church') against its repression.

Speculation about Charlotte Mew's sexuality appears to be rooted in a general perception of her appearance. In *The Life and Eager Death of Emily Brontë* (1936), Virginia Moore expressed the view that Charlotte's 'taste in clothes, walk and physical appearance, though she was small and delicate, hinted faintly of masculinity'.[27] Charlotte was, said Moore, 'passionately attached to her mother and sister; and then passionately attached to another woman'.[28] She did not propose who that other woman might be – an omission that later commentators have attempted to remedy. Moore's comments about Mew were made in passing, to support her hypothesis that (again based on the 'masculinity of her presence') Emily Brontë might also have belonged to that 'beset band of women who can find their pleasure only in women'. The speculation, in Mew's case, has persisted.[29]

Today, her mode of dress is still most commonly defined as masculine, a description that applies specifically to the last decade or so of her life. Davidow describes her routinely dressed in 'a tartan skirt, black velvet jacket, white blouse and soft silk tie';[30] Alida Monro as always wearing in her later years 'a long double-breasted top-coat of tweed with a velvet collar inset'.[31] She was certainly a woman of style, a woman who cared about how she dressed: Alida tells us she insisted on buying her black button boots (in a tiny size two) from the stylish Pinet's of Mayfair, and that in the colder months she favoured 'thick red worsted stockings, which might only be bought from one special shop'.[32] Items mentioned in her will indicate that accessories were also important to her: she left to one friend, Ethel Watkins, 'my scarlet Chinese embroidered scarf', and to another, Kate Cockerell, a diamond brooch and 'my small three drop diamond pendant'.[33] Given that Charlotte routinely associated the colour red with passion (and the pain it created) in her poems and stories, the red stockings and scarlet scarf seem significant.

Around half a dozen photographs exist in the archives of Charlotte in her adult years. In one, taken while she was a young woman, she is wearing a fitted dress; in another, from 1921, a soft white V-neck collarless blouse. In a third, from the same period, she is dressed in a mannish pinstripe coat with a velvet collar (very like the coat that Alida described), worn over a white shirt; tied at her neck, in a large, loose bow, is a soft black satin or silk cravat.[34] This is the image that is most often reproduced and which appears (at the time of writing) on numerous websites. Indeed, it is the image that comes to mind for many people at the mention of her name.

Masculine-looking coats were popular with women at the time. In the autumn of 1922, an advertisement in *The Times* boasted 'Ladies' Tailor-Mades in Men's Winter Cloth Suitings',[35] while the Irish department store Arnott's advertised among its winter fashions for 1923 'ladies' herringbone tweed coats in Dark Grey [. . .] finished with velvet collar'.[36] The following spring, an article on women's fashion in the *Daily Express* announced that the 'mannish high white collar of stiff but exquisitely fine white linen is the latest candidate for honours in the spring collar range. It is shaped in the pattern of a man's double collar [. . .] and is cut away slightly at the front to show a neat and smart black satin bow.'[37] The accompanying line drawing is very like the shirt and black bow worn by Charlotte in the well-known photograph. A month later, a short piece in the same paper noted that 'the most interesting feature of the new spring suits is the return to the ultra-masculine'.[38]

All this is not to say that Charlotte was simply following a trend. On balance, the few accounts we have do suggest that she came to prefer dressing in a more androgynous style as she grew older, perhaps even after fashions had moved on. In a letter written in 1958, a neighbour and close friend of the Oliver family recalled seeing Charlotte at concerts. Although she was writing at a distance of over thirty years, her recollection sounds sure: 'I used to meet Miss Mew when Ethel and I went to music concerts in a hall in Piccadilly. Miss Mew was always very neatly dressed, always in black, but rather like a man – her tie for instance. Being always pale, the contrast was always noticeable.'[39] When Charlotte dressed in this mode it may be that she wanted to signal a sexual orientation, or that she wished to free herself of the constraints of traditional femininity, or simply assert her individuality. It seems likely anyway that she would have concurred with a statement made by crime writer Dorothy L. Sayers in 1938, in response to the charge that male attire was unbecoming on a woman: 'If the trousers do not attract you, so much the worse; for the moment I do not want to attract you. I want to enjoy myself as a human being, and why not?'[40]

Why not indeed? It is sobering to consider what Charlotte might have made of the curiosity surrounding her sexuality. All the evidence suggests she would have struggled to see how it could be relevant to her work. Writing of Emily Brontë, she states her point of view with such heartfelt conviction that it sounds as if she is speaking in part for herself: 'It is said that her genius was masculine, but surely it was purely spiritual, strangely and exquisitely severed from embodiment and freed from any accident of sex.'[41] The comment brings to mind a remark made by Coleridge in 1832 (and later expanded on by Virginia Woolf in *A Room of One's Own*) that 'a great mind must be androgynous'.[42] In Coleridge's vision, the creative mind is an admixture of male and female; in Charlotte's, it is freed of the complication of gender altogether. This – limited as it is to the question of 'genius' – is the clearest expression we get of her views on gender-related issues. She makes no statements anywhere directly about sexuality – still less her own – and to allow her private life to remain private seems the most respectful way to respond to her silence.

Whether because of the Oscar Wilde scandal, or because Harland had rejected 'The China Bowl' (and, possibly, 'The Wedding Day') for publication, or maybe for entirely different reasons, Charlotte never published again in *The Yellow Book*. But she did continue writing. A new story, 'Delivered', followed in July 1895, and Charlotte sent it at once to her friend Ethel Oliver, perhaps seeking a second opinion.[43] The manuscript (recently gifted to me by Ethel's great-nephew, Stephen Oliver) is in draft form: in some places there are words crossed out; in others, there are caret marks where insertions have been indicated, all in Charlotte's own hand.

Essentially a stream of consciousness, the story is strange and unsettling in both tone and content. It follows the thoughts of an unnamed narrator on reading in the papers of the untimely death of twenty-two-year-old Rosamund Weir. Apart from the opening sentence, the whole piece is addressed directly to Rosamund's dead spirit. It quickly emerges that the narrator has an unhealthy obsession with the young woman, whom he perceives as a rare and delicate flower, 'framed not for plucking or for wear'. He recounts the moment in which he first realised that, unbearable as the thought is to him, his beloved must remain unpicked – 'graciously swaying on your stem'. He describes how, with a huge effort of will, he managed to forgo the pleasure of consummating his passion: 'I kept my heart's hand closed in stepping past you, strode quickly and with locked fingers by,' his resolve strengthened by the recognition that Rosamund is a rare and otherworldly creature – 'half fairylike, half saintly', a 'slim, religious sprite', a 'sweet, cloistered fey'. As time goes on, however, his resolve weakens and he makes a 'set but shapeless plan' to seek her out and have his wicked way, whatever the cost. It is at precisely this moment that, 'with a foreseeing sweetness', Rosamund dies, leaving the narrator both unfulfilled and bewildered: 'Who warned you of my coming?' he wants to know. 'What divining angel gained your ear and whispered *Sanctuary*?' Finally, in a chilling moment of revelation, he understands that it was no stranger but his own spirit that 'sped before my body to prepare you'. Now, parted from his spirit, he must live on in body only: he can no more force the dead woman to reply to him than he can 'bid you send the banished partner of my being back to me'.

We do not know how Ethel responded to this strange and unset-
tling story, and so far it remains unpublished, but it is significant
because of the striking resemblance it bears in some of its details to
a poem Charlotte was to publish almost two decades later – and not
just any poem, but the poem that would establish her reputation:
'The Farmer's Bride'. The nature of these resemblances (discussed in
Chapter 12) provides us with another helpful clue to her working
methods; and it would turn out that several other of her stories con-
tained the seeds of future poems. Nobody yet knew that her real tal-
ents lay in the field of poetry – least of all Charlotte herself. But in
pressing on with her stories she was unwittingly stockpiling themes,
ideas and images that would be put to far greater use in years to come.

For the time being there seemed little hope of her making money
from her writing, but money had somehow to be made. She had
already ruled out the idea of marriage, to avoid passing on the fam-
ily's 'mental taint'.[44] But with Fred's earning power failing as fast as
his health, and Henry's medical fees needing to be paid, it looked
increasingly likely that the three Mew sisters would have to make
some real financial contributions of their own. It was already clear
that Charlotte's sporadic earnings could not be depended on, and
Freda (who had turned sixteen that spring of 1895) was still at school.
Though no one could have predicted it, it looked like the family's best
prospects for bringing in a second income might lie with Anne.

8

The World Goes on the Same Outside
1895–1898

Anne Mew – motivated at least in part by the need to find paid employment – had enrolled at the Royal Female School of Art in 1890, when she was sixteen. Among the more expensive of London's private art colleges, it was housed in an eighteenth-century brick building at 43 Queen Square in Bloomsbury, not far from the family home, and could boast of having shown its works in a number of prestigious exhibitions, including the Great Exhibition of 1851.[1] The college was especially popular among aspirational middle-class parents, many of whom saw it as a finishing school for their daughters.[2] The classrooms were light and airy, and there were comfortable 'luncheon-rooms' providing rest and refreshment, and 'an excellent Library containing works on Art, Design and Anatomy'.[3]

Despite its mannerly credentials, this was a serious art training college whose single-sex environment enabled students to focus on their studies without distraction. It had been established in 1842 with the express purpose of enabling 'young women of the middle class to obtain an honourable and profitable employment'.[4] Art was one of the few activities to which a respectable woman (of the sort Mrs Mew expected her daughters to be) might turn if circumstances forced her to earn a living in Victorian Britain, since it involved no physical labour, was not a commercial trade and could be carried out discreetly at home. Even within these confines, a few women went on to make a name for themselves. The renowned children's book illustrator Kate Greenaway studied at a similar institution, the Female School of Art in South Kensington, and used her studies as a springboard to a flourishing professional career.[5]

Now in their twenties, Charlotte and Anne were as close as they had always been; they mixed in each other's friendship circles and covered for each other at home if one of them wanted to stay out late. What they could not predict was the extent to which their lives would bind them even more tightly together in the years ahead, as the family continued to diminish in size and the griefs and secrets they shared continued to accumulate. For now, life at college had opened up a new world to Anne and given her, for the first time, an identity outside the family. She was known to her classmates as Annie, but used her full name, Caroline F. A. Mew, for signing and submitting her work. She was slightly taller than Charlotte, pretty and dainty, with striking eyes which one friend described as 'the most brilliant violet-blue eyes that I have ever seen', but they looked out from under strong brows that were markedly less arched than those of her older sister, giving her a look of calm insouciance.[6] The same friend who had remarked on her eyes thought she bore a distinct resemblance to Marie Antoinette. She was bright and witty and fun to be with, and she proved to be an outstanding student.

On signing up at the Royal Female School, students could tailor their study programmes to whichever path they wished to pursue on graduating. Anne elected, like many others, to work towards the Art Class Teacher's certificate, though it would emerge over the coming years that her real aspiration was to exhibit her work, or at the very least to paint to commission. Such ambitions were generally frowned upon: the consensus was that women were better suited to decorative work than to becoming bona fide artists, creating from their own ideas and imagination. Women – so the argument went – possessed gender-specific skills that made them ideally suited to fine arts and craft work. As one feature writer in *The Spectator* put it, 'The delicate organisation of the weaker sex peculiarly fits them for tasks [. . .] requiring neatness and lightness of hand, nice perception, and tasteful feeling: their natural aptitude, and patience of sedentary pursuits, preeminently adapt them for such occupations.'[7] By the end of the century, attitudes were beginning to change, but the old prejudices were surprisingly tenacious. As late as 1896, a gentleman writer in the leading Victorian art magazine, the *Art Journal*, commented that 'women are doing most excellent work in the Art crafts; so excellent, indeed, that it occurs to me it would be wiser if many who are now trying to win positions as painters and sculptors were to direct their energies and abilities into the less ambitious groove of applied art; success of a quite satisfactory kind might be theirs'.[8]

From the start of her time at college, it was clear that Anne was not the sort of student who would content herself with 'success of a quite satisfactory kind'. Although she never took the institution's top award, the Queen's Gold Medal, her name crops up year after year among the School's list of national prize-winners as her work was repeatedly selected by the external examiners from South Kensington. To win one of the few national prizes on offer was a rare achievement; to do so on a regular basis was rarer still. In 1895, she was awarded the first of three scholarships she was to win, this one the prestigious Clothworkers' Scholarship, of £30 (worth around £2,500 to £3,000 in today's money). The judges added a note that this particular student showed 'considerable talent'.[9] Three years later, in the summer of 1898, she received an accolade that had nothing to do with the School, when *The Studio* magazine awarded her an honourable mention in their design competition for a mosaic frieze. Anne's commended design was playfully titled 'Sea Mew' – a homophone of her name.[10] Later that same year, after she had finished her studies, she was one of a tiny proportion of former students on whom the School conferred a Diploma.

What did Charlotte make of her younger sister's successes? She was herself a talented artist. We have one of the pocket-sized calendars she made for Samuel Chick senior to prove it, with its meticulous pen-and-ink drawing of field workers at harvest time. She was also a highly skilled embroiderer. One example survives: a linen rectangle, measuring ten inches by four, finished with a double border which she hemstitched by hand. The design and detail of the decoration are exquisite: the featherweight linen is decorated with flowers in subtly deepening hues of orange-red that range from the palest bisque through apricot, coral and copper to a deep vermilion; the leaves are rendered in two shades of sage green, the stitches tiny and exact.

She brought a similar level of attention and eye for detail to the scenes she portrayed in her writing. The story which Henry Harland had recently praised so highly – 'The China Bowl' – is full of such visual treasures:

Mother and son sat facing each other in the low-raftered room, where prints of stiff, unlifelike ships, breasting unnatural billows were dotted about the walls. Jenefer's childish sampler, framed, hung by the fire. The careful, brilliant stitches, fitfully lit, set forth between the little stunted trees and comic birds – 'JENEFER PARRIS – aged 13'. [. . .] On a shelf beside it rested the huge Bible, wherein the names of Rachel's dead husband and the children who had followed him were written in her laboured hand. And last came David's name, added in darker ink, such as had chronicled his father's end in the same month and year. Upon the unwieldy book rested the china bowl, brought from the East in their first year of marriage, and used to christen their first child.[11]

With her keen sense of detail and colour, and her precise manual dexterity, Charlotte might perhaps have been a painter, like Anne. But by her mid-twenties – an age when her life might still have gone in many different directions – writing had firmly established itself as her métier.

Throughout the 1890s, Charlotte continued to see her old school friends, many of whom came to study nearby at the university. Harriette Chick followed in the footsteps of her elder sister, Edith, and began her studies in biology there in 1894. Over the next few

years, four more of the seven Chick girls (Margaret, Elsie, Frances
and Dorothy) signed up for degree courses at University College,
London.[12] Rather conveniently for Charlotte, this meant there was
a steady flow of Chick women going back and forth to lectures just
around the corner from her house – almost without pause from 1889
right up until Elsie was awarded her MA in English in 1914. The
Chicks were stimulating company. The youngest, Dorothy, would
graduate in medicine in 1910 and serve as a surgeon in the First
World War; Margaret (whom Charlotte had entertained as a child
with her comical drawings) studied phonetics and worked for many
years as an elocution teacher at Notting Hill High School; Frances
studied chemistry and became the first female medical statistician,
carving out for herself a trailblazing career and being awarded an
OBE. In due course, Harriette would outshine them all: she went on
to enjoy a distinguished career as a bacteriologist and nutritionist, and
in 1944, was made a Dame of the British Empire.

The Oliver sisters were often at the university too. Their elder
brother Frank was currently Professor of Botany there, having suc-
ceeded his father in the post in 1888. Ethel Oliver had returned
to London after her two years at school in York and was now liv-
ing back in Kew. Meanwhile, Winifred was studying at the Slade,
which was then, as now, a part of the university.[13] As for her own
education, Charlotte had been making use of her proximity to the
university to further her studies by attending public lectures. It was
during this phase of her life that she learned to read French to a
standard high enough for her to enjoy novels in the original lan-
guage. Her letters, stories and poems are liberally sprinkled with
French phrases; some even have French titles. Years later, during her
forties, she dug out for a friend a number of French-language novels
which she had clearly owned for some years (including Pierre Loti's
Le Mariage de Loti, *Ramuntcho* and *Le Roman d'un spahi*, Turgenev's
Un Bulgare, Flaubert's *Madame Bovary* and Marguerite Audoux's
Marie-Claire), while lamenting that 'Most of my books have had to

go down to dusty shelves in the basement – as there's no room for them upstairs & are consequently damp & unspeakably dirty – only fit for private use.'[14]

All through her life, Charlotte would be supported by close friends who believed strongly in her gifts as a writer. At this early stage in her career they knew about the story she had published, and already believed she was marked out for greatness.[15] The Chicks and the Olivers, in particular, did their utmost to encourage her. Even so, after her debut in *The Yellow Book* in 1894 – disillusioned, perhaps, by the rejection of her second submission – she didn't publish again for another three years. She had written a handful of stories in the interim ('The China Bowl', 'A Wedding Day' and 'Delivered'), but none of these attempts – and perhaps there were others – had yet found a home. Then, in July 1897, a new story appeared in the popular magazine *The Woman at Home*, a periodical that was about as far removed from the cultural ideals of Henry Harland's *Yellow Book* as it's possible to imagine. Established a year earlier than Harland's magazine and published monthly, *The Woman at Home* was described as 'an enjoyable mélange of letterpress and illustration, fact and fiction, cookery and dress, marriages and nursery chatter, specially adapted [. . .] to the comprehension of women'.[16]

Charlotte's contribution to the magazine, a bittersweet romance entitled 'A Permitted Prayer', came to light during the course of my research, and so far remains uncollected. The action is focused on a hardworking, pretty young typist named Nellie Fenton and the girl's chivalrous suitor, Harry Martin. Nellie's 'demented bear' of an employer, Miss Balleter, ensures that Nellie has little time or energy for romance. Apart from brief dates with Harry on the couple's cherished Saturday afternoons, her days are taken up with either typing at the office or carrying out household chores for her mother. When Harry is called away on business to the north, Nellie catches a bad chill and has to stay home from work. Her condition worsens, and by the time Harry returns from his business trip, Nellie has been dead for five days. The story – a sentimental narrative, full of clichés and fanciful flourishes – seems almost wilfully to eschew the literary skills that were on display in 'Passed'. But it is carefully tailored to the tastes of *The Woman at Home* readers, and Charlotte clearly intended it as a potboiler. Viewed as such it is an undeniable success – as well as a shrewd financial move. *The Woman at Home*, with its tips on fashion and homemaking and a lively gossip section called 'Over the Teacups', was so popular that the initial one hundred thousand print run for the first number sold out within days, and a second edition had to be rushed into print.[17] Fees to contributors were no doubt significantly higher than *The Yellow Book* team was ever able to manage.

The first time Charlotte had sought to publish her writing, she'd needed money badly enough to write to the editor beforehand to enquire about payment. Now, again, her efforts appear to have been driven by circumstance. Her father's stomach problems had been steadily worsening, and there are indications that he believed the end might be in sight. Two months after Charlotte's new story appeared in print, Fred placed the following advertisement in the *Shoreditch Observer* – not once but on three consecutive Saturdays:

To be Sold by Private Treaty. A new Leasehold Building (unfinished) near Shoreditch Railway Station, suitable for adaptation as Workshops and Warehouse, fitted with heating apparatus. — Apply Mr. Frederick Mew, architect, 9, Gordon Street.[18]

Was he trying to establish some further financial stability for the family in the event of his death? It had been some time since he had taken on any architectural work for Kendall & Mew: his most recent commission – a third seaside residential home, this time in Westgate-on-Sea, near Margate – had been completed a whole three years earlier. Commissioned as new premises for the long-established St Michael's Convalescent Home, it was an honourable finale. A handsome, symmetrical building constructed from stock brick, with red brick dressings and central bay windows through all floors, it provided convalescent accommodation for forty men and women, plus a chapel and hall at the rear. Today it is a listed building, still in use as a nursing home. This was Fred's final professional engagement.[19] The fact that he was now hoping to sell the Shoreditch building 'unfinished' suggests that this late, private project was something he had taken on single-handedly and was now too ill to complete.

On Monday 12 September 1898, aged sixty-five, Fred finally succumbed to his illness and died at home in Gordon Street. Charlotte witnessed his death and went to register it the following day. She may also have chosen, in consultation with Anna Maria, the wording for the announcement that appeared in that Thursday's *Morning Post*: 'Frederick Mew, the beloved husband of Annie Mew'. The death certificate recorded 'Malignant disease of the Stomach; Exhaustion'.[20] It was a gruelling end to a life of hard work and much sadness. In reporting the death, the *Journal of the Royal Institute of British Architects* noted that Frederick Mew had been admitted to the institute in 1859; he was one of its oldest associates.[21]

Very few clues remain that might enlighten us about the way Frederick Mew lived his life, or the influence he had on his children. There is a brief mention of him in a letter from his brother Richard in the Isle of Wight to a Mr James Bull in London. It was written in 1843, when Richard was eighteen and Fred was just eleven:

> Dear James, Not feeling inclined to go out this evening, I thought I would let you know how things are with us in the Island. [. . .] Fred is not much altered by his stay in London. He is just as droll as ever – The next time you see him ask him whether he will take a 'little more of the Patent'.[22]

In Victorian Britain, patent medicines were mysterious medical cure-alls whose precise ingredients were undisclosed. Several of them included opium or its derivatives, and they were sometimes given to babies to stop them crying – among them Batley's Sedative Solution and Mother Bailey's Quieting Syrup.[23] That one word 'droll' is the only descriptor we have of Fred from someone who actually knew him, and it gives us a helpful, if fleeting, glimpse of Charlotte's father as a young boy. Taken with the touching reference to a private joke shared between two brothers of quite different ages, it gives the impression of an easy-going boy who enjoyed a good wisecrack: we can imagine the eleven-year-old Fred creasing up with laughter at mention of 'the Patent'. One of Charlotte's Isle of Wight cousins remembered 'Uncle Fred', many years later, walking her with his own children to a Sunday service at the Foundling Hospital. He plied them with facts about the hospital's history on the way, and told them to be sure to pay attention to the music and the sermon.[24] The letters he signed off to his nephew, Walter Mew Barnes, with 'your affectionate Uncle' perhaps provide a final clue.[25] It isn't much to go on, but it does at least suggest a degree of open-heartedness in this most buttoned-up of ages.

A faint picture forms of a man who was hard-working, keen on education, warm and humorous. But in 1953, Alida Monro presented an altogether less flattering portrait: '[He] seems to have been a man who took his responsibilities very lightly. His daughter's account of her early life was one of gaiety and extravagance which she enjoyed to the full. However, he died when she was about twenty-nine, leaving nothing, having spent all his available capital on living.'[26] In the absence of further comment on Fred's habits or personality, Alida's remark emerges as a rare source, and is in danger of carrying more weight than it deserves. Charlotte was already in her mid-forties when Alida first met her. Fred had been dead for some years by then, and Alida knew nothing of his financial obligations or how he spent his 'available capital'. She was only vaguely aware that Charlotte had a brother; still less that he was institutionalised – a fact she said she discovered 'only after Charlotte's death'.[27] Nonetheless, her verdict on Fred's conduct is as damning as it is unequivocal: Frederick Mew was a spendthrift, chipping away at funds he ought to have been stockpiling for his family's future wellbeing. The truth is that Fred had spent many years paying for the care of a seriously ill child – but Alida's impressions can only have come from one source: Charlotte herself.

The role of fathers had undergone substantial change during Fred's lifetime. When he and Anna Maria first set up home together in 1863, Protestant evangelicalism was still a powerful influence on the lives of many British families, and with it came the notion that God was the ultimate, unchallengeable, father figure.[28] It was assumed that the male head of the household would adopt a similar role within the family: he was expected to know what was in everyone's best interest and to ensure that individual family members submitted to his authority. But as new scientific findings (Darwin's in particular) gained popular currency, and belief in the literal truth of the scriptures declined, so the idea of the dogmatic father figure began to look more and more outmoded – even a little absurd. By the end of the century, the same progressive atmosphere that allowed Anne to ride a bicycle and Charlotte to roll her own cigarettes had made the formerly sacrosanct status of fathers far less clearly defined.

It's worth remembering this when considering the family's attitude towards the decisions Fred made on their behalf. All the signs suggest that they were resentful of the amount of money he spent on Henry's care, or became so as the years passed. We know that the service provided at Holloway Sanatorium (to which Fred had moved Henry in 1885) was far from cheap, and in fact philanthropist Thomas Holloway had never intended it as a place to house the long-term insane. It had been conceived as a halfway house from which the *temporarily* deranged could be helped back into their normal working lives. By the time of his father's death, Henry had been confined in total for fourteen years, and the most recent entry in his case notes (written just three months before Fred died) could not have been plainer: 'Absolutely no change,' it read.[29] It ought to have been clear to anyone that Henry was very far beyond short-term help. But Fred wasn't anyone: he was the distraught father of an only son whom he had trained personally in his own profession and whom he dearly wanted to return to the outside world. Added to Fred's grief was the knowledge that the doctors believed 'over study' had led to Henry's derangement in the first place. In continuing to pay the rather steep treatment fees at Holloway, the worst Fred could be accused of is blind optimism. But it's not hard to see why Charlotte and her mother and sisters may have been angry at the amount of money spent on keeping Henry in a place so apparently ill-suited to his needs – especially if there was any truth to Alida's assertion that Fred had spent all his available money on 'living'. Still, the resentment seems unfair, and it's hard to imagine how Fred could have found much time for extravagant entertainment, with all the commissions he took on. He had worked hard all his life, and did his best to provide for his family: he left a total of £2,156 4s 10d in his will – not a fortune, perhaps, but still over three times the amount left by Anna Maria's father back in 1885.[30]

With Fred's death, the immediate family circle was now reduced to four women: Anna Maria, Charlotte, Anne and Freda. The three sisters were twenty-eight, twenty-four and nineteen respectively. Anna Maria was still only sixty-one, but evidently not coping well enough to sort out the legalities of her husband's death. It would soon emerge that poor Freda, the baby of the family, was coping even less well. Whatever Fred's faults, he had held the family unit together, dealing with their occasionally complex legal and business affairs and (as importantly) providing a sense of continuity and emotional stability throughout the various shocks and sadnesses they'd suffered. His passing left a yawning gap at the heart of the household. As different family members set about coming to terms with his death – each with varying degrees of success – there was never any doubt that it should be Charlotte, as the eldest child, who stepped into the breach.

9

City of White Days

1898–1901

To all intents and purposes, Charlotte now became head of the family, and she wasted no time at all in making provision for the future. The earning potential of the dwindling, all-female household was limited. Anne had only recently left college and had not yet found work; in any case her prospective earnings had only ever been intended as a supplement to existing funds. Now that Fred's income had been taken out of the equation, the Mew women decided that a second source of regular funds would be needed. Freda had been worryingly despondent and withdrawn since Fred's death and, for the time being, was staying on the Isle of Wight farm with her father's elder brother, Uncle Richard. In her absence, the remaining women came up with a plan that would allow the family to stay in the Gordon Street house. Less than two weeks after her father's death, Charlotte sat down to write a letter to her barrister cousin, Walter Mew Barnes, whom Fred had routinely consulted on legal matters:

> On thinking over our future we have decided that if it is in any
> way possible we should like to let half of this house, as hereby
> we could keep the greater part of our furniture and possess a
> good address, which is an advantage not to be overlooked, and be
> within reach of the few friends Mama has left to her.[1]

The idea of moving to a less 'good address' was clearly not an option. The main concern here was for Anna Maria, who had to be protected from damaged pride and loneliness at any cost. Ma subscribed to the view expressed in her *Cassell's Household Guide*, that 'the style of a house determines to a great extent the estimate which will be formed of the respectability, class, credit, or means of the occupier'. She did not, however, appear to have much time for the further suggestion that many problems might be spared 'if each man would adapt his mode of life to the actual state of his purse, rather than to his neighbour's supposed opinion about it'.[2]

At the turn of the century, certain elements among the middle classes still frowned upon the taking in of lodgers, but even for them respectable widows in straitened circumstances were a very definite exception to the rule: nobody would have thought any the worse of Anna Maria for renting out her spare rooms at this time. As the years went by, subletting would become commonplace, but for the Mews, the presence of lodgers became – and remained – one more secret to be guarded. They told nobody. Many years later, a close friend of Charlotte revealed just how much the decision had cost the family in terms of pride: 'When I first knew Charlotte, the top half of their house was let to some people, but it was a long time before this was disclosed to me in confidence, as it was felt that such a circumstance was a matter of which to be deeply ashamed.'[3] Practical arrangements cannot have been easy either. The 'use of bathroom' mentioned in Charlotte's letter would have been at best inconvenient and at worst a downright nuisance, as the family got used to the geyser being lit more often and guests traipsing down from the top-floor rooms to use the bathtub.

Why, if it was felt to be so shameful, did the Mews choose to pursue this plan? The £2,156 Fred had left in his will, added to the money from the trust fund that had been set up for Anna Maria six years earlier, on her grandfather's death, seems at first glance a decent enough amount – so decent, in fact, that Mary Davidow argued that the sums 'tend to dispel the prevailing notion that Charlotte Mew's life was a long struggle with poverty'.[4] She is right to suggest that the family had hardly been left in penury but, given the extent of their obligations and the insufficiency of their earning power, they would certainly have had to be prudent. The trust fund provided a net income of around £300 per year; Henry's nursing alone used up around a third of that.

A decision the Mew women made now seems to confirm the strain that the cost of Henry's care was putting them under. On a dull Friday in late October, he was discharged 'uncured' from Holloway Sanatorium and transferred to Peckham House Lunatic Asylum, which took in both paupers and private patients, for whom the institution advertised 'moderate terms'.[5] It was a step Fred had presumably felt unable to take, but it made good sense – financial and otherwise – since the thirteen years Henry had spent at Holloway had seen no improvement at all in his mental health. His bodily condition at the time of his discharge was summarised as 'good', but his final physical examination revealed a number of small bruises on the right side of his chest, beneath his left collarbone and on the upper side of both his forearms, likely self-inflicted. As if this weren't bad enough, the doctor added as an afterthought, 'No other injuries.' For all its gilt decoration and exquisite furnishings, Henry had not been happy at Holloway.

It's possible that there were other factors involved in the decision to move Henry. An enquiry had been ordered by the Secretary of State into the case of Thomas Weir, the twenty-one-year-old former engineer who had died at Holloway four years earlier after being held for several days in 'dry pack' restraints. The report concluded that there had 'clearly been a deficiency of medical attention both in this case and to the patients generally in the retreat, where the need of medical care and supervision is most urgent'.[6] The Weir family's solicitor contended that the dry pack had been used 'simply to save the work of two or three attendants'.[7] It soon emerged that around the same time, a second young man had died while in the institution's care. Henry Foote, also aged twenty-one – and suffering, like Henry Mew, from 'acute mania' – died after being kept in a hot bath for three hours, a method that, according to the asylum's superintendent, was 'usual for violent patients'.[8]

In the midst of the upheaval of Henry's move, Charlotte received a rejection note from the Edinburgh-based *Blackwood's* magazine for her latest short story, 'An Open Door', the tale of a young woman who abandons her fiancé to become a missionary.[9] It sounds an unlikely match for a magazine famous for its horror fiction, but in any case there was little time to dwell on the rejection. In November 1898, Uncle Richard sent news from the Isle of Wight that Freda had become uncontrollably distressed and he and Aunt Fanny no longer felt able to look after her. Instead of sending her back to London, arrangements were made for her admission to a local nursing home called The Limes, on the High Street in nearby Newport.

The traces of Freda's life before this time are so few and so faint that only the haziest of impressions emerges. We know from a school friend of Charlotte's that Anna Maria used to bring Freda (aged about six) to dancing classes at the Gower Street School.[10] Then there is the word-of-mouth description of her from another friend of the family, who judged Freda to be 'remarkable' and 'like a flame'.[11] A possible record of Freda's existence during her teenage years exists in the form of a small notice in a local Worcestershire newspaper. In February 1896, when Freda was sixteen, there is a Miss F. K. Mew listed as a student of Malvern House, a boarding and day school in the beautiful village of Blockley in the Cotswolds; she is among the roll of students who had been successful in that term's Cambridge Local Examinations. Frustratingly, Freda's dates of school attendance fall between the censuses of 1891 and 1901, depriving us of confirmation that 'F. K.' stands for 'Freda Kendall', but if this is indeed Freda (as seems likely), the choice of school may have been influenced by its proximity to the family of Colonel Henry Gillum Webb, whose own daughters were pupils at the more expensive Cheltenham Ladies' College. The Webb and Mew families were close, and the connection went back a long way; the colonel's sister, Sophia Ellen Webb, had been a witness at Fred and Anna Maria's wedding, and the Mews named their second child (the baby who died in Broadstairs, aged two months) Frederick George Webb Mew. More recently, Colonel Webb had been made co-trustee, along with Fred Mew, of the trust that Henry Kendall had set up to provide for Anna Maria and the children. He had a sizeable family home in the village of Ashchurch, conveniently positioned near the railway station, with plenty of room for visitors, and just eighteen miles from Malvern House school.[12]

So: attendance at dance classes, a family friend's estimation of her as 'like a flame', and possible attendance at Malvern House – this is the sum total of what we know of Freda Mew prior to the winter of 1898. Grieving for her father, a hundred miles from her mother and sisters, Freda stayed at The Limes into a second month, and then a third. Then, in January 1899, she climbed up onto a window sill and jumped. According to her case notes, she said afterwards that she had been intending to 'end all', and that she would 'commit suicide sooner or later'.[13] On Saturday 4 February, she was admitted to the private wing of the nearby county asylum, Whitecroft Hospital.[14]

Victorian newspapers are full of stories of patients – especially women – being institutionalised on the flimsiest of grounds, perhaps because their spouses wanted them out of the way or their families were unwilling to put up with their behaviour. Female patients were routinely confined for disorders so widespread that these days they would be considered normal responses to the pressures of daily life – work-related stress, prolonged low mood and generalised anxiety, for instance. An inability to conceive, excessive sexual desire ('nymphomania'), pre-menstrual tension or social transgressions like failure to marry or infidelity ('moral insanity') could all lead to the asylum gates. But Freda's was a different story.

At the time of her admission, the asylum's assistant superintendent, Patrick Taffe Finn, diagnosed 'acute mania', noting that at times Freda made a sudden dash for the windows and that 'She has delusions of persecution at the hands of some Miss ——.' The mention of the words 'delusion' and 'acute mania' must have rung alarm bells for the Mews. The same words had appeared in Henry's admission notes:

'Delusions that the end of the world is coming,' his doctor had written; 'that he is the son of the P. of Wales.'

The asylum had been built on the site of an old farm, positioned roughly at the centre of the island, on the outskirts of Newport. A clock with two dials and a ten-hundredweight bell loomed over its complex of red-brick buildings with hipped slate roofs; and so it remains today, though the buildings have since been redeveloped for residential use. In Freda's day, the clocktower was such a dominant feature of the landscape that to say someone was 'under the clock' meant they'd been admitted to the asylum. Freda was housed along with the other paying patients in a separate building, but their daily life would have been much the same as it was for all inmates. During her first days and weeks there, she did her best to occupy herself, spending long hours with a book open on her lap, gazing at it 'without apparently reading a word' and refusing to answer when spoken to. Every now and then she grew agitated. Just a month after admission one of the doctors noted that she 'seizes articles of clothing the nurses have on and struggles to get them, saying they are hers'. These spells of agitation sometimes lasted for several hours, 'during which she will scratch and bite'. At night-times her erratic behaviour continued: she was caught more than once 'jumping out of bed to get at windows'.

Then a change occurred. By August 1900, Freda was spending most of her days sitting in the same spot, quite motionless, 'never noticing anyone, nor saying a word'. By November the following year, her condition had gone from bad to worse: she was now 'perfectly stuporous' and 'dribbles, unable to attend to her personal wants'. A course of thyroid treatment was tried, but to no effect. In 1902, the attending doctor remarked, without embellishment, that she was 'utterly demented'. She was twenty-three. The last case note we have for Freda, dated November 1909, records that she 'has a funny way of getting up suddenly and dancing across room or airing court – has been up daily and is all the better for it'. Perhaps she was going through the dance steps she'd learned as a young girl. But if there is a note of optimism in this final entry, the doctor's hopefulness was short-lived. Freda never did recover her sanity; she would remain in the asylum for the rest of her long life.

During a time when they were still reeling from Fred's death, Freda's illness sent shockwaves through the family. As for the financial ramifications, a solicitor's letter written in 1921 reveals that out of Anna Maria's annual net income of around £300, she had to find 'roughly 130 pounds a year' for her daughter's care.[15] Once again, Charlotte responded to the financial pressure by picking up her pen. In August 1899, her first literary essay, entitled 'The Governess in Fiction', appeared in *The Academy*. In September, seven months after Freda's admission to Whitecroft, *Temple Bar* published 'The China Bowl' – the most likely candidate for the story Henry Harland had rejected four years earlier on the grounds of its length.[16] If this was indeed the same story, then either Charlotte had altered it in the interim or it contains what now looks like a heart-breaking premonition. On the opening page the backstory of a missing teenaged girl called Jenefer is introduced; she has been lost at sea 'on the darker waves of a dread city, which never washed, as kindlier seas might do, her poor tossed body into the arms of watchers by the shore'. Deprived of her presence, but without confirmation of her death, Jenefer's mother and brother are left in a painful no-man's-land of uncertainty. Unable to grieve properly – still less, to forget her – they spend many evenings keeping a joyless vigil: 'Long they watched for Jenefer [. . .] sitting together in the white-roofed cottage with its four wide windows looking out to sea, and listening for her unreturning feet.'[17]

The placing of 'The China Bowl' was something of a landmark in Charlotte's early writing career. *Temple Bar* had been going for forty years now, and had gradually established itself as one of the least conventional – though most highly regarded – of the literary monthlies. This was the first time Charlotte had appeared in its pages, and over the next six years it would publish many more of her stories, poems and essays. But for the time being, there followed an eighteen-month silence.

A letter written that October of 1900 has recently come to light that suggests Charlotte may have been hard at work on a more ambitious project during this hiatus – a project that, if she could pull it off, would bring in a more useful pot of money than the scraps and scrapings she had garnered so far from publishing in magazines. The letter, from Edith Chick to her fiancé, Arthur Tansley, is written on small creamy sheets of post octavo writing paper in black ink. Discussing the couple's reading habits, Edith expresses her shock and dismay at Arthur's low opinion of Charlotte Brontë's *Villette*: 'I know exactly how a Divine feels when he hears an agnostic.'[18] While she concedes that there is no analysis in the book, there is instead 'wonderful passionate life & can you help loving Paul Emmanuel [*sic*]?' At this point the tone softens, and she confesses that she has recently fallen short of her own ideals by bingeing on the latest Flora Steel novel, *Voices in the Night*.[19] Mrs Steel may be 'a rotten bad novelist', but there is something about her books that Edith nonetheless finds, she says, 'quite fascinating'. It then emerges that Arthur isn't the only person she's been trying to convince of the furtive pleasures of reading Mrs Steel:

I fight Miss Mew pretty frequently on this subject. I think she is becoming impressed. I also make myself systematically hateful to her with regard to her novel and writing generally about once a fortnight, from which you might gather that our intercourse is a little stormy just now. It is not as unselfish as it seems on my part, for I have always maintained that it sheds much more lustre upon an individual to have famous friends than to achieve fame for themselves. Think of how you would figure in all their biographies!![20]

The revelation that Charlotte was working, or intended to work, on a novel is tantalising, though no novel has yet been found, in draft form or otherwise. It is heartwarming anyway to learn that Edith had been pestering her friend to get on with 'writing generally'. Sixteen years after leaving school, Charlotte's ties with the Chicks were as strong as ever. Harriette Chick was continuing with her studies at University College, London, and Edith looked like she might never leave: in 1899 (a decade after she had matriculated), she became the first woman to be made a Quain student of botany. Most of her duties involved assisting Professor Frank Oliver (Ethel's brother) with his research.[21]

If Edith's intercourse with Charlotte was 'a little stormy' around this time, it may well have been because Charlotte understood the wisdom of what her friend was saying, and was exasperated by the fact that her time was too limited and her focus too diverted to do much about it. While Anna Maria was the legal head of the house, it was Charlotte who kept things running, and lately it seemed that there was always some business or other that urgently needed her attention. Earlier that year she'd helped her mother make her will and handled all the resulting correspondence. In the summer, she wrote to the trustees of the Bedford Estate seeking permission for 'the erection of a detached studio' in the back garden of 9 Gordon Street. She was probably intending the studio as a space for Anne to paint in, but the letter admits only to a financial motive: she alludes to the family's 'much reduced resources', consequent on her father's death. In view of those reduced resources, she continues, 'it would be of great service to my mother if she might, with the help of friends, contemplate this scheme for increasing the value of the property'.[22]

Perhaps she was imagining that she too could make use of a studio. It might have offered a welcome escape from the corrosive drip-drip of domestic chores. It might also have provided a useful space in which to write. But while the argument she put forward to the trustees was persuasive – she pointed that the house next door already had such a building in its garden – it seems the estate eventually declined the request. Another four years would pass before Anne finally had her studio, and she would have to walk further than her back garden to get to it.

On Tuesday 22 January, after a reign of some sixty-three years, Queen Victoria died at her Isle of Wight residence, Osborne House. The following day, the *London Daily News* announced the event with the headline 'A NATION'S SORROW'.[23] Two months afterwards, a pair of sonnets appeared anonymously in *Temple Bar*, under the combined title of 'V. R. I'. The first of the pair is subtitled 'January 22nd 1901'. It begins:

> 'A Nation's Sorrow.' No. In that strange hour
> We did but note the flagging pulse of day,
> The sudden pause of Time, and turn away
> Incredulous of grief . . .

The second sonnet, subtitled 'February 2nd 1901' (the date of the Queen's funeral at Windsor Castle), proceeds in a similar vein, and while both poems are unattributed, a notice in the *London Daily News* advertising the March issue of the magazine revealed 'Charlotte M. Mew' as the author.[24]

These were the first of Mew's poems to appear in print, and they indicate the swiftness with which she responded to events (or at least public events) in her writing. But if the timely response is impressive, there is nothing very remarkable about the poems themselves. The unwavering pulse of iambic pentameter demonstrates a degree of technical competence, but the lack of metrical deviation suggests she had not yet developed the confidence that would come with practice. The unvaried pace goes hand in hand with a commonplace sentiment and wilfully archaic diction: 'Then lay not down / Thy sceptre, lest her Empire prove a dream / Of Thine.' The public preference in verse at this time was for conservatism and patriotic fervour. For new young writers seeking an audience, there was little choice but to take note of such preferences. One London newspaper (complaining about a lack of entries for a competition for a poem on the theme of African exploration) even argued that 'It is a young poet's business to be patriotic, and patriotic at the expense of being ridiculous.'[25] If the main aim at this stage was to produce something saleable, then the poems were a success.

It's unlikely that Charlotte spent much time herself reflecting on the niceties of authorial intent: within days of these first poems appearing in print, the family was dealt another devastating blow. On Friday 22 March 1901, just three and a half years after entering Peckham House Lunatic Asylum, Henry Herne Mew died there, of tuberculosis. In a cruel coincidence, it was Ma's birthday. She was sixty-four that day; Henry was just thirty-six. It was an abrupt end that nobody could have foreseen, but alongside their shock and grief, the family may also have felt a sense of profound release. In addition, Charlotte, in particular, may have experienced some guilt over the fact that Henry had caught the infection since his move to Peckham House, which took in paupers alongside private patients, in roughly equal proportion. Disease outbreaks were common in many asylums – especially cholera, typhoid and dysentery, but also diphtheria, smallpox, scarlet fever and tuberculosis. In the more salubrious Holloway Sanatorium, they were comparatively rare.

Henry's burial took place at Nunhead Cemetery the following Tuesday, a day recorded in weather reports as very cold with occasional heavy snow showers. The plain, curved headstone was carved with his name and date of death (no birth date or age), and above that two words in plain sans-serif capitals: 'IN PEACE'. Over a decade later, Charlotte would make the cemetery grounds the setting for one of her most affecting poems. 'In Nunhead Cemetery' is a dramatic monologue addressed to the recently buried sweetheart of a young man, who stands at the graveside with rain sliding down his face, refusing to acknowledge his beloved's death. For all the pathos of the poem, and the derangement of its speaker (driven half mad, as he is, by his loss), the sense of place is precisely rendered – it is a place where the 'quick shadows' of sparrows fall across the lovers' 'low stone parapet' – and it's possible that the remembered snow showers from Henry's burial found their way into the poem as rain:

> It is the clay that makes the earth stick to his spade;
>> He fills in holes like this year after year;
> The others have gone; they were tired, and half afraid,
>> But I would rather be standing here;
>
> There is nowhere else to go. I have seen this place
>> From the windows of the train that's going past
> Against the sky. This is rain on my face –
>> It was raining here when I saw it last.

Nine days after Henry's burial, the 1901 census recorded the extent to which the Mew family had now been reduced: the names of Anna Maria, Charlotte and Anne were accompanied by that of forty-one-year-old Emily Stafford, a 'general domestic' servant. When Charlotte's vibrant essay 'Miss Bolt' – a paean to the family's one-time seamstress – was published in *Temple Bar* the following month, it was a stark reminder of days when the household had been full of children, crowding round the needlewoman and hanging onto her every word 'with childish reverence and credulity' as she regaled them with stories of her many relations.[26]

Charlotte's friends were determined to get her away from her stifling home environment – and the Chick sisters knew just the place. The Chick family hailed from Devon and had been holidaying there for many years, in the picturesque seaside town of Branscombe on England's Jurassic Coast. In 1901, the girls' father secured the tenancy of a large, modern stone-and-flint house called Hazelwood, which quickly became a much-loved second home for the family. Built in the late Georgian style, Hazelwood stands on the side of a steep hill in four acres of grounds, its large bay windows facing south towards the beach and the English Channel beyond. Charlotte was one of the earliest guests (her name first appears in the visitors' book that very year[27]); as time went on, it would become a much-needed refuge for her, a place where she could read and swim, enjoy the fresh salt air and explore the surrounding countryside in the company of close friends, without fear of being judged or questioned. In Charlotte's day a large grandfather clock ticked away the hours, 'echoing peaceably in the hall'. Pear trees were trained up the walls on either side of the front door and a vegetable garden lay to one side.[28] Even today, owned by the National Trust and let to a busy young family, the house has a spellbinding air of serenity. It is a place full of light, with the sea clearly visible from the front bedrooms and the wooded valley of Branscombe stretching westwards.

It was very possibly in the tranquil setting of Hazelwood that a plan to put even more distance between Charlotte and her troubled home life was hatched. In the summer of 1901, she set off with – in her own words – five other 'unmated females' for a seaside holiday in Brittany. The journey was fairly straightforward: throughout the summer months the London and South Western Railway ran a return service direct from Waterloo to St Malo every Monday, Wednesday and Friday afternoon.[29] The train first deposited passengers at Southampton, from where a steamship could be caught at varying hours, according to the tidal pattern at St Malo. Charlotte and her group set out from Southampton in stormy weather, relieved to learn that the conditions at their end of the journey would not delay their departure. In spite of her recent bereavement – and perhaps at the further encouragement of her friends – she travelled with notebook in hand, with a view to working up her observations into a publishable article.

In her account of the holiday, 'Notes in a Brittany Convent', Charlotte avoided naming the six women in her party, referring to them obliquely by their six professions instead. Even so, the women are fairly easy to identify from among her close circle of friends. The Bacteriologist must have been Harriette Chick and the Botanist Edith Chick: Edith refers to the trip in a letter written later that year.[30] The Vocalist was possibly Margaret Chick, with her phonetics and elocution training; the Zoologist Maggie Robinson; and the Humorist Charlotte herself.[31] According to one classmate, Charlotte had enjoyed a reputation as the joker of the pack since schooldays, telling 'amusing stories because she loved to make people laugh'.[32] The identity of the Dilettante is less clear, but Ethel Oliver seems the most likely candidate. Ethel was deeply interested in painting, literature and music, but never made a living, and with her sister, Winifred, she held weekly At Homes for friends, at which they discussed all things artistic.[33]

There is a colourful story about Charlotte larking about to amuse her friends during the crossing. It originated (in print form at least) in a short aside made by Michael Holroyd in his essay on Charlotte Mew, in which he describes a playful remark in one of her later letters as 'an interlude of merriment reminiscent of an occasion in her youth when she had danced in directoire knickers in the cabin of a Channel ferry'.[34] In her biography, Penelope Fitzgerald adds a few details and ascribes the incident specifically to the crossing Charlotte made to Brittany in 1901. Fitzgerald has her heroine performing not just a dance but a knicker-flashing can-can for her friends, and the introduction of boots adds a comic visual touch to the overall picture: 'Although they had a bad crossing she danced a can-can for them in the cabin, in her boots and silk directoire knickers.'[35]

However they amused themselves on the crossing, the small party docked just as dusk was falling, and climbed into a smart four-wheeled coach. The coachman piled up their luggage (sixteen pieces in all) in two separate carriages, and the miniature convoy rattled southwards through the cobbled streets of the town 'like travellers in a dream'. It was dark by the time they arrived at their lodgings, the convent of St Gildas de Rhuys, on the Gulf of Morbihan.

Here was a party of young, lively women, unchaperoned and out for adventure. At thirty-eight, Maggie Robinson was the eldest of the group; the rest were in their mid-twenties or, like Charlotte, just into their thirties. They were by no means raucous, but they were certainly out to enjoy themselves. It was unusual for women to travel unchaperoned at this time, and not everyone approved. The French holiday-makers welcomed their high spirits, but there was one other English party staying at the convent and their disapproval was all too apparent:

A hundred gay *baigneurs*, *baigneuses* – French people all – dined loudly, amicably in the *grande salle*, but we, beneath a ban. Four haughty British stares and one averted glance passed comment, was it on the manner of our advent or our bold unchaperoned front? The leader of the coterie [. . .] (we named her the queen mother) reigned at the head of the long table; on her left, a portly dame with two well-governed daughters acted as applausive audience to the queen mother's flow of courtly reminiscence. On her right, she was supported by her son, known as the *petit abbé*, a slim youth, three parts priest and one part school-boy; the typical Etonian, coated with the mannerisms of an old ecclesiastic, suave and rosy-cheeked, straight of limb but slightly stooping, gliding with felt-slippered feet along the courtyards and corridors, subtilizing thought upon the cliffs, his round blue eyes upon his little book, his black skirts waving in the breeze; with the persuasive cadence, the inscrutable regard, the benedictory hand-clasp of his order.[36]

This unfortunate young man was seen on one occasion 'harbouring a smile at some coarse sally of the Humorist's till, caught by the queen-mother's eye, it stiffened on his youthful lips'.

By contrast, Charlotte loved the Bretons' 'voluble encouragement' and the 'smile of camaraderie' that met her group wherever they went.

She and her companions spent their time walking in the salty sea air along cliff-tops or down on the beach, visiting the church, reading in the courtyard amidst its tangle of fragrant flowers, and in the late evening chatting in the brightly lit salon or listening to the Vocalist performing there. They also expended a good deal of their energy avoiding the over-zealous attentions of a portly, rosy-faced old priest who 'rolled round unexpected corners, cropped up on lonely roads and pounced upon us from dark doorways' in the hope of converting them then and there and in an instant rescuing their souls from their 'lost condition'.

The published account is assiduously upbeat, and perhaps the holiday really was the tonic her friends had wanted it to be. But in the aftermath of Henry's death, the atmosphere back at Gordon Street required a more lasting diversion; Charlotte knew that with a pen and paper, she could travel in her imagination wherever and whenever she pleased. During these dark days, it was a strategy she would employ more and more often. In July, a new story called 'Some Ways of Love' appeared in *Pall Mall Magazine*. Only the fourth she had published, it is a pleasant enough tale, competently written, but the prose style is rather stilted and the plot lacks moral complexity. Of more interest is the fact that in September, a new poem was published in *Temple Bar*. 'To a Little Child in Death' once again uses the archaic 'thou' and 'thine' of the Queen Victoria sonnets, but here for the first time there are glimpses of an original voice. The poem's speaker addresses the dead child as it begins its journey towards heaven, reasoning that the journey ought to be a short one:

> Dear, if little feet make little journeys,
> Thine should not be far;
> Though beyond the faintest star,
> Past earth's last bar,
> Where angels are,
> Thou hast to travel –

By now, Charlotte was comfortable enough to begin to take more risks in her poems. In this one, we find the surprising image of dust being brushed from the faces of babies by the shining hair of angels. The idea is reminiscent of the scene in her first published story, 'Passed', in which the narrator describes how, as she was comforting a stranger who had just lost her sister, the sobbing woman's hair had come unfastened from its clips and 'swept with her involuntary motions across my face'.[37] Over the years, Charlotte returns to the image of hair so often in her writing that it begins to look like an obsession. The word itself is used at least once in almost a third of her poems, and the context is often startling. The young male speaker of 'The Fête' (1916), for instance, asserts with authority, as if he could brook no argument, that 'Only the hair / Of any woman can belong to God.'

By the time her 'Notes in a Brittany Convent' was published the following month (in the magazine's October issue), Charlotte Mew's appearance in the pages of *Temple Bar* was becoming something of a fixture. That same month, she renewed her reading ticket for the British Museum Reading Room.[38] She was writing and publishing more regularly than ever before, but after her experiment with the *Yellow Book* crowd she showed no interest in mixing with other writers; still less in becoming part of a literary set.

The opportunity to do so was certainly there. An article in the *St James's Gazette* in June 1898 recorded that 'Fleet Street has scores of little clubs meeting in taverns, where all the talk is literary shoptalk, and where there are police-court reporters who write novels and sub-editors who write verse.' There were small, supposedly avantgarde groups like the Vagabonds' Club, which went on until the small hours of the morning and was said to invite 'all sorts of literary ladies to its feasts', including those who wrote 'very wicked stories of earth and hell, and cross their legs and smoke cigarettes with their coffee – aye, and even drink whiskey and soda' – although it stopped short of permitting ladies to sign up as members. If boozy evenings in Fleet Street taverns did not appeal, there were more salubrious alternatives: the article's author singles out for mention 'a fascinating little club which in summer abides under the chestnuts and beeches of the park, and on sunny mornings you may see groups of literary people there – perhaps the eminent publisher of fin de siècle works, whose motto might be, "What can I do to shock you?"' – a jibe that could easily have been aimed at Henry Harland, had *The Yellow Book* not folded three years earlier. At the other end of the scale were the older and larger clubs, where ladies might also be invited as guests: the Athenaeum, the Reform, the Garrick and the Savile.[39] There was even talk in the papers of the establishment of corresponding ladies' clubs, and in just a few years, the Ladies' Lyceum (June 1904) and the Ladies' Athenaeum Club (October 1904) would open their doors.[40] Charlotte steered well clear of them all.

With so many demands being made on her, she would have struggled to find the time to network, even had she wanted to do so. But in spite of her brief involvement with the *Yellow Book* crowd, socialising beyond her circle of close friends simply wasn't in Charlotte's nature. Her awareness, and acceptance, of that fact grew as the years went by – and with it an awareness that her lack of connections might in the end damage her reputation. It was this concern that some years later would prompt an apologetic letter to her publisher. She knew a handful of literary people, she told him, and they had written to her privately to express their admiration, but she was unable to ask them to put something in print. 'I am simply not the person,' she explained, 'though for your sake, I wish I were.'[41]

10

The Whole Gay, Unbearable, Amazing Show
1902–1904

In January 1902, Charlotte's maternal aunt, Mary Leonora Kendall, died at her home in Brighton from 'nervous debility and inanition', or what we would now call malnutrition. The death certificate notes that she had been suffering from these conditions for some twelve years, and it was probably an awareness of her deterioration that led her, in the summer of 1900, to draw up a will, with detailed instructions on how her estate (£2,864 17s 2d at the time of death) should be distributed. What is striking about the will is that the first named beneficiary is not a relation but the family servant, Ann Perkin, who had been with the Kendalls for more than thirty years. A sizeable £300 was left to her, 'in recognition of her long and faithful services', along with an assortment of furniture and other household items. To her brother Edward, Mary left £500 in trust, to be invested by her executors for his use. Meanwhile, Anna Maria – who had left the family home to marry shortly after Mary turned eighteen – was bequeathed whatever remained of the belongings: 'all articles of personal or domestic or household use or ornament of which I may be possessed at my death other than the articles hereinbefore mentioned'. The monetary residue of the estate was left to Charlotte and Anne, in equal shares.

Two weeks before she died, Mary had added a codicil to the will, itemising specific gifts for a handful of friends and family members. Ann Perkin would receive a sapphire ring, as well as Mary's long, fur-lined coat; her father's ring and blue enamel studs would go to her brother Edward. No mention is made of Anna Maria in this codicil, and neither was she left any money. It might simply be that Mary was thinking of the longer term, aiming to avoid further death taxes by passing money straight to Anna Maria's daughters. But the fact that no personal gift was set aside for her sister in the codicil seems significant: had relations between the two sisters become strained? The name of their youngest brother, Arthur, is missing altogether from the will. It's likely he had still not been forgiven for bringing the Kendall name into disrepute back in the 1870s, when he burgled the family home. Could it be that Mary was equally ashamed of the mental instability that Anna Maria had apparently passed on to two of her children? And that for some reason she laid the blame at her sister's door? It might even be that Mary Leonora had chosen a life of spinsterhood for herself in order to avoid continuing (in the words of Alida Monro) 'the mental taint that was in their heredity'.[1] If that were the case, her decision to leave money to Charlotte and Anne – who themselves had made a similar choice to remain childless – makes perfect sense. Nothing at all was left for Henry or Freda, though Mary must have known that a gift left in trust for their care would have eased her sister's financial burdens.

Those burdens looked unlikely to lighten any time soon. In the three years since her admission to the asylum, Freda had shown no improvement at all. In most respects her condition had worsened. If she was less combative with the nurses, she still chose to sit in the same spot every day, except now, instead of reading, or pretending to read, she sat with her head hung down, 'requiring everything to be done for her'.[2] There is a strong suggestion throughout her medical notes that she is somehow to blame: that if only she would put in a bit of effort, her prospects might not look quite so grim. If we are right in supposing that the illness that surfaced in Freda and Henry in their late teens was schizophrenia, the treatment they received at the hands of the medical profession was woefully inadequate. In Freda's case, here was a young woman, traumatised by her father's death (and perhaps Henry's too, if she had been told of it), removed quite suddenly from all she had known and loved, and afflicted by a frightening brain disorder that left her confused and very likely suffering delusions and hallucinations that she was unable or unwilling to voice.

It is one of the features of schizophrenia that patients sometimes sit for hours without moving or talking, but Freda's doctors didn't have the benefit of that knowledge. They believed their patient was being wilfully obdurate – maintaining, as they put it, 'a stubborn silence, never uttering a word voluntarily and taking not the least notice of anyone'.[3] Elsewhere they observed, with an unmistakable note of disapproval, that she was 'spiteful at times', 'getting fatter', and 'generally very untidy and resolutely unemployed'. In February, by way of a last resort, they decided to put her on thyroid treatment, a relatively new approach designed for patients who had failed to respond to routine care. The idea was that thyroid, taken as a tablet, started a fever that could be controlled by the physicians, and that in some cases the fever would somehow burn out the mental illness. The drug's results were variable, to say the least, but its unpleasant side effects were more predictable: it caused significant weight gain and induced headaches and 'fine fibrillar twitchings in the tongue, lips, facial muscles and limbs'.[4] There was no improvement at all in Freda's mental condition, either during or after treatment.

How much Charlotte knew of her sister's sorry state at this particular time is unclear, but even without that knowledge recent events had put her under considerable strain. It is striking that this was also the time when her writing began to pick up speed. March 1902 saw the publication of a new sonnet in *Temple Bar*. 'At the Convent Gate' takes the form of an exchange between a young initiate and a would-be suitor. Once again Charlotte was revisiting in this poem a subject she had already described in prose. 'Notes in a Brittany Convent' (published in the same journal five months earlier) had recounted the story of her trip to St Gildas de Rhuys, and now she wove an intricate little fiction around a single figure from that story: a young nun whose 'bright eyes' and 'soft voice' had made a strong impression on her. The poems kept coming, but Charlotte was ill at ease. In April, for the second time in nine months – and subsidised, no doubt, by the money she had just received from Aunt Mary's will – she set off for another holiday abroad.

The destination was Paris, and this time she travelled alone, having arranged to meet up with Ella D'Arcy, her friend from the *Yellow Book* days, who had been living in Paris since 1895. Penelope Fitzgerald has suggested that Charlotte was in love with Ella and went to Paris to be with her, but the proposition seems to be without foundation. Charlotte was an enthusiastic Francophile, and if her decision to visit the capital was influenced by the fact that she had a friend living there, there is no evidence of any romance between them.*

On the afternoon of 18 April, just a few days into the holiday, Charlotte wrote a long letter to Ethel Oliver. 'Physically I have been really better here but mentally tired,' she confided, and in the next breath – as if afraid that mention of her tiredness might cause undue concern – she added, 'but if I wished to get my nerves under control, up to now, thanks to being better, I have done it, and hope that it will last.'[5] Her room, in the Rue de Turin (near Montmartre cemetery), was pleasant enough, with a small balcony that looked out onto the street and the shops opposite, and she relished being 'free and alone', but the boarding house was in a noisy business quarter, the food was lousy and her fellow guests weren't people she wanted to spend time with, though she had made an effort to socialise. There were four German women ('not over friendly'), a Mexican gentleman who spoke English but resented being spoken to, and an older French woman whom she found 'kind, but greasy'. She quickly got into the habit of taking her meals at Ella's lodgings instead, in the Rue du Chat, about half an hour's ride away by omnibus.

---

* An expert on Ella D'Arcy's writings, Professor Benjamin Fisher of the University of Mississippi, has expressed surprise at the suggestion; nor could he recall 'any mention of Mew' in the extensive correspondence he'd seen. 'To be brief,' he told me, 'I have never discovered anything in my researches regarding Ella D'Arcy which would hint of a close relationship between her and Charlotte Mew.' (Benjamin Fisher to the author, by email, 28 October 2016.)

Unlike London, all the trains and buses in Paris were clearly plac-arded with their destinations. But each time Charlotte stepped outside it felt like she was taking her life in her hands. 'It is a danger to be absent-minded crossing the roads,' she told Ethel, 'as the traffic here is simply awful. The heavy two-storied steam trams and innumerable motor cars keep one always on the *qui vive*.' In spite of the traffic, and her low mood, she spent most of her time out and about. The walk from her lodgings to Ella's took her through the Champs-Elysées, which she found 'spacious, gorgeous, airy, altogether luxurious *et tout à fait différent*'.

Ella had asked Flaubert's niece, Caroline Grout, to tea one after-noon. Charlotte was at Ella's lodgings that morning but felt too weary to socialise, offering instead to go out in search of flowers and cakes for the occasion and then giving Ella a helping hand with arranging her room. She confided to Ethel that on arriving in Paris she had found Ella generally 'somewhat in need of someone to look after her' – though she wasn't at liberty, she said, to go into details. She returned to the Rue du Chat for dinner with Ella, and that evening the pair got chatting to two other women seated at their table: one French and the other 'an out-and-out American (very racy in conversation and full of American vitality) who is studying under Marcel to be a prima donna'. 'Marcel' was probably Marcel Journet, the French opera singer who was principal bass at Milan's La Scala from 1915 to 1925. After the meal, the foursome stayed on chatting and drinking till late, the young American singer refusing a cigarette from Charlotte 'with pathetic courage', explaining that she treated her voice as a mother would her cherished child. Saying goodnight to Ella and the rest of the company, Charlotte made her way back to her lodgings and got her first glimpse of the Champs-Elysées at night:

I left E D'A and came along the Champs Elysées looking wonderful with its innumerable lights, and nearly lost my way coming home, as it is difficult to see the names of the streets at night and the omnibus men either cannot or will not help you. They are very surly.

Sometimes one finds a pleasant work girl who directs you very kindly, but my French is so bad it's not easy to understand.

The next morning, she woke to the sound of rain and a craving for hot chocolate. Ella had suggested meeting up in the Parc Monceau, half-way between the two women's lodgings, 'but as it was wet,' Charlotte told Ethel, 'I didn't feel inclined, and waiting for a break, started off by myself in the other direction'. She walked up and down the Boulevard Saint-Michel in search of a *crèmerie*, but found only curiosity shops and book stalls and dingy cafés. Eventually giving up, she explored the rest of the Latin Quarter, where she 'browsed about' for an hour before going on to look around Notre Dame Cathedral, but, still hungover from the night before ('my head was stupid and my eyes tired, and I couldn't look up, etc.'), she was unable to take it in properly. By the time she got back to her lodgings, the sun had come out and she felt bright enough to go down to the salon to make tea in the 'apparatus' that Ethel had lent her. She had told Ella she'd try to show up for lunch, but the morning's exertions had worn her out: 'This afternoon I shall take it easy and not go up to the Rue Chat perhaps till dinner,' she told Ethel, 'though Ella will wonder where I am.'*

---

* Penelope Fitzgerald cites this same letter in support of her theory that Mew was in love with Ella D'Arcy and had gone to Paris specifically to pursue her, but her account contains an important misquotation. She describes how, after waiting for a break in the rain, Charlotte told Ethel she 'started off myself in the other direction ... and prowled about the Quartier Latin' (p. 83). But the word 'prowled' – suggestive of a lovesick unease and predatory frame of mind – does not appear in the original letter. What Charlotte wrote (the writing is clearly legible) is 'browsed', as transcribed by Mary Davidow for her 1960 PhD thesis: 'This morning E D'A wished me to meet her [...] but as it was wet, I didn't feel inclined, and waiting for a break, started off by myself in the other direction; visited Notre Dame and browsed about the Latin Quarter for an hour. It is certainly the most picturesque part of Paris.' (Davidow, p. 283). Fitzgerald's misquotation, her omission of the closing sentence and alteration of 'Latin Quarter' to the more theatrical 'Quartier Latin', puts a different slant on a situation that was in all likelihood devoid of significance.

As the letter continues, it's impossible to ignore the undertow of ennui and disillusionment. The Paris of 1902 was a vibrant and exciting place to be; it was home to artists from all over the world – Picasso, Modigliani and Matisse among them. In the very month of Charlotte's visit (although a few days after she left, so not in time for her to catch it), Debussy premiered his *Pelléas et Mélisande* at the Opéra-Comique.[6] For a young, gifted, independent woman who loved art and music, Paris should have been thrilling. But where she might have seen excitement and opportunity, Charlotte saw only unfriendliness and danger. She disliked the fellow guests at her *pension*, thought the streets perilously busy and the Parisians unhelpful, and in general found very little to enthuse about. Her own analysis of the situation was that, at the time of writing to Ethel, she had had 'no sensations worth recounting', and wondered if 'perhaps I have worn them out'.

The events of the past few years had clearly taken their toll, and this long and important letter gives us a rare chance to see Charlotte's mental processes at work as she tries to tease out what is happening to her in psychological terms. She supposes her inability to respond to her surroundings must be due to the fact that 'I have been living at rather high pressure with not much space for such.' Ethel was one of the few friends Charlotte trusted implicitly, and whose support she could rely on: 'Love to thee who understands', she signs off, with an appropriately Quakerly turn of phrase. But in her present mood, even the act of confiding caused her some anxiety: 'I can't transport my thoughts to England and the things left behind with any sense of reality, and perhaps it is better so, but it makes me seem very egotistic – which I'm not really. It is a queer uncertain mind this of mine – and claims are being made upon it at the moment, which I find difficult to meet.'

Within the space of three years, Charlotte had lost a father and a brother, and had watched her sister fall prey to the same illness that had robbed the family of Henry's presence with such cruel finality. Demands had been made on her from all sides, as she worked to put her family's affairs in order – probates and funerals and investments and arrangements for Freda. The physical strain of those chores can only have magnified the emotional impact of all that had happened.

In spite of these pressures, once back in London, Charlotte continued writing and posting off new pieces for publication. Before the year was out, another story and two more poems had appeared in *Temple Bar*. The November issue carried 'Not for that City', an evocation of a metropolis that never sleeps and is lit by an 'everlasting glare' of sunshine – 'its golden streets and glittering gates ablaze'. What we humans crave, says the poem, is something very far from 'the clamour of [the] never-ending song' offered by such a city. On the contrary,

> . . . if for anything we greatly long,
> It is for some remote and quiet stair
>> Which winds to silence and a space of sleep
>> Too sound for waking and for dreams too deep.

If Charlotte had a model in mind for the city, it's likely she was thinking of Paris, whose own clamour she had been only too happy to leave behind. Certain of the poem's details match those of the district where she'd stayed. The walk to Ella's *pension* would have taken her past the gold-painted 'glittering gates' of the Petit Palais (now a museum of fine art), which had been built just two years before her visit, for the Paris Exposition. But in a poem, the significance of physical details lies in their figurative meaning, and this poem – only her fourth to be published – was the second to include the image of the stair. She would return to the staircase image over and over in her poems, and often, as here, it would denote a walkway to a longed-for silence; a hint, perhaps, at the respite that death might provide.

However alluring the thought of 'a space for sleep' may have been, for now there were the nuts and bolts of life to attend to, and it was around this time that a new member was adopted into the Mew household. Wek (standing for William Edward Kendall) was a noisy and rather badly behaved parrot, for which Charlotte, Anne and Ma soon developed 'an enormous affection'.[7] His name suggests he had previously resided with the Kendalls, and he was likely handed over to the Mews on Aunt Mary's death. Many parrots have a gender bias when it comes to humans, preferring the company of one sex or the other, and there was no doubting this particular bird's preference: in the words of a family friend, Wek, very simply, 'could not stand men'.[8] For the most part, he had been able to avoid them. The Kendall household had been all-female since Henry's death in 1885 – and now he took to his new women-only household with ease, and was rather docile among them. Male visitors, on the other hand, were at risk of having their tea-time conversation drowned out altogether by the bird's persistent squawking. As time went on, Wek became especially important to Ma. For a woman described as having 'few friends' since her husband's death, the parrot's constant presence must have provided a welcome distraction.[9]

Despite the handful of poems she'd published by the winter of 1902–3, Charlotte still thought of herself as a prose writer. In January, two further stories appeared in print, the first of them in the ever-hospitable *Temple Bar* – called, appropriately enough, 'An Open Door'. The story had been rejected by *Blackwood*'s magazine in 1898, and it's not known whether Charlotte had reworked it in the interim. The second, 'The Minnow Fishers', was a very short piece (around 850 words) and appeared anonymously in *The Outlook*, a political weekly that carried a few pages of fiction in each issue; one of Charlotte's favourite authors, Joseph Conrad, was a regular contributor. Mew's story depicts 'three minute and very shabby anglers'

fishing for minnows on the bank of the canal near Maida Vale. The drama of the situation is only revealed when a fourth child is pulled from the water by a passer-by, while the three playmates remain fishing – 'three remorseless specks, intent, oblivious, aloof'. The narrator's shock at the children's indifference escalates into anger when it turns out that the rescued boy is the brother of one of them.

The painterly quality of 'The Minnow Fishers' is heightened by the fact that the three children who are fishing remain unmoving throughout, while the crisis agitates and then closes around them; and it's likely that this story was indeed inspired by a painting. The Scottish painter Robert Gemmell Hutchison had recently exhibited a selection of his paintings at the Royal Society of British Artists' spring exhibition, a show that Charlotte and Anne visited most years.[10] Among Hutchison's works is an oil painting also called *The Minnow Fishers*, which depicts the 'damp dusk' of the story, the 'dingy stretches of the bank' and 'stagnant water' of the canal, and – crucially – a 'tranquil band' of minnow fishers. In the painting, the fourth little boy stands apart and excluded from the others, looking dejectedly at his hands, as if nobody would mind much if he disappeared. If the painting did indeed provide a spur for Mew's story, it gives us a further, intriguing glimpse into her working methods. But the deeper impulse (as with all her work) was rooted in the depths of her psyche; what 'The Minnow Fishers' likely reveals is that Charlotte had at this time a deep horror of inaction, and of its consequences.

Since Fred's death, the normal procedure at Gordon Street had been for one of the two daughters to stay and mind Wek while the other went on holiday, with or without their mother. The previous spring, while Charlotte was away in Paris, Anne had been on caring duty. Now, towards the end of May 1903, it was Charlotte's turn to remain in London while Anne and Ma went over to the Isle of Wight to stay at the rather grand Barfield Lodge in Ryde, which was owned by Fred's sister, Fanny.[11] As Fanny's eldest son, it fell to forty-seven-year-old Walter to take the lead in entertaining his London relatives. On 1 June, for instance – a tranquil summer's day – he shepherded family and three friends together for a trip to Yarmouth, at the other end of the island. A few weeks earlier, Walter (who was often up in London, at his chambers at King's Bench Walk) had paid a visit to Gordon Street to help Anne choose a bicycle, and now she and Walter and friends explored the byways of Yarmouth.

There is no mention of Charlotte cycling, although if Anne had a bicycle, it's not far-fetched to suppose that Charlotte used it too. But that summer at least, she was too busy to spare much time for leisure. Advertisements for the May edition of *Temple Bar* gave notice of a disturbing new story by her entitled 'A White Night', whose contents shed further light on her state of mind at this time. Like 'The Minnow Fishers', the new story focused on the horror of doing nothing when the opportunity to rescue a fellow human being presents itself. The central character, Ella, is on holiday in Spain with her husband, King, and her brother, Cameron, who narrates the tale. While exploring a remote hill town in the dusk, the three venture into a large old church attached to a monastery – 'impressive in its loneliness, its blank negation of the outside world' – and find themselves, after closing time, locked inside. With nobody around to hear their shouts, they resign themselves to spending the night in one of the side chapels, amid the scent of incense and 'a biting chilliness'. Several hours later, very deep in the night, the connecting door to the monastery opens and a line of 'fifty or sixty' monks enters, carrying tapers and accompanied by three priests and a beautiful, small woman dressed in white, who cries out repeatedly in distress as they process towards the altar. There follows a bizarre ritual, which culminates in the woman being buried alive in a hole beneath one of the chancel flagstones while Ella and her party look on in horror but do nothing to stop the proceedings – an omission for which,

Cameron tells us, Ella has 'never forgiven him'. After the monks have left and the sun has risen, the three holidaymakers manage, scrambling on hands and knees, to locate the correct flagstone, but they are unable to prise it up. Reporting the incident to the British Consul later that day, their story is met with sympathy, but the Consul informs them that 'as to *doing* anything in this case, as in others even more remarkable, why, there was absolutely nothing to be done!'

'A White Night' works well as a metaphor for the oppressive forces of patriarchy – the helpless woman surrounded by powerful men and silenced by the system – but while that aspect is certainly present, the narrative also offers up some clues on matters closer to Charlotte's heart at this time. Strange and unsettling as the details are, the story essentially hinges on the failure to rescue a victim whose life is in danger – just as 'The Minnow Fishers' had done. Freda had been at Whitecroft for just over four years now, and Henry had died in the Peckham asylum two years before. If Charlotte had imagined Freda would be gone only for a short while – perhaps until the shock of Fred's death had subsided – it's possible she was expressing in these stories an inward horror of standing by while her sister drew ever closer to the same ignominious fate as Henry's.

Viewed this way, the fact that one of the impassive onlookers in 'The Minnow Fishers' is a sibling of the drowning boy takes on an extra significance. Physical details of the abbey church in 'A White Night' make the connection between convent and asylum hard to ignore: approaching the building, the little group 'counted over thirty windows in a line upon the western side below a central tower with its pointed turret' – a description that calls to mind Freda's asylum on the Isle of Wight, with its own central turret that towered over the accommodation blocks and long lines of inmates' windows. This is how Charlotte depicts the chilling moment in 'A White Night' just before the woman is finally lowered into her burial hole: 'At the last moment, with their hands upon her, standing for a second still erect, before she was committed to the darkness, she unclosed her eyes, sent one swift glance towards the light [...] And then her face was covered with her veil.'

The woman's final beseeching glance would be echoed in the closing lines of 'Ken' – written a decade later – which describe the moment when the speaker watches Ken being handed over to the care of asylum staff:

> So, when they took
> Ken to that place, I did not look
> After he called and turned on me
> His eyes. These I shall see –

Given her habit of inverting genders when drawing on episodes from her life, Ken might easily signify 'Kendall', Freda's middle name (she was the only Mew sibling to carry the name).[12] The homogeneous mass of medical staff who tended to Freda at Whitecroft, and who wrote with such insensitivity about her condition, are not a million miles from the unthinkingly sadistic monks in the story whose 'faces seemed to merge into one face – the face of nothing human – of a system, of a rule'. Did Charlotte feel her beautiful younger sister, as slight in build as the woman in her new story, was in effect being buried alive in the asylum? And if so, did she feel, like the British Consul in her story, that there was 'absolutely nothing to be done' but stand by and watch it happen? In a broader sense, the story seems also to reflect Charlotte's own feelings of being buried under the sheer weight of the adversities life had thrown at her: the bereavements she had experienced, the secrets she must guard and the need to keep the household running come what may, in the face of mounting financial pressure.

That July of 1903, Charlotte (still known as Lotti or 'Lot' to the Chick sisters) was in the seaside town of Branscombe again, for the marriage of Edith to her professor at the newly reconstituted University of London, University College.[13] Edith worked as Arthur Tansley's research assistant, and their romance had been going on, in a gentle way, for several years. On the afternoon of Sunday 26 July, Edith's sister Harriette returned from her own study trip abroad to a house buzzing with preparations for the wedding:

> Got home from Germany to find the house much excited &
> upset. Inspected the wedding presents and the 14 serviette rings
> and in the afternoon, Stopey [palaeobotanist and pioneer of
> birth control Marie Stopes] and Norman and Lot came to tea.
> Stopey was rather sweet on the subject of the D.Sc., amusingly
> so. Norman finally went off at about seven and Lot stayed. E's
> clothes etc the absorbing subject of conversation.[14]

Just how much social contact Charlotte had with Marie Stopes is unknown, but the fact that they were part of the same friendship group (Stopes studied botany at University College, London alongside Edith) may have some bearing on Mew's story. As a feminist pioneer and sexual reformer, Stopes' work in the field of birth control is well known; less well known are her extremist views on race and eugenics. In her 1920 polemic *Radiant Motherhood: A Book for Those Who Are Creating the Future*, she would talk explicitly about the danger to society of the 'vast and ever increasing stock of degenerate, feeble-minded and unbalanced'. These unfortunate individuals were, she said, 'like the parasite upon the healthy tree sapping its vitality', and it was 'the urgent duty of the community to make parenthood impossible for those whose mental and physical conditions are such that there is well-nigh a certainty that their offspring must be physically and mentally tainted'.[15] The connection takes on an ominous significance in light of Charlotte's decision to remain child-free for fear of passing on the perceived 'mental taint' in her family's genes.[16]

On Monday 27th, Charlotte went up to London with Edith, Harriette, their 'Aunty Smith' and 'Stopey' to shop and have lunch. At the end of the afternoon, a select party of well-wishers saw them off on the three o'clock train at Waterloo, laden with five dress boxes. On Tuesday, the Chick women had their dresses fitted 'in a most awful rush' for the wedding, before going up with Charlotte to London again, to the fashionable Frascati restaurant on Oxford Street, where they drank Münchener beer, 'with all due rites & ceremonies', before returning once again on the three o'clock from Waterloo. Wednesday (the eve of the big day) was showery, but – undeterred – the young women picnicked on bread and cheese on the moors outside Colyton, five miles from Branscombe, where they collected heather to decorate the house and then 'sat in the road & behaved in a most unbecoming manner – especially the bride'. That evening, a few more guests arrived at the house amidst pouring rain. 'Weather prospects awful,' Harriette noted wryly in her diary, but the morning of the wedding itself dawned fresh and clear and was spent getting the bride's boots 'heeled and fetched' and decorating the house with flowers. The *Devon and Exeter Gazette* reported that the whole village was *en fête*, having put up banners, flags and even an arch for the couple to walk under. Everything went off well, with a lunch for fifty people laid on back at the house; and in the evening, 'the grounds of Hazelwood House were illuminated, and the Branscombe band performed and were subsequently hospitably entertained'.[17]

On New Year's Day 1904, the Mews gathered in the family church of St Paul's in Barton on the Isle of Wight to pay their last respects to Uncle Richard – 'veteran farmer' and, for a few short weeks, surrogate father to Freda.[18] In nearby Whitecroft asylum, it's unlikely that Freda was even told about the death of the man who had brought her there five years earlier – and if she had been, she would have been in no fit state to take it in: an update in her medical notes around this time observed that she 'never voluntarily moves – dribbles and requires everything done for her'.[19]

Anne returned to the island to stay at Barfield Lodge later that January, just as a new story, 'Mademoiselle', appeared in *Temple Bar* magazine. Its central theme – the predicament of a jobbing artist struggling to earn money from decorative painting – was a subject Charlotte knew well, and it was one that caused her much anguish. Since graduating from the Royal Female School of Art with full honours, Anne had eventually found work with a firm of antique dealers, who paid her a 'sweated wage' to restore painted furniture and decorate mirrors, fire screens, panels and other such items.[20] The work was exhausting, and it was Charlotte who had encouraged her to leave Ma at home this time while Anne went off for a break.

Walter seemed only too happy to entertain his pretty younger cousin without Mrs Mew in tow. On 20 January, he and Anne went walking together, and then for a bicycle ride with Walter's unmarried sister, Marian, the three of them cycling around the seaside village of Lake, past the beach with its sandstone cliffs and sloping golden sands and out towards Westridge Cross. Back at the Lodge that evening, Walter spent a pleasurable few hours teaching Anne how to play whist, on the family's handsome walnut card table. The following morning, Anne and Marian went over to New Fairlee to spend time with Uncle Richard's recently bereaved children, two of whom still lived at the farm. That evening, in his diary, Walter spilled out his feelings about Anne's financial situation. She had brought very few clothes with her, and it appears that Charlotte was sending supplies of one sort or another from London. Given the amount of things Anne borrowed during her visit, the packages most likely contained whatever could *not* reasonably be borrowed – freshly laundered undergarments, sanitary belts, and so on. Walter strongly suspected that the bulky luggage Anne had arrived with was brought for the sake of appearances: 'She came with a large trunk wh. apparently had nothing in it, for she borrowed everything & never had a change of things & was always sending off & receiving parcels.'[21]

Walter had particular reason for concerning himself with his London relatives' financial welfare: he'd been charged with investing the various legacies left to Anna Maria in an attempt to swell the family's coffers; but it was clear to him that what they needed right now – and badly – was working capital. On 16 February, shortly after Anne had left, he wrote to Charlotte, or 'Lottie', as he still called her. Might this not be a good time, he suggested, to call in the 'Wimbledon mortgage'?[22] Charlotte's burdensome position as head of the family is clear: there is no mention of Walter discussing the situation with Anne.

If financial anxieties preyed on Charlotte's mind that winter, she showed no sign of it to her friends. She had a good social life and was enjoying the facilities on her doorstep at University College, London, with the insouciance of a full-time student. Edith Chick, who had now left the university, received a gossipy letter from a friend called Pam in February, informing her that 'When I came down after Botany I found Lott, Maggie [Robinson, who had returned for post-graduate study] and Winifred Oliver in the Common Room, going to tea with Anne at her studio.'[23] Charlotte invited Pam to come along with them, and the outing turned into one of those occasions that are common among groups of close female friends, when everything that is said seems impossibly funny. When Pam admired a sketch Anne had made of a mutual acquaintance, Ida Gutten, she learned that Ida had never returned to the studio since seeing it (so unflatteringly life-like was it). Anne shared the studio with another young artist called Monica, who was out that afternoon, which left the friends free to rifle through her work. Much of it was very good, but a few pieces generated fresh peals of laughter, especially one of a lady depicted in what Charlotte called an 'Himpossible Position'. In the next room along, there was a young man who had turned the place into a bedsit, and Anne described how every now and then the landlady insisted on taking visitors in to see how beautifully he kept his sheets. More peals of laughter.

Pam thought Anne's studio 'simply sweet', but she found herself spooked by one particular object: a plaster cast of an unidentified girl who had drowned herself in the Seine – probably, to judge by the hairstyle, some time in the 1880s. According to popular legend, a pathologist at the morgue in Paris had been so struck by the girl's beauty that he made a wax cast of the face, which became known as *L'inconnue de la Seine*. Copies of it were popular fixtures in artists' studios throughout Europe during the 1900s. But in light of the Mew sisters' childlessness, their ownership of this nameless girl's mask would take on an extra poignancy as time went on. In 'Madeleine', Charlotte has her speaker remark that 'If there were fifty heavens God could not give us back the child who went or never came.' Over the years, the mask would be carefully packed up and transported to each new house they moved to.

That April of 1904, Walter set about calling in a second mortgage on behalf of Anna Maria, but there were signs that he was beginning to weary of Charlotte's anxious enquiries about his handling of the family's financial affairs. When she questioned some of the choices he was making on their behalf, Walter bridled: if she was that unsure of him, ought she not to replace him as trustee of her mother's marriage settlement with someone she actually trusted? On Saturday 18 June, he noted in his diary that 'To-day Charlotte humbly apologizes.'[24]

Anne was staying at Barfield Lodge again at the start of August, when Charlotte's second literary essay, on the poetry of Emily Brontë, appeared in *Temple Bar*. Reading the essay produces the strange impression that Emily is some sort of ghostly double for the woman Mew was growing into, and that we are really reading about the essay's author. Here, she writes with great feeling about 'a soul which has most repelled where least it has been understood' and who was 'perhaps one of nature's outcasts – a self-determined outlaw'; a figure 'hardly human in its self-sufficiency and aloofness, and yet more than human in its compassionate gentleness for the doomed and erring'; a woman who, 'hardly born for earth [. . .] seemed to peer beyond it – craving a clearer vision than it yielded'; a writer who painted a picture of 'surviving life stationed stern and unswaying before the spectacle of murdered joy', and who – perhaps tellingly – 'knew nothing of the passion which breathes and burns in every line'; whose poems, in short, were a 'love-song of a woman who never loved'.[25]

The essay also sheds some useful light on Charlotte's complex feelings about Christianity. The fact that Emily was a 'pagan' did not, so Charlotte maintained, prevent her work from relating, tangentially, to a Christian God; it did so via the human figure of Christ on His crucifix. It was Emily's empathy – an empathy equally evident in Charlotte's own work – for the injured, the sinning and the outcast that connected her poems with the crucified Jesus who stood for all human suffering: 'Only in her infinite forbearance with, and compassion for, the victims of weakness and vanity and passion does she touch that eternally uplifted figure which hangs between earth and heaven to link inseparably the human with the divine.'[26]

In the speculations she makes about the composition of Emily Brontë's poems (or 'self-communings', as she calls them), Charlotte may be revealing something of her own working conditions:

These strange self-communings took shape in intervals of leisure, snatched from prosaic but determined work. Perhaps in the northern twilight of the Haworth kitchen with 'Tabby' knitting by the dying fire. Perhaps in greyer, lonelier dawns, when Emily rose early to the self-appointed labours of the day. For it is notable that this woman, who owned above most women the 'inestimable gift of genius', was one who laid upon herself the simplest duties; that in that poor and Spartan country parsonage it was Emily who, when need came, rose in the bitter winter mornings to do the disabled servant's work.[27]

In the autumn of 1904, the Mews acquired some unusual new neigh-
bours, who were shortly to make literary history. Twenty-two-year-old
Virginia Stephen moved into Gordon Square in October, just around
the corner from the Mews, with her sister Vanessa and her brothers
Thoby and Adrian.[28] Their parents were both dead by this time (their
father, Leslie, had died earlier that year), and the Stephen siblings
were seeking a fresh start, a daring new life away from the stuffy mores
of their childhood home in elegant Kensington. Looking back on this
period some years later, Virginia Woolf (as she had become) reflected
on her feelings about moving to the new house: 'Here everything was
going to be new; everything was going to be different. Everything
was on trial.'[29] The neighbourhood's slightly seedy character made
the house all the more appealing to her. Although the district had
been developed specifically with the upper middle classes in mind, the
gentrification never succeeded in attracting quite enough of the right
kind of clientele, with the result that many of its houses became rental
properties for people passing through the area. From March 1905, 46
Gordon Square would be home to the Thursday-evening gatherings
that evolved, in due course, into the Bloomsbury Group. The eve-
nings were attended by an eclectic mix of Thoby Stephen's Cambridge
friends – among them, biographer Lytton Strachey, artists Duncan
Grant and Roger Fry, art critic Clive Bell, novelists David Garnett
and E. M. Forster, economist John Maynard Keynes, and writer, pub-
lisher and civil servant Leonard Woolf.

It seems extraordinary that for the most productive period of
Charlotte's life she lived a stone's throw from this most famous of
artistic groups, and yet their presence did not impinge on her at all.
It's feasible she may not even have known of the hubbub of literary
activity taking place around the corner, or of the famous writers who
came and went there. If she did know, it's likely that the pressures of

respectability – forced on her by Ma's redoubtable snobbery – would have ensured that she never became a part of their Bohemian set. Virginia Woolf would one day comment that 'After the silence of Hyde Park Gate the roar of traffic was positively alarming. Old characters, sinister, strange, prowled and slunk past our windows.'[30] The observation was made without knowing, of course, that Charlotte Mew was among the strange cast of characters who passed by the windows of 46 Gordon Square. The Stephen siblings had moved from genteel Hyde Park Gate much against the better judgement of their wider family, but they had no regrets; Bloomsbury was, for Virginia, 'the most beautiful, the most exciting, the most romantic place in the world' – and its slightly shady reputation and perpetually shifting population only added to the appeal.[31] But, unlike members of the Bloomsbury set, Charlotte hadn't moved into the area in search of something new and exciting; she'd been there all along. If anyone qualified for the epithet 'Bloomsbury writer', it was her.

11

Waking and Worried Days

1905–1911

With Fred and Henry dead and Freda removed to the asylum, 9 Gordon Street began to resemble 'The Quiet House' that Charlotte would soon conjure in her poem of that name. Anne was out at her studio much of the time, earning money from her furniture job, leaving her sister to oversee the running of the house. For some time now, Charlotte's life had been shrinking to a twofold domestic struggle: to meet their mother's needs and expectations, and to fulfil the family's financial obligations – not the least of which was Freda's hospital bill. It was a quiet and courageous struggle that went on unnoticed by the outside world; and under its heft Charlotte all but disappeared. For the next seven years she flits in and out of our vision – glimpsed mostly in the pages of journals and magazines, although even there her name was beginning to appear with less and less regularity.

Looking back in 1913 on her poems to date, Charlotte described 'The Quiet House' as 'perhaps the most subjective to me, of the lot'; when her first collection was published three years later, one of her reviewers thought it 'the most painful thing in the book'.[1] It paints a sorry picture of a family's daily existence, and it is hard to ignore the biographical weight behind it:

> When we were children Old Nurse used to say,
> The house was like an auction or a fair
> Until the lot of us were safe in bed.
> It has been quiet as the country-side
> Since Ted and Janey and then Mother died
> And Tom crossed Father and was sent away.

After the lawsuit he could not hold up his head,
    Poor Father, and he does not care
    For people here, or to go anywhere.

The 'poor Father' in this opening stanza – who, later in the poem, 'scarcely lets me slip out of his sight' – is surely a surrogate for the mother in Charlotte's real life. The real-life Ma may not have 'care[d] for people' to come to the house, but she had a lot to be thankful for. Her obliging daughters had made significant sacrifices in order to hold on to the 'good address' that was so important to her. But the family was only able to stay on at Gordon Street by living in what might be described as genteel poverty.[2] The house was fast becoming a place in which, as the poem has it, 'nothing lives [. . .] but the fire', and in front of the fire a father (for which we might read mother) who 'watches from his chair' and takes no part at all in the life going on around him: 'Day follows day / The same, or now and then, a different grey'.

The drudgery of domestic life meant that Charlotte, too, was unable to partake as fully as she might have liked in the activities of the outside world. She was, at least, assisted in her work by the domestic servant Jane Elsain,[3] who was thirty-one in 1905, to Charlotte's thirty-six; but these days there were no younger servants – no 'raw girls from the country' – to help with the never-ending round of menial tasks.[4] The upper part of 9 Gordon Street was permanently occupied by this time by what were quaintly termed (in polite society) 'paying guests'. Thomas Norton, a metal merchant, and his wife Elizabeth had the top four rooms, while the Mew women occupied the remaining eight. But they were large rooms, and spread as they were over three floors, they demanded a considerable amount of upkeep. There were fires to be made, hearths to be cleaned, floors to be swept, lamps to be trimmed, furniture to be dusted, laundry to be done, food to be bought, meals prepared, the parrot's bedding to be changed – the list went on. Charlotte was also responsible for dealing with all correspondence relating to household business, collecting the rent and keeping the bills paid. On top of everything, Ma was requiring an increasing amount of attention. Now in her late sixties, she was ageing fast and had become utterly dependent on her daughters for both company and care.

On the rare occasions when Charlotte managed to sit down at her desk, there were constant interruptions from the housemaid. Jane Elsain, it seems, was unwilling or unable to take responsibility for even the smallest decisions; she was forever knocking on Charlotte's door to ask, for instance, 'if she should "finish up" the rice pudding for her dinner? and should she run out for some kippers? or would Miss Lottie mind going herself?'[5]

Throughout her life Charlotte would maintain a complex relationship with the mythical 'Angel in the House' – that idealised emblem of 'utterly unselfish' Victorian femininity whom Virginia Woolf (in 'Professions for Women') famously claimed to have murdered. Woolf's version of the Angel was a paragon of propriety, an annihilator of creativity and expression, a 'phantom' who, as Woolf put it, 'bothered me and wasted my time and so tormented me that at last I killed her'.[6] The danger, Woolf explained, was that had the spectre not been killed, she 'would have plucked the heart out of my writing'. At first glance it may seem that Charlotte failed to square up to her Angel: not once did she seek to turn her back on her familial duties. But hers was a devotion based not on gender but on necessity: she never had the steady 'five hundred pounds a year' that Woolf suggested a woman writer needed to be released from her domestic shackles. What is remarkable is that her writing – and especially her poetry – remained utterly free of the Angel's (and indeed of Ma's) censoring influence. If, when she took up her pen, she heard its voice at her shoulder, cajoling her to write as a woman ought to write, her accomplishment in silencing it was triumphant and absolute.

'Mark Stafford's Wife', the long story she published that January of 1905 in *Temple Bar*, bears witness to this achievement. The novelist May Sinclair thought it had the flavour of Henry James.[7] It also shares a number of details with Thomas Hardy's *Jude the Obscure*, not least of which is a strong resemblance between the two central characters: the young wives around whom the respective tangled dramatic webs are woven. Mark Stafford's assessments of his wife, Kate, as 'a shy, reluctant fay' and someone who 'has a touch of the sprite, a vague atmosphere of mist, of moonlight'[8] might have come straight out of Jude's own mouth, whose opinion of his beloved Sue Bridehead is that her heart 'does not burn in a flame! You are, upon the whole,' he tells her, 'a sort of fay, or sprite – not a woman!'[9] Both heroines ultimately abandon their marriages to return to a previous relationship. In Kate's case she leaves because of what the marriage has cost her, a loss ineffectually captured by the story's narrator, who remarks that 'I can't say how it became chillingly plain to me that some vague virtue had gone out of her.'[10] The seemingly fragile woman who has hidden depths and flees her marriage was a character type that captivated Charlotte. And she was by no means done with her yet.

The next four years are largely silent ones for the biographer; years in which we all but lose sight of Charlotte completely. A brief respite from the oppression of home life came that summer of 1905, in the form of another visit to the Chicks in Devon, and at the end of that year the first of a pair of feature articles, 'The Country Sunday', appeared in *Temple Bar*, to be followed a month later by a companion piece, 'The London Sunday'. Charlotte's contact with her Isle of Wight relations at this time seems also to have dwindled to nothing. Occasional mentions of the Mews in Walter Mew Barnes's diary during these quiet, barely documented years are nearly all of Anne. In November 1906, for instance, Walter went to tea with Anne at her studio while passing through on his way to the city on business. On 1 December, he called in on Anna Maria at Gordon Street and noted, 'Lottie & Anne both in, & the parrot'.[11] It being a Saturday, Anne agreed to accompany her cousin on a shopping trip, to help him choose a present for his sister's birthday, but Charlotte remained at home. This is the only mention Walter makes in his diaries of actually *seeing* Charlotte, and it is about as perfunctory a mention as it could be.

In January 1907, Anne made another solo excursion to the Isle of Wight in bitterly cold weather. Her nine days away were filled with the usual bicycle trips and visits to New Fairlee Farm for tea with her other cousins; this time there was an outing to the town hall to take in a concert by the Royal Marine Artillery band and listen to the rich contralto tones of Kate Fielder, a singer of 'considerable natural endowments'.[12] So far so routine, but in Walter's diary entry for 25 January 1907 we're offered, for the first time, a clue as to what might have been behind Anne's regular visits to the island. The note is short and to the point: 'Anne went to see Freda, who is reported *physically* unwell. M & I joined her at Fairlee to tea. Very cold.'[13] The asylum's medical notes for this day are more forthcoming about the deteriorating condition of the youngest Mew sister: 'Stuporose. Dirty in habits, never speaks or answers when addressed. Resists everything done for her by kicking and biting. Confined to bed from weakness & wasting. In poor health.'[14] 'Stuporose' is a medical term for an unresponsive state from which the patient can only be roused by vigorous stimulation; when the stimulation ceases, the patient slips back into the stupor.

Walter's diaries cover only six years (from 1903 to 1909), but in all likelihood Anne – and probably Charlotte too, earlier on – had been making visits to Whitecroft since Freda first entered the asylum in 1899. There are signs that, after eight years, Anne had become less unsettled by her sister's illness. The day after seeing Freda, she cycled out to Alverstone with Walter and Marian, and watched people skating on 'bad ice' at Sandown waterworks. On the Sunday, the three of them took the ferry to Portsmouth Harbour on Anne's way home. 'Lovely bright gusty day,' Walter noted blithely, in his diary. 'Water tumbly and fairly fizzing.'[15]

Charlotte took the opportunity to escape the anxieties of home life as often as her routine allowed, which is to say not often at all. In the summer of 1907, she went again to Hazelwood in Devon to stay with the Chicks. Since her first visit there in 1901, Hazelwood (along with the Olivers' house in Kew and the Chicks' London house in Ealing) had become a sanctuary; being out of London and beside the sea, it was a particularly diverting one. She went there twice the following year too, in April and September. But the appearance of her name in the house's visitors' book is one of the few traces we have of her movements during 1907 and 1908. Other than that, we know only that at the start of both these years she renewed her six-month ticket at the British Museum Reading Room, allowing her membership to lapse for the second half of each year. With its heating system, circle of high windows and – crucially – its freedom from Ma's demands and the housemaid's frequent interruptions, the Reading Room must have felt like another refuge for Charlotte; one that had the advantage of being close to home.

Whatever Charlotte was doing in the Reading Room at this time, it wasn't resulting in publication. No stories, articles or poems appeared in print in 1906, 1907 or 1908. Could she have been working away on the mysterious novel that Edith Chick had alluded to in 1900? Or perhaps she was writing and sending new work out but wasn't able to find a home for it. *Temple Bar* magazine, on which she'd begun to rely so heavily for publication, had been struggling with readership numbers for some time. In 1905, a young Arthur Ransome (many years off from writing *Swallows and Amazons*) had agreed to take over the magazine's editorship but was unable to save it. It closed the following year, having run to 553 issues; it was in the very last of these that Charlotte's feature 'The London Sunday' had appeared.

Temple Bar's demise was part of a general decline in the popularity of cheap British monthlies; it also marked the close of a chapter in Charlotte's writing life. Periodical publication, and the money it brought with it, would never again be quite so straightforward for her. Beyond *Temple Bar* and *The Yellow Book*, she had so far placed very little in print: a literary essay in *The Academy*, a single short story ('The Minnow Fishers') in *The Outlook* and a sentimental romance in *The Woman at Home* that was so unlike her other work we can suppose it was either an early experiment or aimed solely at bringing in money. Out of this small pool of tried-and-tested periodicals there was one that she was unlikely to submit to a second time. When she had first sent work to *The Academy* a decade earlier, it had been accepted by Charles Lewis Hind, but in 1907, the magazine changed its political direction and editorship when the self-professed 'die-hard' conservative Lord Alfred Douglas took the helm.[16] Douglas is better known as 'Bosie', friend and lover of Oscar Wilde – a connection Charlotte was unlikely to want to foster, especially given her earlier bruising experience with *The Yellow Book* and her aversion to associating (according to a friend) with 'anyone on whom a breath of scandal blew'.[17]

In the summer of 1909, the void in the archives begins to fill again and Charlotte returns more sharply into focus. That summer, she finally managed to get away to her beloved northern France. Her companion on this occasion was almost certainly Elsie Chick, the third youngest of the Chick sisters.[18] Elsie had gone up to study for a BA in English Literature at University College, London in the autumn of 1905 and had already won prizes in English, German and Logic.[19] While Charlotte was fast approaching her fortieth birthday, Elsie had recently turned twenty-seven, and was somewhat in awe of her older friend's literary success, modest as it was at this stage of her career. In due course, she would ask for Charlotte's help with her MA thesis on

Middle English poetry (focusing on Langland's *Piers Plowman*) – in spite of Charlotte's characteristic protestation that this was a subject about which she knew 'nothing whatever'.[20]

Charlotte had a knack for finding things that might be missed by the typical tourist. She favoured local transport in the hope of being ferried to more interesting places than the usual tourist spots, and went out of her way to search for new experiences, filling her letters with descriptions of foreign smells and noises and colour. The frequency with which she engaged the locals in conversation suggests her spoken French was now fairly fluent. During her dispiriting trip to Paris seven years earlier, she had claimed it was 'so bad it's not easy to understand', but as she hadn't returned to France in the intervening years, the apparent improvement is perhaps no more than an indication of her newly buoyant state of mind.[21] Her spirits remained high as she and Elsie made their way west through Brittany, and then followed the coast roughly southwards, stopping at an extraordinary number of places along the way – Dinan, Guingamp, Brest, Le Conquet, Landerneau, Quimper, Fouesnant, Bénodet, Pont-l'Abbé, Douarnenez, St Guénolé and Audierne – and staying for a few days at a time in several of the larger towns and villages.

It's clear from three detailed letters to Ethel Oliver that Charlotte usually took the lead in deciding where to go, in arranging transport and finding rooms when they got there – as might be expected, given the women's difference in age – and that in all her dealings, she proved herself to be both charming and intrepid. In contrast with the correspondence she had sent from Paris in 1902, her enormous zest for life (reinforced, no doubt, by the relief she felt at temporarily breaking free of her ties at Gordon Street) shines through every word she writes in these letters. She doesn't so much sightsee as sight-*hunt*. She believed that 'the right way to see Brittany is to go off the beaten track, i.e., the couriers' carts; and in the little villages one sees the real people – women in strange caps, knitting on the roads while they drive the cow home, and dear little children in costumes – absolutely of the Tudor period – taking refuge under hedges from the automobile rushing by.'[22]

The two friends went first to Dinan and were shocked by the living quarters shown to them by a local resident:

> Going down the one street a poor woman called us in to show her room – a hovel – sand-floored and with wood rafters and walls dripping damp, date 1350, and just as it was then; she had a poor little bed in the corner, a picture of the Virgin, and a broken chair – nothing more – and had lived there alone for fifty years crippled by the damp and cold. 'De la misère,' she said, and so it looked and felt.[23]

The rooms they took in Guingamp the following day must have seemed luxurious by comparison. Charlotte chose one with a view over the river ('heavenly by moonlight on Sunday night'). Their arrival coincided with the town's annual Pardon, and once settled, they headed out to watch: thousands of pilgrims had flooded into Guingamp to pay homage to the 'Black Virgin' in the basilica of Notre-Dame de Bon Secours. Charlotte and Elsie went to the church to get a good view, and watched the procession set off in 'a blaze of travelling lights'.[24]

Towards the middle of July, the fine weather gave way one day to a cold mist and persistent, driving rain. Charlotte stayed inside, putting on all of the few clothes she had with her, one on top of another, and sitting with her tiny feet tucked under the eiderdown. Cooped up in the hotel, she was as blunt as ever in her descriptions of her fellow guests – whether purely for comic effect or not it's hard to tell. Among her fellow travellers was 'a haughty English family who glare but do not speak: Mama, Papa, and New-human-like off-spring',[25] as well as 'the usual Americans and disagreeable English'. In Guingamp, she took against a young American man who had motored his way through France and looked on the Breton folk 'much as one regards the Fat Woman or Bearded Lady at a Fair', telling Charlotte, wearily, that 'it was a job "to find anything noo"'.[26]

The small, quiet fishing village of Le Conquet, lying at the westernmost tip of mainland Brittany, revivified her. The residents wore a distinctive costume, marked by 'wildly bright colours, barbarous tints', and the women wore their hair to the shoulders, so that it hung down from under their caps, giving them, Charlotte thought, an 'unbretonish look, especially in the older women'.[27] But the place itself she found charming, and she regretted only that there were no cabins for bathing (it not being deemed proper for respectable women to be seen on the beach in their bathing suits).

Rushing through Brest *en fête*, with its many flags flying, they arrived next in Landerneau and found it full of shows and caravans set up for its own fête. Exploring alone, while Elsie nursed an upset stomach, Charlotte happened on a large group gathered around a hot-air balloon. The crowd had waited, she told Ethel, six hours for the balloon to go up, and when it finally did, it collapsed almost immediately. The limp balloon seemed emblematic of what one Breton man had warned her in Le Conquet – namely, that Landerneau was a *'ville morte'*. On the plus side, it had, said Charlotte, 'a wonderful quay of immense width stretching out into the beautiful country; and streets of the oldest houses, solemn and deserted, the whole place giving one a sense of space and desolation, very grand and mysterious at night'. Back at the Landerneau hotel, she was handed a letter from Ella D'Arcy, who was still living in Paris and was just off to stay at Beaumont-le-Roger in Normandy. They made no plans for meeting up; Charlotte merely hoped, she told Ethel, that Ella's experience in Beaumont-le-Roger would be 'happier than ours'. Maggie Robinson had also written, but Charlotte was too busy enjoying herself to write back: 'Letter-writing takes up time,' she explained to Ethel, 'and they have only had cards at home for a week.'[28] Quimper, where they happened to be for Bastille Day, enchanted Charlotte almost as much as Le Conquet. On the eve of the celebrations, she and Elsie watched a torchlight vigil being held in the square beneath their window, and the following night, joined a throng of locals on the quayside – a 'crowd of white caps and Breton hats' – to see a cinematograph show.

Never shy of striking up conversations with strangers, Charlotte connected with a good many individual characters that summer. Besides the poor woman in Dinan who had called her and Elsie in off the street to show them her room, she gives us a vivid account of her encounter with a 'ruffian' bus driver in Quimper who happened to be rattling by while the two friends were drinking tea at the hotel window and whom Charlotte persuaded, charging down from the room, to take them 'on a pile of oozing boxes, as the inside was literally crammed', to Fouesnant, where they stumbled on a Breton wedding in full swing.[29] Another night, while she was going down from her room to fetch a candle, she got chatting to the 'short, stout, red-faced' hotel proprietor, who was evidently so taken by this tiny, spirited English lady that he escorted her and Elsie the following day to see his private rose garden just outside Quimper – 'the most amazing place', wrote Charlotte afterwards, 'of gorgeous shrubs, lush grass, and walk after walk of rose trees of every conceivable variety'.[30] The visit made a lasting impression on her and perhaps deepened her fascination with this particular flower. Roses are a recurrent motif in her poetry, but they are not the ubiquitous floral embellishments of Victorian chocolate boxes and still lifes. In Mew's work a rose is as likely to 'stab you across the street' as it is to make you sigh at its loveliness.[31] Her roses are by turns 'terrible', 'passionate', commonplace ('you do not miss a rose'), or bearing the fierce scent 'Of all the sunsets'.[32] They are never merely decorative.

Charlotte's pluckiness usually served her well during her travels. Just once on this trip it proved ineffectual, when she wasted a whole morning arguing with a group of rowdy older children on a beach, after they had first tried to peek at Elsie undressing in her bathing cabin and then buried Charlotte's umbrella in the sand. In spite of her dogged persistence, they refused to tell her where it was. A kind Breton lady eventually returned the umbrella to her, having watched the whole scene from her garden.

Ethel had reported that back home the parrot had been out of his cage and happily wandering about the place, but Charlotte seemed unable to stop herself fretting over his welfare. 'Is Wek to be trusted on the floor, I wonder,' she queried. In Brittany, she told Ethel, she was forever catching sight of lookalikes: 'Did you know it was a Wek country?'[33] Worries about Wek notwithstanding, Charlotte seemed to be enjoying on this holiday a rare respite from the anxieties associated with family and friends. It had to do, she felt, with what French author Pierre Loti called the *ailleurs*, or 'elsewhere'. She had read (in the original French) several of Loti's novels – famous for their richly detailed evocations of the sights and sounds of far-flung places – and her reading had influenced not only her own writing but her whole approach to the art of travelling. Loti himself indulged a lifelong love of travel in search of the *ailleurs*. Charlotte inverted that idea and made London the elsewhere – one she was evidently very happy to hold at a distance:

It is difficult to realize the 'elsewhere' as Loti calls it, here: Tottenham Court Road, & a city with scarcely any sky, while here there is the whole arch of it – the harbour lights at night. One is woken up by the sound of oars plashing and anchors being weighed, and the clatter of sabots up and down the quay. No one hurries about anything. It takes five men to harness the station bus and about 30 to unload a little bit of scrap iron from a sailing boat on the quay. But this is a pleasant sort of oblivion, which ought, even like Christmas, 'come once a year', and while it lasts, it is a blessed rest, a sort of dream snatched from waking and worried days.[34]

The dream, of course, could not go on forever, and back in London there followed three months of 'scarcely any sky' as Charlotte resumed her daily round. Anne went down to stay at Hazelwood in September and traded places with Charlotte the following month. They still felt unable to leave Ma and Wek unattended, and Jane Elsain had too much to do to act as carer and companion for the old lady. In early November, news of cousin Walter's death reached Gordon Street. He had died at home at Barfield Lodge on the 5th, aged just fifty-three. His funeral took place the following Saturday at All Saints' Church in Ryde. There is no mention of any women at all among the mourners who attended the service; even Walter's sister, Marian, appears to have stayed at home. The most likely explanation seems to be an absurd (and even by then rather old-fashioned) notion that women of the middle and upper classes should stay away from funerals in case they were unable to restrain their grief. The risk of allowing female mourners to participate was that they were liable, in the words of *Cassell's Household Guide*, 'to destroy the solemnity of the ceremony with their sobs, and even by fainting'.[35] Though Marian had arguably been closest to Walter, the family was represented instead by his brothers, Edward and George, and his cousins, Richard and Gilbert. The rest of the congregation was made up largely of employees of the Ryde Pier Company (where Walter had been chairman), six of whom were assigned to carry Walter's heavy oak coffin, with its plain silver fittings, into the packed church, and afterwards to the cemetery, where his remains were laid to rest in the family vault.

It was a melancholy start to the darkening days of late autumn, and if any special birthday celebrations took place the following week, for Charlotte's fortieth birthday (on 15 November 1909), they did so unrecorded. But two days before her birthday, she had published a lyric called

'Requiescat' in the leading radical periodical of the day, *The Nation*. The occasion feels momentous, as if it ought to signify a turning point – she had not had a poem in print for some six years – but in fact it was to precede another long silence. Even so, whether by luck or design, this latest poem had found its way into one of the most highly regarded papers of the day. Now in its third year of publication, *The Nation* had been launched on the back of the Liberal Party's landslide success in the 1906 General Election the previous year, and was edited by the free-thinking journalist Henry Massingham, whose political report-age gave him access to some of the innermost corridors of power. He was currently involved in efforts to remove legislative power from the House of Lords. Massingham loved books, but his main interest was in politics, and he intended, he explained in an interview, for the literary pages of his paper to be 'for the general body of thoughtful intelligent readers', rather than for literature lovers alone.[36]

Because of its political focus *The Nation* had been well known outside Britain right from the start. Ella D'Arcy, chancing on 'Requiescat' while browsing through a copy of the paper in France, was so affected that she wrote to Charlotte about it. She found in it, she said, 'the expression of a real & profound emotion', and announced that it would go straight into her private anthology.[37] Ella's admiration for the poem was undoubtedly heartfelt, but it was enhanced by her surprise at learning that Charlotte wrote poetry at all. The two women had known each other as fellow short-story writers, back in the days when both were writing for *The Yellow Book*. 'But you are a poet which I did not know & I beg you very earnestly – not to neglect this finest of all gifts. The poem was a sight realer & more beautiful than any by the Brontë sisters of whose poetical genius you think so much. *Go on producing.*'[38]

'Requiescat' is set on a stretch of beach and addressed to a recently dead sweetheart. In this most unelegiac of elegies, the speaker revels in the thought that everything that continues in the world belongs to the lost beloved (the word 'your' occurs eleven times in the course of twenty-four short lines): the birds, the sea breeze, the salt-scented air, the flowers, the strip of blue at the end of a sea lane – all these things go on in remembrance of the dead lover. The poem finishes by wondering whether the deceased might also – 'strange' as it may seem – remember, in his or her turn, the things of the world; could it be that consciousness remains alive in the world, after the body has left? There is no note of distress or regret; the poem is written in a buoyant, simply rhymed iambic tetrameter, the lines drenched in a zesty, sea-blown brew that is strongly reminiscent of Branscombe, as is evident in the opening stanzas:

> Your birds that call from tree to tree
> > Just overhead, and whirl and dart,
> Your breeze fresh-blowing from the sea,
> > And your sea singing on, Sweetheart.

> Your salt scent on the thin sharp air
> > Of this grey dawn's first drowsy hours,
> While on the grass shines everywhere
> > The yellow starlight of your flowers.

> At the road's end your strip of blue
> > Beyond that line of naked trees –
> Strange that we should remember you
> > As if you would remember these!

> As if your spirit, swaying yet
> > To the old passions, were not free
> Of spring's wild magic, and the fret
> > Of the wilder wooing of the sea!

In a letter written in 1914, Charlotte would claim that she thought 'not much' of this offering.[39] But the poem's oddity lifts it above the ordinary; it is a strangeness evident not so much in the imagery as in the central premise that consciousness might continue its daily exist-ence after death, might remember physical experience – and even go on engaging in some way with the earth's seasonal rhythms. The spirit of the speaker's loved one goes on swaying, as if in time to an unheard music, to the passions it knew while alive, as in thrall as it ever was to the 'wild magic' of springtime. Yet what counted was Charlotte's own opinion. She did not agree with Ella's estimation of the poem as 'more beautiful than any by the Brontë sisters'; nor did she 'go on produc-ing' more poems like it. In fact, she was not to publish anything for another three years. Later, she would tell a friend that she 'did noth-ing' with regard to writing during 1910 and 1911 – though she didn't clarify whether that meant she wrote nothing or simply that she did nothing about sending it out.[40]

'On or about December 1910 human character changed,' Virginia Woolf would write, in her 1924 essay 'Mr Bennett and Mrs Brown'. The precision of the date is deliberately provocative, and Woolf was refer-ring specifically to the advent of Modernism, but the fact remains that numerous political, religious and artistic upheavals were fermenting in Britain around this time; 1910 was a year of unusual turmoil and flux. It began with the first of two general elections, occasioned by a land-mark dispute – much discussed in the pages of Henry Massingham's *Nation* – between the House of Commons and the House of Lords over the 1909 'People's Budget': the Lords had rejected proposals to increase taxation of the rich, provide health insurance for the poor and other progressive measures, and now Herbert Asquith's Liberal government wanted a mandate to get the budget passed. Headlines about a reduced Liberal majority were quickly pushed aside by news of a grisly domestic murder carried out by a north London homeopath the papers dubbed 'Dr Crippen', the establishment of the country's first labour exchanges, the King's failing health, the commencement of Scott's doomed expedition to the Antarctic and the launch of John Mott's ecumenical movement. When Edward VII succumbed to a series of chills and then, at the start of May, a fatal heart attack, his death did not occasion any poems of consolation from Charlotte, as Victoria's passing had done – though that is more an indication, perhaps, of the differing public reaction to the deaths than of Charlotte's own feelings about them, for she was to go on producing occasional poems for significant national events for some time yet.

In the summer of 1911, Charlotte was able to enjoy another brief reprieve from domestic duties: she and Anne had booked a fortnight away in the ancient fishing port of Boulogne, having finally managed to find a suitable companion to sit with Ma and look after the parrot. But the trip made Charlotte anxious: she fretted constantly, full of guilt at having left their seventy-four-year-old mother at home, though she was relieved at least that the notoriously fussy Wek had taken kindly to the new home help they'd engaged. Charlotte had heard – presumably from Ma herself – that the parrot had been depressed by their absence ('poor little soul!').

On 27 June, she wrote another long letter to Ethel Oliver, in which she commented that there 'are no Weks here. It is a town of dogs of all sorts and sizes. They draw the hand carts and play about the quays; and old white horses abound.'[41] Her tone is markedly less light-hearted than in the letters she'd sent from Brittany, as if her spirits had been ground down in the intervening two years. She liked Boulogne 'as well or better than any place I have seen',[42] she said, but her frayed nerves made her less tolerant than ever of her fellow guests. One night, she insisted on 'some nasty people (French)' being stopped from smoking and playing cards in the dining room.[43] She had no objections to either smoking or card playing per se, but to do either in a public space where people gathered to eat was downright antisocial. She also asked for their rooms to be properly 'scrubbed out'. Anne, who (in public, at least) was more reticent than Charlotte, worried that her sister's requests might get them thrown out. 'On the contrary,' Charlotte gloated, 'Madame grasped my hand this morning and asked with a beaming smile if we were satisfied now, etc. – and the stupid little waiter bucked up.'[44]

She spent her days watching the little boats coming and going in the harbour, and playing the occasional game at the casino, aware that something in her nature made her dangerously susceptible: 'attractions of gambling are irresistible,' she told Ethel, 'and I have no money to lose.'[45] She felt 'incurably tired – what the French call fini' – and unable to face the thought of returning to England. She was, she said, 'reluctant to take up "duties and little cares", though I might, and ought not perhaps have left them at all, but I simply could not go on'.[46]

It comes as no surprise to learn that she had not managed to settle to any reading since coming away – 'too tired to even think' – but just before they'd left, a young friend of hers, thirteen-year-old Ianthe Jerrold,[47] had lent her a book of 'Modern Poetry' in which she chanced on 'the most touching poem I have read for years, and which, as far as sentiment goes, I might have written'.[48] It was 'The Old Sceptic' by Alfred Noyes, which opens with the words, 'I am weary of disbelieving', and Charlotte's comment on it perhaps hints at her own thoughts on the subject. The poem's speaker recalls with longing the days when God was the source of all his beliefs. Now that doubt has begun to creep in, he wants only to 'go back and believe in the deep old foolish tales, / And pray the sweet old prayers that I learned at my mother's knee.'[49] It's a sentiment that Thomas Hardy would express again to great effect in his celebrated 1915 poem 'The Oxen'.

Charlotte's writing, too, is freighted with suggestions that she missed the comfort of a firm belief in God. Steeped as she was in the chapter and verse of the Bible, religious allusions suffuse her writing, but the issue of faith is rarely addressed head on. The exception is 'Madeleine in Church' (1916), in which the question of whether it's possible to 'go back and believe' is interrogated at length. Such evidence as exists suggests that she – like Madeleine – was unable to relate to a God who struck her as remote and elusive. It is an indication of Charlotte's precise and original thinking that for her the problem lay as much in doubts over her own visibility to God as in what she could see of Him – a misgiving with which her Madeleine character confronts God directly, in a moving *cri de cœur*: 'What can You know, what can You really see / Of this dark ditch, the soul of me!' In the end, and more and more so as life went on, Mew was chiefly interested in 'Here – not in heavenly hereafters'.[50]

Charlotte and Anne came home that July of 1911 to a country at boiling point: as if in response to the upheavals set in motion the previous year, temperatures had reached a record 98.1°F.[51] What lay behind these political and social changes was – according to Virginia Woolf – a substantial questioning of the power balances that existed between 'masters and servants, husbands and wives, parents and children'.[52] Quiet as things were at Gordon Street, there were signs that changes were afoot there too. On 12 September 1911, Charlotte finally got around to renewing her ticket for the British Museum Reading Room – the first time in three years that she had done so. Was it significant that this was the anniversary of her father's death?

The Mews' finances were in a more parlous state than in the days when Fred, his health failing, had been obliged to sell the warehouse he'd built near Shoreditch station at a giveaway price. Thirteen years on, what would he have made of his daughters' resourcefulness? He would surely have been impressed by the different ways Charlotte and Anne (but Charlotte in particular) had found to stay put in the family house. They had the lodgers, Anne's decorative art job brought in a steady, if modest, income, and there were payments from the investments Charlotte had arranged via their cousin Walter. Now and then they also had a little money from Charlotte's writing. Charlotte

Mew's name had not appeared in print for three years, but there would soon be evidence that she had been following the debates over power closely. Her own contribution, when it came, would be more elegant, more compassionate and infinitely more lasting than any of the anger-fuelled letters that were beginning to fill the letter pages of the more serious-minded papers. Had the time not arrived, those letters wanted to know, for a reassessment of the old patterns of male dominance and female subordination? Were women really predisposed, by nature, merely to follow orders? In November 1909, the Royal Commission on Divorce and Matrimonial Causes had been set up to look into the legal ramifications of such questions. As things stood, only a husband could instigate divorce proceedings. But if a marriage was causing distress, shouldn't either party be allowed to bring it to an end? This was the particular question that caught Charlotte's imagination. Where, in short, should the balance of power between husband and wife properly lie?

A Voice on the Sharp Air

1912

There was a wintry start to February 1912, with severe frosts and even a little snow. Saturday the 3rd dawned bright and clear, if perishingly cold. From her home on the edge of Hampstead Heath a striking young woman of Polish descent, with abundant brown hair and dark eyes, made her way along icy pavements to buy her weekly copy of *The Nation*. Turning eagerly to the back pages, she was delighted to find there a new poem by a writer whose name she didn't know. At nineteen, and yet to meet her husband, and Charlotte's future publisher, Harold Monro, Alida Klemantaski was already a shrewd and enthusiastic poetry reader and was in the habit of flicking straight to the poetry pages of the magazine, but the poem she found that day was unlike any she had read before. 'The Farmer's Bride' by Charlotte M. Mew had her under its spell from the start – so powerfully, in fact, that as she trod her way back to her house in Tanza Road, she began saying the lines to herself and committing them to memory. She did so without the least notion that, in a few years, her life would become permanently linked with that of the author.[1]

A stranger meeting Charlotte Mew for the first time in 1912 might well have taken her for one of the many free-spirited New Women who could now be seen in the streets of most British towns and cities; an older version of the sort denigrated in the letters pages of newspapers as 'the mannish girls of to-day, who dislike marriage, avoid maternity and scorn domesticity'; women whose freedom from the responsibilities of marriage and child-rearing rendered them, in the words of one reader, 'not a support, but a real peril, to any State'.[2] At forty-two, Charlotte was still slim and positively doll-like in stature.[3]

Her once warm brown hair was paler now and the tight curls had softened into a gentle wave; here and there a few white strands were showing. But her eyes, under thick black lashes, were the same deep grey, bright and penetrating. The arch of her brows was as defined as ever, as if raised permanently in surprise. In reality, she was shocked by very little: given her upbringing she was (on the face of it, at least) surprisingly unrepressed. Margaret Chick, for one, considered her 'advanced for the time'.[4] She went where she wanted, unescorted, and – apart from short periods when she managed to quit – smoked her own hand-rolled cigarettes through a long Bakelite cigarette holder.

If Charlotte had followed a more conventional route in life and become a wife, or even mother (assisted, as was usual, by a nursemaid), the irony is that she might have been freer. As it was, fourteen years into her role as head of her household, the 'duties and little cares' she'd talked of the previous summer had become all-consuming. There was nobody to guide her or offer reassurance. Had she been right to fight to keep the family in Gordon Street, in accordance with Ma's wishes? Would the funds from her mother's debentures, the lodgers' rent, Anne's wages and her own paltry earnings from writing be enough to keep them there? And for how long? Freda's medical fees were steadily chipping away at the capital. How might they manage if those fees increased? From the midst of these anxieties there would emerge a work of deftly controlled artifice – a poem so skilfully rendered, so affecting, that it had the ring of real life, and was soon to catapult Charlotte into the literary limelight.

'The Farmer's Bride' is the first of several dramatic monologues written by Charlotte Mew. In the years to come she would stamp her own unique mark on the form, demonstrating her facility for inhabiting the minds and voices of others, especially those who were desolate or deranged. Hilda Doolittle thought her better at the dramatic monologue than almost any other living poet, proposing in a 1916 review that Charlotte Mew 'alone of our generation, with the exception of Mr Hueffer and Mr Frost' had succeeded in the form; and that while she had 'grown a new blossom from the seed of Browning's sowing', she had 'given us a transmutation of his spirit, not a parody of his flesh'.[5] What is extraordinary in this particular poem is that we end up sympathising with two characters on opposing sides of an insurmountable divide – an effect that Charlotte had already attempted in her first published story, 'Passed' (1894).

The poem's title is as carefully chosen as it is charged with significance. If the word 'bride' denotes a newly married woman, or a woman who is about to be married, three years into marriage this one might more accurately be called a wife. But 'farmer's wife' brings to mind a rosy-cheeked, homely sort, if not yet a mother then soon to be one, bustling contentedly about her kitchen and sprinkling grain for the hens in the yard. This woman isn't that: she is a bride still, 'straight and slight as a young larch tree'. And to add to the sense of her evanescence, she is voiceless too.

Over six stanzas of varying lengths, we learn that this fragile young woman is so terrified by her marriage that the previous autumn she escaped under cover of night, only to be tracked down by the farmer and his accomplices and chased over the fields – 'flying like a hare' (and with her hair flying, since this is a poem packed with homophonous double meaning) in the light of their raised lanterns – before being returned to the house, where she has been kept ever since under lock and key. Now safely secured, she is compliant so far as the housework goes, but remains petrified by the thought of physical intimacy, a situation the farmer is barely able to endure now that the Christmas season is nearly upon them and the quietness of a house without children begins to haunt him: 'What's Christmas-time without there be / Some other in the house than we!' The words of the poem are voiced not by the bride of the title, but by the farmer, who seems from the outset *compelled* to speak, out of frustration and despair.

> Three Summers since I chose a maid,
> Too young maybe – but more's to do

At harvest-time than bide and woo.
    When us was wed she turned afraid
Of love and me and all things human;
Like the shut of a winter's day
Her smile went out, and 'twasn't a woman –
    More like a little frightened fay.
        One night, in the Fall, she runned away.

'Out 'mong the sheep, her be,' they said,
'Should properly have been abed;
But sure enough she wasn't there
Lying awake with her wide brown stare.
So over seven-acre field and up-along across the down
    We chased her, flying like a hare
Before our lanterns. To Church-Town
    All in a shiver and a scare
We caught her, fetched her home at last
    And turned the key upon her, fast.

She does the work about the house
As well as most, but like a mouse:
    Happy enough to chat and play
    With birds and rabbits and such as they,
    So long as men-folk keep away.
'Not near, not near!' her eyes beseech
When one of us comes within reach.
    The women say that beasts in stall
    Look round like children at her call.
    I've hardly heard her speak at all.

Shy as a leveret, swift as he,
Straight and slight as a young larch tree,
Sweet as the first wild violets, she,

To her wild self. But what to me?

The short days shorten and the oaks are brown,
    The blue smoke rises to the low grey sky,
One leaf in the still air falls slowly down,
    A magpie's spotted feathers lie
On the black earth spread white with rime,
The berries redden up to Christmas-time.
        What's Christmas-time without there be
        Some other in the house than we!

        She sleeps up in the attic there
        Alone, poor maid. 'Tis but a stair
Betwixt us. Oh! my God! the down,
The soft young down of her, the brown,
The brown of her – her eyes, her hair, her hair!

Mew would later explain to an American critic that the poem was written 'more or less in the dialect of the West of England [. . .] and that in this, *To* is used instead of *At* and the personal pronouns and past tenses of the verbs are ungrammatical'.[6] She had heard the West Country dialect many times on her visits to Branscombe, perhaps while chatting with the Chicks' cook, Emily Perry, or with the gardener, Albert Dean – whose first name his sister pronounced 'Holbert'.[7] And it is the language, rather than the story alone, that makes 'The Farmer's Bride' so compelling. It is a mercurial poem in which the meanings of words are in constant flux, metamorphosing (like the bride herself – now a woman, now a 'frightened fay', now a hare, a mouse, a leveret, a larch tree) under the weight of being looked at. Within the spellbound world of the poem, even the simplest of words – a word like 'down', for instance – refuse to be fixed to a single meaning. In the opening scene, the bride is chased 'up-along across the down'; towards the poem's close, a single oak leaf 'falls slowly down'; and finally, the farmer's voice erupts into an impassioned *cri de cœur* as he pictures his bride's 'soft young down', which he is unable to caress. Like the flighty woman at the poem's heart (who might, we sense, bolt again at any moment), nothing can be relied upon to stay put.

The verse Charlotte had written up to this point had been steadily gaining in subtlety and technical skill, but the surety of her writing seems to have grown remarkably during the silent years in which she'd remained unpublished. It is almost as if her poetry had gathered strength by lying dormant, while she read and absorbed and bided her time. Now she demonstrated a masterly control of tone, rhythm and especially of rhyme – even when those rhymes seemed in danger of over-emphasis. As well as the full rhymes that end each line, 'The Farmer's Bride' resounds with a series of quieter rhymes, echoes and homophones that call to each other from across the stanzas, so that the bride's 'wide brown stare' in the second stanza is answered by the stair that finally separates husband and wife and by her bewitching, untouchable hair. When the farmer's warring emotions – chiefly of pity and frustration – are at their peak, the poem responds by breaking into a clamour of repeated sounds that ring out like a peal of bells: *there, stair, hair, town, down, brown . . .* And nowhere is the emotion more intense than in his haunting final words: 'Oh! my God! the down, / The soft young down of her, the brown, / The brown of her – her eyes, her hair, her hair!'

By contrast, the bride remains *sub silentio* throughout, and we are asked to intuit the intensity of her suffering from what is omitted. It is a brave gamble and one that pays dividends: the young woman's presence pervades every line. She is a recognisable type in Charlotte Mew's work: the figure of the 'shy, reluctant fay' had first appeared in print in her 1905 story 'Mark Stafford's Wife', but there is an earlier version still, in the unfinished story 'Delivered' (1895), in which the central character is described as a 'slim religious sprite', 'no woman, though so tender', and a 'sweet, cloistered fay'.[8] The close echoes of the 'frightened fay' of the poem, who is 'slight as a young larch tree' and whose smile, after marriage, 'went out, and 'twasn't a woman', are clear.

But in other ways, too, this unpublished story reads as a test-ing ground for 'The Farmer's Bride'. Both story and poem coalesce around the idea that there are creatures in the world too ethereal to be touched – or, as the narrator of 'Delivered' has it, 'too frailly formed and delicately schooled for earthly parley'. The much-desired woman of the story – whose very 'presence interdicted contact' – reads as a prototype for the farmer's terrified bride, who is 'happy enough to chat and play / [. . .] So long as men-folk keep away.' And both are surely literary cousins of Hardy's character Sue Bridehead, who is described as 'a slim little wife' and an 'ethereal, fine-nerved, sensitive girl' whose long-suffering suitor, Jude, accuses her in exasperation of being 'a sort of fay, or sprite – not a woman!'[9] Charlotte was an ardent admirer of Hardy's work – she called him 'the King of Wessex'[10] – and she liked his novels as much as she did his poetry. Her open admira-tion makes the deeper correspondences between the farmer's bride and Sue Bridehead all the more intriguing: were the echoes she created in this poem conscious or subliminal. The fact that both women are hor-rified by the thought of carnal relations with their husbands is hardly striking, but what unites them more closely is their absolute refusal to acquiesce: in the words of Sue, 'I daresay it happens to lots of women; only they submit and I kick.'[11]

Given the creative barrenness of the years that led up to it, the appear-ance of 'The Farmer's Bride' seems little short of miraculous. What – beyond a possible rereading of *Jude the Obscure* – might have prompted it? In 1909, a government select committee had been appointed to look into the conditions under which a marriage might be deemed, in the eyes of the law, to have failed. Three years later, Lord Gorell's Royal Commission on Divorce and Matrimonial Causes was nearing the end of its deliberations.[12] The current statutes covering marriage afforded far fewer rights to women than to men, and it was clear to the Commission's members that they were in need of amendment. The law allowed a man to sue for divorce on the grounds that his wife had committed adultery, but women could only obtain a divorce in cases where adultery was combined with cruelty or desertion, or where it involved incest, rape, bigamy, sodomy or bestiality. Now the Commission proposed that husband and wife should, in respect of divorce, be placed 'on an equal footing'.[13] It further recommended that a continuing 'refusal to perform conjugal duties', in cases where there had never been intercourse, should be made sufficient grounds for nullifying a marriage.[14] A young bride who, three years into her marriage, is so terrified of intercourse that she spends her nights '[l]ying awake with her wide brown stare' would surely have qualified.

As a reader of *The Nation*, Charlotte would have been more than averagely well informed about the Commission's deliberations. In 1912, the magazine's pages were full of the marriage question. Just two weeks before her poem appeared in it, an anonymous article entitled 'The New Wife' had questioned the fairness of requiring that wives vow to 'obey' their husbands.[15] One of the letters written in response to the article, by the writer Honora Twycross, summed up the feelings of many readers, who believed that 'The instinct of obedience in woman is difficult to uproot, and she does, as a rule, prefer the headship of a man.'[16] So pervasive was the topic that D. H. Lawrence would comment the following year, 'I can only write what I feel pretty strongly about: and that, at present, is the relations between men and women. After all, it is *the* problem of today, the establishment of a new relation, or the readjustment of the old one, between men and women.'[17]

None of this is to suggest that the debates then raging over the marriage question did anything more than provide a germ for Charlotte Mew's extraordinary poem. She claimed not to be the sort of poet who took much interest in the 'mental processes' (as she put it) that went into the making of her poetry.[18] But when a friend wrote to her asking for help with some verse she had written, Charlotte disclosed her belief that 'the first requirement of poetry' is 'emotion'.[19] She would have empathised with Robert Frost's description of a poem as something that 'begins with a lump in the throat; a homesickness or a lovesickness [. . .] a reaching out towards expression'. That 'reaching out' can be heard in every word the farmer utters; a beseeching, a questing for meaning. It wasn't an abstract political argument but a concrete, emotion-fuelled situation – first imagined and then rendered in excoriating detail – that nursed 'The Farmer's Bride' into being.

But the poem had nonetheless embodied a restiveness in the nation's mood. Large numbers of women were growing increasingly frustrated with the gender imbalance that existed in so many walks of life, most obviously in their exclusion from the right to vote, in spite of years of peaceful lobbying. In the early evening of 1 March – a month after 'The Farmer's Bride' had been published – around 150 suffragettes (Emmeline Pankhurst among them) walked through the streets of London's West End, took out the stones they had been hiding in pockets and mufflers, and began smashing windows. 'SUFFRAGETTES' SPRING MADNESS', screamed the headline of one national newspaper, while another expressed its shock at this 'maenad contingent' of the female population.[20] The authorities wasted no time in locking away huge numbers of them, as securely as Mew's farmer had his bride.

> All in a shiver and a scare
> We caught her, fetched her home at last
> And turned the key upon her, fast.

The poem that Charlotte published later that month was quite unlike 'The Farmer's Bride'. 'The Voice', printed in the feminist monthly periodical *The Englishwoman*, bears more than a passing resemblance to both the setting and central incident of a piece of her short fiction, unpublished in her lifetime, called 'White World'.[21] The story centres on a dying girl who lives with her much older sister and father. One night she is sitting by the fire, as the snow comes down outside, preoccupied by thoughts of the lover her father and sister had sent packing years before, when – miraculously – he returns and leads the dying girl out of the confines of the house and into the snow. The plot then dissipates into a long and punishing journey that ends (we are not surprised to discover) in the girl's death. Both poem and story begin in a room that is silent except for the crackle of a fire, but the poem dispenses with a narrative arc and focuses instead on the passing by of an unnamed visitant, whose presence is signified by a few spare details as the speaker struggles to define it: a 'call', 'a voice on the sharp air', a breath that stirs the hair, a sensation of heat and, finally, the door swinging open as the being ('something swift and tall') sweeps in and out of the firelit room and goes on its way. We never learn the creature's gender, if it has one, or indeed the purpose of its visit, and without these clarifications the poem feels more expansive than the story; and more authentic too, increasing in drama and impact precisely because it remains unconstrained by superfluous explanation. In the aftermath of the visit, the speaker knows only that things cannot go on as they were:

> It left no mark upon the snow,
>> But suddenly, in passing, snapped the chain,
>> Unbarred, flung wide the door
>> Which will not shut again:
> And so we cannot sit here any more.
>>> We must arise and go.
>>> The world is cold without
>>> And dark and hedged about
>>> With mystery and enmity and doubt,
>>>> But we must go
>>> Though yet we do not know
> Who called, or what marks we shall leave upon the snow.

We may pick up an echo of Yeats's 'The Lake Isle of Innisfree' (1893) in that 'arise and go' – a phrase that Yeats himself described as a 'conventional archaism'.[22] But it is likely that both poets were recalling, consciously or otherwise, the King James Bible: 'I will arise and go to my father, and will say unto him, Father, I have sinned against heaven, and before thee' (Luke 15:18). For the most part, though, the diction of 'The Voice' is naturalistic and plainspoken, especially in the cadence of that conspicuously longer final line, whose characters extend across the whiteness of the page like the footprints they are describing.

The sparer, more modern voice that Charlotte used in her poetry was to some extent a natural part of her development as a writer. She began as a prose writer, and when she turned to poetry, her earliest attempts shared some of the antiquated phrasing of her early prose; as time went on, more and more of those archaisms disappeared from her work. But there is an unforced quality and an immediacy in her poetry that is missing even from her later prose, as if her ear were only properly attuned when she was making poems. A look at the beginning of 'White World' reveals the linguistic differences between the two styles:

Firelight lapped the chamber: the flames murmured feverishly,
wasting like waves in futile utterance their wordless life away.
   All was white outside: the sloping fields weighted with millions
of torpid snowflakes bore their load with broad tranquillity.[23]

Disregarding the alliterative clutter of f-, l- and w- sounds in the opening sentence, the writing here is chock-full of modifiers that effectively tell the reader what to think: *feverishly, futile, wordless, weighted, torpid, with broad tranquillity*. How are we to respond when the author has done all the interpreting for us? The poem's descriptors are fewer in number and altogether simpler: a *low* seat, a *small curtained* window, a *quiet* fire. This is writing that suggests, but never dictates, a mood.

෴

'The Farmer's Bride' and 'The Voice' announced Charlotte's return to print. The frequency with which her poems now began to appear in magazines might suggest that, during the silent years, she had in fact been steadily working away and was sending out work from a stock-pile she had amassed, but the poem she published next throws some doubt on that idea. It is also a reminder that poetic achievement rarely progresses along a smooth path of improvement: even the finest of poets have their off days. In the early hours of 15 April 1912, the RMS *Titanic* struck an iceberg and sank off the coast of Newfoundland, on her maiden voyage from Southampton to New York. Two days later, Charlotte dashed off a poem that was unpublished during her lifetime and (perhaps wisely) remains so today. Called simply 'The Titanic', it reads like a throwback to her earliest poetry:

> A challenged God, till man shall prove the stronger
> Strikes whom He will and saves whom He will save.
> Woe to the vanquished! And to whom the glory?

The archaic phrasing and lofty sentiment could hardly be further from the tone of her other new poems.

'The Voice' was to be the first of many Charlotte Mew pieces to appear in *The Englishwoman*, which quickly became an important home for her writing, replacing *Temple Bar* as her most regular outlet. It was a serious-minded and highly regarded shilling monthly, with an emphasis on supporting women's rights, whose mainly political pages were punctuated by literary contributions from the likes of John Masefield, A. E. Housman, John Galsworthy and George Bernard Shaw. In April, it carried a second contribution from Charlotte Mew, an essay entitled 'Mary Stuart in Fiction'.[24] The essay's thorough and meticulous analysis of the subject points to long hours of study in the Reading Room, as Charlotte sat at one of the leather-topped desks, methodically working her way through a stack of books – and indeed the six-month renewal of her reading ticket the previous September would have allowed her access to the library until March 1912, around the time she submitted the piece for publication.

Of the many writers she considers in the essay – French as well as British – Mew is most impressed by Sir Walter Scott, whose 1820 novel *The Abbot* covers the story of Mary Queen of Scots, from her imprisonment at Loch Leven Castle and her subsequent escape from there to her final defeat. Scott represents for Mew 'a robuster, more idealistic age than ours'. Interestingly, what she admires in him most of all is the restraint of his approach: 'When we go back to our old magician, we find [. . .] a fineness of taste in the treatment of emotion, which has long gone out of fashion, a reticence and dignity in human portraiture which is absent from the latest development of the genre.' Comparing Scott's work favourably with the most recent novel under her analysis, Maurice Hewlett's *The Queen's Quair* (1904), she praises Scott for presenting 'a conventional, a classic Mary Stuart [. . .], clothing her instinctively with all that traditional grace and majesty of which Mr Hewlett has cynically stripped her to expose his drenched wanton naked to the storm.'

Reticence, dignity, convention, tradition, grace – it's curious that these qualities should be highly prized by a writer who had such a gift for capturing emotion in its *least* controlled, its most heightened form. So many of the figures Charlotte chose to write about in her poems are similarly exposed 'naked to the storm' – quite literally, in the case of the farmer and his bride, who act out the drama of their differences *en plein air*, tearing through the night fields.

How are we to account for the scathing, uncompromising attitude she displays in her reaction to Hewlett and her unqualified admiration for the restraint she found in Scott? The answer probably lies in the two opposing components of Charlotte Mew's character: an essentially liberal outlook, especially in her attitudes to others, versus an outmoded belief that it was important to keep up appearances at all costs. She remained fiercely independent all her life, but respectability – that most corrosive of Victorian obsessions – was growing more important to her as she progressed through her forties and (ironically) the notion began to lose its hold on the national consciousness. A 'good address' – or at any rate the respect her family commanded – now mattered to Charlotte perhaps as much as it did to Ma. But while she expected that others would judge her by her cover, her own nature was essentially broad-minded and humane. It is abundantly clear from her writing that she had not only sympathy but real empathy for the eclectic cast of drifters, prostitutes and mentally disturbed characters that people her poems and stories. In fact, few things angered her more than the thought of people standing in judgement over others – as witness the gently suppressed undertow of anger in her poem 'On the Asylum Road' (first published in 1916), in which she reminds her readers that the perceived divide between the asylum residents met on the road and 'we merry town or village folk' is no greater than the divide between us and the wildlife which we are happy enough to live alongside.[25] In her personal relationships, too, she stressed the importance of respecting opinions that differed from our own; 'sympathy is not the forcible administration of one's own patent remedy,' she told one friend, 'but a consideration for – even if one cannot understand it – the other person's point of view'.[26]

The 'other person's point of view' was part of Charlotte Mew's psychic make-up: whoever she was, she was also, in a sense, always 'the other person'. The tension generated by the conflicting attitudes inside her lies at the heart of so much that she did, said and created. But where had these values come from? On her mother's side, her grandfather and great-grandfather, Henry Edward Kendall junior and senior, were both distinguished architects who had lived and worked in London and mixed with the social elite. Her father, on the other hand, was the son of an Isle of Wight innkeeper. In point of fact, his background was eminently respectable: he had come from what one local paper dubbed 'a well known and much respected Island family',[27] had attended school in London, as his elder brothers had done before him, and been made an Associate of the Royal Institute of

British Architects at the age of twenty-seven. But Fred had committed the demeaning and irremediable act of falling for his employer's daughter; and Anna Maria never did quite get over the idea that in marrying him she had lowered her own social standing. It could be that Anna Maria's insecurity about her *own* background made her more than usually sensitive to the perceived disparity. After all, there was much in her family's history that might elicit shame in such a woman – a younger brother who had been arrested for thieving, and a question mark over her father's parenthood, for a start. Sensitive as Charlotte was, she could not help but pick up on her mother's expressions of superiority. It's likely that she had absorbed this notion of class difference very young, and carried the warring elements of both her parents within her for life.

In the second week of May, after a spell of intense heat, a dramatic thunderstorm shook London – sharp bolts of lightning announcing a colossal downpour. The following day, the capital woke to a light breeze and a sky 'of the deepest Mediterranean blue'.[28] It was on this Monday 13 May that novelist Catherine Dawson Scott threw a house-warming party at her new home in Southall for around thirty guests, most of them writers. It may have been at this party – at any rate it was certainly this month – that Mrs Dawson Scott first met Charlotte Mew. She had recently moved back to the London area and was keen to re-establish her literary connections and forge new ones. Her belief in the value of socialising in general would lead her eventually to found the now-famous PEN ('Poets, Essayists, Novelists') organisation. A favourite habit of hers was to invite debutant authors to tea; one of the writers she took up, novelist Gladys Stern, remembered her as having a 'maternal passion for lame ducks'.[29] Herself a contributor to *The Englishwoman*, Dawson Scott had almost certainly seen Charlotte's 'The Voice' in the March edition, as well as her essay on Mary Stuart in April. The supernatural overtones of 'The Voice' would particularly have appealed to her: she had a keen interest in all things spiritual and would go on to publish two books on the subject, one a series of spirit messages apparently received by her from the recently deceased president of the United States, Woodrow Wilson.

Mrs Dawson Scott's friends called her Sappho, or Mrs Sappho, after the title of a long poem she self-published in 1889; subsequently, her first novel had been written under the pseudonym Mrs Sappho. Aged forty-seven when Charlotte met her, short and overweight, with a round, cheerful face, Mrs Sappho (as Charlotte would also come to call her) lived with her Irish doctor husband, 'Scottie',[30] and three young children, Marjorie, Christopher and Walter (known as Toby), in a four-storey semi-detached Victorian house near Norwood Green. Mrs Sappho's nature was complex to say the least. According to her daughter, she was 'fiery tempered and loving' at the same time; 'an atheist of outspoken, unconventional views', but also 'sexually inhibited and naïve, old-fashioned in some ways, progressive in others'.[31] Her son Christopher thought of her as 'fat and dumpy', with a fierce and sudden temper.[32] Marjorie remembers how her mother gave little thought to practicality when hiking in her beloved Cornwall: 'She wore trailing velvet tea-gowns both in the house and on her cliff wanderings – woe betide us if we "trod on her tail".'[33]

Charlotte made a strong and immediate impression on Mrs Sappho, who described her in her diary entry for 30 May as 'an imp with brains' and quickly became an ardent admirer of her verse. Though only four years older than Charlotte, she was fully au fait with the workings of the literary world and had an eclectic handful of publications to her name, including novels, plays, a travel book called *Nooks & Corners of Cornwall* and some poetry. She was by now best known as a novelist, but having begun her writing career as a poet, she had remained deeply interested in the genre. Her friendship with Charlotte at this crucial time would do much to help the promotion of her new friend's literary reputation.

The British poetry scene in 1912 was still emerging from what poet and publisher Harold Monro would term the protracted 'numbing effect' of the Victorian era, with its emphasis on patriotic themes couched in a lofty idiom that was popular with a public who read very little contemporary poetry.[34] This was precisely the idiom – devoid of any freshness or originality – in which Charlotte had written her 'V. R. I' sonnets in memory of Victoria, and her more recent poem about the *Titanic*. There were high points in British poetry in the first decade of the century, including Thomas Hardy's verse drama *Dynasts* (published in three parts in 1904, 1906 and 1908) and Yeats's *The Wind among the Reeds* (1899) and *The Green Helmet* (1910). But the tail end of the decade was a period generally marked by stagnation; looking back years later, T. S. Eliot would comment that 'The situation of poetry in 1909 or 1910 was stagnant to a degree difficult for any young poet of today to imagine.'[35]

A long overdue period of change began around 1912, when new work was published that was more in keeping with a world where gramophones were taking their places in living rooms, purpose-built cinemas appeared in many towns and cities, and aeroplanes were seen in the skies for the first time. The change was marked by a new journal dedicated to the field: *The Poetry Review*. A few individual collections of note had also started to appear: in the same month as Mrs Sappho's party, Walter de la Mare's second book for adults, *The Listeners and Other Poems*, was met with universal praise (by 1917, its title poem was being hailed as 'the best poem written during the present century'[36]), and in the autumn, American poet Ezra Pound (who had come to London four years earlier) published *Ripostes*, a book that sowed the seed for a literary trend that he identified and labelled 'Imagism'. The previous year a remarkable poem, 'The Everlasting Mercy', by the popular (and populist) poet John Masefield had caught the public's imagination. Its straight-talking delivery – what one critic called 'a certain brutality of diction'[37] – helped to blow away some cobwebs from the prevailing ideas of what poetry should be: 'If any here won't drink with me / I'll knock his bloody eyes out. See?'[38]

But the most influential publication that year wasn't a single-authored effort; it was an anthology of poets whose work was grouped together under the title of *Georgian Poetry*. The term had been coined by Harold Monro in June of 1911. Having recently returned from a spell in Italy and Switzerland, he had gone to lunch with a poet friend, Arthur Sabin, at the new oak-panelled 'Georgian Restaurant' in Harrods. As the lift doors slid open at the fourth floor, the operator announced the restaurant's name, and on hearing it Monro is said to have commented, 'This is the first time since my return that I have been reminded we are living in a new Georgian era – and, by Jove, Arthur, we are the new Georgian poets!'[39]

The anthology itself was the brainchild of Rupert Brooke and arts patron Edward Marsh. One evening in the autumn of 1912, they hit upon the idea of putting together an anthology drawn entirely from poems published during that year and the last. Marsh became the series editor and Monro the publisher, and by the end of the year all five hundred copies of the initial print run of *Georgian Poetry 1911–1912* had sold out. This was to be the first of five volumes whose express aim, according to Marsh, was to 'help the lovers of poetry to realize that we are at the beginning of another "Georgian period" which may take rank in due time with the several great poetic ages of the past'.[40] A year later, sales figures had reached nearly fifteen thousand. In spite of fairly strenuous efforts in the coming years on the part of Harold Monro to have Charlotte Mew included, her poems would be excluded from all five volumes.

By 1912, then, the poetry landscape, with its emerging factions, had never looked so vibrant – nor quite so divided. The prospect of stepping into this inhospitable terrain for the first time must have been daunting, but for a woman who had recently pronounced herself wrung out by the 'duties and little cares' of her home life,[41] it may nonetheless have presented the possibility of a thrilling escape. From within the oppressive confines of Charlotte's 'dark and gaunt' house in Gordon Street, her situation looked very like that of the lovelorn heroine of her 'White World' story, for whom 'escape became a question and a prayer. Both were to be simply answered. Blackness, hideous and unpitying, bound her. Freedom stood – she saw it plainly – beckoning, awaiting, her, outside in that vast universe of snow.'[42]

In the years to come, Charlotte's poetry would gain her the respect of some influential male writers, but the early champions of her poems were women; without their support, acclaim may have come to her later or not at all. In the light of her exclusion from the heavily male-dominated *Georgian Poetry* series, their backing at this point assumes real significance. 'The Farmer's Bride' had already drawn Charlotte into Mrs Sappho's circle and would win her some important advocates there; it had also secured the lasting admiration of Alida Klemantaski, who would turn out to be more important than any of these new friends. Now she was about to meet a third female patron, who had it in her power to introduce Charlotte's work to that tireless prospector for new poetic talent, Ezra Pound. Her name was May Sinclair.

13

The Din, the Scuffle, the Long Stare
1913

Mrs Sappho's penchant for engineering meetings between fellow writers amounted on occasion to social bullying. In the spring of 1913, she met May Sinclair at a party held by a mutual friend, the Christian mysticist writer Evelyn Underhill.[1] As they chatted, Mrs Sappho decided that May would make a good addition to her circle, and invited her to call on her in Southall for tea. Once back at home, it struck her that Charlotte might like to join them. 'I find in myself a keen desire for Charlotte's stimulating, irritating, keenly interesting society,' she noted in her diary. 'Under the curious husk is a peculiarly sweet, humble nature.'[2] Charlotte initially declined the invitation, explaining to Mrs Sappho that she really didn't want to meet lots of '"clever" & complicated people', adding that 'the fishermen on Boulogne quay are more in my way'.[3] But Mrs Sappho wasn't used to taking no for an answer, and Charlotte eventually gave way. May Sinclair arrived at the house first and was a little nonplussed to learn then, for the first time, that another writer friend would be joining them. But when Charlotte turned up and, at Mrs Sappho's insistence, read aloud 'The Farmer's Bride', 'May was so won over,' Mrs Sappho recorded, 'that she deserted me and they left together and have since called on each other' – leaving their hostess to wash up the teacups.[4]

May Sinclair wasn't petite like Charlotte (whom Mrs Sappho thought resembled 'a French Marquise'[5]) but she was certainly on the small side, and as a young woman she had been pretty, with dark 'smouldering eyes'.[6] Now forty-nine, she had put on weight and her gaze had lost some of its smoulder: one acquaintance who knew her around this time summed her up as 'the consummate unmarried woman, prim and proper, with black, emotionless eyes that exuded a Buddha-like calm'.[7] She was also by all accounts rather humourless and emotionally isolated; Virginia Woolf described her in 1909 as 'a woman of obtrusive, and medicinal morality'.[8] She lived alone in Edwardes Square in Kensington, with a cat called Tommy, on whom she lavished affection; when he finally died in her arms in 1919, after a botched dose of chloroform administered by the vet, she was inconsolable. 'The thought of it & the continual *seeing* of it all over again has poisoned all my walks,' she would tell Mrs Sappho. 'And I can't work. I wish I cd. die; but I'm too strong.'[9] This domestic solitude was unusual for the time, but May was rarely lonely: she was involved in a number of causes and usually had several projects on the go at once. But writing had long been her priority: by the time she met Charlotte, she already had one bestselling novel, *The Divine Fire* (1904), and many other books (mainly fiction), behind her.

Publishing history – and 'medicinal morality' – aside, May Sinclair and Charlotte Mew had many things in common. While they were in their twenties, both women had lost their fathers and been left to take care of ageing and difficult mothers who were obsessed with notions of respectability; both had become fiercely independent in spite of remaining devoted to those mothers, although May had been free of her burden for some time now, since her mother's death in 1901. Both women had also witnessed their siblings falling prey to illness: by the time she and Charlotte met, all of May's five elder brothers had died of congenital heart disease, most of them in early adulthood. 'Those who have left us may be invisible, but they are not absent,' writes St Augustine. And perhaps siblings who have left us are more than usually present: their stopped or altered futures, shared histories and, above all, their shared genes – all these things remain. The fact that Charlotte and May had this experience in common helped cement their acquaintance from the start. But it was Mrs Sappho who had introduced them, and she had no intention of being left out of the equation. There followed a flurry of exchanges between all three writers as they swapped books and poems, read each other's work and sent each other invitations, acceptances and polite refusals to meet in person or attend events.

Early on in this intricate *pas de trois*, May gave Charlotte a copy of the novel she had just published. *The Combined Maze* is a tale of unconventional married life and parenthood, and Charlotte loved it: it was a book, she said, that 'completely got – & kept hold of me'.[10] May called round to Gordon Street on hearing this, and finding her new acquaintance out, she left a note: 'I'm so glad you liked *The Combined Maze*. I never thought you'd read it! It was very nice of you to write to me. Let me try my luck some other Sunday.'[11] Thus began a friendship that, while not particularly long-lived, was to have a profound effect on Charlotte – and on public perceptions of her in years to come.

Mrs Sappho, meanwhile, had been putting some of her prodigious energies into drawing Charlotte closer into her literary circle. In February, she sent her a group of her own poems for comment. Charlotte duly responded, returning the poems with brief comments but protesting, 'I read next to no poetry & understand less.'[12] There was a certain amount of posturing in this response: Charlotte's letters are littered with poetry and prose quotations alike. And if her comment about not understanding it was genuine, it stemmed from a misguided belief that there was something worth knowing about poetry beyond what she had picked up from reading and working with it at close range for many years. She was, in fact, very sure of her own views on the subject – as would become increasingly clear in the months ahead.

What Charlotte's comments reveal is a deep sense of unease about the situation in which she now found herself. Since meeting Mrs Sappho, the number of people who knew her by reputation had broadened considerably, and she was genuinely nervous about being introduced to them all. The writers who came and went at Mrs Sappho's Victorian semi in Southall were not as eminent as those who attended the Stephen siblings' At Homes in Bloomsbury, but they nonetheless included published writers whose judgement Charlotte thought might be important to her future standing. She hadn't been involved with any literary groups since her attendance at the *Yellow Book* gatherings almost twenty years earlier, and Mrs Sappho's literary salons felt like alien territory. But perhaps the thought of missed opportunities was the greater evil, for on the day after writing her fretful letter about her wish to avoid 'clever' people, she arranged to attend another of Mrs Sappho's literary tea parties. She looked forward to it, she said, 'with the usual misgiving'.[13]

Charlotte's visits to Southall seem to have eased her back into sociability and she was soon, for the first time, hosting her own At Home, to entertain a group of people who had written to express an interest in meeting her – 'which invitation I owe to the *Englishwoman* things', she explained to a friend.[14] This momentous occasion was to be held not at the Mews' house (where conversation would be maddeningly interrupted by Ma's incessant demands and Wek's ear-splitting squawking) but at the new studio Anne had secured at 64 Charlotte Street, in the heart of Fitzrovia. About a ten-minute walk from Gordon Street, the Hogarth Studios were housed in a nineteenth-century building, with pedimented windows, that had been let to artists for many decades; Anne occupied No. 7.[15] It was here that, one Saturday afternoon in mid-March, a small group of Charlotte's supporters gathered and exchanged pleasantries, and occasionally contact details, over the tinkle of teacups. As Charlotte handed round plates of éclairs and discussed the plays of Maurice Maeterlinck and his recent Nobel Prize win, she found herself glancing outside at the now familiar view of the street, where at that moment 'the line of lamps, just lit, cut the broken mass of trees in the gardens opposite' where yet more land was being cleared.[16] She thought how much she would like to say about the senseless mutilation of those trees. One of these days, she would get around to writing a poem about it.

Mrs Sappho had asked to see more of her poems, but Charlotte was in two minds about it, especially as most of the newer poems hadn't yet appeared in print. Besides, her friend's praise of 'The Farmer's Bride' had been so excessive that anything else was bound to disappoint. In the end, she posted off a small group, enclosing with them a diffident little note: 'Perhaps when you've read them you will tone down your adjectives,' she suggested.[17] There was one condition attached to the gesture: the verses were not, under any circumstances, Charlotte said, to be passed on. 'I don't really like anyone to see things till they are printed,' she explained, taking Mrs Sappho into her confidence;[18] and besides, these were the only copies she had. Mrs Sappho had previously warned Charlotte that she had 'no sense of honour or decency', and the insistent tone of Charlotte's request for the poems to be sent straight back 'when you've done with them' suggests she had real doubts about how far her friend could be trusted.[19]

From early on in their relationship, Charlotte's dealings with Mrs Sappho were marked by a curious mix of polite reserve and downright rudeness, although she usually took care to temper the rudeness with a kind remark. There was something about the woman that made her wary. But she stayed in touch largely, she told an old friend, Edith Gray Hill, because of Mrs Sappho's children – 'a delightful girl of 14 who does the housekeeping and dressing of the mother to leave her free for literary work, a boy of 10 and a regular Footpad'.[20] The 'footpad' (a colloquial term for a highwayman) evidently referred to the roguish, eight-year-old Toby. Very often Charlotte wrote to ask if she could take the three of them out – to the Coliseum, to London Zoo, to a musical – and then, always, back to 7 Hogarth Studios, or 'the Studio' (as she was soon calling it, capitalising the 'S'), for tea.[21] Writing to Edith now, another thought occurred to her: perhaps, next time Edith was in town with her daughter, some sort of 'children's party' might be arranged. What with Edith's Celia (seven), Elsie O'Keefe's '2 Irish villains' (Maeve, eight, and Manus, four) plus Mrs Sappho's brood of three (Marjorie, Christopher and Toby), they could gather quite a little crowd.[12] At forty-three, Charlotte was nearing the end of her childbearing years – a time when she might naturally be examining her own decision not to be a mother. But her desire to be around children went beyond that. She cherished their unworldliness and sense of fun; in their company there was no need to adhere to difficult social protocols, or to suppress her instinct for the ridiculous.

The same was true in the company of most of her close friends – Ethel and Winifred Oliver and the Chicks, for instance – where she was free to be as ridiculous as she liked. Charlotte's need to escape from the seriousness of her daily life was profound, and it made certain of her friendships enormously important to her. By the same token, she disliked the company of women who allowed themselves to be repressed or somehow diminished after they married. She knew that not all marriages were the same, of course, and that there were some women who managed to 'escape the bit', but in her experience, these were the exception rather than the rule.

A case in point was her old school friend Maggie Robinson, who had finally married in 1909 at the age of forty-six. Maggie had a sharp intellect and had gone on to study zoology and marine biology at University College, London, and then joined the staff there to work in the research laboratory with Edward Browne. Mr Browne was a faultlessly methodical man who kept card indexes in his house for all his books and scientific pamphlets, so that things might be found at a moment's notice. When the couple eventually married, they moved to the small market town of Berkhamsted in Hertfordshire, and Edward carried on much as before: he had a special laboratory built in the grounds of the house so that he could work there, with extra room to accommodate his numerous specimens and growing library.[23] Maggie, on the other hand, had almost entirely given herself up to the niceties of domestic life and now talked of very little else; worse, she seemed to have lost all sense of spontaneity. In July, Charlotte wrote to a friend that she was 'bracing' herself for a weekend at Berkhamsted, 'where the extravagance of cooks, the dearness of vegetables, be all our joy'; she added, as an afterthought, 'Sometimes I thank the little gods that I am not a "married lady".'[24]

Mrs Sappho didn't quite fall into the category of subjugated wife, but she was certainly sheltered by her marriage – comfortably supported, as she was, by a doctor's salary. Whereas Charlotte needed every scrap of income in order to make ends meet, the money Mrs Sappho earned from her writing was a bonus. Charlotte also felt their tastes and outlooks were 'quite different', and she rarely lost an opportunity to say so.[25] When the gift of a novelty necklace arrived in the post, instead of graciously accepting it, Charlotte gave her honest assessment: 'I'm sure I see no beauty in a necklace of fruit pots – full or empty,' she told Mrs Sappho, '& even if I wished, I'm too small to wear it!' But, as ever, she softened the blow with a compliment: 'Sympathy (in the French sense) is sympathy all the world over,' she said, '& yours is very generous & couldn't possibly be put into a pot.'[26]

Her periodic bluntness with Mrs Sappho, good-humoured as it was, touches on something at the heart of Charlotte's whole way of being: she was different things to different people. It's impossible to imagine her, for instance, poking fun at May Sinclair's personal taste, even when she got to know her better. At the moment, the friendship with May was still in its infancy: after an enthusiastic start on both sides, communications had stuttered to a halt. That was largely because May had committed herself to several projects at once: she had fallen into a rhythm of releasing a new book at the rate of one, and often two, a year. She was also busy reviewing and contributing articles for the non-militant Women Writers' Suffrage League, and helping behind the scenes with a number of other causes. That year she had managed to find a necessary bolthole, away from London and the noise of music students forever practising their instruments in the studios near her home. At a quiet guesthouse in Reeth, in the Yorkshire Dales, May shut herself away from the world to write and be among ordinary, unbookish people who didn't know her, in a village sheltered by a line of green hills. Having settled arrangements to go up there later in the summer, she finally sent a note to Charlotte at the start of July: 'Can you – will you – come to tea? Tomorrow, Saturday, at 4.30, or Wednesday 9th at 5? I do so want to see you and know you better.'[27] The invitation was eagerly accepted.

Like Mrs Sappho, May was keen on encouraging and promoting unpublished writers. One of her protégés was Ezra Pound, whose work she'd been supporting since he'd arrived in London as an unknown writer five years earlier, but who was now doing very well under his own steam. In Charlotte Mew – who was both lavishly gifted and almost entirely unheard of – it looked as if she might have found a new project, and the prospect delighted her. May had been so taken by the poem she'd heard Charlotte read aloud at Mrs Sappho's house that she now asked to see others – 'I'm told you've published several every bit as beautiful as The Farmer's Bride,' she said.[28]

In answering May's request, Charlotte showed none of the reticence she'd adopted in her dealings with Mrs Sappho. Among the work she sent to May that summer of 1913 were the three poems she'd published most recently in magazines – 'Requiescat', 'The Changeling' and 'Exspecto Resurrectionem' – plus half a dozen unpublished pieces, including 'Ken', 'In Nunhead Cemetery' and 'The Quiet House'.[29] Together, the group constituted just over half the poems that would appear in her first collection – and if everyone were to respond to them as May did now, Charlotte could look forward to great things. 'I wish I cd. give you any idea of the extraordinary pleasure they have given me,' May gushed.[30] The following day, Charlotte sent a breathlessly excited note to Mrs Sappho – full of dashes – to express her gratitude for the part Mrs Sappho had played in setting things in motion: 'Miss Sinclair said she would send my things to Edward Garnett – Harrison & Pound – I have just replied that I don't want to make use of her – but however it goes – I have firstly to thank you – & very sincerely do – In spite of my "mountain way" I am an antiquely grateful person.'[31]

With her customary efficiency, May now arranged to have copies made of all of Charlotte's unpublished poems so that she could get on with sending them out to editors. She had just one reservation: to her ear there was something awry about the metre in places. 'I know exception will be taken to the apparent lack of metrical technique in some of the poems,' she told Charlotte.[32] May presumably felt she had some authority on which to base her opinion: at the age of twenty-three, she'd published a book of poems entitled *Nakiketa and Other Poems*, under the pseudonym 'Julian Sinclair'. The alias proved to be a shrewd move: May's poetic talents were limited, to say the least, and she soon shifted her efforts to writing novels. The comment she had made about metre was neither needed nor appreciated, and Charlotte responded with barely suppressed indignation: 'Of course I could write smoothly if I chose.'[33] And indeed she could: her 'V. R. I' sonnets, for instance (dull as they are), had been written in the smoothest of iambic penta-meters – not a syllable out of place. Questions of metre aside, May was bowled over by the originality and passion of Charlotte's poems. She couldn't think of 'any living writer who is writing things with such profound vitality in them', she told her new friend, adding, 'with, pos-sibly, the exception of H. D. Lawrence [. . .] And you have qualities of tenderness and subtlety that he has not.'[34] Charlotte was amused by the misnomer – H. D. Lawrence must be 'Another Brother!' she quipped to Mrs Sappho – but she couldn't have been more grateful for the efforts May was making on her behalf.[35]

In bringing her work to the attention of Ezra Pound, May was introducing Charlotte to the most radical quarters of the poetry world. Pound and his close friend, the author and painter Wyndham Lewis, had made it their business to shake the stuffy London cultural scene free of its traditionalist constraints by exposing it to as much avant-garde work as possible. Still in his twenties, Pound was in contact with some influential editors in the US, and after seeing Charlotte's work, he suggested to May that *Poetry* magazine (recently founded by Harriet Monroe in Chicago and fast establishing a reputation for excellence) might be a good place for the poems; he pointed out that it would pay more than Austin Harrison's *English Review*, although there was no reason, he said, why she shouldn't be published in both.[36]

Charlotte was overjoyed that her work was finally being seen – and approved of – by people who held some sway in the literary world. Here, at last, was objective confirmation of her gifts. 'I have been writing polite replies to the "little human praise" I certainly have not warranted lately,' she told a friend – 'all the time struck by the generosity of people who having done big things themselves can find such kind things to say of my little ones. I am now "Charlotte" to Mrs Sappho.'[37] What she omitted to say in this letter was that her desire for recognition was mixed up with a sense of deep unease at the thought of losing some of her highly cherished privacy. But she was well aware of the paradox: in fact, it was precisely this tension of both wanting and not wanting to push herself forward that now kindled a poem that Charlotte said she preferred 'to anything I have done, though I don't know why'.[38]

Set in the confines of an 'over-heated house', 'Fame' depicts some-one newly famous mixing with a crowd of deferential acquaintances and hangers-on. As the poem progresses, we learn how much the speaker longs for 'the sweetbriar air' of their old, simpler life; but to remove themselves from the newly discovered glamour of fame seems an impossible prospect: now that they have grown used to the 'long stare' of their admirers, would they really be able to live without it?

> Sometimes in the over-heated house, but not for long,
>> Smirking and speaking rather loud,
>> I see myself among the crowd,
> Where no one fits the singer to his song,
> Or sifts the unpainted from the painted faces
> Of the people who are always on my stair;
> They were not with me when I walked in heavenly places;
>> But could I spare
> In the blind Earth's great silences and spaces,

The din, the scuffle, the long stare
    If I went back and it was not there?
Back to the old known things that are the new,
The folded glory of the gorse, the sweetbriar air,
To the larks that cannot praise us, knowing nothing of what we do,
        And the divine, wise trees that do not care.

The rest of the poem describes the speaker's hypothetical rejection of fame, and then resolves into a disturbing image of a stillborn lamb – the embodiment of a different, smaller dream that the speaker has recklessly abandoned, 'ghostly and pitiful and white', in favour of the glitz and glamour of fame.

May's efforts to place Charlotte's poems followed a period in which Charlotte had been busy on her own behalf, and with gratifying results. On 17 February, a single edition of *The Englishwoman* had featured both a new poem ('The Changeling') and the first part of an ecological essay entitled 'Men and Trees (I)', which maintained that 'the London trees are all prisoners of men, some unreasonably mutilated like the lopped crowd in Greenwich Park, while, now and then, there is a wholesale massacre such as that of the seven hundred in Kensington Gardens, which took place, no one knows why, some thirty years ago'.[39] In March, the companion piece, 'Men and Trees (II)', denounced mankind's loss of connection with nature in the current age of the 'Culte du Moi', and quoted the Japanese artist Yoshio Markino looking back on his own childhood: 'When I leaned against a tree, I felt I was a tree.'[40] On 22 March, a second poem, 'Exspecto Resurrectionem', was published in the American journal *Living Age*.[41]

In terms of her writing, this was the busiest, and most stressful, time of Charlotte's life so far. That spring of 1913, the excitement of seeing the reaction to her new poems, the nervousness caused by meeting so many new people (after what had been, in effect, a long period of social hibernation) and the demands of her home life led to a bad spell of sleeplessness. Charlotte put it down largely to the pressure of constantly having to labour away at her family duties. 'The doctor won't give me sleeping stuff,' she grumbled to a friend, 'so I am fighting it out myself with the selfish resolution to put business and domestic cares absolutely behind me for a time.'[42]

That she thought it was selfish to take a break from her exhausting chores seems as sad as it is revealing. But why had the doctor refused to prescribe a sedative? Was there a concern that she might misuse the medication? Had she done so in the past? Certainly she would have had occasion enough to ask for it. She had been under considerable strain ever since Fred's death had forced her to take on the role of materfamilias fifteen years earlier, but in any case hers had never been the most relaxed of temperaments – nor, indeed, had her home environment ever provided much chance to relax. In the opinion of at least one of her friends, she smoked 'in order to calm her nerves',[43] and seemed always to need something to absorb the nervous energy within her. She wore a signet ring on the little finger of her right hand, which the same friend remembers her twirling 'round and round in the most fascinating manner by moving her third finger against it'.[44] That particular gesture had replaced her schoolgirl habit of spinning around on her feet ('a sort of pirouetting, as it were'[45]) while she talked. But since those days, she had developed a characteristic nervous tic: now when she spoke, she kept her head cocked on one side, and from time to time shook her head towards her left shoulder.

She was badly in need of another holiday, and some time during that spring of 1913 she managed to get away to Dieppe.[46] The town in those days was still relatively unknown to foreign tourists – an old Norman seaport, with a fish market and castle and a bustling square, the Place du Puits Salé, whose famous Café des Tribunaux had been painted by Walter Sickert some time around 1890. Dieppe had once been a firm favourite of the *Yellow Book* crowd, and it is entirely possible that Charlotte had visited it then too, when she was in her twenties. Its casino had proved particularly popular with many of the *Yellow Book* authors.[47] Charlotte was by no means immune to its charms herself, but she recognised it for the danger it was and, having 'no money to lose', did her best to keep away.[48] She had booked into the Hotel du Commerce – 'not stylish nor comfortable', but it had the advantage of being only £10 a day.[49] She could have had an even cheaper room at the Normandie – 'but really one must be here – the Square is a pure delight & when one hasn't too many holidays, it makes all the difference to be in the right place'.[50] Here, while the bells of St Rémy Church tolled out the hours, she sat down and began an extraordinary poem full of excitement, menace and foreboding, which she titled 'The Fête'. Voiced by a traumatised sixteen-year-old boy, the poem recounts how four days earlier, as the boy sat watching the circus, a dazzling trapeze artist had entered the arena on a horse and, on the last night of the fair, led him into the woods, where '*The Enchanted Thing*' (evidently a seduction of some kind) took place. In retrospect, the whole episode, as unsettling as it was 'enchanting', seems to have been preordained:

> In the *Place d'Armes* all afternoon
> The building birds had sung 'Soon, soon,'
> The shuttered streets slept sound that night,
> It was full moon:
> The path into the wood was almost white,
> The trees were very still and seemed to stare . . .

'The Fête' is as crammed with spectacle as the circus tent where the boy first lays eyes on his seductress. Among the first objects to enter the poem's arena are a 'wood that sees' and a square crossed, with equal consequence, by a 'tiny funeral', the shadow of a bird, and the '*demoiselles*' of the local convent school, who shoot the speaker a glance as they walk by, warning him that physical contact is '*défendu*' – forbidden. The speaker's young heart 'pelts and beats' with the rain against the window-glass as the tension builds, and we are given plane trees coming into leaf and a 'singing wind' that swings down from the stars to saunter through country lanes until, at the crux of the poem, the night of the circus arrives, with its smells of animals and dust and roses and the captivating woman who enters the tent standing on a white horse and flying a bird 'on the wing / Of her white arms'. Everything in this poem is potently, mercurially alive. When he got to see it a year later, Ezra Pound decided that he liked it so much he wanted it for *The Egoist*, the avant-garde literary magazine where he was poetry editor.

For the moment, May Sinclair had hit an impasse with the poems she was trying to place. 'Mr. Harrison seems to have run away with the idea that *all* yr poems have been published elsewhere, because of the notes attached to some of them,' she explained to Charlotte. 'I expressly told him that this was not the case, but that I was sending him all of them so that he cd. judge yr quality better.'[51] May hadn't yet heard back about the poems that had been sent to *Poetry* magazine either, but was lunching with Ezra Pound the following day and would let Charlotte know if there was any news.

Meanwhile, Charlotte had also been talking over some of her poems with her old friend Edith Hill, who, though only five years her senior, had taught Charlotte maths at the Gower Street School and now lived on private means in Sydenham, having married a wealthy gold-and-silversmith. One of the two poems under discussion was 'Ken', which – like 'The Farmer's Bride' – dealt with a much-de-bated topic of the day: how should those members of society who were deemed 'mentally deficient' be accommodated? Should they be housed in asylums or allowed to live in the community?

Details of the 1913 Mental Deficiency Bill had been widely reported in the papers in recent months, and the discussions and arguments surrounding it would rage on until the act was passed, in November 1913. Two years earlier, Home Secretary Winston Churchill (one of the early drafters of the bill) had spoken out in favour of the compulsory internment of 'mental defectives' in labour camps. He preferred, in fact, the option of sterilisation for such people, but that would have been costly. The 1913 Act categorised the mentally ill into four distinct groups: idiots, imbeciles, the feeble-minded and moral defectives. There was already provision for the first two of these categories to be forcibly placed in institutions, and the question of segregation for the latter two was an area in which feelings ran high. A letter sent to the *Fifeshire Advertiser* in the autumn of 1912 summed up the feelings on one side of the debate: 'The idea of segregating and imprisoning human beings, who harm none and are able to work for their living, simply because they have some peculiarity which may be described as mentally deficient, is abhorrent in the extreme.'[52]

Ken, the eponymous subject of Charlotte's poem, was precisely the sort of person under discussion: a young man who 'ploughed up the street, / Groping, with knarred, high-lifted feet', more often than not trailed by some child or other, under the illusion that 'all the children and the deer, / Whom every day he went to see / Out in the park, belonged to him.' But for the adults in his home town, he is an embarrassing nuisance. 'God help the folk that next him sits / He fidgets so, with his poor wits,' they tut. Even so, he lives affably enough alongside them, in a 'gabled house facing the Castle wall', until his removal to an asylum – effected, we can't help feeling, by one or more of those gossiping neighbours. In the final two stanzas, the poem asks the reader to consider the implications of such an action:

> But in that red brick barn upon the hill
>   I wonder – can one own the deer,
> And does one walk with children still
>   As one did here –
>   Do roses grow
> Beneath those twenty windows in a row –
>   And if some night

When you have not seen any light
They cannot move you from your chair
What happens there?
I do not know.

So, when they took
Ken to that place, I did not look
After he called and turned on me
His eyes. These I shall see –

Why should the mentally ill *not* have roses growing underneath their windows? It's an important political question; but what makes the poem come alive is the vividness of its setting – a 'place of bells and cloisters and grey towers' where children dart from doorways in the twilight and call to each other through the town's crooked streets; the poem's direct tone, which compels us to listen; and, too, the strangeness of the imagery – the 'red wounded stars' of Ken's eyes, for instance, as he turns his anguished gaze on the speaker, all the light gone out of them. Where do such images come from? They cannot be worked out or learned. Charlotte's poems are full of unexpected likenesses of this kind, drawn from a place deep inside her and transformed, through her unique sensibility, into lucid images of universal resonance.

Such rich metaphorical connections require from the writer a degree of independence from plan or method; a readiness to take a leap into the unknown. And if the resulting images have the appearance of spontaneity, they are also hard won. What is it that makes an artist able to reach for such originality, or indeed want to? The answer in Charlotte's case is that she was writing about things that mattered deeply to her. The 'red brick barn' with its 'twenty windows in a row' in 'Ken' is reminiscent of the red-brick Whitecroft Hospital, with its long lines of inmates' windows, where Freda was housed, and the question about what happens in such a place when a patient cannot be moved from their chair is one that Charlotte must have asked herself about Freda, who presented with precisely this symptom. Catatonic immobility is typical of certain types of schizophrenia; mutism is another symptom, and the poem also notes of Ken that 'He scarcely spoke, you scarcely heard, / His voice broke off in little jars / To tears sometimes.' A selection of comments from Freda's case notes suggests that her condition had at the very least provided details for the poem, and that she may have been a direct inspiration for Ken. The staff caring for her reported, among other things, that she 'sits doubled up in a chair'; 'never voluntarily says a word to others'; 'will sit in the same place as long as left, with her head hung down'; and 'remains in the same attitude as long as left and never says a word'.[53] The echo of Freda's middle name, Kendall, in Charlotte's naming of her luckless character must surely be more than coincidence.

Charlotte and Edith also discussed 'In Nunhead Cemetery', set in the place where Charlotte's brother Henry had been buried twelve years earlier. Edith felt unsure, she said, about the ending, in which the bereaved young man – already deranged by grief – loses grip of his senses completely and decides he prefers the company of the dead to that of the living. In the last line he reaches the unsettling conclusion that if the gravedigger would only uncover the buried bodies again, they would not die a second time – and they would make excellent company:

> I shall stay here: here you can see the sky;
> The houses in the streets are much too high;
> > There is no one left to speak to there;
> > Here they are everywhere,
> And just above them fields and fields of roses lie –
> If he would dig it all up again they would not die.

Was this a little too much, Edith wondered? Would the poem not, perhaps, work better without it? Charlotte's answer was emphatic, and it gives us another glimpse into just how sure she was of what she was doing in these new poems: 'The last verse which you find superfluous', she explained, 'is to me the most inevitable (and was written first) being a lapse from the sanity and self-control of what precedes it. The mind and senses can stand no more, and that is to express their failure and exhaustion.'[54] Charlotte was aiming for exactly the kind of dissolution that had so discomfited her correspondent; having witnessed just such a lapse from sanity, on more than one occasion, she knew it rang true.

Late on in the summer, May Sinclair was preparing to go up to Yorkshire again. She would be away for two months, and in her usual manner – and, no doubt, in an effort to clear the decks for writing – she was fastidious about tying up loose ends before she set off. This included consolidating the arrangements she'd set in motion for the placing of Charlotte's work with various editors and magazines. She now sent back to Gordon Street any copies of poems she no longer needed, and she informed Charlotte that Ezra Pound had sent three of the poems to *Poetry* in Chicago: 'You will no doubt hear from the editor or from him,' she told her.[55] She passed on Pound's address in Kensington ('in case you want to write to him or send him more poems'). Austin Harrison at the *English Review* had all the poems that were not with other editors, and May had instructed him to write directly to Charlotte about them. She also left her own address in Yorkshire, where she planned to be 'till the middle or end of October'. That was all straightforward enough; but she signed off this valedictory note with such an air of finality that Charlotte wondered if she was drawing a line under the friendship and intended not to see her again.

> I wish I cd. have come & seen you before I left – but I've been frightfully rushed and was in the country all — [illegible]. Good-bye and Good Luck.
> Always very sincerely yrs, May Sinclair.[56]

A short while later, May wrote to correct the impression: 'My dear Miss Mew, My handwriting must be more illegible even than I thought it, or my powers of expression hopelessly impaired by my miniature removal.'[57] In returning the poems, she had merely been thinking that the duplicate typescripts would be safer with Charlotte than they would be in her own hand luggage; she had kept further copies of all of them for herself at home. She expressed her pleasure at having had the chance 'to do anything for you and for yr splendid work', and then she got to the heart of the matter:

> As for 'good-bye' I never dreamt it wd. be interpreted 'Goodbye for ever.'! But it is my own fault if – going to Yorkshire and Scotland for two months – I write as if I were bound for the North Pole. In November – I hope – we meet, if you are not too disgusted with my style!
> always very sincerely yrs, M. S.[58]

May would write several more letters to Charlotte that she signed off with 'Goodbye & Good Luck', and none of them heralded an absence of more than a few weeks: it was clearly no more than a quirk of phrasing, but it is perhaps understandable that Charlotte took it for more on this first occasion. None of Charlotte's letters to May has survived, and without seeing Charlotte's replies it's difficult to gauge just how hurt she was by this particular exchange, but the carefully apologetic tone of May's second letter suggests that she *had* been hurt. Nonetheless, she was evidently in light enough spirits in the second half of August to leave London for 'a world of garden parties'– which, she reported to Mrs Sappho afterwards, had 'greatly amused me & worn out my clothes'.[59]

But the confusion that had arisen from May's 'Good-bye & Good Luck' letter left the writer wary of causing further offence, and in September she wrote again from Yorkshire: she hoped Charlotte wouldn't think her 'an awful brute' for not having asked her to visit

Reeth,[60] but she had gone up to Scotland for a break and stayed longer than intended, which meant that she now had only a week or two to work up the early chapters of her new novel, *The Three Sisters.* 'I'm not behaving worse to you than to the other friends I wanted to have here!' she assured Charlotte.[61] If Charlotte thought she had any special claims on May's affections, that comment put her straight.

Meanwhile, Charlotte found herself declining Mrs Sappho's invitations with increasing frequency. In June, she had written to say she wouldn't be able to make it down to Southall again for the time being as she had 'more the next week or two than I can manage to get through'.[62] In mid-July, she said she had intended to come down the following day '– but I have been going at it rather hard lately & may have to take a rest.'[63] Behind the polite refusals was a growing irritation with Mrs Sappho's supposition that she could show Charlotte off to her friends like some sort of fairground curiosity. Reverting to Mrs Sappho's proper name, Charlotte let off steam to Edith Hill: 'Mrs Scott asked me to go down last Saturday to recite the poems to some literary friends, and in my brightest way I replied that she had mistaken me for little Tich or Margaret Cooper at the piano, and impolitely declined.'[64] Charlotte remained civil with Mrs Sappho but she steadfastly refused to be bossed about – especially when assumptions appeared to have been made about her availability: 'Thank you so much for ticket herewith returned. I would so much have liked to come but have an engagement at 1 for the whole afternoon so it couldn't be worked in.'[65] And no, thank you, she wouldn't come down to Cornwall in September as she already had two invitations (one from 'very old friends' – the Chicks – who, she explained, had a house in the West Country) 'which make it impossible for me to say anything but a grateful – regretful – "No Thank you" to yours'.[66]

There were other grounds for irritation, and even mistrust. Mrs Sappho had been right to warn Charlotte back in June that she had no sense of honour or decency. Instead of keeping Charlotte's unpublished poems to herself, as she had been asked to, she'd passed them freely among her friends, and in so doing had, as Charlotte put it, made her a 'jest & a byword' not only within Mrs Sappho's circle but with 'the small points of it' that touched Charlotte's own. Charlotte's response to this betrayal of trust seems remarkably gracious: she simply told Mrs Sappho that if she weren't 'so large & sweet', she wouldn't be able to forgive her for it. But that was not to say she condoned the behaviour: 'please you mustn't go on doing it as it makes me feel such a dreadful ass & that you know – no one forgives!'[67]

Charlotte had a great deal more self-control than in the days when she had snapped her nursemaid's parasol in two after she'd been whacked with it for misbehaving. However much cause for annoyance her new friends gave her, she seemed to remain loyal to them, willing to undertake all sorts of small kindnesses in return for the faith they showed in her. She undoubtedly had her limits of tolerance, but neither Mrs Sappho nor May Sinclair had yet reached them. At the start of November, Mrs Sappho was due to have a minor operation. Charlotte offered to meet her from it, and wrote a few days ahead to check on the arrangements: 'But you say you are due at George St at 4 – shouldn't I then fetch you at 4:45 (not 3:45 as you say) as I didn't bargain to attend the operation, or shall I be there at 4:30 & wait, looking over Punches, till you appear?'[68]

Though the friendship was slightly newer, Charlotte was equally willing to put herself out for May. In the same week as Mrs Sappho's operation, she offered to address a pile of circulars that had been printed to advertise London's new Medico-Psychological Clinic, the first public clinic in Britain to use psychoanalysis for the treatment of nervous disorders. May had been hard at work for some time securing both funds and suitable premises. She'd told Charlotte that her niece had come over to help with the circulars but had got bored after sticking seven stamps onto the envelopes.

The Bugle Hotel in Newport, Isle of Wight, where Charlotte's father
Frederick was born on 14 March 1832.

Charlotte's great uncle,
Benjamin Mew, set up the first
family brewery in 1814.
W. B. Mew, Langton & Co. was
established in 1873.

Frederick and Anna Maria Mew in 1863, the year of their marriage.

'Lotti' (LEFT) and Anne Mew in January 1878, aged eight and four.
Charlotte was fiercely protective of 'my little sister' throughout her life.
The pair remained close allies and friends and lived together for over
half a century, until parted by death.

Henry Mew in January 1880,
aged fourteen.

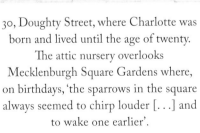

30, Doughty Street, where Charlotte was
born and lived until the age of twenty.
The attic nursery overlooks
Mecklenburgh Square Gardens where,
on birthdays, 'the sparrows in the square
always seemed to chirp louder [. . .] and
to wake one earlier'.

The Mew family's parrot,
William Edward Kendall,
known as 'Wek'.

Charlotte with six of the seven Chick sisters in the garden of the Chicks' home in Ealing in 1889. Standing, left to right: Mary (16), Edith (19), Harriette (14) and Margaret (12). Seated: Frances (6), Charlotte Mew (19) and Elsie (8).

Charlotte's beloved headmistress, Lucy Harrison, in 1890. A pupil at the school commented of her, 'I remember just how it felt when Miss Harrison came into the room, bringing with her, as she always did, a serene sense of freshness and space and of august things. And how swiftly we fell to work, fired by that noble earnestness.'

Charlotte Mew in her twenties.

BELOW Aerial view, taken *c.* 1920, of the environs of University College London, showing the position of 9 Gordon Street, the Mews' family home from 1890–1922.

ABOVE Charlotte Mew's first publication, a short story called 'Passed', appeared in the second issue of *The Yellow Book* when she was twenty-four.

ABOVE A calendar handmade by
Charlotte Mew. Her friend Margaret
Chick revealed it was 'one of many which
she made for my father over the years'.
(Margaret Chick to Mary Davidow,
17 September *c.* 1960)

Embroidery designed and worked by
Charlotte Mew on featherweight linen;
the double border is hemstitched by hand.
Charlotte embroidered many such cloths
as gifts for her friends, and besides being
a highly skilled needleworker was also a
talented sketcher and pianist.

Anne Mew in 1897, aged twenty-three, who Charlotte said had '100 times my pluck and patience – & her very own definite gift – all going to seed – & to me its [*sic*] heartbreaking'. (CMM to Catherine Dawson Scott, 12 March 1914)

Freda Mew in August 1896, aged seventeen, two years before she became ill.

The County Asylum on the outskirts of Newport, Isle of Wight, *c.* 1904. Freda was admitted in February 1899, at the age of nineteen, and remained there until her death in 1958.

Catherine Dawson Scott, *c.* 1913. Known to Charlotte as 'Mrs Sappho', Dawson Scott shared Mew's poems widely with her literary friends and acquaintances (including May Sinclair) during 1913 and 1914, but the friendship was short-lived and ended on bad terms.

May Sinclair, *c.* 1910, with whom Charlotte enjoyed an intense, if brief, friendship. Sinclair introduced Mew's work to a number of influential editors, including Ezra Pound.

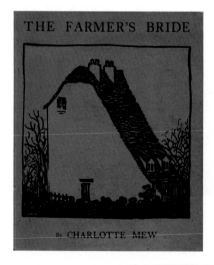

The front cover design of *The Farmer's Bride* (1916), with its illustration by Claud Lovat Fraser. Charlotte commented of the roof that she 'certainly never saw one like it & I don't think any wall would support it'. (CMM to Paul Lemperly, 31 August 1921)

Sketch of a maidservant attaching slippers to a gentleman's feet, included in letter from Charlotte Mew to Alida Monro, 29 May 1918.

Charlotte's publisher, Harold Monro. He was a great admirer of Mew's poetry and did his best to promote it, in spite of their occasionally awkward professional relationship.

Sydney Cockerell in 1917, aged fifty. 'Has anyone remarked that, were the centre figure in Tudor dress, – Behold! Shakespeare? I saw it at once.' (CMM to Sydney Cockerell, 28 December 1921)

or toasted cheese? & if not will you make a final effort to eat or drink something — ? A written reply un necessary — but an immediate sertice would respectfully be requested. The aesthetic arrangement of this Flat are probably matters of one so of us immortals but I really believe you would run a better chance of general survival in a Boarding House.

E. M. K.

Letter excerpt (CMM to Alida Monro, 7 November 1918) showing sketch of a boarding house dining table and attendants. Long hours in the Poetry Bookshop during the war years had taken their toll on Alida's health and Charlotte now joked to her that she might 'run a better chance of general survival' were she to move into a boarding house.

In 1921 (LEFT) and c. 1922 (RIGHT): Charlotte retained an interest in fashion all her life. She had a strong sense of style and many different ways of dressing. She insisted on buying her black button-up boots (in a tiny size 2) from Pinet's in Mayfair and left several items of jewellery and accessories to friends in her will, including a scarlet Chinese embroidered scarf, a diamond brooch and a three-drop diamond pendant.

Hogarth Studios, 64 Charlotte Street: the Mews' last address, where Charlotte nursed her sister Anne through her final illness. The flat they occupied (no. 7) was originally secured as a studio for Anne's painting, but over the years the sisters had many guests to tea there. A bed was first installed in the early 1920s – 'into which', Charlotte told Sydney Cockerell, 'you can turn when you lose your last train – if it's not too short!' (CMM to Sydney Cockerell, 8 March 1922)

The gravestone of Charlotte and Anne Mew in Fortune Green Cemetery, Hampstead. The inscription, from Dante's Purgatorio, reads 'Cast down the seed of weeping and attend'.

Watercolour of Charlotte Mew by her friend Dorothy Hawksley.
Painted in 1926, two years before Mew's death, this was the only
portrait she sat for.

Now she thanked Charlotte for her offer of help with the chore, told her it was 'sweet' of her, but declined the offer: 'I wouldn't put that burden on my friends.'[69]

As the days shortened towards the tail end of 1913, Charlotte's pace of publication showed no sign of letting up. But her mood plummeted – in part because of her decision, on 4 September, to quit smoking. A fortnight later she was complaining that going without cigarettes had reduced her 'to a state of misery & stupidity beggaring description'.[70] Perhaps it was Molière's comment that nobody who lives without tobacco deserves to live (*'qui vit sans tabac, n'est pas digne de vivre'*) that prompted her own theatrical pronouncement to Mrs Sappho: *'Je veux mourir'* ('I want to die').[71] Meanwhile, the 18 October issue of a new political weekly, the *New Statesman*, edited by Clifford Sharp, included a long memoir piece by her, based on the family's beloved nursemaid Elizabeth Goodman and titled 'An Old Servant'.[72] May said she admired the 'story' greatly and hoped there would be others of its kind, adding, abstrusely, '– and others, not of that sort'.[73]

In November, *The Englishwoman* featured the sixth and final piece of Charlotte's writing to be published that year: a sonnet entitled 'Péri en Mer' ('Perished at Sea').[74] She had subtitled it 'Cameret' – misspelling the town of Camaret-sur-Mer, a short day trip from Quimper, where she'd stayed with Elsie Chick on their 1909 tour of Brittany's west coast. It is a sad little poem, in which the speaker reflects on how, since her spiritual death some years earlier, she has been walking through the world as a 'homeless ghost'. She pictures her friends gathering around her deathbed, all of them unaware that her soul had died many years ago, at a moment so precise she is able to pinpoint it and bring it alive again in rich, painterly detail:

That night in summer when the gulls topped white
 The crowded masts cut black against a sky
Of fading rose – where suddenly the light
 Of Youth went out, and I, no longer I,
Climbed home, the homeless ghost I was to be.

'Péri en Mer' had been conceived around the time of Charlotte's fortieth birthday; now her younger sister had arrived at that milestone. Anne turned forty on 19 November 1913, and if she was, by this stage in life, reconciled to her lot, Charlotte still thought it a terrible iniquity. She felt her sister's talents were being frittered away on monotonous work that kept her mired in unwarranted obscurity. Anne was, she told Edith Hill, 'perfectly heroic about having no work of her own to send in anywhere – but I feel it rather keenly'.[75] The latest census schedule (for 1911) had listed Anne's occupation as 'decorative artist' – a respectable enough profession, and some might think her lucky to have her steady job with the furniture company. After all, the expressed, primary objective of her alma mater had been 'first, to enable young women of the middle class to obtain an honourable and profitable employment'.[76] But unlike the ne'er-do-well artist in Charlotte's story 'Mademoiselle' (who is similarly employed but hopelessly lazy), Anne was both industrious and talented, and – a fact that Charlotte found hard to live with – her earnings were badly needed. While Charlotte's fictional artist, Antoine, allows himself to be bankrolled by his adoring mistress, Anne's income was absolutely fundamental to keeping the family installed at their Gordon Street address.

A week before Christmas, Charlotte did consent to visit Mrs Sappho again, and apparently had such a good time that she ended up leaving far later than intended, but was duly 'punished', as she put it, by having to wait an hour at Southall station for the last train because Mrs

Sappho had given her the wrong journey times. She had told her family she'd be home by seven, and when she finally arrived, Anne and Ma were waiting up and greeted her 'in panic & dressing gowns'.[77]

In the lead-up to Christmas, she had also managed to set some time aside for embroidery, and now she sent a little linen cloth to May Sinclair, decorated with an assortment of tiny animals from land, sky and sea. The letters she sent out with her presents suggest that she had made something similar for Mrs Sappho, but with so much on her mind, she'd wrapped it up with the package that went to Edith Hill. Mrs Sappho opened her own package (full of toys for the children) two days before Christmas, and wrote to ask about one of the gifts: was the book meant for her? Charlotte replied in something of a dither:

> Yes – the book was – is – for you – but an enclosure (also for
> you) must have gone in Mrs. Hill's package of books & toys &
> I may get it back. Four days of directing envelopes & doing up
> parcels from noon till midnight – with only an hour or two's sleep
> between must be my apology for mixing things up.[78]

With all the emotions that Charlotte had experienced of late – the excitement of having her work read and admired by her contemporaries; her bewilderment at the thought that May had meant to put an end to their friendship; the sleeplessness, the garden-party socialising – it was Anne for whom she reserved her deepest feelings, and Anne's welfare that most concerned her. As Christmas drew nearer, so Anne's workload had increased, leaving her no time even to buy presents – let alone wrap them. She arrived home late on Christmas Eve, exhausted and with the beginnings of a nasty cold. Charlotte was deeply saddened by her sister's working conditions, but in practice there was very little she could do except, as she explained to Mrs Sappho, help with the consequences: 'My sister could not get an hour off from her work even on Xmas Eve – so I had to do her shopping too this year & what I could for her when she got home dreadfully fagged – & ill with a chill got by working in a freezing room. Her boss is a first-class devil.'[79]

The unfairness of Anne's situation was to cause Charlotte greater distress in the coming years than any fleeting anxiety over her friendships or her writing. At times it would become almost too much to bear. 'I am credited with a more or less indifferent front to these things,' she wrote; 'the fact is that they cut me to the heart.' [80]

14

Our Little Wind-blown Hearts

1914

It was a legend in the Mew household – or so she told Mrs Sappho – that Charlotte was 'cynically indifferent' to Christmas good wishes and parcels. That year she had received an 'alarming' heap of books, nightdress cases, diaries, hat-pins, pen-wipers and scent-bottles – 'to acknowledge as prettily as I can', she said. But Mrs Sappho's particular gift, which she'd opened on Christmas Day morning at the breakfast table, was an exception: 'It is true I have few wishes & not many needs but red china of that particular kind is a (hereditary) passion, & I suppose the chief "need" of all of us is just that generous remembrance of our real selves that you have sent me.'[1]

May Sinclair was also busy acknowledging Christmas gifts. On New Year's Day, she wrote from her Yorkshire retreat to thank Charlotte for the 'lovely & dear little cloth with its birds & beasts & fishes' that she had embroidered. May planned to be back in London in two days' time and would pay a visit to Gordon Street the following day, though Charlotte was not to stay in especially. The rest of the letter was less cheering: the American magazine, *Poetry*, had rejected the group of Charlotte's poems sent to them by Ezra Pound. It's possible the rejection had been provoked by yet another flare-up of an ongoing dispute between Pound and Harriet Monroe over the magazine's editorial policy. Delivering the news, May told her that both she and Pound were 'so disgusted' with the magazine they had ceased to have anything to do with it, although in fact Pound would continue as a roving editor for the publication for five more years.[2]

Charlotte was undeterred, and in February 1914, she completed another new poem. 'The Forest Road' is addressed to a much-loved

woman asleep in her bed – a fact that has led some critics to con-
clude that this is a lesbian love poem; but there is another, more likely,
explanation for its genesis. Mary Davidow (drawing on the informa-
tion she had gathered from Charlotte's friends and relations) stated
categorically that it sprang from the sad plight of Freda's death-in-life
existence in the Isle of Wight asylum, and from Charlotte's struggle
with leaving her there.[3] That reading makes sense of lines that other-
wise remain quite impenetrable. The physical setting is a room, where
the speaker is sitting or lying beside the poem's addressee. Beneath
the room's window is a forest road, stretching away into the distance
– and here, once again, Charlotte recycled an image she'd used pre-
viously in her prose writing. An almost identical road appears in the
article she'd published the previous March, 'Men and Trees (I)' – itself
the memory of a real road in Fontainebleau:

> But even modern, tourist Fontainebleau has not thrown off the
> forest spell. There is a village on one of the great roads where at
> nightfall the pigmy houses and their trivial lights are quite unreal.
> Nothing is real but the infinite vague road stretching away world
> without end between the infinite black wall of trees.[4]

That same wall of trees makes an appearance at the start of the
poem, except that here the line is skilfully broken in such a way as to
suggest that the 'breathless road between the walls' may – for a brief
moment in that magical hiatus at the line's end – be the walls of an
asylum corridor:

> The forest road,
> The infinite straight road stretching away
> World without end: the breathless road between the walls
> Of the black listening trees: the hushed, grey road
> Beyond the window that you shut to-night . . .

Some of this monologue is spoken directly to the sleeping woman, while other passages read as pure soliloquy. As the speaker grieves over the sleeper's enforced confinement, she revisits memories of happier, and freer, times – moments when, for instance, 'if I smiled you always ran to me. / Now you must sleep forgetfully, as children do.' It's easy to imagine Freda – almost ten years younger than Charlotte – running towards the warmth of her big sister's arms in childhood, especially now that she had reverted to a virtually childlike state. The mood of protectiveness that pervades the poem brings to mind an earlier passage from Charlotte's memoir writing. In 'Miss Bolt', she had recollected a moment when the word 'dead' was spoken for the first time in front of her other sister, Anne; on that occasion, Charlotte had instinctively 'bent and kissed the word away'.[5] The speaker of 'The Forest Road' wishes she could do the same for the appalling fear that the sleeping woman is suffering:

> . . . Oh! hidden eyes that plead in sleep
> Against the lonely dark, if I could touch the fear
> And leave it kissed away on quiet lids –
> If I could hush these hands that are half-awake,
> Groping for me in sleep I could go free.

But as the poem winds towards its close, she still hasn't managed to move beyond imagining the moment of departure:

> . . . If I could leave you there –
> If, without waking you, I could get up and reach the door – !
> We used to go together.

Once, maybe; now, they remain where they are, unhappily confined, while the speaker hears from time to time a 'singing on the road / That makes all other music like the music in a dream', calling her away. In an impassioned, if ghoulish, conclusion, it transpires that the singing is coming from the speaker's own soul. If this is indeed an asylum ward, it is not too fanciful to see the 'quivering snow' in these closing lines as the sheet under which the second woman lies sleeping – a sheet whose physical counterpart may once have been smeared with blood from Freda's suicide attempt:

> . . . Then lie you there
> Dear and wild heart behind this quivering snow
> With two red stains on it: and I will strike and tear
> Mine out, and scatter it to yours. Oh! throbbing dust,
> You that were life, our little wind-blown hearts!
>   The road! the road!
> There is a shadow there: I see my soul,
> I hear my soul, singing among the trees!

The heart is loaded with protean meaning throughout Mew's work, but perhaps nowhere quite so memorably as in 'The Forest Road'. Elsewhere, it is 'a place of palaces and pinnacles and shining towers', an architect – and receiver – of emotion but also, principally, a physical organ. The heart in a Charlotte Mew poem 'pelts and beats'; it may be 'buried', 'lame', 'slowing down', 'broken', 'wind-blown' or stilled against the 'sweet earth'. In poem after poem she reveals it to us in all its many guises: 'wild', 'guarded', 'heavy', 'empty', 'quivering', tugged at by 'tiny fingers' or 'beating in space'. But only here is the bereft speaker moved to strike and tear it out altogether; only the loss of *this* beloved impels in her the desire to fling it down alongside its 'dear and wild' companion and look on as the two throb together in the dust.

The name Freda derives from the Old Norse *fríða*, meaning 'lovely, beautiful', and from the noun *friðr*, meaning 'peace'. Freda had once been considered the loveliest of the three Mew sisters, with her calm, disarming gaze, vibrant personality and abundant chestnut-coloured hair. Now she was neither lovely nor at peace. How painful it must have been for Charlotte to 'reach the door', walk through it and leave her behind, mindful of the time when they used hardly to notice doors and doorways at all as they passed through them together, two sisters going about their ordinary business.

In spite of the anguish that is evident in 'The Forest Road', in those early months of 1914, Charlotte was generally in high spirits, though her good mood was tempered by the frustration she felt at trying, again, to do without cigarettes – '& as I write I weep!' she moaned to Mrs Sappho.[6] The attempt she'd made to give up in the autumn had evidently come to nothing. This time she immersed herself in reading. First on her list was Joseph Conrad's latest novel, *Chance*, which she was taking slowly because she couldn't bear the thought of finishing. 'Life gets lit & lifted up always when I'm reading Conrad,' she enthused.[7] There were certain passages, she said, that played over in her mind, including one in which Charles Marlow, the narrator, declares, 'Never confess! never! never! [. . .] a confession of whatever sort is always untimely. [. . .] How many sympathetic souls can you reckon on in the world? One in ten, one in a hundred – in a thousand – in ten thousand?' Charlotte had not forgotten Mrs Sappho's small but hurtful betrayal the previous summer – how her friend had bandied about her unpublished poems as if she had never been asked not to – but if Charlotte, in quoting the Conrad passage, had meant to prick Mrs Sappho's conscience, it had no effect. May had described to her Charlotte's new poem about the teenage boy at the circus, and now she was desperate to see it. Charlotte sent it, but begged her not to repeat her previous insult by passing the poem round to all her friends: 'Here is *The Fête* with comment enclosed. Please return both when read – & ne me rendez pas encore dam' ridiculous – s'il vous plait!'[8]

Mrs Sappho's successful acquisition of the poem now resulted in a display of duplicity that was remarkable even by her standards. After reading it, she asked May for her thoughts on it, and in answering that question, May was naïvely candid – both about 'The Fête' and about Charlotte's work in general:

> About Charlotte Mew: I think *The Fête* is the most wonderfully *conceived* thing that she has ever done. When she read it aloud to me I thought it the most wonderfully achieved. When I read it to myself I found it difficult & obscure, and the versification, which she made all right in her broken, dramatic manner, seemed somehow all wrong. As wrong, as faulty in structure & form as *The Farmer's Wife* [*sic*] is right, line for line & word for word. It absolutely needed her voice, her face, her intonation, & vehemence to make it carry. I think she's got to find a form which will be right without those outside aids. [. . .] But the passion & the vision & the psychology of the thing are beyond words![9]

May and Mrs Sappho had evidently been discussing Charlotte as if she were a star pupil whose rough edges it was their responsibility to knock off – and Charlotte was perhaps partly to blame in this, for putting it about that she was a poetic ingénue. But Mrs Sappho's motivation for what she did next can only be guessed at: she wasted no time in showing May's comments to Charlotte, who was unsurprisingly taken aback. Why had May written to Mrs Sappho to criticise the poem without expressing the same reservations to Charlotte? A fortnight later, to the day, May sent news from Yorkshire that Ezra Pound wanted to take 'The Fête' himself for the avant-garde magazine *The Egoist*.[10] On the subject of her own opinion of the poem, she remained silent.

The letter Charlotte wrote to May has not survived, but judging from May's reply, Charlotte must have decided to ask her outright about the comments she'd sent to Mrs Sappho. The response was embarrassingly contrite: May now bent over backwards to praise the poem. What she had thought was missing from it was never 'vision, it was not passion, it wasn't any of the great things that mark poetry

– the poem is full of them – is alive with them'. Her previous conclusion that something about 'the metric' was missing had been arrived at 'probably because I read it all wrong'; she now felt that it was 'my own ear & my own senses that were in fault', especially since 'in all your other poems that I know, yr rhythm, yr metre, the structure of yr phrases and the pace & stress were always suited to the emotion or to the picture, so it will be here'.[11]

If Mrs Sappho's motive in passing on May's private comments to Charlotte had been to create a rift, then she was to be disappointed. Charlotte acknowledged that May had not been entirely candid but told Mrs Sappho she hoped she herself could see beyond people's 'weaknesses & poses'; after all, very few people were entirely without them. She threw in a quotation from G. K. Chesterton to illustrate her point: '"we are all stricken men" one way or another,' she said; 'the only thing I have no mercy for is hardness & deadness – & this lady has been kind to me'.[12] Her balanced assessment of this incident brings to mind the moments in her writing when she steps back to present a situation from opposing sides. But while she did her best to remain level-headed, her last word on the subject betrays her irritation at Mrs Sappho's behaviour: 'I don't think there's anything quite so deadly', she told her, 'as "giving people away".'[13]

On 11 March 1914, the Mews' maid, Jane Elsain, announced 'suddenly & calmly' that she had to go home and nurse her mother, which would normally have left Charlotte with all of Jane's jobs to do, but to her great joy a 'priceless char' had turned up at just the right moment – heaven-sent, said Charlotte, 'like manna from the clouds'.[14] In spite of Mrs Sappho's underhand nature, Charlotte continued to confide in her, and she now revealed just how badly she was feeling about her sister. Her unhappiness over Anne's lack of opportunity seemed to grow in direct proportion to her own success:

I simply hate telling her about these verses – because she's had no chance whatever, & has 100 times my pluck & patience – & her own very definite gift – all going to seed – & to me its [*sic*] heart-breaking – & she would be furious if she knew I was saying it – & hasn't the least idea that I feel it acutely – so little do we people who spend our days together know each other![15]

In those pre-war years, Anne's workload was such that she rarely had time to socialise, and Charlotte found herself more than once writing to a friend on her behalf. Each time, she took great pains to ensure that the refusal should not sound like a rebuff: 'Anne is so sorry she can't come to you on Friday – but having only one free day a week she gets booked up a long while ahead – so I hope you'll give her another chance.'[16]

Meanwhile, Mrs Sappho had asked Charlotte once again to come and read for her friends in Southall. Having initially protested ('how I hate it – the performing monkey!'[17]), she gave way, though not with especially good grace: 'Tell me what time & what to wear – perhaps you'll get me a dress for the occasion!'[18] On Monday 16 March, a select group gathered in Mrs Sappho's parlour (with what Charlotte, in her teasing fashion, called its 'Railway Waiting Room idea of dec-oration'[19]) and made themselves comfortable as they settled to watch Charlotte read her poems.

The stormy weather on the journey over from Gordon Street had done nothing to calm her nerves, and her intentions to quit smok-ing had come to naught, as they often did when she had something stressful to contend with. And reading her poems aloud *was* stress-ful, because she set such great store by it: she believed that all verse gained from being spoken aloud '– & mine particularly – I suppose – because it's rough, though my ideal is Beauty'.[20] A quiet chatter went on while she sat down, placed her freshly rolled cigarettes and matches on a little table in front of her and busied herself with her papers. Among the tiny audience that day were Mrs Sappho's painter cousin, Kathie Giles, and Evelyn Underhill. As the women talked and waited, their eyes went again and again towards the tiny figure of Charlotte, neat and diminutive in her tartan skirt and black velvet jacket. At length, she looked up and, with a characteristic toss of her head and a moment's pause, began. *It is the clay that makes the earth stick to his spade . . .* The first few lines were a little hesitant, but she quickly forgot herself and, pausing to smoke between poems – and sometimes between stanzas – she gave them 'In Nunhead Cemetery', 'Pécheresse', 'The Fête', 'The Quiet House' and a handful of others. The room had fallen absolutely quiet, and now and then a sniff could be heard as one or other of the listeners stifled a sob. 'I think this ought to be a marked day in all our lives,' Mrs Sappho wrote afterwards in her diary. 'It was an enchanting hour!' At the end of it all, Evelyn Underhill turned to her hostess and pronounced her verdict: 'Magnificent!' Beyond that, she was lost for words.[21]

Buttoning up her coat in the entrance hall, Kathie Giles told her cousin, 'I will go to the ends of the earth any time to hear your Charlotte tell her poems – she is a modern piper, and I will follow her piping.'[22] A few days later, Mrs Sappho received a letter from Evelyn:

> My dear Mrs. Scott, I feel as if I departed yesterday without thanking you, but really an hour with Miss Mew is like having whiskey with one's tea – my feet were clean off the floor! Heavens, what a tempest she produced – the most truly creative person I have ever come near. [. . .] I hope to heaven I shall be able to make Scott-James print her stuff.[23]

Journalist and critic Rolfe Scott-James was at that time editor of the highly regarded *New Weekly*, and Evelyn Underhill would stay true to her word.

May Sinclair hadn't been at the Southall reading, but Charlotte had read a few poems aloud to her in private, and she was as impressed as everybody else: 'you read furiously well: I never knew anybody who cd. get out the passion of a thing as you can,' she told Charlotte.[24] That month while she was up in Yorkshire once again, May received news that a buyer had been found for her place in Kensington. It was partly the noise of practising musicians in neighbouring studios that had made a bolthole necessary in the first place, and she was determined that her next house would be, above all else, somewhere quiet. She told Charlotte she was on the lookout 'for part of a house where there are no musicians' and which cost no more than £50 or £60. Would Charlotte let her know if she heard of anything that fitted the bill?[25]

Charlotte – ever keen to help – set to work, scouring the papers and then visiting a shortlist of properties to check they were in a suitably quiet neighbourhood. When she reported back on her findings a few days later, May was horrified: it was, she said, 'perfectly angelic of you to go & take all that awful bother', but 'I never dreamed of even hinting that you sd. run round, I only thought that perhaps you might hear of something and let me know. [. . .] And all my days I shall be haunted by a vision of you, small, & too fragile by far for the hideous task, going up and down those infernal houses.'[26] What she'd neglected to tell Charlotte the first time round was that she had other friends 'scouring St John's Wood' for her, and that there was already a tentative plan to share a house there with the daughter of one of them, if the right place could be found.[27] And found it was: a neat little Georgian house on the corner of Blenheim Road and Abbey Road, near the future site of the famous recording studio. May arrived back in Kensington in mid-March and began the arduous process of packing up house ready to move. 'When I'm settled,' she told Charlotte, 'I hope you will come and see me.'[28]

Evelyn Underhill had been so impressed by Charlotte's reading at Mrs Sappho's house that on Monday 30 March, she visited her at home in Gordon Street, most likely with a view to gathering poems to send to Rolfe Scott-James for the *New Weekly*. Charlotte took the opportunity to read aloud 'The Forest Road'. As Evelyn listened, she said she *thought* she liked it, but 'couldn't quite take it in at a first reading', and asked if she could keep hold of it for a while.[29] Writing to Mrs Sappho two days later, Charlotte revealed this was her 'first attempt at unrhymed stuff' and gave her own verdict on the poem: 'I don't care for it,' she announced – although with what degree of sincerity it's hard to know.[30] When Evelyn had spent some time with the poem, she decided that on second thoughts *she* didn't care for it either. Mrs Sappho liked it very much and told Charlotte that her doctor husband thought it so deeply realised he was convinced the writer must herself be mad – a verdict Charlotte found hilarious: 'a professional point of view,' she quipped to Ethel Oliver.[31]

Sharing her poetry with literary friends and acquaintances was useful if Charlotte wanted it to be published, but she found the resulting hullabaloo oppressive – opinions and offers to help place the poems flying this way and that – and by now she was feeling the need to get away again. A repeat of her trip to Dieppe the previous Easter would be ideal. She bought herself a ferry ticket for 4 April, and asked Mrs Sappho if she'd like to bring Marjorie or Christopher over for the following weekend so that they'd be there for Easter Sunday. Having made these arrangements, there seemed to be a hundred and one things to do before leaving – a heap of letters to answer 'about people's oculists & landladies',[32] and Elsie Chick's MA thesis on Middle English poetry, which Charlotte had promised to look over. She finally got around to that three days before she set off.[33]

Her second-class cabin, in a new English boat called the *Paris*, was 'quite luxurious – done up in chintz & really airy'[34] – which was just as well because the sea was far from calm. When she got to the Hotel du Commerce, she found Clemence, the chambermaid who had looked after her the previous year, still there, and it took her no time at all to settle into holiday mode. This time her room had a rooftop view that was perfect for her old habit of people-watching by the window: 'by sitting on trunk or window ledge I see the place – as pleasing as ever,' she told Ethel Oliver.[35] While the weather was lousy, it seemed as good an occupation as any. But Charlotte couldn't have cared less about the weather: she was simply 'glad of the quiet – doing or doing nothing as one likes'.[36]

Even at this distance, though, she hadn't quite managed to escape the noise her startling new poems had generated; the difference was that here she felt blissfully unconcerned by it. She had recently heard from Evelyn Underhill that Rolfe Scott-James wanted to take some of the poems she'd sent him. Charlotte was pleased, of course, but in her 'more or less somnolent state', the complicated business of publishing poems seemed very far away.[37] She was, she confessed to Mrs Sappho, 'in a mild state of stupour [sic] for the moment & can't believe I ever wrote any'.[38]

When the weather cleared and she ventured out into the streets of Dieppe, she was soon engaging with the locals again. While standing around on a corner near the harbour, she was invited into a little raftered room in an eighteenth-century house where people of assorted ages were making nets: '5 very old & one middle-aged/young woman & 2 year old son & the young sailor'. She stayed chatting with them for the rest of the afternoon. In this unadorned room, with its straightforward, purposeful activity and its 'shelves packed with twine & lamps hanging from the rafters & everyone so simple & friendly',[39] she was in her element. She could think of no better place to be. And place was unusually important to Charlotte Mew, both as a private person and as a writer. It was also a major stimulus for her work: 'I should never have done "The Fête" verse if I hadn't been here last year,'[40] she reflected to Ethel, and to Mrs Sappho she said that 'One realises the place much more alone, I think – it's all there & you don't feel it through another mind which mixes up things.'[41] That level of focus – which Charlotte found only when she was by herself – was fundamental to her creative process; she might wish it otherwise but knew by now that 'we can't choose the working of it'. The problem was that her sharpened perceptions led to a crushing sense of hopelessness if she found herself unable to create something from them. 'Probably if I don't get to work,' she confided to Ethel, with poignant self-awareness, 'I shall have a fit of the usual blues.'[42]

So far her mood had been remarkably tranquil. Beneath her window there was 'a continual patter of feet & pipe of little voices [. . .] which makes me think of Toby – who would go out in a boat with me if he were here – no one else would get me into one!'[43] Once again it was the company of children she craved – their lack of complexity and their inexhaustible capacity for fun. In the poor quarter of the town, she had come across a group of fishermen's children playing a game chalked out in numbered circles and squares, and asked them to explain the rules – 'which they did very sweetly & politely' – for which she thanked them with a silver piece and instructions to buy some sweets with it.[44] Mrs Sappho's children never did come to Dieppe (plans had already been made for them to be in Cornwall that Easter), but Charlotte arrived home to two boxes of cowslips, which they had collected for her from the seaside. She told them the flowers would remind her 'not only of Cornish cliffs – but French cliffs – where at Dieppe they were growing – all gold – on the steepest slopes'. She wished she could be there with them now, or in Cornwall, 'poking about chimney pots & putting my nose – with a lighted candle (not on my nose!) into caves with you. If you would have let me? but instead I have some beastly business to see through here – my sister in bed from over work – & a dull dinner party thrown in tonight.'[45]

At the start of spring, Charlotte suggested calling in on May Sinclair with Mrs Sappho so that they could see the new house in St John's Wood together, but May had other ideas, confiding to Charlotte that 'I'd ever so much rather see you when you were by yr.self.'[46] And with that, she invited Charlotte to supper the following Saturday, 9 May. 'The Fête' had just been published in *The Egoist*, and May was still feeling contrite about her criticisms of the poem. Supper would be the perfect opportunity to tell Charlotte 'how entirely I admire [it] now that I see it in print'.[47] Doing so might have been awkward with Mrs Sappho present, since May had given her an altogether different verdict on the poem. In her anxiety to make amends, May now went even more overboard with her praise, claiming that, on reflection, she thought it 'one of the best, if not *the* best thing you have done yet; & that is the highest praise that can be given it'. She signed off 'Till S— and After', making it as plain as possible that she very much wanted to continue seeing Charlotte.[48]

From her earliest days of acquaintance with Mrs Sappho, Charlotte had expressed a fear of getting involved with 'complicated' people, and when Mrs Sappho had shown her May's criticism of 'The Fête', it had seemed to her that May was one of the most complicated of all. During the course of that Saturday evening supper, some sort of awkward discussion took place, in which Charlotte asked May a direct question. We don't know what that question was, but we do know that, for the time being, May left it unanswered. It seems likely that the two women would have talked about May's changing reaction to the poem at some length. By now, a discomfiting note of mistrust had evidently entered the relationship: the smallest misunderstandings could lead to tedious discussions about what had really been meant. May felt the need to defend herself against the charge of complication; in fact, she thought *Charlotte* was the complicated one, and wrote afterwards to say so:

Not by way of an 'answer' but as a general statement, may I assure you that I really have *not* a complicated mind, but in some ways rather a simple one, & when I say 'I want to walk with you to Baker St. Station,' I mean I want to *walk*, & I want to walk with *you*, and I want to walk to Baker St. Station. The act of walking is a pleasure in itself, that has no ulterior purpose or significance.

Better to take things simply & never go back on them or analyse them, isn't it?

I (who am so complicated) took it all quite simply & was glad of it – of your being here, of yr talking to me – well, why can't you do the same?

The rest of the letter was more chatty. The new house considered itself 'honoured and blessed', May said, 'by yr. having come to it'.[49] Her comment about walking to Baker Street might have been no more than a figurative illustration of her 'simple' turn of mind; or she might actually have asked Charlotte if she could accompany her on the half-hour walk from the house to the station. If so, had Charlotte interpreted an offer of company as an expression of romantic interest? And did it lead, as Penelope Fitzgerald has suggested, to some kind of pass being made? 'What is certain', writes Fitzgerald, 'is that there was an uncontrolled physical confession of furious longing, desiring and touching which terrified May' – an assertion that seems to have originated in gossip.[50] The letters themselves contain no suggestion of a confession – still less an advance. Whatever did or did not occur that evening, May's annoyance did not last long or go very deep: she asked Charlotte to 'try [her] luck again on Tuesday 19th, 4.30, when I've asked the Aldingtons & Evelyn Stuart-Moore' – try her luck, that is (presumably), with getting an answer to her question.

Charlotte's poetry continued to flourish. At the end of May, 'Fame' was published in the *New Weekly*; in June, another new poem, 'On the Road to the Sea', appeared in *The Englishwoman*; and the following month, the *New Weekly* featured its second Charlotte Mew poem, 'Pécheresse' ('The Sinner') – about an abandoned lover who remains ruinously faithful, and waits at the quayside thinking of nothing else but her 'one night [. . .] one short grey day' of intimacy.

In September, she produced an intriguing short lyric entitled 'Smile, Death', which may not merit particular attention were it not for the fact that it provides the best evidence we have of Mew's working methods. Remarks she made to friends suggest that she carried poems in her head before committing them to paper. During the summer of 1913, for instance, she had told both Edith Hill and Mrs Sappho that she had in mind then things that were 'rather unmanageable, and possibly too big to pull off'.[51] She left behind no rough drafts of poems in their early stages; these she presumably destroyed. Perhaps they formed the scrawled-on paper spills that Alida and Anne had watched her rolling up and feeding into the parrot's cage.[52]

However, a few handwritten manuscripts do exist which show poems near – not quite in – their final form. 'Smile, Death' is the most detailed example. What makes this particular document special is that it is accompanied by a corrected typescript and a final, clean typescript, so that we're able to see the poem in two interim stages. The handwritten draft is copied out neatly with a thick-nibbed fountain pen, in blue ink, as if Charlotte intended it to be legible enough for her typist to read. From these three documents it's possible to piece together a history of the poem's making as it found its way towards its final form.

In 1904, Charlotte had remarked on the 'power of vivid personification' demonstrated by Emily Brontë in 'Self-Interrogation'. The third stanza of that poem begins 'Time stands before the door of Death, / Upbraiding bitterly'. In these lines, said Charlotte, 'The massive figures of Time and Death – two familiar deities – stand visibly before us, and we are confronted by a picture that Watts [British symbolist painter G. F. Watts] might well have painted: abstractions take shape and force themselves upon our vision almost before they can arrest our thought.'[53]

But Brontë's image pales alongside the chilling characterisation in Charlotte's lyric, in which death is personified as a fellow skater, come to speed the speaker out of this world and into the next. On 17 September 1914, Charlotte sat down to write out that first neat draft of the poem, and in the opening line, she gives Death a face and commands it to smile:

Smile, Death, I shall smile as I come to you

The opening words had fallen instinctively into a loose, mainly dactylic pentameter ('*Smile, Death,* I shall *smile* as I *come* to *you*'). As the poem found its way, that bouncy metre took a firmer hold in the second line:

Straight from the *road* & the *moor* I must *leave* be*hind*

This worked well – each stressed foot like the physical foot of the skater pushing off as the speaker pictures herself going smilingly to meet her ruinous escort. But now what she wanted to convey was the majesty of the moor's wide open space, and for that, the dactyls and neat pentameter of the opening lines were all wrong. She switched instead to a longer, predominantly iambic line:

Nothing on this great earth was ever like that wind-swept space

This was close, but when she'd finished writing the poem out, she came back to the line again. Reading the whole thing through, the rhythm here sounded frustratingly uneven. She crossed out the word 'ever'. It seemed to her, too, that 'wind-swept' struck a false note: it suggested desolation, but this was a place the speaker had cherished, a place far from the cluttered confinement of human existence; from deadlines, decisions and unpaid bills, friendships, and chores to be done. The moor was a place where all this could be lifted away in an instant by the wind: it wasn't so much windswept as wind*blown*. She drew a line through 'wind-swept' and wrote the new word in neatly over the top. With these two amendments in place, she was satisfied enough to pass it on for typing.

It was only after she had collected the poem from her typist's office (opposite the British Museum) that the poem settled into its final, chilling form, for it was at this stage that she made a number of amendments that, though small, at once heightened the poem's sense of immediacy and overall force. Writing less neatly this time and in a different pen, with a finer nib, she scored firmly through the word 'shall' in the first line, and with that one deletion she reframed the whole poem in the present tense. Death was waiting for the speaker *right now* – watching as she skated willingly towards it – and if it was watching, then she would welcome its gaze:

Smile, Death, see I smile as I come to you

That insertion of 'see' – inviting, as it does, Death's undivided attention – is disquieting, but the most unnerving moment in the poem comes in the penultimate line, when we learn that the expression on Death's face is not, as we might have expected, one of menace or unthinking evil but of *kindness*. Charlotte now made the odd, but brilliant, decision to place the line in parenthesis, as if it were merely an aside; she then added an exclamation mark to communicate the speaker's surprise – and allow the reader to share in it. The poem would remain unpublished during her lifetime, but its two short stanzas made a thrilling addition to her posthumous collection, *The Rambling Sailor*:

Smile, Death, see I smile as I come to you
Straight from the road and the moor that I leave behind,
Nothing on earth to me was like this wind-blown space,
Nothing was like the road, but at the end there was a vision or a face
   And the eyes were not always kind.

  Smile, Death, as you fasten the blades to my feet for me,
On, on let us skate past the sleeping willows dusted with snow;

Fast, fast down the frozen stream, with the moor and the road and
the vision behind,
(Show me your face, why the eyes are kind!)
And we will not speak of life or believe in it or remember it as we go.

Anne was coming home from work ill more and more often, and that
spring of 1914, she finally decided she'd had enough: 'she couldn't phys-
ically stand it any longer,' Charlotte told Mrs Sappho, and now they
wanted to spread the word that Anne was available for lessons in draw-
ing and painting. She had already signed up her first pupil – a lady who
worked in the music halls and was, said Charlotte, 'all hat & sealskin
outside & general grub underneath'.[54] Freedom from her furniture job
would make a tremendous difference to Anne, both in terms of her
health and her creativity: by the end of June, she was happily working
on a commission which left her no time to take on some suitable work
that Mrs Sappho had seen advertised in the *Pall Mall Gazette*.[55]

The commission must have gone some way towards easing Charlotte's
uneasiness over her own continuing success and the social engagements
that occasionally accompanied it. In early June, May invited her to the
Women Writers Dinner, due to take place on the 22nd of that month.
She wrote from Yorkshire to explain that she'd been left with spare tick-
ets after two American friends had pulled out at the last moment. In this
and every subsequent letter, May addressed her as 'My dear Charlotte'
– and if she would consent to come, May told her, her attendance would
'rob the occasion of much of its horror'.[56] Now celebrating its silver jubi-
lee, this year's event was to be held at the opulent Criterion restaurant
in Piccadilly. In the meantime, May planned to be back in St John's
Wood on Wednesday 17th and would be free of work by the weekend, if
Charlotte should care to come over to her on the Saturday. Charlotte did
care to, and she also agreed to the jubilee dinner, a carefully orchestrated
occasion where guests were encouraged to read through the 'Hints on

Etiquette' printed on the back of the table plans before going in to din-
ner. She found herself among those advised that they should refrain
from smoking until after the royal toasts had been made.[57]

In contrast with the warmth of May's letters to Charlotte, a fragment
reported from Mrs Sappho's diary suggests May resented Charlotte's
attention on at least one occasion during that summer of 1914. I have
been unable to trace the diary for this period; the entry exists only in
quoted form in Marjorie Watts's biography of her mother, *Mrs Sappho*.[58]
According to Watts, Charlotte spent the afternoon and evening of 12 July
(three weeks after the Women Writers Dinner) with May at her house
in St John's Wood, and Mrs Sappho learned something about her after-
wards that horrified her: she noted in her diary that night that 'Charlotte
has been bothering and annoying May.'[59] The entry goes on to reflect
more generally on the relationship between genius and sexual desire:

> All the geniuses I have met have been unsound sexually . . . Ella
> d'Arcy was immensely over-sexed, practically a prostitute.
> Charlotte is evidently a pervert. Is then genius merely one form of
> sex? Genius creates, just as sex does, and in genius perhaps the sex
> instinct is always atrophied, flawed, damaged, because all the real
> stuff is gone into the genius.[60]

If the quotation can be taken at face value, then precisely how
Charlotte had been 'bothering and annoying' May must remain a
matter of conjecture. All we know is that Mrs Sappho considered the
behaviour perverted – although given that Mrs Sappho's daughter
described her as 'sexually inhibited and naïve', it may not have taken
much to shock her.[61] If Charlotte had indeed made a pass at May, that
would no doubt have been enough to offend Mrs Sappho's narrow sen-
sibilities. At any rate, from this date regular correspondence between
Mrs Sappho and Charlotte ceased abruptly. Charlotte and May, on the
other hand, continued to meet and to write to each other as usual.

15

This Dark Ditch, the Soul of Me!

1914–1915

At 11 p.m. on 4 August 1914, Britain announced it was at war. The declaration came after Germany failed to give an assurance that it would respect the neutrality of Belgium, as an independent kingdom, and then proceeded to invade it. 'Germany tried to bribe us with peace to desert our friends and duty,' the *Daily Mail* reported the following morning. 'But Great Britain has preferred the path of honour.'[1] The country was plunged into a frenzy of patriotic fervour as Britain's army and navy were mobilised, and reserve battalions and regiments sprang up everywhere. 'TO THE MANHOOD OF BRITAIN', bellowed one headline, in an appeal to the nation's menfolk. 'The whole Empire is ringing with the call to arms.'[2]

James Chick, brother of the seven Chick sisters, was among the first to enlist. He went out to France in September and worked as a non-commissioned officer throughout the war, rising to the position of company quartermaster sergeant. His bravery in Flanders would earn him a Meritorious Service Medal.[3] His sister Dorothy wasn't far behind him. She had only recently qualified as a surgeon, but in January 1915, she would leave for the Serbian front, as part of Mrs Berry's Anglo-Serbian Medical Unit.[4] Gilbert Mew, the youngest of Charlotte's Isle of Wight cousins, was living in Canada when war broke out. He signed up as a private with the 8th Battalion Canadian Infantry, went out to France in February 1915 and was wounded in the Vimy Ridge assault on the first day of the Battle of Arras in 1917. He died four months later from his injuries and is buried in Béthune Military Cemetery.

May Sinclair was also swept up in the early war fervour. Ever the joiner, she wasted no time in enlisting for work with a volunteer ambulance corps that had been set up by one of the board members of the Medico-Psychological Clinic, Dr Hector Munro. For a short while she did what she could in Belgium, distributing food to the crowds of refugees in Ghent and assisting with the wounded. But she was so ill suited to the task that after just seventeen days Dr Munro sent her home and wrote to the War Office to ask them 'not to allow her to rejoin'.[5]

In due course, Charlotte too would play her own small part in the war effort, but for the time being, the declaration of war barely registered in her all-female household and life went on much as before. The thought of leaving Ma and Anne to fend for themselves while she threw herself into some dangerous scheme to support the troops was, in any case, inconceivable. May would go on to fictionalise her own wartime experiences in Belgium, but she never talked about them to Charlotte, who received a postcard from her that Christmas that read, simply, 'All good wishes for Xmas & New Year.'[6] At the end of December, Charlotte heard from a friend, Blanche Crackanthorpe, that her son Oliver had come home wounded from the front just a week before Christmas. Letting him go for a second time would be hard to bear: 'When our men went forth we knew nothing of trench-life,' Blanche confided; '& now we know, we ask ourselves how are we going to stand the second starting & parting.'[7] Thus began Charlotte's first-hand knowledge of the catalogue of sons, husbands and fathers who went off to fight and failed, so often, to return.

She nonetheless began the New Year of 1915 in good spirits, and with a determination to be as helpful to her friends as they had been to her. Her particular skills were currently much in demand: the war, it seems, had made a poet of everyone. At the start of January, Charlotte sat down to write a considered response to a short lyric that Edith Hill had sent her – a response that would be, she began, 'chiefly on the technique, as given the quality of emotion – the first requirement of poetry – it seems a pity this should suffer for a certain want of it, when it can be got with work and patience'.[8] Two years earlier, she had told Mrs Sappho, 'I read next to no poetry & understand less.'[9] The detailed critique she now offered Edith Hill gave the lie to that claim once and for all:

> So, first, I notice that rhyming the last 2 lines you haven't done this with the 2 first – perhaps permissible – though it gives an effect of carelessness & as the whole is written in 4-lined, & not free, verse I think the last 2, though uneven, might better be equally uneven, i.e. having the same number of syllables; while you have 12. 18. 16. 20. etc etc. [. . .] You certainly give, as you mean to, a strong sense of loss & sacrifice – even though, if I may say so, the personal seems rather to overshadow the universal i.e. the sense of fellowship with other women [. . .] And then too, I think however strong the emotion is, one ought to test it – asking oneself here, whether in fact 'wounded & missing' justifies the same measure of despair as 'killed in action' which might eventually be denied to the wounded & missing who often get back [. . .] All this, I fear, sounds very carping mais j'ai passé par là & know how one is carried away, and at the same time if one is to do good work one must accept the discipline which can be got, while the emotion is given to one, & shouldn't be sacrificed to the lack of it.[10]

She appears to have been far gentler on May Sinclair when she turned up at Gordon Street on 3 January with a poem she had written in French. Anne was out of the house at the time – 'spending a cruelly wet weekend at Berkhamsted' with Maggie and Edward Browne – and the three hours Charlotte and May spent alone together passed quickly in earnest discussion and light-hearted joshing.[11] But if May's intention had been to impress Charlotte with her poem, the attempt fell rather flat: Charlotte immediately detected in May's offering an unmistakable echo of Verlaine's 'Sagesse' ('Wisdom'), which ends with the following quatrain:

> Qu'as-tu fait, ô toi que voilà
> Pleurant sans cesse,
> Dis, qu'as-tu fait, toi que voilà,
> De ta jeunesse?

The lines might be translated as 'What have you done, you there, constantly crying, tell me, what have you done with your youth?' May's poem – also composed of four quatrains and also structured in tetrameter alternated with shorter lines, similarly rhymed *abab* – was titled 'La Morte' ('The Dead Woman'). It begins:

> Qu'avez-vous de vos beaux jours, ma chère,
> Les jours qui vous aimaient?
> Et de vos joies, les âpres, les amères,
> Qu'avez vous fait?[12]

The metre of May's opening is less precise than the Verlaine and her French is not quite correct. The first line is missing a main verb, but the general sense might be rendered, 'What have you done, my dear one, with your best days, the days that loved you? And what of your joys, the keen ones and the bitter ones? What have you made of those?'[13] With Charlotte's help, she rewrote the verse, inserting a main verb in the first line, and altering the second line to a simpler and more affecting sentiment:

> Qu'avez-vous fait de vos beaux jours, ma chère,
> Vos jours qui sont passés?[14]

('What have you done, my dear one, with your best days, your days that have passed?')

When Charlotte had pointed out the resemblance to Verlaine, May was initially evasive. She left Gordon Street that afternoon with a copy of Charlotte's *French Poets* and a greatly heightened regard for her friend's poetic powers. Three days later, she came close to admitting the Verlaine influence, though she maintained that the imitation was subconscious: 'there's no doubt that that verse – that perfect verse – of Verlaine's must have been the thing that haunted me, so that my poor verses haven't even the merit of originality!'[15]

Charlotte had thoroughly enjoyed working with May on her poem, and had taken the opportunity to read aloud the start of a remarkable new poem of her own, 'Madeleine in Church'. May was bowled over by what she heard: this latest poem contained, she said, 'depths & depths of passion & of sheer beauty' and she was anxious that Charlotte should go on with it.[16] 'Finish – finish yr. Courtisan [*sic*]. She's magnificent. The last verses are all there – coiled up in a lobe of yr. brain asleep & waiting to be waked – just like darling Tommy in his basket. Possibly you'll hear them stirring in their sleep & soon after the poem will finish itself.'[17]

The intensity of May's enthusiasm was understandable. 'Madeleine in Church' takes the standard Victorian trope of the usually silent 'fallen woman' and gives her a voice, so that instead of deliberations on the nature of female debauchery, we get one particular woman's point of view as she reflects on her past relationships with a series of lovers – Monty, Stuart, Redge, Jim . . . Madeleine directs her words to God but speaks them from a candlelit corner of the church, far from the altar and its imposing crucifix:

> Here, in the darkness, where this plaster saint
>   Stands nearer than God stands to our distress,
> And one small candle shines, but not so faint
>   As the far lights of everlastingness
> I'd rather kneel than over there, in open day
>   Where Christ is hanging, rather pray
>   To something more like my own clay . . .

The impression, right from these opening lines, is that we are eaves-dropping on the woman's private thoughts as her mind jumps from one insight or memory to the next. Those lifelike vacillations account in part for the poem's length (at 222 lines, this is the longest of all Charlotte Mew's poems); but the philosophical content is artfully single-minded, focusing on a handful of key ideas: the comfort of religious faith, the price of over-indulgence and the difficulty of relating to a God who seems distant and elusive even in incarnate form –

> Oh! quiet Christ who never knew
> The poisonous fangs that bite us through
> And make us do the things we do . . .

Madeleine's question is not so much 'How can I perceive You?' as 'How can You perceive *me?*'

> God holds You, and You hang so high,
> Though no one looking long at You,
> Can think You do not suffer too,
> But, up there, from your still, star-lighted tree
> What can You know, what can You really see
> Of this dark ditch, the soul of me!

Her persistent envisioning of Christ as almost (though 'not quite') human makes Him seem immediately more accountable, and more deserving of her anger – a stance that Charlotte herself adopted and would hold right up to the end of her life. In this poem, she takes the ubiquitous image of Jesus as shepherd to His erring flock and interrogates it: yes, we might indeed return to His fold, 'like any flock of baa-ing sheep', but only once He has 'shorn, led us to slaughter, torn the bleating soul in us to rags'. What our souls are bleating for, says Madeleine, is life itself, in all its sensual vibrancy – 'The thick, close voice of musk, / The jessamine music on the thin night air, / Or, sometimes, my own hands about me anywhere', 'the lights, the colours, the perfumes', the 'gemlike wines', 'the scent in every red and yellow rose /

Of all the sunsets'. To illuminate the question of Christ's responsibility, the shadowy figure of Mary Magdalene – normally consigned to a bit-part – is set centre stage as a living, passionate woman:

> How old was Mary out of whom You cast
> So many devils? Was she young or perhaps for years
> She had sat staring, with dry eyes, at this and that man going past
> Till suddenly she saw You on the steps of Simon's house
> And stood and looked at You through tears.

In an extraordinarily intimate portrayal of the scene in which Mary Magdalene washes Jesus's feet, Madeleine pictures 'the wet cheek lying there' on the bare foot; and how afterwards Mary's perfume must have clung to Jesus 'from head to feet all through the day' as He went about his business. 'Madeleine in Church' shows Mew using her exceptional imaginative gifts to dazzling effect, writing with a power and assurance that she herself could hardly have foreseen in the days of her well-mannered 'V. R. I' sonnets.

From the outset, Charlotte had declared this new poem 'possibly too big to pull off',[18] and she had clearly been struggling to find an ending for it. Without May's encouragement at this critical juncture, who knows if the task might finally have defeated her? Given the strength of feeling that had developed between the two women, May's enthusiasm would perhaps have counted for more than anyone else's. The ending of the poem, when it came, reiterated Charlotte's personal belief that as humans we are all physical beings before we are anything else, set apart from each other by the degree to which we experience – or allow ourselves to experience – the physical life. *Sentio ergo sum*: I feel, therefore I am. In Charlotte's time, it was generally believed that prostitutes were the victims of their own rapacious sexual appetites; her Madeleine may not be a prostitute, but she is certainly a fallen woman, in the Victorian sense, a woman who has lived her life delighting in sex and other sensual pleasures, and for that, she remains resolutely unrepentant. Through all her enquiries and uncertainties, Madeleine's refusal to 'be content with the tame, bloodless things' or to apologise for her own human nature remains intact. It's from that position of defiance that she is finally able to say of her namesake, Mary Magdalene: 'She was a sinner, we are what we are: the spirit afterwards, but first, the touch.'

As elsewhere in her work, Charlotte's religious interest here is almost wholly confined to the second person of the Trinity; in this poem she addresses him directly, in an incriminating second-person voice, driving that 'You' home by repeating it in quick succession and echoing the word in pulsing full rhymes ('knew', 'through', 'do', 'too'). When, in the final stanza, she resorts to 'He', we read it as a signal of her disillusionment. In the end, her Madeleine is unable to be consoled by the divine because she is too distressed by Jesus's meek acceptance of his physical death – and by his refusal or inability to acknowledge her own existence:

> I cannot bear to look at this divinely bent and gracious head:
> When I was small I never quite believed that He was dead:
> And at the Convent school I used to lie awake in bed
> Thinking about His hands. It did not matter what they said,
> He was alive to me, so hurt, so hurt! And most of all in Holy Week
> When there was no one else to see
> I used to think it would not hurt me too, so terribly,
> If He had ever seemed to notice me
> Or, if, for once, He would only speak.

'Madeleine in Church' was not the first dramatic monologue voiced by a fallen woman. Among its predecessors were Christina Rossetti's 'The Convent Threshold' (1858) and Dora Greenwell's 'Christina' (written in 1851, though not published until 1861). Augusta Webster's 'A Castaway' (1870) broke new ground by blurring the usual distinctions between good and evil, civilised and depraved; it is a poem which, as Angela Leighton has pointed out, ghosts at least one passage spoken by Mew's Madeleine.[19] But nobody brings this Victorian trope quite so vividly – or humanly – to life as Mew does in her drifting and richly evocative *tour de force*, in which the artful vagaries of metre and thought seem forged by spontaneous emotion, the sentiment born of a fierceness that is all Mew's own. Most significantly, her Madeleine stands alone in remaining throughout utterly unrepentant; she has no need of – or desire for – redemption. The poem resonated strongly with readers once it was published, and perhaps especially with female readers, some of whom were haunted by individual lines. Six years later, a new friend of Charlotte, Florence Hardy (wife of Thomas), would write to tell her that 'In our little conservatory for two years I have grown white geraniums because of two lines in "Madeleine in Church". I had never seen "the dreams upon the eyes of white geraniums in the dusk" before.'[20]

The war showed no signs of ending early, as many had anticipated it might. Now that the winter months of early 1915 gave way to spring, the turning of the seasons took on an extra poignancy. Towards the end of March, *The Bystander*'s woman-about-town, 'Blanche', wrote a fictional letter to her cousin in the colonies, in which she wondered aloud about the effects of spring in war-torn Belgium:

SPRING, Spring, beautiful Spring – it's here, really and truly here, and sweet as only Spring in England can be – even in wartime. It arrived in the Park last Sunday week. [. . .] Nature takes no account of even war, and she's as busy as ever with her yearly work of re-clothing the world in a soft green gown of ravishing beauty except, I suppose, in those dreary and desolate places that the fires of war have scorched and blasted. And even there she is trying her hardest, and not altogether vainly: you can see catkins on the trees and buds on the bushes even here and there in the firing line, so they tell me.[21]

The Bystander was one of several weekly tabloids that had soared in popularity since the outbreak of war, and whether Charlotte saw this particular feature or not, towards the end of May she expressed the same idea, with rather more originality and economy, in a poem that was initially titled 'Spring, 1915':

> Let us remember Spring will come again
> To the scorched blackened woods where all the wounded trees
> Wait, with the old wise patience for the heavenly rain . . .

This short poem, nine lines in total, ends with the arresting image of the bereaved sitting with their 'great Dead, hands in their hands, eyes in their eyes', utterly blind to the changing seasons around them.

On 31 May 1915, after several failed attempts, the first bombs from Zeppelin airships dropped on London – 120 altogether. Seven people were killed, thirty-five injured, and forty-one fires were started. Standing close to King's Cross and Euston stations, Gordon Street was at high risk of attack, but for the time being, Bloomsbury was spared. Meanwhile, even the village of Reeth, deep in the Yorkshire countryside, had prepared itself for Zeppelins: 'No lights allowed to show in the village or the country round!' May Sinclair told Charlotte.[22] But still she found the place 'heavenly': she had recently been walking on nearby Fremington Edge when a foal came tentatively over to her outstretched hand and began nuzzling and sucking her fingers, and then 'laid its darling muzzle in my hand. [. . .] Well, well – there's a War, & when I think of it I think: what a place for German artillery along Fremington Edge!'[23]

London did not seem quite so heavenly, nor quite such an unlikely target. Late in the evening of 8 September 1915, Charlotte may have heard, as others did, the eerie throbbing of a Zeppelin flying over Bloomsbury, its bulk blotting out the night stars. A circular paved area in Queen Square commemorates the spot where the first of several bombs exploded that night.[24] No one in the vicinity was injured, but the explosion blew out hundreds of windows, filling the streets with broken glass. A little further east, more bombs lit up the skies as buildings burned and flames leapt as high as the dome of St Paul's.[25] The 1915 Zeppelin raids were the first of their kind in Britain, and they had a deeply unsettling effect on those who lived through them. Returning to Bloomsbury after one such bombardment, and finding her neighbour's house in ruins, American poet H.D. (Hilda Doolittle) described the scene: 'We came home and simply waded through glass, while wind from now unshuttered windows made the house a barn, an unprotected dugout,' she wrote to Norman Holmes Pearson. 'What does that sort of shock do to the mind, the imagination – not solely of myself, but of an epoch?'[26]

By the time of the September bombardments, Charlotte had already written a second war poem. Perhaps as a consequence of the 31 May Zeppelin raids, 'June, 1915', written just days after 'Spring, 1915' (now retitled 'May, 1915'), is less straightforwardly optimistic than its sister poem. It bemoans the indifference of the 'broken world' to the thrill of early roses appearing: in the poem, nothing could be further from the minds of wartime Londoners, as they go about their business among the 'veiled lamps of town'. When we encounter a shiny-haired child, he seems at first a troubling embodiment of innocence: entirely unaware of the horrors of war, he is reaching up to pick the first rose of June in some 'green sunny lane', far out in the countryside. But the last two lines effect an abrupt volte-face and transfigure the child into a moving emblem of hope:

Or what's the broken world to June and him
Of the small eager hand, the shining eyes, the rough bright head?

Lines like these, unashamedly emotive as they are, were out of kil-
ter with the ideals of the fashionable Imagists, whose poems were
tightly pared back in terms of both sentiment and verbiage. But in one
respect 'June, 1915' accords closely with the principles of Imagism: the
preference for the telling concrete detail over abstractions. In focusing
on the single image of a child reaching towards a rose, Charlotte's
new poem followed – as indeed does much of her poetry – what Ezra
Pound had dubbed, in 1911, 'the method of Luminous Detail'.[27]

May and Charlotte remained in close contact during this time, but
their relationship – marked by a certain awkwardness from its earliest
days – continued to show signs of strain. Charlotte was unusually
quick to take offence with May, who routinely found herself on the
back foot, doing what she could to placate her difficult friend. One
such episode followed the recent publication in *The Egoist* of an essay
by Harold Monro in which he had questioned some of the ideals of
the Imagist movement.[28] A short response by May in the following
edition (awkwardly entitled 'Two Notes. 1. On H.D. 2. On Imagism')
defended the Imagists' aims and applauded their efforts to move away
from the unrestrained 'passion' of other poetry.

The efforts May went to, in her attempt to set things straight,
suggest that Charlotte was deeply offended by the article. They also
reveal just how keen May was at this stage to protect the friendship
from the corrosive effects of misunderstanding. She began by employ-
ing some straightforward damage limitation. 'About the Imagists – I
used the word "passion" in the limited sense of that wch. tears its hair,'
she explained; 'a lot, not all, but a lot of the Victorian "passion" was
hair-tearing . . .' But sensing that her friend was unlikely to fall for
feeble distinctions between the wrong and the right sort of passion,
May now executed a wholesale about-turn – arguing that passion
was, in fact, an essential ingredient for poetry. 'The precise criticism
that I sd. have applied to the Imagists – if I'd been out that day for
criticism – is that they lack strong human passion. [. . .] In writing

to Richard Aldington I said, "Some day you will have an emotion that the 'image' will not carry; then where are you?"'[29] Finally, for good measure, she threw in a bit of undisguised flattery. 'I know one poet whose heart beats like a dynamo under an iron-grey tailor-made suit (I *think* one of her suits is iron-grey) & when she publishes her poems she will give me something to say that I cannot and do not say of my Imagists.'

There is something in May's tone here – the impression it leaves of someone who is placating a spoilt and needy child – that captures the unhealthy dynamics of her friendship with Charlotte. But the two women continued to meet up, both alone and in wider company, and May took as keen an interest as ever in Charlotte's writing. In the middle of June, she invited Charlotte 'to sup with me on Saturday at 7.30 – bring *Madeleine* & *The Haymarket*?'[30] The latter is a short, impressionistic prose piece about the origins of Cumberland Market in London. May wrote a couple of weeks later from Yorkshire to say how much she 'loved' it: she thought this was precisely the sort of thing Charlotte should be concentrating on at the moment. 'I wish you'd do a lot of these things,' she said, '& Hay cd. come out in a volume of sketches. You are amazingly lucky in that your prose is as beautiful as your poetry.'[31] 'The Haymarket' had first appeared in the *New Statesman* over a year earlier, and in the intervening months Charlotte had written nothing but poems. Contrary to May's suggestion, it was to be the last prose piece she would publish.

Alida Klemantaski, the young woman who'd memorised 'The Farmer's Bride' while treading home through the frosty streets three years earlier, had lost none of her enthusiasm for the poem, although her life had changed a good deal since then, largely as a result of her meeting Harold Monro, editor of the quarterly periodical *Poetry and Drama*. At thirty-six, Harold had already achieved one of his great dreams:

to open a shop dedicated solely to poetry, a place where poets could meet and share their work, and where poetry lovers could encounter that work. The Poetry Bookshop in Devonshire Street – 'five minutes from the British Museum', as the fliers proclaimed – had first opened in January 1913. Customers were welcome to browse the books at their leisure, there was no obligation to buy, and seats were provided for anyone who wanted to sit and read at greater length. They would find on the shelves, so the adverts boasted, 'copies of nearly every book of English and American poetry published, as well as most of the important reprints and new editions of standard authors and a large selection of foreign books and periodicals'. The Bookshop quickly established itself as an important venue for poetry readings. Over the years it would host performances by W. B. Yeats, Edith Sitwell, Walter de la Mare and Ford Madox Hueffer (who changed his Germanic-sounding surname to 'Ford' after the war). But Monro's ambitions for the best poets of the day went beyond providing a stage for their readings: ultimately, he wanted to publish them.

Alida had met Harold Monro early in 1913, two months after the Bookshop opened, and when his secretary, Gertrude Townsend, left at the end of that year to get married, Alida took over all the duties Gertrude had performed in helping to run the shop – and introduced some fresh ideas of her own. One of the first things she did was to tell Harold about the poem that had so 'electrified' her in the winter of 1912.[32] She recited it to him now from memory, and after hearing it, he asked for a letter to be sent to the author enquiring if she had any more poems and whether she might be interested in publishing a book of them. By way of reply, Charlotte sent them 'The Changeling', along with a self-effacing and unnecessary note saying that it 'might or might not be liked as much as "The Farmer's Bride"'.[33] But Alida liked it very much and wrote back to say that she proposed to read both poems at the Bookshop one Tuesday or Thursday evening in November. If Miss Mew would care to join them, she would be most welcome.

It was already dark when Charlotte set off through the lamplit streets that winter of 1915. It was also bitterly cold for the time of year – the coldest November on record. At the far end of Queen Square, she continued on into a 'dark slummy street' full of litter and stray cats. This was Devonshire Street; she had never had much cause to notice it before. The shop was positioned about halfway down, on the right-hand side – a three-storeyed, eighteenth-century building with a large leaded window fronting the street. As she walked towards it she could hear the gentle thud, thud of the goldbeaters at the far end of the street. She stopped in the yellow light that spilled from the shop's window; in case she were in any doubt that she'd come to the right place, glossy black lettering over the lintel announced THE POETRY BOOKSHOP. Inside was an assortment of characters browsing the shelves or standing in small groups, deep in conversation. Alida Klemantaski stood among them, with one eye on the door: the readings were due to start any moment and she had been looking out, with some agitation, for the arrival of her new guest. The moment of that arrival struck her so forcibly that she was able to recall it in detail over sixty years later:

At about five minutes to six the swing-door of the shop was pushed open and into the room stalked Charlotte Mew. Such a word best describes her walk. She was very small, only about four feet ten inches, very slight, with square shoulders and tiny hands and feet. [. . .] When she came into the shop she was asked: 'Are you Charlotte Mew?' and her reply, delivered characteristically with a slight smile of amusement, was: 'I am sorry to say I am.'[34]

16

The New and True Note of Genius
1916–1918

The Poetry Bookshop's separate reading room, in a yard at the back of
the shop, had once been one of several goldbeaters' workshops dotted
along Devonshire Street. With its whitewashed walls, exposed beams
and dark-blue-curtained windows, it had the air of a village meet-
ing-house. It held no more than about sixty seats, arranged in rows,
but these usually afforded ample provision: by 1915, two years after
the readings had started, the average attendance was around thirty-five.
There were exceptions, of course: when Yeats had read from his own
work in the summer of 1913, 'in his famous sing-song chant, head back,
hands clutching his lapels, pince-nez perched precariously on his nose',
forty customers had to be turned away.[1] The curtains were kept drawn
even in the lighter months so that the room was always in semi-dark-
ness, and in a space at the far end stood the reading table, illuminated
by the glow of a green-shaded oil lamp. Once a week, at around 6 p.m.,
the appointed reader – sometimes an actor, sometimes a guest poet,
often Harold Monro himself, or Alida – appeared in the lamp's small
pool of light to read a selection of poems. Having noted that the audi-
ence's attention was liable to wander after about forty minutes, Monro
insisted that no event should last longer than thirty-five. After each
poem, the audience apparently made their response clear enough for
him to be able to note it in his register of readings. Pound's 'La Fraisne',
recited by Monro at one of the early events, was 'well received as usual',
while Shelley's 'Intellectual Beauty' (a favourite of Monro's) was sum-
marily deemed a 'Failure'.[2]

So it was that Alida came to be reading two of Charlotte's poems
in her 'rich contralto' voice one icy November evening of 1915.[3] From

the point of view of both publisher and fellow poet, Harold Monro could not have been more grateful to his young assistant for bringing Mew's work to his attention. At the time, he was grieving for a much-loved friend, Basil Watt, who had lived for a little while in rooms above the Bookshop and been killed at the Battle of Loos in September. The loss awakened in Harold not only a deep sorrow but regret for the extinguishing of beauty and sexual potential, as is evident in 'Carrion', one of four poems inspired by Basil's war service:

> . . . Your head has dropped
> Into a furrow. And the lovely curve
> Of your strong leg has wasted . . .
>
> . . .
>
> No coffin-cover now will cram
> Your body in a shell of lead . . .

Now the thrill of discovering a new poet went a little way towards distracting him from his grief, and less than a month after the reading, he and Charlotte were discussing the idea of bringing out a collection under the Poetry Bookshop's own imprint. At this point, Charlotte had seventeen poems that she felt held together strongly as a group and were worth publishing. Wartime costs probably discouraged Monro from offering a contract for a full-length collection (paper was in short supply and expensive), but in any case, he thought Mew's poetry would be a good candidate for his latest enterprise. He believed that the whole business of buying and reading poetry ought to be less precious, and less intimidating, for potential readers. Soon after the Bookshop opened, he had begun issuing a series of rough-and-ready publications in three formats: slim pamphlets, slightly more substantial booklets which he called 'chapbooks', and 'rhyme sheets'. The latter, measuring six to eight inches wide and up to two feet high, featured single poems decorated with hand-coloured illustrations at the head and the foot of the text, and in time they proved immensely popular. In such forms, Monro maintained, poetry could be 'sold anywhere and everywhere, carried in the pocket, read at any spare moment, left in the train, or committed to the memory and passed on'.[4] Already, the new poetry chapbooks were selling in decent numbers, and what he now proposed to Charlotte was that they bring out *half* of her poems as soon as possible, in chapbook form, with a view to following up with a second chapbook later. Charlotte initially agreed to the arrangement but almost immediately changed her mind. She wrote to Monro on 14 December 1915 to tell him she believed her poems would 'run a better chance' in a single volume, and to ask him to consider publishing them as a regular book after all: 'For as I told you – these verses hang together, for me, & mark a period – & on second thoughts I am reluctant to have them divided into (say, roughly) two half dozens, published with the interval of a year between as was last suggested. You see, I really don't want to split them up or have them hanging on.'[5]

May Sinclair was not impressed by this decision. Having settled into the role of Mew's literary adviser, she now let her friend know, in no uncertain terms, that she had made a wrong move. Could Charlotte not see that this was probably her only chance of having the poems collected at all, at least for the foreseeable future? What's more, it was Monro's only chance to publish them, given that the costs of bringing out a conventional book were clearly beyond him; to deprive him of that opportunity was grossly unfair. 'Harold Monroe [*sic*] is such a benefactor to poets, & so honest & sincere, & cares so awfully for what he *does* care for that he deserves encouragement,'[6] she wrote in a cross little note delivered two days after Christmas. She didn't think for a moment that there was any danger of Charlotte sticking to her decision: it was simply evidence of inexperience, or else an instance of wrong-headed stubbornness. 'Do change yr. mind about it, there's a dear,' she counselled, with all the condescension of a disappointed teacher.

Charlotte ignored May's advice, and by mid-January 1916, had an agreement for all seventeen poems to be published together under the title *The Farmer's Bride* and was sending through corrections, asking for time to consider the order of the poems, and discussing a design for the front cover. It was at this point, too, that she asked for a blank dedication to be inserted, followed by a short epigraph:

> To ———
> He asked life of Thee & Thou gavest him
> a long life: even for ever & ever.[7]

The quotation is from verse four of Psalm Twenty-one in the Book of Common Prayer; Mew altered the normally capitalised 'H' in 'Him' to lower case in order to indicate a human recipient of the verse. The identity of that recipient is unknown, but Val Warner may be right in speculating that it was Henry.[8] The fifteenth anniversary of Henry's death was fast approaching, and Charlotte's fierce protection of her family's secrets would have prevented her from naming her elder brother outright. Such privileged information was certainly not the sort of thing she wanted to discuss with her publisher, who never was told of Henry Mew's existence.

There were production problems from the outset. The abnormally long lines of some of the poems meant that the standard book size would not do, since Charlotte was absolutely insistent that the lines should not be broken by overturning the excess words; nor did she want individual verses to be split across pages. By February, Monro had run into a further problem: a compositor at the printers in Clerkenwell was refusing to set 'Madeleine in Church' – all six and a half pages of it – because he felt the poem was blasphemous. He may have objected purely on moral grounds; more likely he was concerned about possible legal ramifications. Three months earlier D. H. Lawrence's *The Rainbow* had been seized by police and burned, after being described in court as 'a mass of obscenity of thought, idea, and action throughout, wrapped up in language which [the prosecuting lawyer] supposed would be regarded in some quarters as an artistic and intellectual effort'.[9] Charlotte's poem was hardly a mass of obscenity, but its eponymous narrator begins by asserting her preference for the ear of a little plaster saint over that of God, and goes on to confront God directly: is it His will, she demands to know, 'that we should be content with the tame, bloodless things' when there is so much beauty and desire in the world? Artistic merit aside, 'Madeleine in Church' is a text in which a woman talks candidly to God about her tortured soul, her sensuality and her numerous past lovers, and the compositor would take no part in promulgating it. The upshot was that a different printing firm would have to be found. Charlotte did her best to remain upbeat: 'I think your printer must be a spiritual brother of the Editors who refused Ken because they "believed in the segregation of the feeble-minded",' she quipped, '& after this, one can't expect the advocates of early marriages to buy *The Farmer's Bride*!'[10]

Monro was beginning to feel he had bitten off more than he could chew: there were, he now told Charlotte, extra expenses involved in producing the poems that he couldn't have foreseen, although he omitted to say precisely what those expenses were. At the same time, he was struggling with his own difficult feelings about the war and fears of being drafted: two of his staff would be called up for service in six weeks' time, and he suspected he might have to follow soon after. By and large, he viewed the conflict as an irritating interruption to his work at the Bookshop, prolonged by the ineptitude of politicians who might have brought it to an end with a bit of skilful negotiation; but he would not refuse to fight, if asked. He suggested putting off publication of *The Farmer's Bride* until after the fighting was over, but Charlotte felt the times were so abnormal that no one could possibly say when the war might end. Her view was that Monro was duty-bound to honour their existing agreement, and in early March, she wrote to tell him so:

> I quite appreciate the difficulties which have arisen but your
> suggestion to modify the agreement by postponing publication

till after the War, seems to me, as things are, practically an
indefinite postponement; & as my negotiations with you last
autumn prevented my making any arrangement with another
publisher to bring out a book this Spring – I should like the
agreement to stand.[11]

The offer she now made to 'relinquish such royalties as might
cover or help to cover the increased cost of production' suggests that
she still had much to learn about the earning power of poetry: even
with its bestselling titles, the Poetry Bookshop was lucky to make
much of a profit.[12]

Negotiations with her new publisher had not got off to a good
start, and Charlotte now felt thoroughly miserable about the book.
'Such satisfaction as I might have had [. . .] is very definitely clouded
by the fact that it is being published reluctantly – at an unreckoned
cost,' she complained.[13] In the end, Monro agreed to go ahead with
a print run of one thousand copies (although only half were to be
released for the time being), and the job was transferred from the
high-principled Clerkenwell printers to the Westminster Press in
Covent Garden. Charlotte's notes reveal, once again, just how sure
she was in her artistic intentions. She was absolutely clear about how
she wanted her poems to look on the page and was exasperated by
the typesetters' apparent lack of attention to detail. By late April,
with some degree of frustration, she was sending back final proof
corrections –

which I hope the printers will attend to as they are really
important & this is the third time I have tried to get the same
line of the Fête to run on – & if the muddle they have made of
the end of the F. B. (also corrected in the last proof) remains it
will spoil the poem.
    The two lines run together on page 36 and break in verse on
page 38 are also bad mistakes – but when verses intact in last

proofs are broken up in these, one feels doubtful & only hopes for the best.[14]

Like the heads of the Hydra, as soon as one obstacle had been dealt with, two new ones seemed to grow in its place. On 11 May, *The Globe* announced that the Poetry Bookshop would shortly be releasing 'two cheap books, "The Farmer's Bride," by Charlotte New, and "Over the Brazier," by Robert Graves, as well as seven broadsheets of "Blake's Songs of Innocence"'.[15] The comical substituting of 'cheap' for 'chap' and the misspelling of Mew's surname were the latest in a long sequence of inauspicious errors, so that when, on 28 May, Charlotte opened a package containing her six, error-free author copies of the finished book, it seemed little short of a miracle. The cover illustration, printed in black on elegant slate-green card, was by Claud Lovat Fraser, and showed a thatched cottage with an unfeasibly steep pitched roof. Ever the architect's daughter, Charlotte would later comment that she 'certainly never saw one like it & I don't think any wall would support it'.[16] The gable-end, facing the reader, was blank except for a tiny door and, high up in the attic, a single window, behind which it was easy to picture the farmer's captive bride in the middle of the night, scared and impossibly young, 'lying awake with her wide brown stare'.

In sharp contrast to her difficult business interactions with Harold Monro, relations between Charlotte and Alida could not have been more amicable. Right from their first meeting at the Poetry Bookshop a close friendship had sprung up between them, and over the coming years, Charlotte (the elder of the two by some twenty years) would become an important confidante for Alida, providing not only wise words but also a vital dose of humour when it was needed. Alida maintained that 'no one could be more warm-hearted and witty in her talk and in her friendship' than Charlotte, and began confiding in her almost from the start, about the intense feelings she harboured for her boss and the delicate complexities involved in sharing those feelings.[17] The fact that Charlotte was unmarried and had little – perhaps no – experience of romantic entanglements did not seem to matter. Harold was not entirely unresponsive to Alida's expressions of affection, but neither did his interest extend quite as far as she would have liked. Alida knew that he had an estranged wife and a young son away at preparatory school, but what she didn't yet know was that his erotic feelings were chiefly for members of his own sex. Deeply private, and prone to spells of depression, Harold was nervous of Alida's ever more candid professions of adoration, which she conveyed in frequent letters: 'If I had a god to worship I believe it would be you,' she told him.[18]

Harold Monro and Alida Klemantaski had first met at a Poets' Club dinner in March 1913 – a formal, evening-dress affair, to which Alida had been invited by the club's founder, who admired her warm reading voice and wanted her to recite some of Harold's poems. Alida was the granddaughter of a Polish refugee and his Jewish wife, a heritage that accounted for her striking, decidedly Slavic appearance and led Virginia Woolf to describe her (when they met in 1935) as 'a handsome swarthy Russian looking woman'.[19] Intelligent and capable, she had briefly worked for the suffragette cause, and at the time of her meeting with Harold, was looking for something meaningful to do with her life in the longer term. Her initial plan had been to become a doctor and use her medical training to help rescue prostitutes from a life of ill health, but her encounter with the Poetry Bookshop crowd put an end to those ambitions.

Harold was seventeen years Alida's senior – almost twice her age when they first met – good-looking, deep-thinking and visionary. After hearing her at the Poets' Club, Harold had invited Alida to read at the Bookshop. By the time of her second reading there, in June 1913, she had realised she was in love, and when Harold suggested she join him in the Bookshop as his assistant, she had jumped at the chance. From her earliest days at the shop, she had thrown all her youthful energy into work that was neither easy nor particularly interesting to her. Unlike that of her predecessor, Gertrude Townsend, Alida's involvement with the Bookshop went way beyond what might be expected of an average secretary. A friend of Harold's remarked on how quickly she took over 'the most soul-destroying practical details' connected with the running of the shop – making it possible for Harold to leave the premises for days and weeks at a time.

More often than not, he used his new-found freedom to stay alone at his hilltop retreat in Ascona.[20] In the early 1900s, this quiet Swiss fishing village, on the shore of Lake Maggiore, had become home to a colony of free-spirited utopians who lived on a vegetable-only diet in the woods below Harold's mill house on Monte Verità – 'Hill of Truth' – unburdened by modern accoutrements, including clothes. It attracted a number of famous visitors, including Herman Hesse, Carl Jung, Isadora Duncan and Paul Klee. In time, the colonists came to adopt a doctrine of 'erotic liberation' taught by Austrian psychoanalyst Otto Gross, who, in 1907, had a passionate affair with Frieda Weekley (future wife of D. H. Lawrence) and whose countercultural beliefs would find their way into Harold's writing.[21]

Alida had very little idea of what went on in Ascona, and apparently chose to overlook Harold's frank confession in an early letter to her that when it came to relationships, he was 'absolutely faithless'.[22] In the spring and summer of 1916, she was so panicked by the prospect of his imminent drafting that she found it difficult to eat. It wasn't long before her fears were realised. Harold had barely time enough to see *The Farmer's Bride* into print before he was finally called up for service. In July, he began training at Handel Street barracks, after being appointed as second lieutenant in the Royal Garrison Artillery. To Alida's great relief, he was confined to home duties.

The barracks were only a ten-minute walk from the Bookshop, but Harold's hours (5 a.m. to 6 p.m.) left him little time, and less energy, for Bookshop business – or, indeed, for Alida. The shop's clerk, Mr McDonald, had also been drafted into the army, but there was still a bookkeeper, a housekeeper, a Swiss maid, an office boy and a part-time salesman on the staff, and it was Alida's job to manage them all in Harold's absence. It did not come easily to her, and she agreed to do it solely to please Harold; knowing he was married had done nothing to dampen her feelings for him.[23] For the remainder of the war, she took over the running of the shop completely, organising the weekly poetry readings, managing the shop's complex finances and oversee-ing the publication and distribution of *Georgian Poetry*. When boxes of the third anthology arrived from the printers, she stayed up until four in the morning making up packages for various booksellers, and then hired a wheelbarrow to transport the parcels to the distributor in Goswell Road. On seeing this particular volume (*1916–17*), Harold commented that the omission of Charlotte Mew was 'of course again a conspicuous flaw'.[24]

In spite of his difficult hours at the barracks, he found time throughout that summer of 1916 to correspond with Charlotte. At the end of July, two months after her book was published, he wrote to tell her it was 'going dead': nobody seemed to be interested in reviewing it.[25] Charlotte took the news hard and was profusely apologetic. She had expected one or two decent reviews to appear, she explained, because while she didn't know many 'literary people' those she did know had written to say how highly they thought of the book – but 'there it stops'.[26] Even if she knew them better, she went on, 'I couldn't ask them to get me notices, because I am sim-ply not the person, though for your sake, I wish I were.' The 'one or two more or less influential people', who had been full of praise for the book included *The Nation*'s Henry Nevinson, who had declared the poems 'magnificent', but it seemed (at least through the prism of Charlotte's anxious and mistrustful mind) that nobody was pre-pared to commit their opinions to print. The poet Gerald Gould, who wrote for the *Herald*, had promised her a notice, but that hadn't materialised either. Gould would go on to become fiction editor of the *Observer* and was a talented and perceptive literary critic; a review from him would certainly be worth having.

Whatever the reasons, it looked (or so he said) as if Monro might be left with a stack of remainders. He told Charlotte that they numbered around 850, but in fact only 500 copies of the initial print run of 1,000 had been bound by July, and 150 of those had already sold. For a relatively unknown poet publishing for the first time, these figures were perfectly respectable, and must have been in line with Harold's expectations. He nonetheless wasted no time in communicating his disappointment; Charlotte (who knew nothing about sales figures) was, she said, 'truly sorry'.[27] She was in fact puzzled by the book's failure to make more of an impact. Granted, there was a war on, but she didn't think that could be wholly responsible, considering 'what & how other verses are noticed'.[28]

As it turned out, both publisher and writer were being a little premature in their assessment of the book's reception. Gould's promised notice appeared in due course at the start of August, and it could hardly have been better. Charlotte Mew was, he said, 'one of the few living writers who can give one what may be called "the authentic thrill"'.[29] He urged readers to push on through moments of complexity, because 'with Miss Mew, as so often with poets occasionally difficult, the best passages are after all radiantly simple'. He found the atmosphere of the book 'rare and elusive', and many of the poems 'strange, queer, eerie, ghostlike'. 'The Changeling' was, he said, 'a poem so beautiful that I will not try to find epithets for it'; 'Ken' was 'powerful, pitiful and horrible'; 'Madeleine in Church' addressed 'the profoundest of human and religious problems', and 'The Pedlar' (a bittersweet lyric that imagines the speaker's 'ghost' self redressing a missed opportunity and kissing the object of her desire on the lips 'as ghosts don't do') was 'magical and romantic'.

But it was Gould's astute identification of the book's essence that might have pleased Charlotte most of all: her insight into the 'raptures and – still more – the horrors that beset childhood' was, the critic felt, 'so keen as to be positively painful'. For Charlotte Mew – private individual and poet alike – the two extremes were often inseparable, and Gould recognised this at once: 'pain is a constant note of these poems,' he observed; 'the poet seems unable to disentangle life, or beauty, from pain.' He found in the intermingling of these emotions an artistic integrity that was missing from so much contemporary verse, and ended his piece by instructing readers not to take his word for it:

> Let me insist, in conclusion, that you must get this book for yourself if you care at all for the developments of originality in modern verse. You will be either fascinated or bemused by the rich and elaborate strangeness of atmosphere; you will be puzzled often, and sometimes, perhaps, shocked, but I do not think you will fail to recognize the new and true note of genius.[30]

This extraordinary praise must have gone a little way towards making up for the lack of interest from other quarters. Charlotte was happy enough, at any rate, to post a cutting to May, whose own response was rather deflating: after acknowledging that she was 'immensely pleased' by the review, she went on to say how much better it would have been if Gould had written in J. C. Squire's *New Statesman* rather than the *Herald* – 'but if only Squire will do it himself, that will be better still'.[31] She assured Charlotte she was doing all she could for the book. Harold Monro had provided her with review copies which she had duly sent out to Squire and a number of her other contacts, including Rebecca West for the *Daily News*, William Courtney for the *Daily Telegraph*, Clement Shorter for *The Sphere* and H.D. (Hilda Doolittle) for *The Egoist*. And then, once again, she tempered this good news with the comment that, in the accompanying letters she'd sent out with the books, she hadn't always poured praise on the poems, but instead had carefully tailored her comments 'according to the idiosyncrasies of the reviewer'.[32] This seemed to be the way with May

Sinclair, at least in her dealings with Charlotte: what she gave with one hand she took away, time and again, with the other. She ended by warning Charlotte not to be disappointed if the response was poor: it was, alas, 'very difficult to get Poetry reviewed at present', she cautioned – 'unless it's written from the Trenches!'[33]

Three weeks after this correspondence, May sent a brief update in a short and rather inconsequential letter that turned out to be the last she would send; or the last, anyway, that Charlotte kept. She began the letter with the news that H.D. was definitely writing a piece for *The Egoist* – and 'it ought to be very good indeed'.[34] She went on to praise H.D.'s courage in calmly accepting the conscription of her husband, the poet Richard Aldington. The recent extension of the Military Service Act had finally made married men eligible, and Aldington had duly enlisted in the 11th Devonshire Regiment, setting off, at the end of June, for the regimental base near Wareham. He was scathing about his fellow soldiers, appalled by their lack of interest in culture and art, hated life in the camp and dreaded being sent to the front. He fretted about what a long absence from cultural life might do to him, explaining to fellow poet Amy Lowell that once away from it, 'One sees [. . .] the supreme importance of literature, the one imperishable record of the human soul.'[35] H.D. did what she could to keep her husband's spirits up, visiting him, staying nearby at Corfe Castle and encouraging friends to write. May Sinclair seemed baffled by her efforts, remarking that since Britain wasn't H.D.'s country, this wasn't really her war – 'and yet she behaves as if it were'.[36] How, May wondered, could H.D. bear to risk losing her husband for the sake of a country that wasn't even hers? And for that matter, how could her husband bear to risk his life for a war he didn't approve of? 'I can't imagine anything more awful than being sent into the trenches to fight for a cause you don't believe in – unless it is the state of mind that doesn't believe, & that can imagine that anything that's been thought or written (written in the last twenty years, anyhow) more important than the winning of the war!'[37]

Because this is the last communication that has survived between Charlotte and May, it is tempting to search it for clues that might help explain their subsequent estrangement. The precise cause remains a matter for conjecture. Did May's comment about the war hint at a divergence of opinion from Charlotte's own attitude? We simply do not have enough information about Charlotte's relationship with May to know how these words were intended, or how they were taken. The war itself put many friendships under strain, and perhaps the most likely explanation is that the women simply drifted apart. By this stage, their relations had cooled almost to the level of a business connection, with May acting as unpaid publicist for the book, and for some while now her letters to Charlotte had ceased to contain anything very personal. The days when the pair had wrangled over the semantics of a passing comment, or whiled away whole afternoons, their heads bent over compositions of French poetry, had long passed.

But May's advance notice of H. D.'s review proved to be accurate. It appeared the following month, in September 1916, but it emerged that the author had used most of her word count as a platform for her own musings on the nature of originality. She gave no indication of having read any of the poems in *The Farmer's Bride*, except 'Madeleine in Church', from which she quoted twenty-three long lines before asserting that 'Miss Mew has chosen one of the most difficult forms in the language – the dramatic lyric' and that she was one of only three poets (along with Robert Frost and Ford Madox Hueffer) to have succeeded in this form, having 'grown a new blossom from the seed of Browning's sowing', following the master 'without imitating him'.[38] After May had set Charlotte up to expect something 'very good indeed' from H.D., this must have felt to her rather half-hearted. She may well have been disappointed by the lukewarm appraisal, and if she said so, that in itself could have been enough to cause a rift between the two friends. At any rate, the correspondence between Charlotte and May now dwindled away to nothing.

In February of 1917, out of the blue, Charlotte received an invitation from her old friend Mrs Sappho to come and read to members of her newly formed To-morrow Club. Charlotte replied that she was 'quite incapable of it' – or indeed of any public appearance on any stage.[39] It was now, she added, a full nine months since *The Farmer's Bride* had been published and she couldn't remember receiving any invitations to read at the time – when, for the sake of publicity, such invitations had been most needed. She was glad, she said, to hear of the success of Mrs Sappho's recently reissued novel, *Madcap Jane*, and offered her congratulations, but her tone – while polite – was unmistakably cool. In her usual manner, Mrs Sappho tried once again to persuade her to come and read, but this time Charlotte was unyielding on the subject – an attitude that Mrs Sappho apparently found 'disappointing'. Charlotte retorted, pointedly, in a final letter written on 24 June 1917, that 'People are only "disappointing" when one makes a wrong diagnosis.'[40] It's possible she was referring to the falling-out that had occurred almost three years earlier, when Mrs Sappho had noted in her diary that Charlotte had been 'bothering and annoying' May, and promptly ceased to have anything to do with her. If so, then now, at last, Charlotte had the opportunity to say her piece on the matter: the conclusions Mrs Sappho seemed to have drawn about her were, quite simply, 'wrong'. Mrs Sappho would occasionally attempt to draw Charlotte into other of her schemes in years to come, but Charlotte invariably sent flat refusals to all such invitations; she found it impossible to forgive Mrs Sappho for the hurt she had first inflicted and then refused to acknowledge.

Friendship was hugely important to Charlotte; but not all her friendships were alike. Some – such as those she enjoyed with Ethel Oliver and many of her childhood friends – were characterised by intimacy and a deep, mutual understanding; others by disparity and contradiction. Throughout her adult life, she had made two types of friend: the one stable and sustaining, and the other springing from her involvement with this group or that. The latter may have quickly outgrown their expedience, but they nonetheless served a purpose. Ella D'Arcy had been one such friend; Mrs Sappho and May Sinclair were others. Shorter-term friendships like these provided Charlotte with a safe outlet for the contradictory and headstrong part of her nature that had led her to snap her nursemaid's parasol in half as a little girl. They were also, very often, beneficial to her writing career.

Whether by design or accident, it was just as Charlotte's newest friendship, with Alida, had got under way that her involvement with May and Mrs Sappho petered out entirely. By the summer of 1918, she and Alida were close enough for Alida to feel able to leave Joggles, her beloved white West Highland terrier, overnight at Gordon Street for the first time. On that occasion, the dog had to be dropped off with the housemaid, Jane Elsain, since Charlotte was out making visits to soldiers' wives on behalf of the local War Pensions Committee. The voluntary work Charlotte did for the committee had taken over from her work at Miss Paget's Girls' Club, and involved verifying the needs of claimants who had applied for a 'separation allowance' or widow's pension. Years later, Alida would recall Charlotte telling humorous – if slightly unkind – stories of her encounters during these visits:

> I remember the zest with which she once described her arrival
> in some back street slum, and her knocking at the door, only to
> be faced by a harridan, with a man's cap worn back to front and
> a heavy bobbly shawl, towering above her and demanding what
> she wanted. When told the name of the woman who was sought,
> the harridan turned and went half-way up the flight of stairs,
> shrieking in her strident voice, 'Tell the lidy upstairs there's a
> person 'ere who wants to see 'er.'[41]

In the late afternoon of 29 May, Charlotte told Alida that she had '11 pigsties from Primrose Hill to Kings X' to visit that day and had not yet had lunch.[42] The description hints at a lack of compassion for the difficult circumstances of these women – an insensitivity that is perhaps surprising given the empathy she shows, and would go on showing, for the unfortunate and dispossessed in her poems and stories. On the other hand, her exasperation is easy enough to understand: the war pensions work was both difficult and time-consuming. The demographic gender imbalance in Britain had been greatly accentuated by the war: the 1921 census would record 1.72 million more women than men in England and Wales, an excess which the newspapers dubbed the 'superfluous two million'.[43] The list of Charlotte's scheduled visits must have seemed endless.

Looking after Joggles for the weekend must have seemed to Charlotte a small favour to be asked in the light of all that Alida had done for her. She knew it was Alida's personal appreciation of her poetry that had secured its publication in book form; how and when that event might have happened otherwise could only be guessed at. But in future years the friendship was to prove still more helpful to Charlotte, altering the landscape of both her professional and personal life. Alida's position at the Poetry Bookshop put her in contact with publishers, editors and other influential literary figures – as well as poets: Rupert Brooke, H.D., T. S. Eliot, Robert Frost, Amy Lowell, Wilfred Owen, Ezra Pound, Edward Thomas and W. B. Yeats all passed through the Bookshop's doors at one time or another.

One warm Tuesday morning in June 1918, a middle-aged gentleman, in waistcoat, suit and tie, with a close-cropped beard and kind, intelligent eyes, walked into the shop and engaged Alida in conversation about various contemporary poets and how they were faring during these difficult war years. He was Sydney Cockerell, Director of the Fitzwilliam Museum in Cambridge, and Alida seized on the opportunity to enthuse about Charlotte's poems. After listening with obvious interest, he left the shop to go and look at a group of paintings at Christie's auction house, with a view to acquiring them for the museum; but his conversation with Alida stayed with him, and that evening he made the following entry in his diary:

> Went to London by the 8.30. Went to the Poetry Bookshop to see Miss Klemantaski, with whom I had an interesting talk about the way in which the various living poets are selling – & about Charlotte Mew, who has published one small book of remarkable poems. She lives near Gower St & her life (she is about 43) is spent in attendance on an old mother.[44]

Charlotte was in fact approaching her forty-ninth birthday at the time. When she heard of Sydney Cockerell's interest in her work, she sent him (at Alida's prompting) a manuscript copy of her book. She might have been still more delighted had she known that Cockerell counted among his own close friends Thomas Hardy, whose writing she had admired for many years, and whose complex fictional characters had helped shape her own most famous creation, the farmer's bride. Cockerell was two years older than Charlotte – 'bald, bearded and spectacled', as he had once portrayed himself to John Ruskin.[45] In time, Charlotte would come up with a more telling description: he looked, she thought, like Shakespeare in modern dress.[46]

17

Witnesses to the 'Real Thing'

1918

When Sydney Cockerell had taken up his post as Director of the Fitzwilliam Museum in Cambridge in 1908, the place was in a mess. Good paintings hung alongside bad, all from widely different periods and countries, and in the display cases, collections were crowded together according to no particular scheme. 'I found it a pigstye [*sic*],' he later wrote, with customary brio, and 'I turned it into a palace.'[1] At fifty-one, he was by now a familiar figure in the museum's galleries, in his dark blue serge suit and crisp, wing-collared shirt. He'd journeyed a long way from his family's early vision of him as a merchant in his father's coal business.

Sydney's passion for collecting had begun when he was a boy – with mosses, butterflies and other insects and, later, fossils and shells. After a good education at St Paul's in Hammersmith, he left school at seventeen, as expected, to work for the family firm. From that point, his life might have followed a secure but predictable path, had he not had the initiative to start, at around the same time, a correspondence with one of his boyhood heroes, artist and thinker John Ruskin. He sent Ruskin a carefully labelled selection of his rarer shells, together with details of their provenance written out in impossibly neat handwriting. Ruskin was both impressed and intrigued; he described his new acquaintance to a friend as 'a very remarkable young man – so sweet & thoughtful – & of high scientific power too', and after a brief correspondence he invited Sydney to holiday with him in France.[2] So began a new collecting passion: for the rest of his life Sydney would be a collector of friendships, with men and women for whom he had a special admiration. After

Ruskin, he had set his sights on William Morris, and in due course became his personal secretary.

Sydney's habit extended to chronicling key details from his own life, which he noted down over the years in a series of slim green or blue cloth-bound pocket diaries in his tiny, elegant hand – so tiny in places that a magnifying glass is needed to read it. Since his visit to the Poetry Bookshop that warm June morning of 1918, Charlotte Mew and her poems had been very much on his mind. A fortnight later, he went up to London on business at the Victoria & Albert Museum and lunched with Lady Margaret Sackville, herself a poet and currently engaged in an affair with future prime minister Ramsay MacDonald. Whatever else they talked about, it was Lady Margaret's interest in Mew that Sydney chose to record. 'She shares my admiration of Charlotte Mew's poems,' he noted in his diary that evening, with obvious satisfaction.[3]

Charlotte was extremely gratified by Cockerell's interest in her poems – enough to have posted him a manuscript copy of *The Farmer's Bride*, for which Sydney – ever punctilious – sent a cheque by return of post, along with a note in which he reiterated his admiration for the poetry. A week later, he wrote in more detail, once again lavishing praise on the poems, but this time suggesting that she take another look at the ending of her poem 'The Farmer's Bride' and consider a revision. Charlotte thanked him for 'the practical interest you are good enough to take in my small production' but suggested his admiration may have been less forthcoming had he known 'what an unadaptable person you were dealing with – really incapable – even if Barkis was willin'' – to go back on anything once written – to rewrite a line of it'.[4] In her casual allusion to Dickens (Barkis is the cart-driver in *David Copperfield*), she was sending a signal that, though she had only recently published a book, she was no literary novice in search or need of advice. The rest of her reply was heavily seasoned with further literary references; and if the approach seems defensive, it is also understandable. Quite how

Cockerell thought Charlotte *would* be willing to go back and alter a poem that had already won her widespread praise is hard to imagine, especially since by this stage it had been published without alteration both in a journal and in her own book. The subtext of her reply was clear: there would be no further discussion on the matter.

> I could only change my Farmer by making him someone else – as, so far as I had the use of words, they did express my idea of a rough countryman seeing & saying things differently from the more sophisticated townsman – at once more clearly & more confusedly. I am afraid, too, that the point you touch on is more than merely technical – as it seems to me that in the 'cri de cœur' (I use your phrase) one either has or has not the person, & if the author is not right here he is wrong past mending – judged by Flaubert's implacable – 'Le mot ne manque jamais quand on possède l'idée.'[5]

Though her tone is scrupulously polite, confidence shines out from this concise and erudite response, which she sent by return of post. Her quotation of Flaubert's remark – that the word never fails once you have the idea – indicates the degree of trust she placed in her own poetic instinct and in the subconscious's ability to supply the necessary language. But she was grateful at least to Cockerell for turning her thoughts to the concept of the 'cri de cœur', and came up with two further examples that she thought illustrated his meaning very well. The first is from Alexandre Dumas's novel *La Dame aux camélias*, in which the main character, the courtesan Marguerite Gautier, is on the brink of death when she receives a visit from the lover she thought had abandoned her and declares, *'Je veux vivre!'* The second example is spoken by Mrs Gamp (in Dickens's *Martin Chuzzlewit*) who, having generously filled her teapot with gin instead of tea, looks on with increasing indignation as her tea-guest, Betsey Prig, helps herself to twice her share; when Mrs Gamp can stand it no longer, she stops her guest's hand and shouts, 'No, Betsey! Drink fair, wotever you do!' Neither of these examples has anything like the subtlety of the dangerously suppressed emotion that causes the farmer's outburst in Mew's poem, but her point was that 'in both cases, one has not only the cry but the gesture and the accent'. She was in no doubt that she too had succeeded in capturing her farmer's gesture and accent. 'And so', she concluded, 'one goes on – calling up the witnesses to the "real thing" & finds oneself in delightful company.'[6] The following day, Sydney was suitably repentant: 'Of course you are wholly right,' he conceded. 'When I had posted my letter I realised my impertinence in suggesting a revision of such a beautiful and spontaneous work of art and I know that I deserve a wigging.'[7]

With this exchange, the tone was set for a correspondence and friendship that would last for the rest of Charlotte's life. She and Sydney at once recognised in each other a preference for candour over flummery and empty words. There were some who thought Sydney brusque and outspoken to the point of rudeness; but then there were some who thought the same of Charlotte. Sydney was undoubtedly a kind soul, and several times used his forthrightness to speak out in defence of others, protesting publicly, for instance, against the long hours and exhausting duties of nurses. Charlotte's difficult domestic situation, her diminutive stature and her obvious courage in the face of it all brought out in him a deep protective instinct, and with it a desire to help make life better for her.

In July, a few days after their discussion about literary *cris de cœur*, Charlotte was enthusiastically agreeing to Sydney's suggestion that he call round to see her – if, that is, he was prepared to wait a while. As the war rumbled on, the task of ensuring that there was enough money to keep the family at Gordon Street and to pay for Freda's care had become increasingly challenging, and it was decided that the family would have to free up the ground-floor rooms for a second set of tenants. Charlotte was now in the process of moving the family's belongings to the basement in preparation. 'For the next few weeks,' she explained, 'I am arranging nothing.'[8] Sydney immediately understood the situation. 'Your last letter conveyed a hint that you would like a rest and I quite intended to wait,' he reassured her.[9] The fact that he both recognised and respected her need for breathing space boded well for the future of the relationship. It was the absence of precisely this kind of empathy and respect for privacy that had sounded the death knell for her friendship with Mrs Sappho.

While he waited, Cockerell began to send Charlotte's book round to his friends, and soon forwarded to her a response from the poet Wilfrid Scawen Blunt, which Charlotte claimed to find 'doubly interesting since you say that the opinions & axioms expressed in it seem to you very sound.'[10] In picking up on the word 'axiom', she was singling out a particular comment in the letter. Blunt had complained of her habit of 'writing sometimes as a man & sometimes as a woman which I consider a great mistake as it always takes away something of the poem's full sincerity.'[11] He went on: 'A woman ought *always* to write like a woman, notwithstanding the temptation there doubtless is to invert the rôles. It is an axiom with me that sexual sincerity is the essential of good emotional work.'[12]

It was apparently one thing for the likes of Tennyson (in 'Mariana') and Dante Gabriel Rossetti (in 'The Blessed Damozel') to write in the voice of the opposite gender, but quite another for a woman poet to do so. Blunt was a close friend of Cockerell's, a wealthy aristocrat and something of a ladies' man whose own 'sexual sincerity', in a personal sense (he had a string of illicit affairs during his marriage), may have been questionable.[13] But even Blunt conceded that Charlotte had 'the great merit which few of her contemporaries possess of making one feel in each piece that she has something to say which is worth saying'.[14] A. E. Housman also found in the poems 'much that is good', but again felt the need to offer advice, and again his objection to Charlotte's work stemmed from her gender. The problem was, he said, that 'as female poets are apt to be, she is too literary, and puts in ornament which does not suit the supposed speakers'.[15]

To his credit, Sydney never swayed from his own unalloyed admiration of the poems and he continued to be a strong advocate for them. In that respect he had entered Charlotte's life at just the right moment: without ever asking for the favour, she had relied to a large degree on her friends to disseminate her work among their own circles – first there had been Mrs Sappho, then May Sinclair, Alida and now Sydney. While he quietly continued to spread word of her poetry in Britain, it was beginning to find admirers further afield on its own account. In late August, she received a letter from Professor Lewis Chase of the University of Rochester, New York, asking for help with a lecture series he was planning to give on contemporary British poets. Might she be able to furnish him with some pertinent facts about her life and working method, he wondered – including information on her early environment, her literary loves and masters, circumstances 'which tend to induce in you the mood of composition', and her theory and method of revision?[16] Charlotte's response was polite but firm: 'I regret that I cannot send the information you ask for as I have never taken enough interest in my mental processes (such as they are) to analyse them.' But she also gave sound artistic reasons for demurring: 'I think too that the chief, if not the only, value of any work of art is precisely that quality in it which is independent of influences or, as you say, "recuperations" and that the critic or reader is more likely to discover this than the writer – since lookers-on are said to see most of the game.'[17]

Reading through Charlotte's correspondence during these years, it's often easy to forget there was a war on; she mentions it directly just a handful of times, and even then only in passing. London itself was not badly damaged (there were only thirty-one air raids on the capital during the entire war), and in the letters that have survived there are no direct references to the political background, the conflict of nations or the scale of the slaughter. That is not to say that she didn't think about these horrors or discuss them with friends, but the disruption to her home life was small enough to allow her to continue with her day-to-day activities – and with her writing, though she was no longer able to publish in magazines.

The first letter we have after the outbreak of war is dated January 1915, when the fighting was clearly on her mind; she talks of one friend's war-wounded son and of spending the evening with 'an old servant' whose fifty-two-year-old husband was just going out to fight.[18] But by then, the drill halls, barracks and army training camps that sprang up all over London in 1914 and '15 had already become part of the fabric of her daily life. She must many times have walked past volunteers drilling in Russell Square – an activity memorialised by Edward Shanks:

> *Form four-rs! Form two deep!* We wheel and pair
> And still the brown leaves drift in Russell Square.[19]

Charlotte's few personal comments on the conflict, along with her trio of war poems, suggest that she was appalled and saddened by the fighting and the calamitous loss of life that resulted. The third of the poems, 'The Cenotaph', would not be written until after the war's end. It comments eloquently on the death-in-life experience of those who had lost loved ones, contrasting distant fields where 'the wild, sweet, wonderful blood of youth was shed' with homes where 'watchers by lonely hearths' have 'more slowly bled'. But Charlotte had no father, brothers or sons fighting in the war. Sydney, the one man she was close to at this time, was forty-seven when the conflict started – too old for conscription. He had remained in Cambridge, doing his bit for the war effort – at one point conducting parties of wounded around the colleges – but most of his time was spent at the Fitzwilliam: after arranging for some of the smaller artefacts ('the ivories, coins, gems, enamels and finer manuscripts') to be safely stored away, he had kept the museum open.

At the start of September 1918, Charlotte finally got around to fixing a date with Sydney, for tea at Hogarth Studios. So it was that amid the paint pots, as the tea was poured and drunk, Sydney made up for his unwanted critical advice and charmed both the Mew sisters with his manner and the genuine interest he showed in them. They were touched, too, by his offer to wash up afterwards – though, characteristically, they declined it. Charlotte suggested that next time perhaps he'd like to come to the house, 'where, for the moment, this [the washing-up] is done for us'.[20]

Over tea, Sydney had shared the news that his friend Thomas Hardy had been hugely enjoying Charlotte's poetry and had expressed a wish to meet her. Sure enough, within weeks, Charlotte heard from Hardy's wife, Florence, who confirmed 'the immense pleasure your poems have given my husband': 'It is a long time since I have known him so engrossed by a book, as by *The Farmer's Bride*. It now lies by him on his study table and I have read all the poems to him – some of them *many* times – and shall probably read them to him many more times.'[21] Hardy was seventy-eight years old – 'not a young man & he cares to see but few people nowadays', Florence explained; but he did want to meet Charlotte, if she felt up to making the 'tedious journey to Dorchester from London'.[22] Charlotte was, she said, astonished and thrilled in equal measure that 'Mr. Hardy has given a thought to *The Farmer's Bride* and its writer'.[23] She would, of course, be delighted to visit – when time permitted for both parties. Thus the general idea was settled that Charlotte should visit the Hardys at Max Gate, their home in Dorchester, though for the time being the plan remained in embryo.

Over the following months, Sydney called regularly on Charlotte, adding her to his list of London friends to be visited. On 12 October (a 'wretched day of drizzle'), he went to tea for the first time at

Gordon Street and 'talked with her for two hours, chiefly about lit-
erature', before taking both Mew sisters out to dinner.[24] Other times,
Charlotte and Sydney would take the short walk to Alida's flat in
Millman Street for tea. Before long, he was sending her tickets to
talks or exhibitions. Charlotte knew that, for the good of her soul,
she needed to get away from the house and all its attendant stresses
from time to time, and Sydney's exhortations for her to do so usu-
ally met with little resistance. They went together to the theatre, to
films at the New Gallery cinema in Regent Street, or to dine at Les
Gobelins, the excellent restaurant that adjoined the cinema, on the
corner of Heddon Street. When Sydney visited the Gordon Street
house, he sometimes brought with him a book of poems that he
thought Charlotte should read: one such was *An Echo of the Spheres*
by Mrs Charlotte Bain – a collection of poems that had been rescued
from oblivion by the poet's son, the popular fantasy writer F. W. Bain.
Charlotte was less sure about the poems than Sydney appeared to be,
but even before reading the book, she had told him (in a now familiar
refrain) that 'It is no use asking me for any sort of critical appreciation
– least of all of poetry – as that is beyond my powers & was "never
among my crimes".'[25]

That November of 1918, Sydney brought Charlotte a copy of
the Ashendene edition of *The Song of Songs*, printed on vellum and
hand-decorated by his wife, Kate, who (before marriage, children
and then illness intervened) had been a gifted and much sought-
after illuminator and calligrapher, known professionally as Florence
Kate Kingsford. Charlotte was entranced by the craftsmanship –
exquisite illustrations rendered in vibrant colours and gold leaf.
It was the first contact (albeit indirect) between two women who
would become very dear to each other later in Charlotte's life. But at
the moment, Kate Cockerell was battling her own demons. In recent
years, she'd had to turn down work because she was struggling with
her hand coordination, and in 1916, the doctors had diagnosed her
with multiple sclerosis. By 1918, she was devoting all her time to

looking after the couple's three children: Margaret (then aged ten), Christopher (eight) and Katharine (seven).

In the end it was left to Charlotte to arrange a date with the Hardys. The first, tentative plan for an autumn visit had been cancelled after Florence wrote in October to say that Thomas had come down with a chill and been warned that 'he must have complete rest and quiet and see no one'.[26] But she wrote at the same time to Sydney, telling him how embarrassed she was to put Charlotte off with this 'bungling excuse' and confiding the real reason: her husband had told her, in no uncertain terms, that 'owing to the scarcity of coal we cannot entertain any visitors until next spring – when fires are over'.[27] A few weeks earlier, at the end of September 1918, the Germans had been forced into retreat, but even after the armistice in November, the effects of rationing and shortages would continue to be felt for some time, with notices from the Coal Controller regularly appearing in the papers to impress on the public 'the necessity for strict adherence to their rations'.[28]

In December, however, Charlotte took matters into her own hands: 'my plan for meeting the knocks of winter is to forget there are such things as spring and summer,' she explained. She would therefore like to come down the following Wednesday, and unless she heard otherwise, would be at Dorchester station on the 4th at 4.14 p.m.[29] Florence Hardy replied immediately to say she would come to the station to meet her, unless it was raining very hard – in which case, she said, 'would you ask for a fly to take you to Max Gate – there will be one there ordered by us'.[30]

The tiny figure that alighted onto the platform was not at all what Florence had been expecting. Charlotte was ten years older than Florence, but – 'What a pathetic little creature!' Florence wrote to Sydney afterwards. 'One longed to be kind to her and look after her.'[31] Charlotte's first impressions of Florence are unrecorded. She was Hardy's second wife, and at thirty-nine, exactly half her husband's age – young enough to be his granddaughter. Now four years into their marriage, the couple had held a quiet ceremony two years after the first Mrs Hardy, Emma, had died in her attic bedroom at Max Gate. It wasn't easy for Florence living in the shadow of that death. Strained and complex as the first marriage was, it had lasted thirty-eight years, and Emma's death had occasioned in Hardy an enormous outpouring of remorse and a searing, elegiac sequence of poems. Florence and Thomas now lived on at Max Gate with a badly behaved white Highland terrier named Wessie, on whom they both doted.

Charlotte was aware of at least some of this background, as the carriage approached the large, red-brick house which Hardy, a trained architect, had designed himself, in the Queen Anne style. Behind a rather austere frontage, Max Gate's interior was modest: two bedrooms, two reception rooms, a study and smaller attic bedrooms, with a kitchen and service rooms at the back. The house had neither gas nor electricity, and no telephone at this time (one would arrive in 1920, which Hardy resolutely refused to answer); it was heated by coal fires and lit by oil lamps. But Charlotte was beside herself to be there and, at the Hardys' invitation, stayed on an extra night. In spite of Thomas's concern over fuel shortages, they had lit a large and welcoming fire, and conversation flowed freely, punctuated by the demands of Wessie. Charlotte 'talked all the time', Florence reported to Sydney. 'We never have had anyone here who talked so much, from the moment I met her at the station.'[32]

Back in London, Charlotte sent the Hardys a handwritten copy of her poem 'On the Road to the Sea' and a wistful note that 'In London streets I still seem to be looking at Dorchester trees and walking about with all the good things under them.'[33] From this time on, Florence made a habit of letting Charlotte know whenever she came up to London (sometimes to see doctors, on account of her fragile health), and the pair would do their best to engineer a meeting.

Two years had passed since the publication of *The Farmer's Bride*; they were years that had marked something of a sea-change in Charlotte's life, and she now said goodbye to 1918 with some important new friendships in place and with the new domestic arrangements at Gordon Street finally settled. She was able to report to Florence that a second set of lodgers had at last been safely installed, with the help of 'a little heap of sweeps and "chars" and white-washers'.[34] She omitted to say that the whole family, along with their maid Jane Elsain and Wek the parrot, had been forced to decamp to the house's cramped basement in order to accommodate the lodgers; ever after, guests would be asked for tea only rarely.

18

I Have Been Through the Gates

1919–1920

That New Year of 1919, Alida invited a small group of women poets to her flat, with the particular aim of introducing Charlotte to the eccentric aristocratic poet Edith Sitwell, then aged thirty. Sydney Cockerell happened to drop in on the party after dinner and recorded in his diary, 'Much good talk, chiefly about poetry.'[1] But Sitwell came away with quite a different impression. Though she admired Charlotte's work, she had evidently found her reticence off-putting: 'What a grey tragic woman – about sixty in point of age, and sucked dry of blood (though not of spirit) by poverty and an arachnoid mother. I tried to get her to come and see me, but she is a hermit, inhabited by a terrible bitterness, and though she was very nice to me, she wouldn't come.'[2] Sitwell wasn't known for her tact, but Charlotte was in fact only forty-nine; the strains of the passing years were perhaps beginning to tell on her appearance. The other member of that evening's party was the poet and suffragette Madeleine Rock, who had spent time in Holloway prison for smashing windows. After being squeezed beside Miss Rock on a sofa all evening, Sitwell reported that she was 'extremely fat and exuding a glutinous hysteria from every pore'.[3] Whatever Edith Sitwell's feelings about Charlotte as a person, she continued to be an advocate for her poetry, noting in one 1921 review that Mew was 'utterly unselfconscious, and she never spares herself; there is no self-protective weakness in her'.[4]

Florence Hardy would no doubt have agreed. She had been discussing 'On the Road to the Sea' with some of her Cambridge friends – among them, the philosopher Goldsworthy Lowes Dickinson, diplomat Arthur Elliott Felkin and novelist E. M. Forster – and she wrote to Charlotte to ask her a question 'which I hope you won't think silly'.[5] The whole group had been caught up in a heated debate about the gender of the poem's speaker. 'All the men say it is a woman – I and another of my sex say it is a man who speaks.'[6] Charlotte responded at once with her own take on the poem: 'On the Road to the Sea represents to me a middle-aged man speaking – in thought – to a middle-aged woman whom he has only met once or twice.'[7] Her use of that tiny aside 'to me' is revealing: she believed that once a poem was finished and out in the world, the writer's intentions for it were no more valid than other people's interpretations.

In February, Charlotte received news that Dorothy Chick, the youngest of the seven Chick sisters, had died of flu, aged just thirty-five. Her funeral took place on 4 March at Haven Green Baptist Church in Ealing and was attended by a great many friends – Charlotte and Anne very likely among them. In his sermon, the pastor suggested that the congregation had 'become inured to death', having witnessed, for the past four years, so many 'bereaved homes and darkened lives'.[8] But there was, he noted, something particularly tragic about Dorothy's death. Her medical career had been meteoric in its achievements, and it was ironic that, having faced all the horrors of war in Serbia and returned unscathed, she'd died in peacetime in a London hospital. After the final hymn, 'God Moves in a Mysterious Way', the mourners processed out to a stirring rendition of Chopin's Funeral March.

Harold Monro's miserable army career at last came to an end in March, releasing Alida from her stewardship of the shop. Charlotte ('Aunty Mew' in Alida's letters to Harold) had done what she could in his absence by helping Alida put the finishing touches to the Bookshop's rhyme sheets, which went for a penny more when the illustrations were coloured. She had got into the habit of collecting a batch to work on at home; just before Christmas, she had told Alida to 'do me up a roll which I will look in for'.[9] She constantly urged her young friend to keep warm and eat more, suggesting, at various times, 'bread and milk', 'toasted cheese', 'a good teaspoonful of powdered cinnamon in one breakfast cup of boiling milk', 'stewed veal cooked with an onion' and 'stewed prunes'.[10] The last few years had left Alida physically and mentally drained, and her doctor now prescribed a long rest – a prospect that unsettled Harold less than she would have liked. 'I loathe going away from you,' she wrote to him, shortly before his return to Devonshire Street. 'Do you understand in the least?'[11] Thankfully, on this occasion her good sense won out, and on 27 March – the very day Harold was officially demobilised – she left for an extended holiday on the Sussex coast.

Spring turned to summer and 'Now that the trees are green,' wrote Sydney in May, it was the perfect time for Charlotte to come and stay with him and Kate in Cambridge.[12] Going away anywhere was never straightforward for the Mew sisters: they were still taking it in turns to be on duty at home, looking after Ma and helping Jane Elsain with the chores. Just after Easter, Charlotte had managed to get away for a brief visit to Alida in Sussex, and now Anne was about to leave for a short break of her own – 'but when she comes back – if the trees are still green, I hope to be able to run down to Cambridge (thank you) probably toward the end of June'.[13] When June came, she went instead to Maggie and Edward Browne's place in Berkhamsted. However dreary she found Maggie now that she was married (and her talk was chiefly of 'the extravagance of cooks, the dearness of vegetables'[14]), she was an old and trusted friend, and her house – like the Olivers' houses in Kew and then Isleworth, or the Chicks' in Branscombe – was something of a haven.

It would be another two and a half years before Charlotte finally travelled to Cambridge, but in the meantime, Sydney continued to visit her and to do what he could to keep up her spirits and promote her work. On 16 May, he brought Siegfried Sassoon to have tea with her at Hogarth Studios. Sassoon had been taking a course with the Officers' Training Corps in Cambridge when he first met Sydney, in August 1915; it was an introduction that would make a lasting impression on the young poet:

I spent several evenings at his house – evenings made memorable by the wonderful books he showed me – and from which I returned to my camp bed in Pembroke College in a trance of stimulation after having handled manuscripts of D. G. Rossetti, William Morris and Francis Thompson. [. . .] On those Sunday nights in the quiet candle-lit room he seemed a sort of bearded and spectacled magician, conjuring up the medieval illuminated missals and psalters on which he was a famous expert, and bringing my mind into almost living contact with the Pre-Raphaelites whom I had worshipped since my dreaming adolescence.[15]

Since then, Sassoon had seen active service on the Western Front and had been decorated for bravery, given convalescent leave for gastric fever and sent to Craiglockhart military psychiatric hospital near Edinburgh – not suffering from shell shock, as so many of the hospital's patients were, but after delivering a letter in protest of the war to his commanding officer. On his discharge from the hospital he had resumed fighting, until a head wound in July 1918 ended his army service. He was now in the process of rounding up forty or so of Thomas Hardy's friends for a private compilation that he planned to present on Hardy's birthday at the start of June – an initiative Sydney felt sure would please the great man very much.

Charlotte readily agreed to take part, and contributed a short and simple lyric called 'Song', which would later be published in *The Athenaeum*. Sydney offered to get it set to music, only to discover that Charlotte had already composed a setting herself: 'I think I shall be content with my own little air – if I ever get it written out,' she told him.[16] By her own admission the poem (which rhymed 'knoweth' with 'goeth' and 'faileth' with 'availeth') was 'not quite 20th century!'[17] Nor was it her finest work, but the thank-you note Hardy sent in response to the gesture was, said Charlotte, 'as precious a bit of paper as I am ever likely to possess'.[18]

In July, she published another new poem on the theme of lost love in the opening issue of Harold Monro's latest venture, a periodical called *The Monthly Chapbook* (later renamed *The Chapbook*). It's possible that 'Sea Love' had been conceived during Charlotte's Easter break by the Sussex seaside with Alida, but she chose in any case to have her speaker tell the story in the West Country dialect she used for so many of her poems. It lends to this one an air of unselfconsciousness perfectly fitted to the situation, in which we find ourselves eavesdropping on a woman who has returned to the same stretch of shore where she recently stood with her sweetheart in the early, heady days of the relationship, when both lovers believed that their love could have no end:

> Tide be runnin' the great world over:
> 'Twas only last June month I mind that we
> Was thinkin' the toss and the call in the breast of the lover
> So everlastin' as the sea.
>
> Heer's the same little fishes that sputter and swim,
> Wi' the moon's old glim on the grey, wet sand;
> An' him no more to me nor me to him
> Than the wind goin' over my hand.

Sassoon was enthralled by this deft little storytelling lyric and took it with him down to Cambridge when he visited the Cockerells in August. He could hardly have failed to be impressed: in just eight lines Mew manages to suggest not only the story but the back-story of a passionate affair, introducing the reader to the speaker in such a way that to enter the poem feels like an act of intrusion. The reader's reward, as they step onto the shoreline beside that speaker, is to experience with her a quiet but magical performance. The second half effects a sudden diminuendo as the all-consuming pulse of the tide in the opening stanza dwindles to the faintest 'splutter' of 'little fishes' and the ephemeral flutter of a breeze passing over the speaker's moonlit hand. Sydney was equally captivated, but when he wrote to Charlotte about it, she responded with her usual self-deprecation: 'I am glad you liked the dialect poem in the down-hearted Chapbook.'[19]

Charlotte's friendship with Sydney was not without its tensions, and her reactions to him were complex, as they were with so many of the friends she made during adulthood. Sydney's closeness to Thomas Hardy was, perhaps, the biggest draw for her. She also appreciated hearing from him about the daily lives of a great many interesting people, without the practical difficulty of having to meet them in person. 'Nothing makes you forget to share your good things & sweeten the world by so doing,' she told him.[20] She was especially curious about one of his more unusual correspondents: a Benedictine nun called Laurentia whom he had met on a visit to Stanbrook Abbey in Worcester. Charlotte was, she said, 'rather envious of her cloistered peace' but she also felt keenly for the nun's friends, who abhorred the fact that Laurentia was hidden away in a monastery and hoped that she might one day change her mind and leave.[21] Charlotte's empathy for the friends was probably coloured by experience: she had recently had an impromptu visit from her favourite Isle of Wight cousin, Gertrude Mary, who, having worked as a hospital nurse for some years, had called in at Gordon Street 'with the sudden announcement that she was going into a convent', leaving behind a sister who was 'practically alone & I fear broken-hearted' – a comment that seems, at least in part, to convey Charlotte's own feelings on the matter.[22]

That autumn of 1919, she turned down yet another invitation to stay in Cambridge – in spite of a promise that there would 'be next to no-one in the place, if you want to maintain the sensation of London in August'.[23] Sydney's promise was a response to a comment Charlotte had made about the blessed quietness of London during the holiday season, when there were 'No callers – no-one expecting me to call, or minding, by their gay sea waves, whether or not their nice letters get answered.'[24] But the strength of Charlotte's resistance, sustained over so many months, suggests there may have been further issues, beyond the usual burden of her domestic duties, that prevented her from going to Cambridge. A few years earlier, she'd written to Mrs Sappho, from the straightforward calm of Boulogne, that she would 'really die of exhaustion if I had even to try to keep step with "clever" & complicated people'.[25] Cambridge, of course, was full of such people.

It may have been the social aspect of the visit that bothered her: Charlotte's pressing need for privacy meant she was uncomfortable spending protracted spells of time with any but her closest friends – friends who, crucially, knew of Henry and Freda's existence. True, she had made an exception for the Hardys, but Thomas Hardy was one of her literary heroes – and she had had to steel herself for the visit. Her first instinct was always to safeguard the family's secrets and protect them from the sort of gossip that would have so upset Ma, and the result was that over the years she had turned further inwards. But she had, too, a natural inclination towards seclusion that Sydney (gregarious even with strangers) may have found difficult to understand. Her love of privacy went back at least as far as the bad-weather days of her childhood, when she had pulled aside the heavy, fringed cloth of the nursery table and retreated inside.

Sydney's frequent invitations were beginning to exasperate her, and eventually there was nothing for it but to lay her cards on the table:

As to Cambridge, Dear and very kind Mr. Cockerell, I am not going to Cambridge (or to Oxford, for which I've just had an invitation) or to any other strange houses, or to see any other strange people, for the good of my soul or body, any more than your Sub-Prioress, for the good of hers, is going back into the world, which perhaps both of us know well enough.[26]

At times she found his persistence trying, and once or twice she made it clear to him. In February 1920, Sydney took the unusual step of voicing his own mild objections to *her* behaviour: 'Why so touchy?' he responded, after she'd reprimanded him for sending tickets she couldn't use and hadn't asked for, 'When I am merely seeking a means of providing you with three hours of exquisite artistic sensation and happiness.' It was uncharacteristic of him to take this defensive stance with Charlotte, and for a few paragraphs he continued in the same vein, testing, for the first time, how she might deal with his criticism:

Why so diffuse? when 'No, and be damned to you' would have said the same thing in six monosyllables.

Why so proud? This morning I stood for over 3 hours in a queue of people who were buying tickets for themselves and for friends at a distance. I cannot see that Cambridge is open to reprimand for this admirable custom, or that, if Gower Street disapproves of it, the manners of Gower Street are superior to those of Cambridge.[27]

Charlotte responded to this rhetorical posturing with a long silence, so that in April, Sydney was forced to write again, ten weeks after his first letter, to ask if he was 'still in disgrace'.[28] This time she relented and, without mentioning the incident or the silence, told him simply, 'Yes, please do come & see us in your next free time.'[29]

It's possible that without Sydney's perseverance Charlotte would have allowed the friendship to peter out, as she had done with other of her recent connections, but she was probably not so much angry as exhausted. It is easy to imagine just how wearying and demoralising it must have been for the family to surrender another floor of their home to strangers and retire to the dark, damp space of the basement. Charlotte had previously stored only her books there, rendering them 'damp & unspeakably dirty – only fit for private use', and now that they'd moved there to live she suggested to Sydney that perhaps he might one day 'put up with a cookshop supper at the Studio as our dungeon here is too cramped for visitors'.[30] It was hard for the whole household, but especially for Charlotte, to whom, as head of the family, the others (Jane Elsain, Anne and the ever-fault-finding Ma) turned unrelentingly for guidance and reassurance.

Charlotte may have dreamed of the sort of seclusion offered by a monastic life, but her sense of familial duty put paid to any serious thoughts of escaping. That autumn of 1919, her system was under particular stress: she was, as she told Sydney, 'nerving' herself to face the winter, 'which gives my beloved London her best effects, but shrivels *me* up!'[31] In mid-September, Jane Elsain took a holiday and Charlotte found herself busier than ever. Besides the extra house-work, she was plagued, once again, by business letters – 'which,' she said, 'if I had it, I would give anyone £600 p.a. to write for me'.[32] As temperatures dropped and her workload increased, it seemed almost inevitable that she would fall prey to some sort of illness. By the time Florence Hardy invited her down to Max Gate again in October, she was feeling too drained to contemplate it, and wrote to apologise that 'the result of one or two attacks of "flu" is that I have now to stay & take things quietly at home.'[33]

Winter had fallen quickly that year. A reporter in the *Globe* noted how almost overnight, in the second week of October, Londoners had swapped their light autumn clothing for overcoats and furs, and bus drivers had put on their khaki scarves and leather driving mitts. 'One of the most unexpected results of this swift descent of winter', wrote the *Globe* reporter, 'was a number of colds and beginnings of influenza which seemed to attack everyone.'[34] Unexpected because the official line was that the deadly 'Spanish flu' pandemic was now in abeyance in Britain. In reality, it was very far from being over and would even-tually result in five times as many deaths globally as the war itself.

Prime Minister David Lloyd George had contracted it in September 1918, though the papers – prevented from propagating demoralising news stories during the war – reported that the premier was merely suffering from a chill that he might have averted had he not been insistent about 'setting an example in coal economy' by refusing to light a fire in his room.[35]

Lloyd George, fifty-five at the time of his illness, survived, but worldwide the virus killed upwards of fifty million people, affecting every continent. In the UK, it was brought back by soldiers returning home from France, and if Charlotte's flu episodes were part of the 'Spanish' strain, then it may have been her age that saved her. The virus was particularly aggressive among the young, triggering a deadly response in their more vigorous immune systems – a feature that goes some way towards explaining why, of the seven Chick sisters, it was the youngest, Dorothy, who had succumbed the previous February. Reports of Dorothy's death had drawn attention to her age: 'It is painfully sad that one of the few lady doctors of the land should die at such an early age as 35,' one paper lamented.[36]

While the war receives only a handful of mentions in Charlotte's letters, that September of 1919, the *Westminster Gazette* published her third poem on the subject. The final peace agreement between Allied and Associated Governments and Germany had been signed at Versailles in June, bringing a formal end to hostilities and prompting a spate of commemorative activity, including the erection of memorials across the country. Charlotte's new poem, 'The Cenotaph', appeared two months after the first (temporary) London Cenotaph was unveiled in Whitehall. Designed by Edwin Lutyens, the structure was inspired by the *cenotaphia* ('empty graves') of classical archaeology, which were built to commemorate absent remains. It's possible that the poem depicts a completely imagined construction – an example, as has been suggested, of what John Hollander calls 'notional ekphrasis'. Certainly the memorial described in it is quite different from the plain London monument – an undecorated space onto which millions of people could project their own stories and emotions about the war. Charlotte's Cenotaph (with its statue of 'Victory, winged' and its 'stairway, at the foot') was not that. But in July, a French catafalque had been erected near the Arc de Triomphe, to serve as a saluting point for troops during the *quatorze juillet* Victory March. Although the whole edifice was dismantled after the parade, a large photograph of it had appeared that summer of 1919 on the front page of the *Illustrated London News* and in *The Graphic*. It showed huge emblematic figures of Victory, with outstretched wings, poised above a small flight of steps, just as depicted in the poem.[37]

On a handful of previous occasions Charlotte had marked events of major national importance by writing a poem: the passing of Queen Victoria, the sinking of the *Titanic*, the war. Such events seemed to awaken her conscience; it was as if she felt she had a duty as a poet to mark them. Many of her other subjects – marriage, religious doubt, the segregation of so-called 'moral defectives', the incarceration of the insane – happened also to be issues of national concern, but their chief interest to Charlotte lay in their connection with her personal life, and those of people close to her. The few times when she did write specifically to mark a public event, it rarely resulted in her best work, but 'The Cenotaph' is a notable exception.

Her friends certainly thought so. Sydney relayed the fact that Siegfried Sassoon admired it as much as he did himself. Charlotte was clearly pleased by these compliments and quipped (with her customary diffidence) that it was 'a mercy for your friends that C. M. only breaks out, & then mildly, about once in seven years!'[38] She added that 'there is nothing in the *Cenotaph* except the little experiment of the last three lines which you spotted: & since you don't complain of it I suppose it has come off'.[39] In those lines, she imagines the planned cenotaph standing in a bustling market place –

While looking into every busy whore's and huckster's face
As they drive their bargains, is the Face
Of God: and some young, piteous, murdered face.

From this time on, the poem suggests, no business transaction could take place without the traders sensing behind their customers' eyes the steady, accusatory gaze of the murdered soldier, and of God. This wasn't the first time Charlotte had written about the image of an ever-watchful 'Face'. In 'The Country Sunday' (1905) a thick, concealing sky hangs between us and the Face, which, 'watching us invisibly, we somehow fail to see'.[40] The unsettling sensation of being answerable to an observer, and therefore never quite alone, was something Charlotte had experienced since childhood, when her version of an ever-watchful and terrifyingly exacting deity had, so she wrote, 'judged in those old days my scamped and ill-done tasks [. . .] and still, with wider range, it views and judges now'.[41]

By late 1919, *The Farmer's Bride* was selling much better, and the Poetry Bookshop was making plans for reissuing it. Harold Monro felt that arrangements could also be made, 'subject to certain conditions, for its publication in America, at the same time as its re-issue here'.[42] Five days before Christmas, Charlotte learned that Houghton Mifflin had offered to publish the book in the States but that Harold had turned them down, on the grounds that he could probably get a better offer elsewhere. His preference was for the book to be placed with the more prestigious Macmillan Company in New York. Why, Charlotte wanted to know, had she not been consulted? Houghton Mifflin would certainly have been, she said, 'good enough' for her.[43] To be published in the States was (as it remains today) a significant milestone in the career of a British poet. What restraint, then, must

Charlotte have mustered to acknowledge that if Harold's idea of getting Macmillan to do it were to succeed, 'you will, as you say, be doing better'.[44] Charlotte now revealed that the vice-president at Macmillan in America had written to her back in May expressing an interest in her work. He'd told her that since *The Farmer's Bride* had already been published in England, 'the American copyright is therefore lost', so it would be 'inadvisable' to bring it out in the States.[45] However, he added, if she would care to send her next volume to them 'to let us consider its publication, I should be much gratified'.[46]

There was still a chance they might be persuaded by the official proposal Harold now sent, but three months into the new year of 1920, he got a formal response. The answer, at least for the time being, was no. It was a decision, said Charlotte, that 'confirms my regret that Mssrs Houghton Mifflin's offer for it was not accepted'.[47] Macmillan was impressed by the book but, sure enough, had turned it down on the grounds of copyright.

Under different circumstances Charlotte would perhaps have been more openly aggrieved with Harold, but Alida had just informed her (out of the blue) that she and Harold were to marry. From her own dealings with Harold, Charlotte thought him pompous, secretive and self-important, but she did her best to keep her thoughts to herself, and on 27 March, the wedding went ahead at the register office in Holborn, with no guests except the two strangers who'd been drafted in to act as witnesses. Charlotte was unable to keep from sounding a note of caution in her congratulatory message: 'Dear Alida,' she wrote, 'With all my heart I wish you luck, happiness & if it's not fatally bad for you your heart's desire.'[48] She was probably less shocked than Alida when she learned later that Harold had hurried off straight after the wedding to 'stay with a friend' for the night.[49]

The Monros' wedding did little to interfere with business as usual at the Poetry Bookshop. Among other things, Harold was now proposing to issue a second edition of *The Farmer's Bride*, to be published that autumn of 1920, this time in 'boards' (hardback). The idea now was to add a number of new poems, with a view to asking Macmillan to regard it as a new book and bring out an American edition under the title of *Saturday Market*. Charlotte was doubtful of her prospects, and she had still not forgiven Harold for failing to consult her over the Houghton Mifflin offer. She felt that in professional matters things ought to be done formally – in a way that demonstrated respect for the work – and that the author ought to be included in discussions from the outset. 'I shall be sorry if this last opportunity of an American edition should be missed together with chances now gone by,' she told Harold now.[50] In the event, the scheme came off, and by October, Charlotte was preparing to sign an agreement with Macmillan, bringing to a close ten anxious months of negotiation.

Charlotte had a group of ten additional poems assembled for the new book, and in July 1920, one final lyric, 'I Have Been Through the Gates', appeared as the opening poem in the thirteenth issue of Harold Monro's *Chapbook*. In eight lines, this electrifying poem communicates – like others written during this period, in particular 'Sea Love' (July 1919) and 'Song' (October 1919) – a sense of profound loss. Its speaker describes entering the glorious gates to the beloved's heart and then, as if recoiling from danger or in revulsion, creeping 'back, back', the heart having become, chillingly, 'a place with the lights gone out, forsaken by great winds'. But the opening is one of the most jubilant lines that Mew was to write: 'His heart, to me, was a place of palaces and pinnacles and shining towers'.

Did Charlotte have a specific lost love in mind? Did the poem stem from a heaping-up of personal grief accrued over many years? Or was she writing on behalf of everyone who had lost a sweetheart in the war? There is even the possibility that the poem is not about a romantic love at all but about Henry, whose broken spirit had lain for so many years imprisoned behind the literal gates of the asylum, forever abandoned by 'the heavenly rain, unclean and unswept'. The answer is probably not clear-cut, but whatever its impetus, the poem rings out with the anguish of an abandoned dream, and its sentiment spills into the longest lines Mew had yet made – twenty-seven syllables, in one instance – as if the enormity of feeling could not possibly be contained by anything shorter. Clearly, she was making no concession this time round to the difficulties such lines had caused for the typesetter of the book's earlier edition.

> The walls are standing to-day, and the gates: I have been through
>   the gates, I have groped, I have crept
> Back, back. There is dust in the streets, and blood; they are empty;
>   darkness is over them;
> His heart is a place with the lights gone out, forsaken by great
>   winds and the heavenly rain, unclean and unswept,
> Like the heart of the holy city, old, blind, beautiful Jerusalem,
>   Over which Christ wept.

The crucial thing about the poem's location – a place 'through the gates' – is that it is imagined and romanticised ('as we see things in dreams') before it is actually encountered. Cambridge academic John Newton has noted that the poem shares something with Jude Fawley's idealisation of the university city of Christminster in Hardy's *Jude the Obscure*, and with Jude's bitter disappointment upon finally arriving at the city – a disappointment that matches, perhaps, the abandoned hopes that Charlotte and her family had once harboured for Henry. Like Christminster, Mew's utopia is compared with the holy city and populated with towers that soar heavenwards; it rises before our eyes from a few, carefully chosen words: 'I remember the trees, and the high, white walls, and how the sun was always on the towers'. Though utterly different from that of 'Sea Love', the setting of 'I Have Been Through the Gates' is conjured with the same extraordinary concision. Both poems show Mew working at the height of her powers. In one respect, it is astonishing that she travelled to such places from the dark, damp confines of her Bloomsbury basement. But the dominant mood of the poems is one of disillusionment: in both cases we encounter a dispirited figure in an empty landscape, standing among the ruins of an idyll they once believed in.

On a fine day in late August, Sydney paid an unannounced visit to the Mews' basement, and was shocked by the conditions in which they were living. He insisted on taking Charlotte out to supper, noting simply in his diary that evening that 'She was not well & they evidently have a great struggle, with a tiny income.'[51] It may have been this visit that set him thinking about a campaign to establish a pension for her – a scheme that would at least alleviate her financial difficulties. For the rest, there was very little he could do except offer diversion. He thought the letters of his friend Georgiana Burne-Jones might provide her with a welcome distraction and left them with her to read. Georgiana was the wife of the Pre-Raphaelite painter Edward Burne-Jones and, for a while, a close friend and confidante of George Eliot, as well as William Morris, John Ruskin and others – but the last letter she ever wrote, before her sudden death earlier that year, was to Sydney.

Returning Lady Burne-Jones's letters the following month, Charlotte remarked that reading them had been like listening in on two friends in intimate conversation, so that 'even to a stranger the silencing of such a living voice – at the end – came as a shock. But,' she continued, 'between friends, one on this side & one on that, perhaps there is no real silence & often I think such speech as was once heard here gathers force & beauty when it comes to be heard only with the inward Ear.'[52] That idea, of death as an amplification of all meaningful noise, very likely had its roots in a passage she had first encountered in George Eliot's *Middlemarch*, in which the narrator observes that 'If we had a keen vision and feeling of all ordinary human life, it would be like hearing the grass grow and the squirrel's heart beat, and we should die of that roar which lies on the other side of silence.'

Towards the end of her own life, Charlotte would echo Eliot's words again, as she looked back on the time when she finally visited Sydney and Kate in Cambridge: 'What you gave me at Cambridge that fortnight can't be told this side of silence,' she would explain to Kate.[53] In the meantime, there was plenty still to hear. Details from the same *Middlemarch* passage had appeared in her 1913 poem 'The Changeling', in which the child speaker attributes her distracted air to a heightened sensitivity to the sounds of the world – and it's hard not to see the changeling as a version of Charlotte herself. She believed all her life that though an acute tuning-in to the world might be painful, the pay-off was that the committed listener got to experience so much that might otherwise be missed. And if there were some who settled for less as they grew older, Charlotte – like her 'Madeleine' – refused to be content with the 'tame, bloodless things' of the world. Now that she had turned fifty, her powers of perception and her receptiveness to life's richness were still a match for the girlhood powers she had once intimated through the voice of her changeling:

> Sometimes I wouldn't speak, you see,
> Or answer when you spoke to me,
> Because in the long, still dusks of Spring
> You can hear the whole world whispering;
> The shy green grasses making love,
> The feathers grow on the dear, grey dove,
> The tiny heart of the redstart beat,
> The patter of the squirrel's feet,
> The pebbles pushing in the silver streams,
> The rushes talking in their dreams,
> The swish-swish of the bat's black wings,
> The wild-wood bluebell's sweet ting-tings,
> Humming and hammering at your ear,
> Everything there is to hear
> In the heart of hidden things . . .

19

Minuit Sonné and Not Half the Day's Work Done!

1921–1923

Once she had corrected the final proofs for the new, expanded edition of *The Farmer's Bride* and returned them to her publisher, Charlotte found herself in an unusually relaxed frame of mind. If book publication had taught her anything, it was that the writing life involved a whole new set of responsibilities, all of them unpaid: engaging in discussions about typesetting and page format, proof-reading and correcting, responding to permissions requests from anthologists and negotiating the tiny fees that went with them – the list at times seemed endless. She had found the task of amending proofs and ensuring her amendments were incorporated especially exasperating: the whole process had been, she said, a 'muddle'.[1] But the business side of the new edition had at last been put to bed and with it the pressure to produce new material also passed.

Charlotte now gave herself licence to get back to what she liked doing best – which is to say visiting the Reading Room to read, make notes, think and experiment. At the start of February 1921, she renewed her ticket, and not even Sydney's wearisome enquiries after new poems could put a dent in her mood. 'Alas: poor verses – if they were made as puddings are one could regularly serve up one a week,' she told him airily, throwing in a bit of Shakespeare for good measure: '"Things without remedy should be without regard" & I have been playing with plasticine instead.'[2] Sydney would have recognised the quotation: this was Lady Macbeth, soothing her husband in the wake of his first murder – and if the association was far-fetched, the message was perfectly clear: in this rare moment of relative calm, Charlotte would not be harried.

When the new book arrived in the post, she was relaxed enough to comment to Alida that it looked 'very cheery in new blue coat'.[3] Florence Hardy received a copy shortly afterwards and read all the new poems aloud to Thomas, before reporting back to Charlotte that he 'liked "Sea Love" perhaps the best'.[4] But she was concerned to see that Charlotte had altered a line in 'On the Road to the Sea' from 'I who make others smile' (as it had appeared in *The Englishwoman* back in 1914) to 'I who make other women smile'. Was the change the result of Florence's comments on the uncertainty of the speaker's gender? If so, then she rather regretted making those comments: 'There was', she reflected now, 'something alluring in each reader supplying his own idea.'[5]

The simultaneous appearance of the book in the States under the title of *Saturday Market* meant that reviews began to appear on both sides of the Atlantic at the same time. In London, *The Sphere* had asked for a photo of the fifty-one-year-old Charlotte, but she didn't have one – and, she told Alida, didn't really see why one was needed. 'It's only because I don't want to part with it that I'm not asking them to have J's [Alida's dog, Joggles's] instead.'[6] With some reluctance, she agreed to sit for a photograph, from which she looks out at us, thoughtful but relaxed in a crisp white collarless blouse with a deep V at the neck, her hair – now almost entirely white – drawn back softly from her face and forehead, the arch of her brows as pronounced as ever. Beneath the photo, *The Sphere*'s reviewer enthused that the book's title poem was 'full of that thrill and charm which only the very best poetry can give'.[7] Elsewhere, *The Spectator* admired Mew's 'wonderful degree of craftsmanship',[8] and Edith Sitwell, writing for the *Daily Herald*, felt the new edition had been enriched by the eleven poems added to it – each one of which brought us, she said, 'face to face with truth, whether we like it or not'.[9] In the States, a review by Marion Strobel took up over three pages of *Poetry* magazine, while the *New York Times* drew attention to Mew's facility with the dramatic monologue: 'It is as if the poet put on other lives as we put on garments,' the reviewer marvelled.[10]

In July, a letter arrived from the New York poet and critic Louis Untermeyer. The previous spring, Siegfried Sassoon had visited him and his wife, Jean, and read aloud to them the long poem 'Madeleine in Church' – 'with a beauty that no professional elocutionist could ever attain,' he explained.[11] The Untermeyers had immediately sent off for a British copy of *The Farmer's Bride*, and since receiving it they had been relentless in insisting to anyone and everyone who would listen that an ignorance of Mew's poetry was 'little short of criminal!'[12] The recent appearance of *Saturday Market* in the States had brought for them 'a wave of relief not unmixed with triumph'. He was writing now to ask for permission to include three of Charlotte's shorter poems in a new edition of his *Modern British Poetry*, along with a brief biographical gloss. This was the beginning of a sustained crusade on Untermeyer's part to spread the word of Mew's poetry in America and to write publicly as often as he could about her unique gift.

When the anthology eventually appeared, the standard background details were missing from Charlotte's introduction. She had no doubt replied in her usual way to Untermeyer's request for 'a line or two of biographical matter', but a condensed version of one of Untermeyer's glowing reviews made up for the absence.[13] There were no hard feelings on his part: if Charlotte should ever care to visit the States, their New York apartment had, he said, 'a Steinway piano, books and two ardent admirers of Charlotte Mew' to offer.[14] Over the years they continued to correspond, albeit sporadically, Untermeyer remaining unerringly appreciative and respectful. Was Charlotte aware, he asked her on one occasion, that Sara Teasdale – 'one of our finest lyricists' – was also an admirer of *The Farmer's Bride*?[15]

The poetry was also being discussed in Europe. That November of 1921, the American writer and editor Alfred Kreymborg sent, from Rome, the inaugural issue of *Broom, An International Magazine of the Arts*, which had been launched with the aim of introducing Americans to European avant-garde artworks. Perhaps Charlotte might care to contribute a poem for a fee? In response she posted off 'Here Lies a

Prisoner', a five-line lyric that had almost certainly been prompted by the twentieth anniversary of Henry's death earlier that year.[16]

> Leave him: he's quiet enough: and what matter
> Out of his body or in, you can scatter
> The frozen breath of his silenced soul, of his outraged soul to the
>   winds that rave:
> Quieter now than he used to be, but listening still to the magpie chatter
>   Over his grave.

Alongside this new interest from European and American quarters, Charlotte's work was being reproduced at home more widely than ever. During 1921–2, it appeared in five important British anthologies – among them, Thomas Caldwell's *Golden Book of Modern English Poetry*, which was part of the bestselling Everyman series. The demand for her poems had been a long time in coming, and when the American *Bookman* printed her 'To a Child in Death', she wrote to Sydney to let him know, adding excitedly that the editor was 'asking for more – God help him!'[17] Louis Untermeyer happened to see the poem in the *Bookman* that month and sent an admiring note to Charlotte, signing it off with 'Strength to you – and your large & flexible line.'[18]

What Charlotte had not foreseen was that her newfound renown would also make her fair game for attack. In the August of 1921, a parody titled 'The Circus Clown' appeared in *Punch*. It was the work of E. V. Knox, known to the magazine's readers as 'Evoe'. The opening draws on images and phrasing from 'The Fête' and 'The Quiet House':

> The moonlight drips on the parlour floor;
> I shall go mad if no one wipes it up.
> When I was one year old Nurse used to say,
> 'It's no more use to cry when milk is spilt

> Than cry about the moon.' There were big bars
> Across the nursery window. You said once,
> 'Life is all bars on which we beat in vain
> Praying for drinks.' I smiled when you said that.[19]

Knox had been writing his parodies for some time, and a number of male poets, including Thomas Hardy and John Masefield, had fallen prey to his pen; but the secure literary reputations of such poets rendered the parodies harmless – even flattering. As the first woman poet to be given the Evoe treatment, it was different for Charlotte. For one thing, Knox had not thought it necessary in any of the previous spoofs to advertise the poet's gender. But *Punch* already had something of a reputation for caricaturing the figure of the New Woman in its cartoons, and in keeping with that tradition the Mew parody veers uncomfortably close to personal mockery, ending with the line 'Ah, God! why did they make me bob my hair?' Charlotte at any rate viewed the exercise as an attack; she was deeply hurt by it, and the hurt lingered for some time. 'I expect you saw Punch's parody of August 24th, a delicate & humane reduction of CMM to pulp,' she wrote to Sydney, almost a month later.[20]

In spite of her growing reputation, Charlotte was still being excluded from volumes in which she ought, in the opinion of many, to have been represented. When J. C. Squire sent Thomas Hardy his *Book of Women's Verse* in January 1922, Hardy commented that he was 'rather disappointed to find you had omitted Charlotte Mew – the greatest poetess I have come across lately, in my judgement'.[21] It's likely that Charlotte's work was simply too novel for Squire, whose tastes were well known to be on the conservative side; contemporary critic Frank Swinnerton described him as 'all in favour of traditional forms of verse'.[22] More annoying, certainly as far as Harold Monro was concerned, was Mew's absence from the fifth and final volume of Edward Marsh's *Georgian Poetry*. The first three volumes had included no female poets at all; the fourth (published in 1919) featured four poems by Fredegond Shove, whom literary history has now all but forgotten. Monro had pointed out the year earlier, in *Some Contemporary Poets*, that in the current climate 'Success depends on knowing the right people' – and Shove moved in all the right circles.²³ Her aunt was married to Ralph Vaughan Williams, who helped promote her work by setting four of the poems to music, and her mother was a cousin of Virginia Woolf. This latter connection would have counted with Marsh: he, Leonard Woolf and Fredegond's husband, Gerald, were all members of the small, tight-knit intellectual society known as the Cambridge Apostles. In 1919, there were three poets in the group, and all three (Rupert Brooke, James Stephens and Robert Trevelyan) had featured in the opening volume of Marsh's series. The latest number also contained seven poems by the aristocratic Vita Sackville-West, who, once again, was at the heart of the Bloomsbury set. Charlotte Mew, of course, had no such connections.

The depressive episodes Charlotte suffered from as an adult (she called them 'the usual blues'²⁴) seemed always to be triggered by specific external events; the problem was that those events were so numerous. In the four years since they'd met, Sydney Cockerell had become a vital part of her support network, as indispensable to her as Ethel and Winifred Oliver, the Chicks and other older friends. His rather simplistic, upbeat way of viewing the world could, at times, be irritating to her; but it was also very often – and particularly when she felt herself to be on the verge of a depression – just what Charlotte needed. Both of them knew this, without having to say as much. In September, he took her to see a short film by Charlie Chaplin called *Shoulder Arms*, about an army private who goes on a daring mission behind enemy lines. It was, said Charlotte afterwards, 'a truly delightful evening. [. . .] Didn't you like best of all the camouflaged hero sprinting away from the fat German between the trees?'[25] She confided to Florence Hardy that she would take a Chaplin film over some of the more worthy objects that Sydney pressed upon her, any day: *Shoulder Arms* was, she said, 'a far, far better thing I thought than the Dooms Day Book – kindly lent me by S. C. C. which I found quite indigestible'.[26] But her gratitude to Sydney was profound and heartfelt: there was, by now, she told him, 'so much to say thank you for that I can't say it at all'.[27]

Film outings with friends were helpful, but what Charlotte also needed was total solitude and a change of scene. With Ma more fragile and demanding than ever, it took both her daughters most of their time to look after her. Charlotte had, in addition to her care duties, the administrative side of things to see to. However hard she worked, she never quite got through her list of daily tasks: 'Minuit sonné and not half the day's work done!' she told Sydney one late December night, with barely suppressed panic.[28] For some while now she had been in the habit of staying up past midnight to finish her work: most of her letters were written between 1 and 2 a.m. ('my free time'); the problem was that by then she was really only up to sleeping.[29]

With Anne also needing time away from Gordon Street now and then, the two sisters continued to stand in for each other, as they had always done. When her turn came for a break that autumn of 1921, Charlotte took herself off to spend a few days in Salisbury, where she had once stopped for half an hour between trains to sit in the Cathedral Close. What she remembered above all was the sound of the rooks, and she had come down now, she told Florence Hardy, 'to hear them cawing again'.[30] It was an unusually warm October, and the hypnotic pull of the 'elsewhere' quickly worked its magic: before long she was reporting that 'in the sunshine with the red street & the grey spire' the place was 'like a dream city'.[31]

But the little holiday was all too brief a respite from the drudgery that awaited her back home. For friends, the Mews' daily existence, lived out in the stale air of the Gordon Street basement, was hard to witness, but their calls invariably lifted Charlotte's spirits. Outings to the friends' houses, when Charlotte could manage it, were more valuable still. The memories of such occasions were, for her, she said, 'like great coats hung up, to reach down & get warm in on cold days, with snow on the ground'.[32] Sydney knew this and never gave up issuing invitations. That difficult winter of 1921/2, he and Kate invited Charlotte to Cambridge to see in the New Year and make a weekend of it. Anne fell ill again at Christmas but had rallied enough by the 28th for Charlotte to feel able to confirm the visit. She arrived in Cambridge at around six on the evening of Saturday 31st and walked with Sydney to his spacious town house in Shaftesbury Road. It was a far cry from the dark, damp sickroom atmosphere of Gordon Street. In the warmth of a study lined from floor to ceiling with books and hung with sumptuously patterned William Morris curtains, Charlotte chatted with the Cockerells about their favourite artists, admired more of Kate's illuminated manuscripts and gradually got used to the luxury of not having to jump up at the sound of Ma's voice to rearrange pillows or attend to her personal needs.

In her thank-you note, Charlotte enclosed a postcard of a work by the French symbolist painter Eugène Carrière, with the comment that 'I believe his idea was – as far as possible – to paint pure emotion.'[33] The words could almost be a statement of intent for her own work. Like the near-monochrome faces Carrière painted, which gaze out from their canvases with expressions that capture something beyond the mere appearance of the sitter, the words of Charlotte's characters – the haunted, the heartbroken, the desperate and the destitute – confront readers head on with their unembellished depictions of how things really are.

This time she returned home to a fresh set of challenges. The Mews had been at 9 Gordon Street for some thirty years, and now that the lease was approaching its end, the Bedford Estate had written to ask that they either 'make good the dilapidations or pay their value'.[34]

Since Walter Mew Barnes's death in 1909, the family had employed the services of Layton's solicitors in the City. Hugh Layton now suggested to the estate that in view of Mrs Mew's financial position and advanced age (which he gave as 'about 90', though she was in fact seventy-seven), the family be released from any liability on condition that they vacated the property ahead of time, 'on Ladyday next'.[35] In British and Irish tradition, Lady Day used to be one of the four 'quarter days', days on which school terms started, servants were hired and rents collected. It fell on 25 March – which would leave the Mews just over two months to find new accommodation. Nevertheless, some sort of arrangement had to be made, and this (if they could get the estate to agree) seemed the most workable option. Ought it not also be taken into account, asked Charlotte, that ten years earlier the family had spent – of their own volition and without prompting – 'at least 100 pounds' on improving the house's drainage by removing the old brick drain and having a modern system installed? Yes, it ought – and Layton passed the information on, along with his opinion that paying for more house repairs at this juncture was out of the question. Mrs Mew's trust property brought in a net income of approximately £300 per year; out of that sum the Mews had to pay not only rent and rates but Freda's hospital fees (around £130 per year), doctors' and vets' fees, food, clothes and other daily living expenses. 'We understand that one of the daughters does some occasional light work,' Layton explained, 'which brings her in a very trifling income' – and he was probably referring to Anne rather than Charlotte.[36] The estate decided to cut their losses and quickly agreed to the terms.

For some time now Sydney had been turning over the idea of arranging a civil list pension for Charlotte. At the end of the previous year, he had called in on her at Hogarth Studios, and it was probably at that meeting, on 17 December 1921, that he first told her about the plan. At any rate, it was the first time Charlotte had opened up to him about the true extent of her problems. She seems to have used the occasion to confide her biggest secrets of all: that she had other siblings, besides Anne; that they had been sent to asylums many years earlier; and that her beloved elder brother was no longer living. The following day, she sent him a note, emphasising the need for the conversation to remain confidential: 'I have told practically no-one about our affairs & don't mean to till "the hend",' she told him, her flippancy failing to hide the anxiety behind her words.[37]

She had kept the fact of Henry and Freda's existence from all the other friends she'd made in adulthood: Mrs Sappho, May Sinclair – even Alida. Why did she single Sydney out for special treatment? It's likely that he needed to get an idea of Charlotte's income and expenditure for the civil list application – a matter it would have been hard to discuss without Charlotte revealing the heavy expense of Freda's upkeep in the asylum – but even taking that into account, her confession indicates the degree of trust she now placed in him. Loyal as ever, Sydney made no mention of the matter in his diary, a detail that is as significant as it is touching: ever the archivist, he kept his diary with the full intention of its being seen by future generations interested in the many famous artists and writers with whom he mixed. Careful as he was to protect Charlotte's privacy and keep the more upsetting details of her private life to himself, hearing them had strengthened his resolve; he left the studio that cold December afternoon determined to press ahead with plans for a civil list proposal.

The Mew family's ill health extended that winter to the one non-human member of the household. Wek had not been in the best shape for some time now and had recently fallen prey to bumblefoot, a persistent foot infection that was failing to respond to treatment. Without effective medication, the condition quickly worsened and his sores turned into painful abscesses. When he was no longer able to stand on his perch, the parrot man at London Zoo advised that it would be kindest to put him to sleep – but neither Charlotte nor Anne could bring themselves to do it. Since Wek hated for men to come near him, a male vet (and there was no other kind) was out of the question. Among their friends, the animal-loving Alida seemed the obvious choice and, with some hesitation, she agreed to step in. When it came to it, she found the ordeal so unnerving that she was able to recall, over thirty years later, the 'terrible moment when I was led by the two sisters to a room at the back of the house in complete darkness except for a candle'.[38] She performed the necessary deed with the aid of a chloroform-soaked sponge and several large blankets to seal off the surrounding air, and left the room to wait for the chemical to take effect. When she returned, with a small box, to retrieve the corpse, she reached her hand into the cage – 'only to receive a smart nip on the finger which nearly caused me to scream hysterically'. She had to steel herself to reach in again and take hold of the poor bird by its neck, clutching it until it fell completely limp.

Knowing that they would be moving to a new house before long, Charlotte and Anne resolved to bury Wek in the Oliver family's back garden in Isleworth, where they would be able to visit whenever they wanted.[39] And if this were a fairy story, as the sisters placed the little box in the ground, they might also have been able to lay to rest with it all the worst times from the family's years at Gordon Street – the deaths of Elizabeth Goodman, their father and then Henry, and the havoc wreaked by Freda's sudden removal to the asylum. But it is not a fairy story and the ghosts of absent loved ones – and of the area surrounding Gordon Street itself – continued to haunt Charlotte, as would soon become clear from her poetry.

It wasn't until early March 1922, just a few weeks before Lady Day, that Charlotte finally found somewhere suitable to live and began making the necessary arrangements. The top two floors of 86 Delancey Street, on the northeast edge of Regent's Park, comprised '2 rooms & 2 attics & a doll's kitchen'.[40] Some of the heavy, dark-wood furniture with which the Mews had filled the Gordon Street house had been sent into storage when the second lot of tenants moved in, but there was still far too much to fit into the new lodgings. They had one of the beds put up in Anne's studio, with the idea of staying there if they were out late in town. Sydney too was invited to use it – 'if it's not too short!' – whenever he found he'd missed the last train back to Cambridge.[41] Ma insisted on taking to Delancey Street the large, round, gate-legged table, her six Adam chairs and several valuable mirrors. Even after moving the surplus into storage, Charlotte anticipated it would be 'a perfect scuffle to get out & in'.[42] It seemed little short of a miracle when, on 21 March, they managed it.

In many ways, the new home was an improvement. In Gordon Street, the tall houses opposite their own had blocked out much of the light. The view from the front room at Delancey Street delighted all three of the Mew women: through the trees they could see a convent, whose green shutters made Charlotte think of France. When Sydney visited a week later, on a day of cold sleet showers, he was relieved to see that the new quarters, though 'more restricted internally', had 'great external advantages of air and movement over the house in Gordon St'.[43] Charlotte soon took up her old habit of window-watching whenever she got the chance. Four years of living below ground level had deprived her of that treat, and now she made up for lost time. She loved especially the constant whirl of activity: 'carts & cabs & people & snorting trains going by below – & birds chirping above it all'.[44] By the end of May, the trees from the Delancey Street windows were 'a dream of greenness & movement – with the birds flying over – & we are so flooded by sunlight that by day I suppose we shall have to shut them out, at any rate while it's 88 in the shade'.[45] She had recently been thrilled to see 'the full blast of Bank Holiday under our window – airballs, ice & lemonade & fruit stalls & Punch & Judy – all under the trees – &

greatly it pleases me, though it makes the eggs boil over & the house "contrary"!'[46]

For all that, the move was not quite the fresh start it might have been: while her surroundings had changed for the better, Charlotte's long list of chores and obligations had actually increased. Jane Elsain, in common with many other domestic servants after the war, had left the Mews for better-paid employment elsewhere, and with no maid at the new house, life was, said Charlotte, 'more difficult' than ever.[47]

Meanwhile, life was also becoming increasingly complicated for Alida. Harold seemed always to be depressed these days, and Alida now confided in Charlotte that he was drinking heavily and spending as little time as possible in the new marital home in Heathcote Street – very near, as it happened, to Charlotte's childhood house in Doughty Street. Alida was beside herself, but the more she pleaded with her husband, the worse things seemed to get. In fact, they had not been right for some time. In February the previous year, the couple had left abruptly to stay in a house Harold had bought on the French Riviera. When she heard of the sudden departure, Charlotte had taken it as a good sign, assuming the decision had been made on a romantic impulse. She'd imagined her young friend – not quite a year into her marriage – playing the tables at nearby Monte Carlo and promenading about the place 'much painted, with a bright green parasol'.[48] In reality, Villa des Oliviers was a tiny, sparsely furnished cottage, perched high above a town on the narrow ridge of Cap Ferrat, from which Alida eventually sent back reports of flu and gastritis, a cold, 'matless' kitchen floor, and a severe toothache that had plagued Harold ever since they'd arrived. When she thought things couldn't get any worse, she'd made the discovery that for some months Harold had been seeing a young soldier whom he referred to as 'J'. Confronted with this knowledge, she could no longer ignore the real reason for her husband's long-standing unhappiness – as well as his lack of interest in the physical side of their relationship.

Charlotte felt desperately concerned for Alida ('I wish you would now pack up & get home intact,' she told her[49]), and angry with Harold about his apparent lack of concern for his wife's wellbeing. It was not in Charlotte's nature to allow personal feelings to interfere with business, but after hearing about the shenanigans in France she let her irritability show during an exchange with Harold over one of her poems. She had recently sent him 'The Rambling Sailor', for the latest edition of his *Chapbook*. This ballad-style poem – about a sailor pursued through quays and backstreets across the globe by the tireless figure of Death – would one day become the title poem of her posthumous collection. Like many other of her character poems it is written in dialect, but here the incongruous, sing-song rhythms of a nursery rhyme lend the storytelling a menacing edge. The opening stanza outlines a scenario that will provide a platform for Death's own words:

> In the old back streets o' Pimlico,
> On the docks at Monte Video,
> At the Ring o' Bells on Plymouth Hoe
> He'm arter me now wheerever I go.
> An' dirty nights when the wind do blow
> I can hear him sing-songin' up from sea:
> Oh! no man nor woman's bin friend to me
> An' to-day I'm feared wheer to-morrow I'll be,
> Sin' the night the moon lay whist and white
> On the road goin' down to the Lizard Light
> When I heard him hummin' behind me.

Charlotte was annoyed, when Harold sent her a second set of proofs to check, to see that he had left in a spelling that had been wrongly standardised, in spite of her previous request to change it back to her original version: 'If I have not made the correction clear in the last line but one, the word should be spelt *wheer*,' she told him (instead of 'where'). It was essential that the mistake be put right before publication, she added – '& perhaps you would be kind enough to do so?'[50] Harold quickly saw to it and the poem proved a great success: when the *Literary Digest* reported on *The Chapbook*'s return to publication (after a suspension of nearly a year) it was Charlotte Mew's poem they chose to reprint – prefaced by the comment that it 'scarcely seems the work of a feminine mind'.[51]

On 8 August, Sydney looked in on Charlotte and tried to persuade her to come down the following week to the village of Southwater in West Sussex, where he would be holidaying with his family. He had asked his painter friend Dorothy Hawksley along too, and Charlotte readily agreed to join the little group, but she had recently begun experiencing symptoms of weakness and at the last moment wrote an apologetic note to Kate Cockerell to say that her heart had 'gone wrong again' and she wasn't up to the journey. She had first complained of 'an old heart weakness' in a letter to Sydney in the summer of 1919.[52] 'I really ought not to make engagements & rarely do,' she told Kate now – 'but it would have been very nice for me to have had a quiet day with you.'[53]

By the following week, she was barely well enough to leave her attic room 'or properly get through the daily round here', she told Sydney, and now Anne was ill in bed as well.[54] Sydney sympathised but did his best to change her mind: he felt that what Charlotte really needed was to get away from it all. The invitations kept coming, and Charlotte kept turning them down. Each time she did so she experienced a fresh surge of guilt: there was nothing she hated so much as feeling like a nuisance to her friends. 'Short of taking down the entire frontage of my "house" to expose the inside,' she told Sydney, '– if I could or would do so – I'm afraid I can't convince you that I should not repeatedly say No to such an extraordinarily good friend if I could say Yes. And it does not make a not too easy existence easier to have so often to say it.'[55]

In October, both Anne and Ma succumbed to a nasty virus and Charlotte, in spite of the heart condition she complained of, found herself filling hot-water bottles, tucking in blankets and making endless warm drinks and bowls of broth. Ma seemed to be wasting away before their eyes, her tiny, birdlike frame swamped by the outmoded clothes she still insisted on wearing. Then, on a chilly Friday, two weeks before Christmas that miserable December of 1922, the old lady fell and fractured her thigh. Charlotte called in a local doctor, Dr Horatio Cowan of Fitzroy Square, who examined Mrs Mew and was not at all hopeful about the prognosis; he told Charlotte and Anne they should prepare themselves: Ma's condition was likely to deteriorate, and possibly quite rapidly. Septic pneumonia was mentioned, as well as heart failure – 'or something unforeseen'.[56] Arrangements were made for a medical attendant to come in during the day to change dressings and check on the wound, but the equally fragile condition of the Mews' finances meant that a live-in nurse was out of the question. Charlotte never begrudged the time it took to tend to Ma; she only wished she could forestall the inevitable. When Ethel Inglis (a new friend whom she had met via the Hardys) had lost her sister the previous month, Charlotte's note of condolence had been tellingly heartfelt, offering something beyond the usual empathy and platitudes: 'I think we miss in a special way those who have been more or less dependent on our care – & shut in from the free & active life which only comes to them – as it were – through windows.'[57]

Despite her daughters' attentive care, Dr Cowan's prediction proved accurate, and Ma's condition worsened almost overnight. Charlotte now arranged for her to be moved into St Peter's Harbour in Kilburn, a home for aged and infirm women run by an Anglican sisterhood. It had been set up specifically for women who either had no one to care for them at all or (as in Ma's case) could not afford round-the-clock nursing. For the modest sum of thirty-five shillings a week, patients were able to enjoy the comfort and peace of a well-ordered hospital at a fraction of the normal cost.[58] For Charlotte and Anne, it was peace of mind of the most complicated kind.

Sydney continued to call in at Delancey Street. He did so unannounced on Valentine's Day 1923, a windswept day of snow, sleet and fog, and was rewarded with supper and, as he noted afterwards, 'a very kind welcome'.[59] In April, he went with Charlotte, Anne and his eldest daughter, Margaret (now fifteen years old), to a matinee of a hugely popular Italian puppet show that was playing at the beautiful Scala Theatre, opposite Anne's studio. His assiduous kindness meant a great deal to Charlotte, but it also puzzled her: she couldn't understand why he bothered at all – 'seeing that a long barren chain of "thank yous" is all you ever get for it'.[60] Sydney said he believed friendship to be 'precious beyond all words [. . .] a plant that withers if it be not heedfully tended',[61] and when it came to Charlotte, apparently no amount of tending was too much for him. These days he very rarely went out with his wife: it was seven years since Kate had been diagnosed with multiple sclerosis and her movements had become so restricted that she was by now a virtual recluse. Sitting beside Charlotte in darkened theatres and at restaurant tables, it's possible that Sydney's feelings for her had grown into something more than friendship. The pair had known each other for nearly five years. 'And don't you think it is time – next time – that you dropped the "Miss" for C. M. or something similar?' she asked him now.[62] The impeccably mannered Sydney replied just three days later, as if he had been waiting some time for the invitation, 'My dear Charlotte, Yes of course, but may I be Sydney? I have long ceased to think of you as Miss Mew . . .'[63]

Now that Charlotte was no longer charged with the all-consuming task of looking after Ma, Sydney thought it would be a good time for her to meet Walter de la Mare, whose support with the civil list application would be invaluable. Even if that scheme were to come to nothing, it would do Charlotte no harm to widen her circle of acquaintances. The 1921 edition of *The Farmer's Bride* had caused a small stir of excitement in poetry circles, and Sydney felt that Charlotte should take full advantage of the attention while she had it. He told her that if she would only agree to issue an invitation to de la Mare for tea at the studio, he would take care of the rest. De la Mare accepted the invitation at once and a date was set for early May – although Charlotte, diffident as ever, remained uneasy about the arrangement. She felt certain that it was being done purely as a favour to Sydney, and out of 'a rather rare delicacy or courtesy' on the part of the illustrious poet, who surely had better things to do with his time.[64]

In the event, it was Charlotte who had to cancel the arrangement. The day before de la Mare was due to visit, the Mew sisters received a telegram from St Peter's Harbour with the news that Ma was now dangerously ill with bronchitis. Everyone knew that, at eighty-six years of age, Ma's chances of fighting off this latest assault were slim. Sydney went up as soon as he heard and found Alida with Charlotte and Anne at the studio, doing what she could to help and console. A week later, Charlotte reported that her mother was getting 'weaker from day to day – & for the last ten has hardly been expected to see another.'[65] With her immune system compromised, the infection that had triggered Ma's bronchitis spread quickly through the blood into all parts of her body. Both daughters were with her when, on 12 May 1923, she finally passed away. It was Charlotte who went to register the death – just as she had done with her father twenty-five years earlier. There was so much to arrange, in fact, that she left it to Anne to write round to their friends. 'The funeral will probably be on Wednesday,' she told Sydney. 'Charlotte is very upset & much to do, so hopes you will forgive her not writing.'[66]

'All women become like their mothers. That is their tragedy.' So Oscar Wilde had written in *The Importance of Being Earnest*, and whether Charlotte was aware of it or not, she had inherited a number of traits – including attitudes and opinions – from her mother. In particular, Ma's much-expressed view of Fred as someone who lacked sufficient breeding to fulfil his responsibilities as a husband and father had hardened, with the passing years, into family myth, so that as the Mews sank deeper into poverty, Fred's memory had become increasingly tarnished. Likewise, Ma's belief in the need to maintain respectability at almost any cost meant that Charlotte held on to the notion long after many of her contemporaries had abandoned it. Ma had been with Charlotte and Anne almost every day of their lives, and for all her faults, her daughters had loved her deeply, as she had loved them. Whatever excuses Anne passed on to friends for Charlotte's lack of contact in the aftermath of Ma's death, the truth was that for the time being, Charlotte wasn't ready to let them into this most private and devastating of griefs.

It comes as something of a surprise to learn that throughout the traumatic period of Ma's illness, Charlotte had found time to write and send out poems: the time she had spent in the Reading Room 'playing with plasticine' had evidently paid off.[67] The previous October, a simple twelve-line lyric titled 'Old Shepherd's Prayer' had been published in the first-ever issue of the *New Leader*, the weekly paper of the left-leaning Independent Labour Party.[68] Its editor, Henry Brailsford, had set out with the aim of soliciting contributions from the best authors of the day, and the likelihood is that he had written to Charlotte to ask for a poem – an indication, perhaps, of the esteem in which she was now held in certain quarters. Walter de la Mare's 'The Widow' was the only other poetry to appear in that issue, and though neither poem was overtly political, the paper itself most certainly was. Charlotte wasn't given to discussing politics in her letters to friends, and her own political beliefs are largely unknown. But her memorable and damning evocation of the effects of the First World War on the natural world in 'May, 1915', for instance – of 'scorched, blackened woods, where all the wounded trees / Wait, with their old wise patience for the heavenly rain' – was very much in keeping with the *New Leader*'s position on such matters. Unlike the Parliamentary Labour Party, the ILP had adopted and maintained a resolutely anti-war stance, refusing to lend its support to the war effort throughout its entire duration.

At the start of 1923, three months after 'Old Shepherd's Prayer' was published, Harold Monro's *Chapbook* carried one of the finest poems Charlotte would write. It was on a topic about which she had already written in prose form – the felling of trees to make way for new buildings – and once again, it had been occasioned by a recent memory. In the green, open space of Endsleigh Gardens, very near the Gordon Street house, a number of mature London planes had been cut down in preparation for a large building that would serve as the new headquarters for the Quaker movement. In 'The Trees are Down', Charlotte presents the undertaking as a piece of theatre – as well as a brutal act of cruelty. From within the house, she had heard the workmen's cries, the grating of the saws, the crash of branches as they fell, and imagined that, after every blow of the axe and scrape of the saw, her own heart had been struck 'with the hearts of the planes'. In the closing lines, she takes the reader right up close – inside the felled trees themselves – and lists the noises they 'must have heard' as they lay dying on the ground: the fall of rain, the flight of sparrows and the sound of insects creeping through the grass.

It is not for a moment the Spring is unmade to-day;
These were great trees, it was in them from root to stem:
When the men with the 'Whoops' and the 'Whoas' have carted the
    whole of the whispering loveliness away
Half the Spring, for me, will have gone with them.

It is going now, and my heart has been struck with the hearts of
    the planes;
Half my life it has beat with these, in the sun, in the rains,
           In the March wind, the May breeze,
In the great gales that came over to them across the roofs from the
    great seas.

> There was only a quiet rain when they were dying;
> They must have heard the sparrows flying,
And the small creeping creatures in the earth where they were
lying –
> But I, all day, I heard an angel crying:
> 'Hurt not the trees.'

Shortly after this poem appeared, *The Sphere* published a brief, painterly lyric called 'In the Fields', where once again an image of trees – this time comfortingly redeeming – is foregrounded: 'Under old trees the shadow of young leaves / Dancing to please the wind along the grass'. Read alongside 'The Trees are Down', the image provides yet another example of a conviction that can be found everywhere in Charlotte Mew's work: the knowledge that – in the natural world at least – after death comes renewal. During that early part of 1923, a fourth new poem, 'Fin de Fête', was printed, also in *The Sphere*. Its lines are spoken, just as in 'In Nunhead Cemetery', by a grieving lover standing at the graveside; and for the theme, Charlotte returned to an idea she had drawn on many times before – the peculiarly Evangelical notion, learned at her nurse's knee, that pleasure cannot be had without paying for it; or, as she had put it seven years earlier in 'Madeleine in Church', that 'joy and pain, like any mother and her unborn child were almost one'.

Sweetheart, for such a day
> One mustn't grudge the score;
Here, then, it's all to pay,
> It's Good-night at the door.

Good-night and good dreams to you, –
> Do you remember the picture-book thieves
Who left two children sleeping in a wood the long night through,
> And how the birds came down and covered them with leaves?

So you and I should have slept, – But now,
　　Oh, what a lonely head!
With just the shadow of a waving bough
　　In the moonlight over your bed.

There is something Hardyesque in the intimation of lost opportunities that pervades the final stanza, and in that image of the branch's shadow 'waving' over the moonlit grave, with its solitary occupant below. The words might almost be spoken by Sergeant Troy at the graveside of his illicit but only true sweetheart, Fanny Robin – or indeed by Hardy himself to his beloved Emma. Sure enough, when Hardy saw the poem, he copied it out from the magazine and kept the copy on his desk, where it stayed until the end of his own long and emotionally complex life.

20

This Rare Spirit

1923–1924

Charlotte had been knocked sideways by her mother's death. She told Kate Cockerell that she didn't know if she would 'ever again feel altogether here'.[1] A similar sentiment appears in 'The Trees are Down', in which the speaker prophesies that once the plane trees near her old house have vanished, 'Half the Spring, for me, will have gone with them.' Her sense of self was deeply rooted in the things that mattered most to her, and what mattered most of all – as is evident from her letters, her poems, virtually everything she wrote – was her family. Thus, in the state of numbness that now followed the end of her mother's life, she explained to Florence Hardy that 'as yet I don't know how much of my own has gone with her'.[2] She was grateful, of course, that Ma was no longer suffering but drew no comfort at all from her friends' reminders that the loss was unavoidable and expected. Over the years she had devoted an increasing proportion of her time to caring for her mother and, relieved so suddenly of the responsibility, she felt not only uprooted but superfluous.

Her frustration with the platitudes offered by well-wishers spilled out in a note to Sydney: 'It was foreseen – a deliverance for her – & as everyone tells us, for us "inevitable" – but with all that, my Mother's death is for me a stupefying blow – & I feel like a weed dug up and thrown over a wall.'[3] She may have had in mind here a phrase from 'Her Last Lines' by Emily Brontë, a poem she had singled out for praise in her 1904 essay, in which the various religious dogmas that humans believe in are judged 'Worthless as wither'd weeds'.[4] Charlotte's friends recognised the significance of the moment and were deeply concerned, but nothing they wrote or said seemed to help. Florence Hardy passed on her husband's 'kindest regards and deep sympathy' and hoped that Charlotte would now 'take a good rest'.[5] But how could she rest with so much to do? A fortnight later, when Sydney enquired as to whether she'd been able to follow Mrs Hardy's advice, she shot back, 'No. I haven't had my "rest" – it is 1.15 a.m. & I've spent the day hunting for legal documents – and da capo tomorrow.'[6] To make matters worse, she was suffering from a severely inflamed throat, a condition that 'tons of tabloids & mixtures of every colour in the paint-box' had so far done nothing to alleviate.[7]

Finally, a month after Anna Maria's death and just two months after moving into the new house, the Mew sisters were able to shut up the top floor of Delancey Street while Anne went off to Dorset for a week with friends and Charlotte went to stay with the Olivers. The Oliver parents had died while the war was on (Hannah in 1914 and Daniel in 1916, after a brief bout of flu), and Ethel and Winifred now lived by themselves in Isleworth. Staying with them in their quiet, 'Quakerly' house always made Charlotte feel, she said, 'that I ought to find the Lake of Galilee round the corner instead of trains to the Chiswick Empire cinema'.[8] It was the sort of house she might have liked to live in herself. There were paintings by the Pre-Raphaelite artist Arthur Hughes on the walls, an abundance of books properly arranged on bookshelves and a beautiful inlaid grand piano. The Oliver sisters asked Charlotte to treat the house as her own while she was there. They cooked for her, brought her cups of tea and encouraged her to rest as much as she could. She quickly got into a routine of spending half the day in bed and then going out into the June sunshine to read *The Times* in the large, west-facing garden where Wek was buried.

Sydney, meanwhile, was busy on Charlotte's behalf. In the summer of 1923, he met several times with Siegfried Sassoon to discuss the possibility of securing a civil list pension for her. Sassoon was immediately persuaded and threw his full weight behind the scheme: on 6 July, he went in person to see the influential poet and biographer

Edmund Gosse, who agreed, with some reservations, to add his name
to the petition. Sassoon noted in his diary that evening that Gosse
had not shared 'the high opinions expressed by Hardy, de la Mare,
and Masefield', but he suspected the reticence came partly from the
fact that Gosse 'isn't very well-disposed towards S.C.C.'.[9] By con-
trast, Masefield told Sydney it would give him the 'greatest pleasure'
to support the scheme, adding that Mew's was 'the one mind, now liv-
ing, in the least comparable with Emily Brontë's for depth and fire'.[10]
De la Mare, too, said it would be 'a privilege and happiness'.[11] Gosse
insisted the signatories be limited to what he somewhat immodestly
called 'the big four' – namely himself, Hardy, Masefield and de la
Mare – on the grounds that to include more would be to dilute the
overall impact of the application.[12] In the end, Sydney concurred, and
thus the matter was settled: John Masefield would write the letter and
pass it round to the others for approval and then signing.

On a searing hot day in mid-July, Sydney caught the train to London
with the sole purpose of updating Charlotte on progress with the pen-
sion application. A few days later, he sent her a copy of the appeal:

We, the undersigned, send you this Memorial, to recommend
Miss Charlotte Mew for a Pension on the Civil List.

In our opinion, Miss Mew is the most distinguished of the
living English women writers. Her work stands alone in power,
quality and suggestion. There has been and is nothing like it.

As she is a poet, writing poetry of a rare kind, she may not be
widely known for many years. We feel that it would be a wise
and gracious act, worthy of a great people, to give to this rare
spirit the means of doing her work until the world can appraise
and reward it.[13]

'If nothing more should come of it,' Sydney couldn't help comment-
ing, 'I think you may consider that you have had two very considerable
pats on the back.'[14] He was referring to Hardy and Masefield, rather

than to the self-aggrandising Gosse, who, in the end, declined to sign the petition. But it was incredible to Charlotte that *any* of these great writers should be speaking out on her behalf. The following weekend, she took the train from Liverpool Street to Cambridge to stay with the Cockerells for a second time – a journey of around an hour and a half. We cannot know the detail of her thoughts as she watched the sidings and warehouses of London slide past the windows and flatten into patchworks of fields, but we do know that she was in a general state of agitation. She was deeply touched by Sydney's kindness (the latest instance 'in the long & amazing list of yours for one of the most undeserving of created things') but couldn't decide if it was more 'like a dream or a nightmare' that someone should go to Downing Street on her account.[15] And while she would not allow herself to believe that Prime Minister Stanley Baldwin might take the petition seriously, neither could she stop herself thinking about what it would mean for her if he did.

In Cambridge, the sensation of being away from her normal surroundings and in the company of good friends helped settle her mind. After tea with Kate and the children, Sydney walked Charlotte to the famous Botanic Garden, where the pair strolled in the evening sun beneath the giant redwoods, cedars and pines that lined the main walk, and then on down to the lake. They knew each other well enough by now to enjoy the sort of companionable silence that is the preserve of close friends. 'We sat on the grass looking at the waterlilies,' Sydney noted later in his diary, with touching simplicity.[16]

Two days after Charlotte returned to London, Sydney went to Downing Street to consult the prime minister's secretary, Patrick Gower. That same day, Gower solicited the advice, in turn, of the secretary of the Royal Literary Fund, expressing his own opinion that 'To judge from the names of those who support the application it would seem to be a pretty strong case.'[17]

It was during that same hot summer of 1923 that Sara Teasdale visited England. Towards the end of July, she went for lunch with Walter de la Mare and his young wife, Elfrida, and it's more than likely that Charlotte's name cropped up in conversation, as a week later Teasdale sent a letter to Delancey Street. Charlotte had already heard from Louis Untermeyer that Teasdale was an admirer of her work, but she nonetheless expressed her 'wonder that my small book should have pleased you' and invited the American poet to tea at Hogarth Studios the following Thursday, 9 August, at 4.30 p.m.[18] It was not the most successful of meetings. Teasdale reported to her husband afterwards that 'Miss Mew apparently . . . lumps all Americans together as a bustling vulgar lot.'[19]

At the start of October, Charlotte managed a short holiday by the sea in Charmouth, Dorset, but returned feeling as drained as ever. The inflamed throat she had complained of in June had worsened as the weather turned colder, and failed to respond to any of the standard treatments. In November, at her wits' end, she took it upon herself to treat the infection with hydrogen peroxide. She could have bought a mouthwash from the chemist, containing just the right proportion of peroxide, but a home-made solution could be made up for a fraction of the cost, and in 1920s Britain, self-administration of such solutions was de rigueur for thrifty homemakers: the woman's page of one contemporary paper, for instance, enthused that when a small amount of peroxide 'is poured into a tumbler of water the foaming frothy liquid penetrates all the crannies, and keeps malevolent germs at bay'.[20] The problem was that the mixture Charlotte made up was many times too strong, which not only exacerbated the symptoms but made the original condition harder to examine. Still, as far as he could tell, Mew's doctor could find 'nothing malignant'. A Harley Street specialist confirmed that opinion and prescribed complete rest. The official diagnosis, as Anne reported afterwards to Sydney, was 'chronic inflammation of the throat, tongue and pharynx, and general exhaustion, caused by worry'.[21] Sydney was more than a little alarmed by the episode: 'I don't know what you might have done to yourself with that ridiculous peroxide,' he scolded.[22] And whether he was more concerned for her physical or mental wellbeing is hard to tell. At any rate, for once Charlotte was contrite, replying that she was 'glad to have done with Medical Adventure for a time'.[23]

In time-honoured fashion, Sydney was up in London less than a week later doing his best to take Charlotte's mind off the whole sorry business. They went with Anne to see a bizarre winter variety show at the Scala performed by a visiting Russian troupe and featuring peasant songs, Cossack dancing, surreal staging (in the middle of one song, miniature mountain goats appeared, passing along the head of a gorge) and a scene in which statues of Catherine the Great and three of her leading subjects came to life on the top of a monument set in a ballroom full of ghostly dancers. One of the London papers remarked that the show's wide appeal – 'its laughter, its colour, and its happy imaginativeness' – made it 'peculiarly attractive at this grey season. And there is not even the wrinkle of a highbrow in the whole thing.'[24] That would have suited Charlotte very well: when it came to entertainment, the lower brow, the better. Among the things she saw during 1923 and '24 were Charlie Chaplin's *The Pilgrim*, a stage play of *Peter Pan* (to which she took Sydney's younger daughter, Katharine), a second Italian marionette show and a silent western called *The Covered Wagon*.

Having cheered Charlotte up with the Russian show, Sydney might have congratulated himself on doing his bit and returned to Cambridge with an easy conscience, but he sensed that she was in real need of him that winter. He wanted to do all he could, and if that meant making a pest of himself, then so be it; anything that might forestall a full-blown depression was worth the risk. After Charlotte declined to take him up on his offer of another weekend in Cambridge ('with a fire in your room and breakfast in bed'[25]), he took matters into his own hands and posted a short note informing her that on Wednesday 5 December, he was taking her and Anne to lunch at Les Gobelins to meet Walter de la Mare. John Masefield had also been invited but he, apparently, could not leave 'his Oxford hill-top' before the New Year.[26] In the event, Alida Monro and Florence Hardy made up the party and more than compensated for Masefield's absence. Charlotte was delighted by 'how well Mrs. Hardy was look-ing – and she was, too, so friendly. But so was everybody —.'[27] The lunch was such a 'tremendous success', in fact, that the little party sat on at their table talking till gone three in the afternoon.[28] It was clear to everyone that Charlotte and de la Mare had taken an instant lik-ing to each other, but Charlotte was probably unaware of quite how much of an impression she'd made. De la Mare confessed to Sydney afterwards that 'Somehow my prevision of Charlotte Mew was totally different from the reality. I remember all her talk, but when I try to repeat some of the stories she told me, somehow I lose all the essence. She just knows humanity – one of the rarest things in the world.'[29]

On a bright Saturday in late December, four days after Christmas, Charlotte received a letter from Whitehall.

> Dear Madam,
> I am desired by the Prime Minister to inform you that, on his recommendation, the King has been pleased to award you a Civil List Pension of £75 in recognition of the merit of your poetical works.[30]

Sydney had been notified at the same time, and Sassoon ('over-joyed at the news') wrote to him immediately to offer his sincere thanks 'for what you have done for one who surely stands with Emily Brontë and Christina Rossetti', adding, 'What an extraordinary world – that can produce these superb Mews & Lawrences.'[31] He meant T. E. Lawrence, whose recently published *The Seven Pillars of Wisdom* (1922) he had been reading.

Charlotte's own reaction to the news was more complex – her excitement at being granted the pension mixed with a good dose of humility and self-doubt: 'I ought not to have it & did not expect it,' she told Sydney. 'I have done nothing to deserve it or everything all you good people have done to get it for me.'[32] But she also told him that a cloud had been lifted: 'For the past six months I haven't allowed myself to look at the future – but here comes the help that may let me do that again.'[33] She sent off her formal acceptance at once, promising to observe Patrick Gower's request to keep the information private until an official announcement was made in parliament the following August. Then she wrote letters of thanks to her sponsors, starting with Thomas Hardy, to whom she stressed once again that 'from head to feet [. . .] I know myself to be unworthy of it'.[34] In his response to Charlotte's thanks, Masefield graciously pointed out to her that 'it was your work that won the recognition, not any words of mine'.[35] Meanwhile, Sassoon told her that, while it was good news, he felt she deserved 'a more generous reward from the country you have served so nobly by your poetry'.[36]

Five years after the war, Sassoon was still reeling from the trauma of it, and it was perhaps with its horrors still fresh in his mind that he now made a claim in this letter for the importance of the poet's role that was nearly as lofty as Shelley's assertion (in 1840) that 'poets are the unacknowledged legislators of the world'. Sassoon's experience of combat, and his anger at the incompetent management of it all, had left him with complex and conflicting feelings about the war and its aftermath. It was the responsibility of poets, so he maintained, to shine a torch into the darkest corners of this troubled post-war era and to use their special insight with the utmost care:

> In an age like this, poets [. . .] carry the world on their shoulders, so it seems to me. And in their eyes the future of civilisation struggles to survive. I wish more of them were as intensely aware of their responsibility as you are, & sustained it so nobly. Forgive this effusiveness, but I feel very strongly about what you have done in verse.[37]

Charlotte's reply to this piece of unabashed rhetoric was touchingly optimistic: if poets did carry this present world on their shoulders, she said, then 'perhaps the one way of not letting it down is to hold it high'.[38] She told him she'd been rereading Robert Louis Stevenson's *A Child's Garden of Verses*, a choice that made perfect sense to Sassoon now that he had got to know her better. Children were important to Charlotte not only because she enjoyed their company, but because she remained loyal to the child-self within her own psyche. She had once written that her own childhood had left her 'mysteriously and without farewell'.[39] The time she spent with children as an adult perhaps allowed her to encounter it again for a brief spell. She often went to great lengths to form connections with children: with Mrs Sappho's, whom she'd taken on outings to the Coliseum and the zoo, with the fishermen's children in Dieppe, who had stopped what they were doing to explain their games to her; and now with Sydney's children. What she shared with them above all was a lack of guile and an irreverent sense of mischief. That January of 1924, she wrote directly to thirteen-year-old Katharine Cockerell to talk about final arrangements for their trip to see *Peter Pan* and asked for her love to be passed on to 'Chimpey', Katharine's brother (whose real name was Christopher). A plan was settled on: before the play, Sydney would take both children to the Science Museum and then bring Katharine to meet Charlotte at the Adelphi Theatre. Science was a special interest of Chimpey's; in a few years, he would be studying mechanical engineering at Cambridge. He would go on to invent the hovercraft.

As winter turned into spring, Charlotte's health faltered once again, and she allowed herself to be talked into a few weeks' rest with those 'two good Samaritans', Ethel and Winifred Oliver. This time she spent her days 'watching the blue tits in the garden & when everyone is out

– composing hymn tunes on a nice piano'.[40] The 'nice piano' was in fact an inlaid Broadwood grand that had once belonged to Christina Rossetti. Ethel, who had studied music in Italy after leaving school, had become a gifted pianist: she could play her way through difficult Beethoven sonatas with ease and worked for some time as deputy organist for her local church, St Mary's.[41] Charlotte's early musical gift and general passion for music had also endured. She played the Broadwood whenever she could, and at least one of her poems, 'Song' (1919), was 'written for music' that she composed herself – though she was, so she told Sydney, 'not musical enough to get [the notes] onto paper'.[42]

When Sydney called on Charlotte after she'd returned home, he found her still 'looking very ill and worn'.[43] By late April, she had rallied slightly, in time for her and Anne to pass a quiet but pleasant Easter in London – 'the first without our Mother', Charlotte pointed out to Florence Hardy, but 'brightened by a most lovely bunch of spring flowers from Mrs. Inglis'.[44] Florence wasn't convinced by the exaggeratedly upbeat tone of this letter, and issued another invitation to Dorset; if Charlotte didn't want to come down specially, she and Anne were always welcome to break the journey at Max Gate if they were 'going west' any time.[45] Alida also asked her down to Sussex for a week or so in August, to stay in a cottage she was renting for six months, on her doctor's advice, at Sidlesham Common; two years earlier, she had been diagnosed with a patch on the lung, and her work in the Bookshop, combined with anxiety over Harold's excessive drinking, was doing her no good at all.[46] She promised Charlotte 'perfect peace in the garden, with six dogs, one cat & no human disturbances'.[47] In the end, Charlotte took up neither of these offers, but on the last weekend in May, she did make it to Cambridge again, and on the Sunday came downstairs to find that Sydney (who'd had to leave the house before she woke) had lit a welcoming fire in his study and laid out a pen, inkpot and slabs of paper for her – '& so in the warmth of it all I got off my letters', she told him afterwards.[48]

In between his visits to Charlotte, Sydney frequently sent tickets for her and Anne to see exhibitions, talks and plays. So it was that the

Mew sisters found themselves sitting one hot July afternoon in the elaborately decorated auditorium of the New Theatre in St Martin's Lane, watching George Bernard Shaw's *Saint Joan*. Shaw had written the play for his friend Sybil Thorndike, whom he cast in the central role. The production was generally considered a success, but Charlotte found it more humorous than poignant. She had enjoyed it, she reported to Sydney, but 'in a rather unexpected way':

> – much as one does a Revue at the Hippodrome, though Miss Thorndyke [*sic*] did us out of her songs & dances – perhaps because it was 86–87 in the shade. I can imagine how fine the trial scene would be if the awful & splendid Ecclesiastes weren't trying a Musical comedy actress for cheeking the Court & wearing breeches. The last act ought to have ended with a fox-trot & the French & English flags brought in by the daughter of Herodias on a charger.[49]

Humour was not at all what Shaw had meant to convey, but Charlotte wasn't alone in objecting to the play's unconventional portrayal of its medieval heroine. T. S. Eliot, who had been at the opening night, thought Shaw's was 'perhaps the greatest sacrilege of all Joans: for instead of the saint or the strumpet of the legends to which he objects, he has turned her into a great middle-class reformer, and her place is a little higher than Mrs. Pankhurst'.[50] Charlotte had never been keen in general on art that tried too hard to be worthy. She'd rather be entertained by a good comedy, and indeed had recently been to see William Congreve's *The Way of the World*, with Millamant, the female lead, played by Edith Evans, an actress Charlotte judged to be 'the most enchanting & wonderful person I've seen on the stage for ages'.[51] Congreve's comedy seemed to Charlotte 'sacred drama' compared with *Saint Joan*.

Sydney's attentions meant that Charlotte never had to go long without cultural stimulation of one kind or another. But these days, the interesting thoughts she voiced in her letters in response to such entertainments apparently represented the extent of her creative output: somewhere along the line she seemed to have lost the habit of shaping her thoughts into verse. It was almost a year and a half since her most recent poems, 'Fin de Fête' and 'In the Fields', had appeared in *The Sphere*, shortly before her mother's death. Had she really stopped writing, or was she simply choosing to keep the work to herself? To judge, again, from her letters, it would seem that there were no problematic business concerns occupying her at this time, as there so often had been in her life, and the heavy responsibility of caring for Ma had also finally been lifted. On the other hand, she never seemed to be entirely well these days: she continued to complain periodically about her 'old heart weakness' and of general colds and flu, and there was also the troubling throat problem, brought on (in the specialist's opinion) by stress and general exhaustion – and no doubt, too, by grief. But in the past she had continued writing through all this and worse. Could it be that when her mother died, the part that had 'gone with' the dead woman was an essential part of Charlotte's writing self?[52] Or if she *was* managing to write a little, perhaps it was the civil list pension that prevented her from sending her work out for publication. She could never quite believe she deserved the distinction, which made her feel, she said, unworthy 'from head to feet', and in the months and years to come it would become clear that she felt under enormous pressure to produce new work in order to justify it.

Whether writing or not, to the outside world it appeared that the life she lived after her mother's death was measured out if not quite in coffee spoons (to borrow Eliot's phrase), then in the cinema and theatre trips that Sydney arranged for her, in lunches and teas, in bouts of illness and spells of recuperation at the houses of close friends. The impression is of someone with time on her hands, of the kind enjoyed by some of her wealthier contemporaries, but Charlotte's leisure hours were born more of a bewildered numbness than of indolence.

She was also spending an increasing amount of time looking after her sister. Anne's health had been fragile for a number of years. In 1921 (during the wrangle over the dilapidations on the Gordon Street house), the family's solicitor had described her as 'very delicate' and 'a great expense' to her mother.[53] She suffered from persistent back-ache and seemed always to succumb to whatever bug was currently doing the rounds. Everyone had thought all that would improve once she stopped working for her 'first-class devil' of a boss at the firm of antique dealers – and certainly, long hours stooped over pieces of old furniture and surrounded by paint fumes can't have helped – but when she finally handed in her notice, the symptoms continued.[54] The only difference, three years on, was that Charlotte seemed to be unwell almost as often as her sister. But it was typical of both of them that they continued to see friends and carry on as if their poor health were nothing more than a background nuisance, one more burden to be endured. When Sydney took them out to supper at the Etoile in Charlotte Street that summer of 1924, they asked him back to the studio afterwards, where they sat talking till gone eleven. 'Both ladies looked to me miserably ill,' Sydney confided in his diary afterwards, 'but their talk was excellent.'[55]

In 'Miss Bolt', Charlotte had described a fictional alter ego, 'Miss Mary', bending down to the little sister on her knee to kiss away the word 'dead' because she thought the girl too young to hear it – though 'Miss Mary', at seven years old, presumably was not. Almost half a century had passed since their early childhood days, and Charlotte was still very much playing the protective older sibling to Anne. A second invitation for the sisters to join Sydney and a friend for supper one late summer evening met with a qualified response. Charlotte explained that Anne had a prior engagement but that she herself would be delighted to come – only she hoped they would understand that she needed to be back at the house before Anne returned, as 'I don't like leaving her alone in it at night.'[56] It was Anne who, in many ways, became the 'sig-nificant other' in Charlotte's life as the years rolled by and their shared cargo of griefs and privations accumulated. In Charlotte's short story 'Elinor' (unpublished during her lifetime), the unorthodox and friend-less female narrator makes a stark and revealing statement about her sister: 'I did not miss companionship; she was sufficient – all in all to me,' she says.[57] The Mew sisters may not have been friendless, but by this stage of their lives Charlotte and Anne, now fifty-four and fif-ty-one respectively, had become 'all in all' to one another too. For both of them, their closeness had very likely supplanted the need for other deep attachments; even, perhaps, for romance.

In October, Florence Hardy was up in London again for health reasons of her own. She was staying at what had become her preferred nursing home, Fitzroy House, while recuperating from an operation to remove a tumour on her parotid gland that the doctors feared might be can-cerous. In spite of the circumstances, her mood was positively buoyant. She told Sydney it was a relief to be away from the airless atmosphere of Max Gate: how she was dreading the winter there, 'its dismalness', and how she hated the dark, heavy furniture that filled the place.[58] At the nursing home she had a steady stream of visitors – her sister Eva, Charlotte and Anne, Dorothy Hawksley and Virginia Woolf among them. On one occasion that autumn, Woolf and Charlotte met briefly at Florence's bedside, and no doubt exchanged the usual pleasant-ries, but apparently nothing more significant was said: the encounter remains only as a short note in Woolf's diary.[59]

Florence seemed to view her time at Fitzroy House almost as a vacation, and spent her days there composing cheery letters. They included one to Charlotte, written early in the morning (after she had 'watched the dawn & listened to the milk carts rattling by') about the 'magnificent poems' Charlotte had sent her in manuscript.[60] The most recent of these, 'Fin de Fête', had been written some time ago, but all were new to Florence. 'Here Lies a Prisoner' was a favourite, she said, and she longed to take it home to show Thomas, if Charlotte would allow her: '<u>Will not lose it</u>, I faithfully promise,' she assured her friend, underlining the phrase – before quickly changing her mind and asking if she might copy it out instead. Charlotte had also sent two more of the poems she'd written since the new edition of *The Farmer's Bride*: 'The Rambling Sailor' and 'The Trees are Down'. 'How T. H. would love that,' Florence enthused about the last of these. 'But I fear if he read it never again would one bough be lopped of [*sic*] the trees that hem us round & make some of our rooms so dark & depressing.' And then, not wanting to end on that gloomy note, she added that she thought there was 'no other living poet man or woman – who could have written just that poem'.[61]

Painter Dorothy Hawksley had become part of Charlotte's small circle of friends almost as soon as Sydney had introduced them in the spring of 1922. She lived a quiet life with her mother, a brother and a sister in Hampstead but exhibited her work regularly at London's Royal Academy and the Paris Salon. Charlotte thought Dorothy 'very cheerful & smart & vigorous', and her work 'delightful in an unusual way'.[62] She appreciated especially Dorothy's willingness to include Anne in their social engagements. Anne had been there the first time Sydney brought Dorothy round to Hogarth Studios, when the little group of four had stayed chatting happily until late. 'As for the Cockerell–Hawksley evening,' Charlotte enthused to Sydney afterwards, 'it's a long enough time since I had such a delightful one.'[63] Charlotte and Anne were both subsequently invited to Dorothy's own studio in St John's Wood, close to Lord's cricket ground – an experience that Charlotte said would 'give Anne no end of pleasure, of a sort that nothing else does'.[64] Dorothy worked mainly in watercolours, occasionally oils and tempera, and Anne appreciated her work apparently without any of the envy or resentment that might be expected from a fellow artist whose own opportunities had been so limited by circumstance. 'We're going to see Miss Hawksley's last masterpiece on Friday,' Anne told Sydney on one typical occasion, 'and are greatly looking forward to it.'[65]

In recent months, Charlotte had spent an increasing amount of time in Dorothy's company, and that December of 1924, she was part of a small party Sydney got together for a pre-Christmas lunch. Originally, he had booked a table for seven at Les Gobelins – to include himself, his wife Kate, Charlotte, Anne, Dorothy Hawksley, Siegfried Sassoon and Sassoon's book designer friend Stephen Gooden. In the end, Kate (who was up in town for a doctor's appointment) decided to head back to Cambridge before lunch: the whole of London was covered that day in a dense yellow 'pea-soup' fog – the worst there had been in years – and staying out in it wasn't likely to do her condition any good.

Charlotte and Anne weren't exactly in full health either that winter and, as they edged their way along the pavement to Heddon Street, the fog (made up largely of soot particles from coal fires) stung their eyes and made them cough. At the junction of Oxford Street and Regent Street, an acetylene flare had been lit to serve as a guide for the buses, cars and tramcars crawling by, and its yellow flame cast a ghostly glimmer over the street and filled it with shadows. When they stepped into the cosy lobby of Les Gobelins, it was like stepping into a different world. A fortnight before Christmas, there was a festive mood in the air; the food was excellent, as ever, and not ridiculously overpriced (a three-course table d'hôte lunch for three shillings and sixpence), and the talk at the table was good-humoured and lively. Siegfried Sassoon and his friend were on especially good form. Charlotte and Sassoon, seated beside each other, fell easily into conversation, and by the end of the meal Sassoon had promised, much to Charlotte's delight and 'in the most Xtian way', to come over to Hogarth Studios two days later to help her with some 'exhausting Americans', whom she had felt duty bound to invite to tea.[66] These were the Untermeyers – Louis and his wife, poet and singer Jean Starr – whom Sassoon had introduced to Charlotte's work four years earlier. Jean was due to give a recital at London's Aeolian Hall the following week.

For Charlotte, the only thing that marred the afternoon at Les Gobelins was Kate Cockerell's absence. Afterwards, while Anne made her way back to Delancey Street, Charlotte stopped off at the studio to attend to some business and from there she wrote a letter to Kate. She told her she had been wise not to stay out in 'this infernal fog', which had, she said, 'made a little hell of London the last 3 days & at this moment (4pm) seems to be getting blacker'.[67] Even so, next time Kate was up for a medical appointment, it would mean the world to Charlotte if she could manage just a quiet talk at the studio, which was, after all, only a five-minute cab ride from Harley Street; and she was welcome to bring whomever she liked to tea – 'as long as they aren't "highbrows"', she added, because they gave Charlotte 'a worse headache than simple fogs'.[68]

The comment was made partly for Kate's benefit: in spite of her extraordinary artistic gift, Kate was shy, hated writing letters (much to Sydney's consternation, she couldn't spell properly) and felt ill at ease with the many academic acquaintances her husband brought to the house. But Charlotte's remark was also heartfelt: she dreaded the impending visit from the Untermeyers, even knowing Sassoon would be there to help her. Like Kate, these days she was happier in the company of close family and friends, or away from human contact altogether, surrounded by the incurious natural world she had evoked so succinctly in her poem 'Fame' – 'the larks that cannot praise us, knowing nothing of what we do, / And the divine, wise trees that do not care.' The thing she liked most about the Delancey Street house was that she could look directly out at the trees of Regent's Park. Inside the house she did what she could to bring the outside nearer; she had recently got into the habit of climbing up onto the bed to put breakfast out on top of the skylight in her attic bedroom before retiring – 'for the family of starlings who come for it early,' she explained, 'with a great patter & scuffle & always to time'.[69] If only human visitors were as easy to cater for.

349

Siegfried Sassoon arrived at Hogarth Studios ('angelically') a short time before the Untermeyers were due, to help set things up, and found Charlotte in a state of some agitation. The worst thing about strangers, she had confided to Kate, was that she had to conceal from them the fact that she was 'now a shattered wreck'.[70] On the surface of things, her life was easier than it had been for some time, and yet she felt more drained than ever – a state she herself ascribed to a viral infection: 'a sort of permanent Influenza [. . .] for which no remedy seems to exist'.[71] Thankfully, when her 'exhausting Americans' materialised, they turned out to be not exhausting at all. In fact, Charlotte took an immediate liking to them. 'They were unusually quiet & nice & friendly,' she reported to Sydney afterwards, '& all three gave me a very pleasant time.'[72]

Many years later, both the Untermeyers (who were by then no longer married) recalled the visit in their separate memoirs. Together, their short accounts provide two of the most detailed first-hand descriptions we have of Charlotte at this or any other time of her life. Louis talks, intriguingly, of a parrot, and while there's no other mention of such an animal, it could be that Charlotte and Anne had been unable to get used to a house empty of Wek's noisy presence and had bought a replacement. He prefaces his account by declaring his estimate of Charlotte as 'one of the most original and least appreciated poets of the period'.

> The few poems of hers I had read arrested me not only because
> of their beauty but because of their fusion of lonely fantasy
> and impending tragedy. Something of the same combination
> emanated from Charlotte Mew's own presence when I saw
> her in a dingy room in Bloomsbury. She was a tiny creature,
> several inches less than five feet, with contradictory features.
> The mischief that played fitfully about her mouth was denied
> by darkly haunted eyes. Moreover, her essential femininity was
> contradicted by a mannish double-breasted jacket topped with a

velvet collar which made her look like an epicene revenant from the eighteen-nineties. Like Amy Lowell she smoked incessantly and cultivated pets – her favourite was a thin, violent parrot in contrast to Amy's seven huge English sheepdogs – but there any resemblance between the two poets ended. Amy Lowell's energy and income matched her enormous girth; Charlotte Mew's stamina and finances were as frail as her body. Similarities and idiosyncrasies, however, were forgotten when she spoke. Hers was a voice that was delicate and precise, as fine and firm as the extraordinary poems in *The Farmer's Bride*. [. . .] It was a desultory conversation punctuated with screams from the parrot. My hostess served strong black tea and retreated from any references to her background, her way of life, or her family.[73]

Jean's description is much briefer. She begins by emphasising that Mew's nature is 'best deduced by a reading of her poems', and makes no attempt to define that nature. What she does give us is a brief snapshot of her encounter that December of 1924 which, for a moment, sets Charlotte Mew before us – in all her complexity, all her temperamental and physical incongruity – with a spine-tingling immediacy:

We met for tea at Miss Mew's flat in London, and immediately I felt a wave of almost electrical attraction. I still recall the impact of that white and narrow face, the bones showing almost as luminous through the flesh [. . .], framed in glistening white hair and punctuated by dark, burning eyes in which the tragic sense was deep-seated, but which could brighten instantly with her ready humour.[74]

21

The Thing Is Found

1925–1928

Florence Hardy found her return to Dorset and the 'dismalness' of life at Max Gate every bit as depressing as she'd feared it would be. Charlotte felt for her, and with the authority of someone speaking from experience, she told her that 'everyone must find his own special weapons for fighting the blues & the will to fight it must never flag'.[1] She recommended something to keep the hands busy – wood-carving, modelling or basket-making, 'or really any kind of handcraft'.[2] They may not have been the most original of suggestions but neither were they bland conciliations: it was an approach that had been effective for Charlotte in the past – perhaps, she suggested, because of the way it 'both strengthens & rests the mind by turning it with some new winder or unconnected channel'.[3]

But Charlotte's own mood that January of 1925 was less than buoyant. On the 15th, Sydney went to Hogarth Studios to collect a drawing of Kate's and found Anne working on a new painting there in preparation for the Royal Academy's annual exhibition. As it happened, Anne was glad of the chance to speak to Sydney alone. She told him that Charlotte had been fretting about her poetry and not sleeping well. Sure enough, when he called in at Delancey Street, he found Charlotte 'in a panic because she had been able to produce no more poems'.[4] Over a cup of tea, it emerged that she'd been contemplating giving up the civil list pension altogether; it was the only thing that might relieve the terrible pressure she felt under to justify the honour. Sydney told her that the pension involved no obligation whatsoever to create anything new; it had been awarded to her on the merit of past work, and to give it up would be absurd. He came away feeling their chat had left Charlotte 'much relieved'. But he must have known that if that was true, then it was only partly so: when they walked together afterwards to Dorothy Hawksley's studio, he suggested she should stay on and chat to Dorothy with him, but try as he might to persuade her, she 'would not come in'.[5]

She had at least one poem ready for publication. That month, the *Nation and Athenaeum* published the bleak 'Moorland Night'. And if the spirit of Emily Brontë is apparent in the poem, the extraordinary sensory detail and abrupt telescoping of perspective – apparent from the opening lines – are entirely Mew's own.

My face is against the grass – the moorland grass is wet –
  My eyes are shut against the grass, against my lips there are
    the little blades,
      Over my head the curlews call,
  And now there is the night wind in my hair;
My heart is against the grass and the sweet earth; – it has gone still,
  at last.
      It does not want to beat any more,
        And why should it beat?
      This is the end of the journey;
        The Thing is found.

It's sobering to reflect on all the adversities that might have caused Charlotte to write such lines. She presents us here with the portrait of a person turning in on herself even as she gives herself up, with a profound sense of release, to something greater. Here is a speaker so disillusioned with the larger picture of her life that she shuts her eyes on the lush expanse of moorland stretching away in all directions to feel instead a handful of tiny grass blades against her lips; a speaker who welcomes the feel of her heart slowing to a halt against the 'sweet earth'. Meanwhile the mysterious 'Thing' has been found. Charlotte had capitalised that word once before, in her 1914 poem 'The Fête'.

But then it was the 'Enchanted Thing' and seemed to represent a physical embodiment of the force of life – in the form, specifically, of a young man's first sexual encounter. In 'Moorland Night', the Thing that is found is almost an inversion of that idea: it is the final, blissful cessation of all life's human concerns, a melting away of boundaries, a yielding to the larger cycle of life. As the poem unfolds, the speaker eventually rises and leaves 'The Thing' behind, but with the hope that 'One day the quiet earth may give it back'.

If 'Moorland Night' reflected Charlotte's mood that cold, wet winter of 1925, with the lengthening of the days her spirits became a little lighter. Spring had always had a powerful lifting effect on her mood: 'There is something new in the old heavenly air of Spring,' she'd written in 'The Fête'. Elsewhere, she'd talked of its 'wild magic' and its power to restore our engagement with the natural world – how 'in the long, still dusks of Spring / You can hear the whole world whispering'.[6] So it was that in mid-May, when she received an invitation from the Hardys to visit them at the start of June, she replied immediately that she would be 'proud & pleased' to accept, and hoped there might be an opportunity this time 'to see the Garden & even sit in it'.[7] Her first visit to the Hardys had had to be postponed at the last moment. Now, once again, Florence wrote at the eleventh hour with the news that eighty-five-year-old Thomas was unwell, and that the doctor had recommended complete rest, with no visitors. Charlotte's kind response to the last-minute change of plan prompted Florence to send a long, confiding letter, full of gratitude: 'It is so good of you to be thoughtful and understanding about T. H. Most people are inclined to take up this attitude: "Oh, I shan't tire him. Other people may do so, but it's impossible that he should be tired of *me*." Our kind S. C. C. is rather like that, thoughtful as he is in other ways.'[8] But Florence ought not to have been surprised. Charlotte was keenly sensitive to other people's complexities and predicaments, in part because she had so many of her own. She had nonetheless been looking forward to a change of scene, and a few days later she wrote to Sydney, asking if he and Kate would have her at Cambridge instead. It must have struck Sydney as an interesting turnaround from the days when Charlotte had repeatedly rejected his own steady stream of invitations, but he replied at once that of course they'd be delighted to have her.

She took the train down on the afternoon of Saturday 13th, and this time found her own way to the house. The weather remained hot and cloudless for the entire weekend, and she was delighted to discover that the university was celebrating May week – the students in high spirits after an arduous round of exams. On the Monday, after supper she walked with Sydney across the fen to the Backs, where they stopped to look at the new Clare building – 'beautiful in the evening light'.[9] Crossing the Garret Hostel Bridge between the colleges of Trinity and Trinity Hall, they looked down on the illuminated paths of Trinity and its trees hung with lanterns for the May ball, of which they later 'caught a glimpse' through the doorway of the marquee.[10] The visit was exactly the tonic Charlotte had hoped it would be.

Siegfried Sassoon brought out a new poetry collection that spring, privately printed in a limited edition of ninety-nine copies. The elaborate title – *Lingual Exercises for Advanced Vocabularians* – suggested an element of self-mockery, and if Sassoon was uncertain about this particular offering, then many of his friends, including Charlotte, were inclined to agree. On receiving her copy, she wrote Sassoon a careful letter: she singled out a few poems for praise but said she found the satirical verses, in which he took pot shots at sitting targets like the Anglican clergy and 'Lady Lucre', less successful. Sassoon's war poems had been written with a genuine sense of urgency and anger; now Charlotte felt he'd taken a wrong turn. She knew he was capable of more, and she implied as much. After joking that she hoped his next book might be 'in words of one syllable', she drew his attention to the advice George Sand had given to Flaubert: '*Occupe-toi davan-tage du fond*' – first take care of the basics.[11]

Later that same year, Heinemann issued Sassoon's *Selected Poems*, which included all of his best-known war poems, and this time Charlotte was effusive with her praise. She talked of the poetry's 'beauty & horror', and of how that horror was counterweighted by the 'vision & loveliness' of poems like 'A Poplar and the Moon', a simple ten-line lyric that memorialises a passing moment. In fact, there was so much richness in the book, she said, that it 'may come to be one of those books of Escape [. . .] which one reaches up for any time after midnight – & of which – anyhow on my small shelves – there aren't so many'.[12] This final verdict would have meant a great deal to Sassoon, coming as it did from a writer whom he would later describe as 'the only poet who can give me a lump in my throat'.[13]

It may have been Siegfried Sassoon who first introduced Charlotte's work to Lady Ottoline Morrell, society hostess and influential patron of the arts. She and Sassoon had first met in 1916, after she read his 'To Victory' in *The Times* and asked a mutual friend (journalist and art critic Robert Ross) to bring the young soldier-poet to visit her when he was next on leave. Lady Ottoline had made it her business to befriend a number of writers in recent years – T. S. Eliot, W. B. Yeats and Virginia Woolf among them – whom she invited down to stay at her country mansion, Garsington Manor in Oxfordshire, or to the literary salons she held at her London townhouse in Bedford Square. Woolf left a vivid description of her in one of her letters: 'There used to be a great lady in Bedford Square who managed to make life seem a little amusing & interesting & adventurous, so I used to think when I was young & wore a blue dress & Ottoline was like a Spanish galleon, hung with golden coins & lovely silken sails.'[14]

While staying at Garsington that August of 1925, Sassoon was amused to hear his hostess reading out a letter at the breakfast table from the Poet Laureate, Robert Bridges, thanking her for sending him Charlotte Mew's poems. Soon afterwards she wrote directly to Charlotte and asked if she might be permitted to call in at Delancey Street for tea. Charlotte replied that it was 'truly nice' of her to think of visiting, and the tea date duly took place, at 4.30 p.m. on 11 September.[15] It seems to have been the only occasion on which the pair actually met, but over the years that followed Lady Ottoline continued her pursuit, determined to add the elusive Miss Mew to her collection of exotic writers.

As another year drew to a close, it brought with it the usual round of winter ailments; and once again it was Anne who was hardest hit. When Sydney knocked on the door of Delancey Street a week before Christmas, he got no answer: Charlotte was out shopping, and her sister ill in bed. But two days later, perhaps as part of her own determined effort at 'fighting the blues', Charlotte cheerfully reported to Sydney that the cold weather had its upsides. The previous evening a blue tit – 'lost in the fog', Charlotte supposed – had found its way into the front room and 'spent a comfortable night, without fuss,' on the curtain top, before departing the following morning.[16]

The visitation clearly delighted her, and perhaps she even took it as an omen of better times ahead. The birds that appear in her poetry have an element of otherworldliness about them, their voices songs from another realm, like the gulls that appear in the haunting and unearthly 'In Nunhead Cemetery' that are embodiments of 'The old sea-captains' souls'.[17] 'The word of a bird is a thing to follow,' the speaker tells us in 'The Changeling'. But for now, there were the practicalities of the human world to think about. Charlotte and Anne spent that Christmas of 1925 with 'a friend at Hampstead' – almost certainly the figure painter Katherine Righton, who had remained close to both sisters since her days at the Royal Female School of Art with Anne.[18] They stayed on for a few days after Christmas itself, returning to Delancey Street on the 29th to find a present waiting for Charlotte. It was a book of Emily Brontë's poems, signed by Lady

Ottoline. If Ottoline had been hoping to win Charlotte over by the gesture, or to draw her into some sort of a dialogue about the poems, then she was to be disappointed. Charlotte's thank-you note was polite enough, but it consisted of a single sentence, followed by the briefest of sign-offs: 'All good wishes for 1926.'[19]

Dorothy Hawksley would paint Sydney many times over the years – much to his delight – but in 1926, she managed, against the odds, to persuade Charlotte to sit for a portrait. The resulting watercolour, in blue, grey, pale pink and flesh tones, shows its subject looking weary but thoughtful, a puff of white hair framing her fine features and heavily lidded eyes, her head leaning on one small hand.[20] Now held by the National Portrait Gallery in London, this luminous painting is the only one that exists of Charlotte Mew. Since she had been so reluctant in the past even to sit for a photograph, its existence is evidence perhaps more of her affection for Dorothy than of a desire to share her image. Dorothy had recently been busy with other paintings too. That year she was one of the featured artists in the Royal Academy's annual exhibition. Anne had sent in three compositions of her own, but none had been selected, and the day after the show's opening, Charlotte wrote to apologise to Dorothy ('Ever Dear D') for not attending: 'being rudely cast out,' she explained, she and Anne had 'egotistically forgotten' that one of Dorothy's paintings was on display.[21] Her Japanese-influenced *Daphne* depicts the naked, sylph-like naiad peeping out from a laurel tree, and was singled out for praise in *The Sketch* for its 'delicate fantasy' and imaginative treatment of the myth.[22] For Anne, meanwhile, who had left college with a string of prizes to her name, and who had been struggling for years to find proper time to paint, the disappointment of her latest rejection must have been acute.

Since her panic the previous January over her inability to write, Charlotte had stopped sending new work of her own out, but now

– ironically – her poems seemed to be appearing everywhere. The year before, Louis Untermeyer's revised *Modern British Poetry* had included five of her shorter lyrics, plus a fulsome introduction, which began 'One of the most amazing figures in modern poetry is Charlotte Mew. She has published only one book, yet that one small collection contains some of the finest poetry of our times.'[23] As well as being a commercial success, the anthology was widely used in schools and colleges across the United States, and other editors soon began to take note of Charlotte's work. In March 1926, 'The Farmer's Bride' was included in an American anthology intended specifically for undergraduates. Charlotte loved the thought that her poems were being introduced to this vibrant new audience; she told the volume's editor how thrilled she was 'to be represented in a book for American youth'.[24] At 9 p.m. on Friday 27 August, Alida and Harold Monro broadcast a selection of contemporary poems on BBC radio in a fifteen-minute programme slotted in between two performances by the J. H. Squire Celeste Octet.[25] The programme was billed in the papers as 'Short poems, chiefly humorous', and among the selection was Charlotte's decidedly unhumorous 'Sea Love', which Alida recited in her sonorous voice.

Charlotte had told Sydney that she'd been unable to produce any new poems, but that summer – against the odds and twelve years after her last prose piece had appeared in print – she began work on a long story called 'Aglæ', set in Brittany. When Aglæ's younger sister Germaine marries a local fisherman, the three live on happily together in their 'little yellow house with its red pointed roof': 'it was a great thing for the house when she brought Raymond into it,' the narrator tells us. Raymond seems happy enough with the arrangement too: 'If anything pleased him [. . .] he would seize Germaine by the waist, kissing her half a dozen times, waltzing her round the room, and afterward come up behind Aglæ's chair, to kiss her too, once, perhaps, on the hair, on the forehead.'[26] The story contains moments of deep tenderness; the style – in contrast to the hyperbolic prose of Charlotte's early stories – is poetic but uncluttered:

> A great peace, from the sky to the water, hung over the harbour: the boats were moored, empty and silent and without lights. It was Easter night; they would not go out till morning: the masts just stirred, they were never really still; the stillness was over the sky and the town and the harbour though there might be a breeze bearing out at sea.[27]

Agläe's new brother-in-law is from a family of 'broad, straight men' whose faces are 'browned and roughened by the wind', and Agläe loves in particular his 'sweeping black lashes' and 'intensely blue child's eyes'.[28] Germaine bears a daughter, Odette, who shows more affection for her 'Tante Agläe' than for her mother – an attachment that intensifies when Raymond dies in a freak boating accident and Germaine, too quickly, takes a new lover. One stormy night, in the aftermath of Raymond's death, Agläe sees his face appearing behind hers in her bedroom mirror. He tells her, simply, how pretty she is, at which she dissolves into tears – 'her whole body was shaken with sobs'. As she creeps back into bed beside Odette, Raymond lies down next to her –

> [. . .] and towards morning when the wind had dropped and Raymond was gone, it came to her that if he had still been there she could have touched him; that though he might never come to her like that again he had been there; he was not dead, he was alive because she was alive, and because he had been there alive with her, it seemed for a moment as if she could never die.[29]

And if the loss of what might have been is painful to Agläe, she draws consolation from her unattached state. She has, after all, the memory of Raymond, yet remains answerable to no one: 'I belong to myself,' she tells us, as if realising it for the first time; 'it is all that I have. I have never been touched. No – only by Raymond, so lightly – and – here in that room, on the hair, on the forehead.'[30]

The latter part of the manuscript (clearly at an earlier stage of composition than the opening pages) trails off into disorganised paragraphs in barely legible handwriting. But the story is significant for its exploration of the inner life of a woman who – like Charlotte herself – experiences great depths of passion that she is either unable or unwilling to express. The document, now in the British Library, is marked, in Charlotte's handwriting, 'abandoned, October 1926' – by which time the decline in Anne's health had pushed all other concerns aside and dictated a change in the sisters' living arrangements.

In the meantime, in September, a short lyric, 'Do Dreams Lie Deeper?', was published in *Atalanta's Garland*, an anniversary publication for the Edinburgh University Women's Union. The poem had been solicited by Herbert Grierson, who had also managed to secure contributions from Virginia Woolf, Katherine Mansfield and Walter de la Mare. When Charlotte had responded to Grierson's initial request for work, she'd described the poem as a 'scrap of verse',[31] but he was delighted with it. Though not one of her strongest pieces, it nevertheless poses a typically original and peculiar question: what happens to our dreams after we have been buried? The male speaker (himself dead and buried, though awake for the duration of the poem) talks of his dreams as his children, with lives of their own – which means that their eyes don't necessarily close when his do:

> And what sunrise
> When these are shut shall open *their* little eyes?

The personification of the dreams is straightforward enough, but what makes the image feel strange is that the dreams – products of the speaker's mind – are independent of the speaker; so independent as to be unaffected by his death. Strange as it is, the poem's internal logic makes particular sense when applied to the life of the artist, whose dreams for their work may well be realised after the artist's death. Charlotte Mew's own life and death would be a case in point. The hoped-for sunrise signals a moment of discovery, a shedding of light on the dreamer's true artistic worth. Once the 'little eyes' of his dreams are opened, the deceased is endowed with something akin to the ancient Greek notion of *kleos* (fame or heroic glory that lives on after death), an honour accorded to soldier and poet alike. Fittingly, this was the last poem Charlotte would publish.

It was decided that London was doing Anne no good at all. At the end of the summer of 1926, Charlotte arranged for the furniture – the heavy gilt mirrors and the Adam chairs and oak table that Ma had insisted on bringing to the house – to be taken into storage at Shoolbred's department store on the Tottenham Court Road, and set about shutting up Delancey Street. Now that Ma was dead, there was no longer any need to keep up with the expense of 'a decent address', and the sisters intended to look for somewhere smaller once Anne was properly recovered, but for the moment they had no more definite plans than to escape London before winter began.

The city of Chichester, on the south coast, was close to the sea and the beautiful Sussex Downs; more importantly, it was a decent distance from the soot-filled air of the capital. Alida had looked around for somewhere suitable for them last time she was in Sussex but could only recommend hotels. '*I* rather fancy the Northgate,' Charlotte told her, 'but A thinks rooms would be "quieter" – so I've been writing furiously to various matrons for some, so far with poor results. If I can I shall go Thursday and look round.'[32] In the second week of October, she found rooms in a house near the cathedral and made arrangements to move in as soon as possible. Before leaving, they called in on

Dr Cowan in Fitzroy Square, who advised against Anne travelling; for the time being, he wanted her where he could keep an eye on her. 'As the Doctor is keeping Anne in town we are at the moment rather hung up,' Charlotte told Sydney, '– but still hoping to get away later.'[33]

Anne rallied slightly, and when they finally got down to Sussex at the start of November, their lodgings, and Chichester itself, surpassed all expectations. St George's House wasn't just close to the cathedral but directly opposite it, and they whiled away most of their time relaxing in their rooms or in the garden, 'watching the Cathedral starlings very happily'. Charlotte took the opportunity to catch up on some reading (she was gradually 'draining' the shelves of nearby Barrett's bookshop), and Anne got as much rest as she needed, sketched and made nightcaps for them both to keep them snug in the chilly autumn nights.[34] Almost all their lives the sisters had been forced to take separate holidays so that Ma would always have one of them close at hand. Now they were able to spend some proper time together, and the experience, for both of them, was among the happiest of their lives. They had no intention, so Charlotte told Sydney, of settling down in London again 'till the Spring or till Anne is definitely better'.[35] In fact, Charlotte said she would 'gladly stay on in the pleasant old house hard by the Cross'. But the priority was Anne's health, and all else must follow from that: 'everything just now is uncertain except that we go up to a friend in Bucks for Christmas'.[36]

Instead of going straight from Chichester to keep this engagement, they stopped off in London so that Anne could attend a hospital appointment, returning to Hogarth Studios and the 'roar & rush' of London life on 16 December.[37] Dr Cowan had arranged for Anne to see a specialist, who now told her, two days before Christmas, that there was 'no hope'. It was cancer of the womb, and it had already advanced beyond the stage at which they could offer any helpful treatment. And in any case, he added, by this point she wasn't strong enough for them to risk it.[38]

On Christmas Eve, the sisters set off in a state of numbness for the house of their old school friend Maggie Browne, in the quiet market town of Berkhamsted, and somehow made it through Christmas. Up until that moment, neither of them had known there was anything seriously wrong. But Maggie and her husband Edward were so alarmed by the thought of Anne returning to the studio that they insisted on paying for her to be moved somewhere where she could be properly cared for. Charlotte accepted the offer, but it must have wounded her pride to do so: few things were more painful to her than the idea that she wasn't able to take proper care of her little sister. Back at Hogarth Studios, there was a letter waiting from Sydney, in which he also offered his help in finding 'more comfortable quarters than the studio' for Anne.[39] The somewhat defensive tone of Charlotte's reply is as sad as it is evident: 'We should not have been grubbing here but that it has all been so sudden & we were caught.'[40] She was at least able to tell Sydney that arrangements had already been made: Anne was to be admitted to a nursing home in Nottingham Place, a twenty-minute walk from the studio. Sydney understood the need for sensitivity at this time, and he was aware that his desire to help could sometimes be interpreted as interference, but that never stopped him from speaking out if he thought his advice might be helpful. His concern now was as much for Charlotte's welfare as it was for Anne's.

It is a huge relief for me to know that she is having all possible care & attention. So what it must mean to you I cannot measure. I do hope you are not subsisting on tea & cigarettes. With that good restaurant so near you it is not so difficult to get food that you can eat – & all your strength will be needed in the coming weeks. It may just enable Anne to turn the corner, supposing the diagnosis to be as wrong as another I heard of on Friday.[41]

But Anne was by now so weak that when Sydney asked if there was anything he could take her by way of reading material, he was told it would have to be something simple and 'light to hold'.[42] Weak as she was – and faint-spoken and unnervingly thin – Anne seemed to Charlotte 'amazing. The brutal finality or fatal silence of Doctors doesn't move her,' she told Sydney. 'She simply says "I am all right" & is talking of coming out in 3 weeks' time.'[43] Both sisters must have known that the odds were against it, but Anne's optimism, fuelled by her Catholic faith, was contagious, and somehow Charlotte allowed herself to be swept up. So it was that 1927 proceeded with the Mew sisters caught up in a form of *folie à deux*, an unspoken pact of shared denial in which Sydney, to some extent, colluded. In spite of everything, his idea that the official diagnosis ('a hopeless case of cancer') might be wrong began to look like some kind of miraculous possibility.[44]

During the ensuing weeks, Sydney was a regular visitor at the nursing home. On 19 January, he found Anne sitting up, dressed in her day clothes, and remarked that 'she did not look like a dying woman'.[45] On the 26th, Charlotte renewed her Reading Room ticket at the British Museum, and at the same time the extraordinary decision was taken to move Anne into a room at the Etoile hotel and restaurant, a stone's throw away from the studio in Charlotte Street. She made the move on the last day of January, and when Sydney visited her there two days later he found her 'up, very thin but cheerful & pleased with her room'.[46] A month later, Anne was still arranging to do things: 1 March had been set aside for Katherine Righton to accompany her to the Royal Academy so that she could 'have a shot at the Stevens room'.[47]

Charlotte, meanwhile, had recently been to see a new silent film, *The Constant Nymph* – 'or Nip, as our Housekeeper calls it'.[48] Described by *Tatler* as 'one of the big dramatic successes of the year', it was based on a bestselling novel of the same name by Margaret Kennedy, about two teenage girls who are in love with the same man.[49] At the other end of the cultural spectrum, she also visited, that February of 1927, a new exhibition of Flemish paintings at the Royal Academy and came away elated – she would have liked to take van der Weyden's *Portrait of a Lady* away with her to hang on her own wall – although owing to her height, she had had, she told Sydney afterwards, only 'a partial

view' of the exhibition itself, '& a thorough one of a great many peo-
ple's backs'.[50]

The slightly manic, carnival atmosphere ended abruptly, late one
evening at the end of March. Anne was at the studio when something
happened that alarmed Charlotte enough for her to call Dr Cowan
out there and then. She doesn't say what, only that Anne had become
'suddenly worse', but given that the cancer was in Anne's womb, it
may have been a frightening bleed. The doctor came and helped make
Anne more comfortable, but he refused to sanction the idea of return-
ing her to the Etoile. What he really wanted was for her to go back
to the nursing home – and the sooner the better – but Anne said she
couldn't face it, and with some reluctance Dr Cowan agreed that for
the time being she could stay on at Hogarth Studios. Charlotte now
found herself in the impossible situation of nursing a patient in the
late stages of cancer by herself, with the most basic of facilities, in
what was essentially a bedsit. By this stage, the cancer had spread to
Anne's liver, and she was now so weak that she wasn't up to very much
reading, or even talking.

The only thing that brought her some relief was David Garnett's
new novel *Go She Must!*, which Charlotte read aloud to her, chapter
by chapter. It charts the life and loves of a country vicar's daughter
named Anne Dunnock and her eventual escape from provincial life.
Most of the story is set in the fictional village of Dry Coulter in rural
Cambridgeshire – a mercifully long way off from the stuffy confines
of the studio. 'The elm trees were so beautiful; it was because of the
elms that she loved Dry Coulter. Soon the spring would come, soon
the snowdrops would cluster thickly under the garden walls, and every
day that passed improved the quality of the birdsong.'[51]

Charlotte thought the novel 'a lovely piece of landscape painting'
and hoped that visualising the countryside might be doing Anne
some good. 'I would give almost anything for her to have a sight of
Spring trees & a breath of sweet air,' she told Sydney, '– but the gods

are against it.'[52] Almost a month went by with them struggling on in this way, until, on 25 April, Anne was admitted to a second nursing home. This one was a little further away than the last, in Kilburn, but the improved surroundings made the longer journey worthwhile. Anne was given a large, bright room 'with two windows & outlook on trees & sky'. Just as importantly, she seemed, said Charlotte, to be 'with kind people'.[53]

Friends began to visit and send flowers. A box of pansies arrived from Kate Cockerell; Sydney sent lilac (which was, Charlotte told him, 'such a rest from the reds & blues & yellows, giving a quiet sweetness in the room which is full of sunlight & blessed by trees'[54]); Alida, away in Scotland for part of May, visited once; Katherine Righton more often. Charlotte herself was now spending all day with Anne and getting back to the studio late. 'If there is mercy,' she told Alida towards the end of April, 'it can't be long.'[55] But the days dragged on into weeks, and at the end of May, Charlotte wrote a note from the home to bring Alida up to date: 'Anne is still here – if one can say so of such a shadow & the last 2 days has not had much pain – or much sleep.'[56] Charlotte was dismayed that the noise from an adjacent garage was reducing the effectiveness of Anne's injections, 'as after these there must be 10 minutes quiet'.[57] But at least she seemed, for the most part, to be out of pain.

From now on it was a matter of waiting for the final release, though nobody seemed to know when that would come. One evening in June, Charlotte returned to the studio after a long day at Anne's bedside to find yet another card from Lady Ottoline, and sent a brief but unambiguous reply to explain that there was 'no chance' of meeting at the moment – 'as my sister is dangerously ill in a Nursing Home & I spend all my time with her & consequently have none for seeing anyone else'.[58] Six days later, at midnight on Saturday 18 June, 'after 3 terrible days & nights', it was over.[59] The cause of Anne's death was given as 'Carcinoma of the uterus and liver. Haemorrhage and Exhaustion.'[60] She was fifty-three.

When Sydney had written to ask when and where the funeral would take place, his letter – along with many others received during that nightmarish week – went unopened. He wrote a second time to say that, as Charlotte hadn't replied, 'I judge that you would prefer to face that harrowing ordeal with only the oldest of your friends – otherwise I should be there.'[61] Again, the letter was met with silence – an oversight for which Charlotte afterwards asked his forgiveness, explaining that she hadn't sent him details because she knew he 'hated funerals & had to go to so many'.[62] Around twelve people attended the service, on the Thursday following the death, at Fortune Green cemetery in Hampstead. Most of the mourners had invited themselves. They included Ethel and Winifred Oliver, and one of Anne's painting models – 'too sad to speak' when Charlotte went over to her afterwards. 'And people who barely knew my little sister sent handfuls of flowers,' she told Sydney, with obvious pride –

> But how exquisite a spirit it was or how dauntless only I can know who knew what she had to fight & how she fought it – & so much more of that grace of thought & deed than her oldest friend could know. I remember the lifelong endurance of all sorts of pain – the effort – the gaiety – the endless Kindness – the passion for every honest & lovely thing & then to think that at least she is saved from even more difficult days that might have come.[63]

Charlotte's only consoling thought here – that Anne had been spared future suffering – chimes with what she had once written about Emily Brontë, namely that death was 'not a problem because it was the end of problems'.[64] Charlotte had long thought of death as a kindly presence – a presence she often envisaged in human form: 'Show me your face,' she'd written in 'Smile, Death'; 'why the eyes are kind!'[65]

What did it mean to Charlotte to lose her sister at this point in her life? The sister with whom, for over half a century, she had shared not only her living quarters and the occasional holiday, but her hopes and fears, her friends, nearly every meal and film, theatre show and tea party she had ever been to? More significantly, they had both known the experience of being unmarried women, and women with artistic ambitions, in an age when to be either was frowned upon. They had suffered the same losses and weathered financial hardship, alongside the increasing restrictions that caring for Ma had entailed. Perhaps most distressing of all, Charlotte had lost the last person in the world with whom she shared the full secret of Henry's and Freda's illnesses; the one person with whom she could speak openly about them, as often as she liked, without shame or fear of reproof. When her mother had died, she had told Kate Cockerell she didn't know if she would 'ever again feel altogether here'.[66] With Anne's death that feeling must have been multiplied many times over.

'What is better than to love and live with the loved?' So asks George Eliot in a letter to Lady Lytton, upon the death of a much-loved friend. She continues: '– But that must sometimes bring us to live with the dead; and this too turns at last into a very tranquil and sweet tie, safe from change and injury.'[67] It is among the quotations that Charlotte had copied out years earlier in her broad-nibbed fountain pen in the British Museum Reading Room. But if she had found consolation in the idea in the wake of other deaths, Anne's death was to be a different story. After the funeral, she went back to the Oliver sisters' house. A neighbour of the Olivers later recalled seeing her around this time, dressed from head to toe in black, and remarked on how her 'big black hat couldn't hide the grief-stricken face'.[68] Charlotte was inconsolable, unable to sleep. Her nerves became more and more frayed, in spite of the Olivers' attentive care.

Lady Ottoline called in person at Hogarth Studios that week in the hope of catching Charlotte at home; finding her out, she wrote a letter, which went unacknowledged. A few days later, she tried again, armed with flowers that she was forced to leave with the housekeeper. This time Charlotte lost her temper and let Lady Ottoline know that her attentions were not welcome: 'as [the letter] hasn't been answered,' she fumed, 'I hoped you would understand – as nearly everyone else has been good enough to do without my saying so, that I am only seeing & writing to old friends. I came here to some – for quiet after a long strain & a great blow some six weeks ago.'[69]

In August, she was at Hogarth Studios 'on & off' while she began the task of 'sorting & lifting & tearing up too & trying to start the inevitable business which I have done for one or another of my people since 1898'.[70] That business had started with her father, whose death she had both witnessed and reported; then Henry, her mother and now Anne. Each time, it had been Charlotte who registered the death and afterwards took care of the flood of paperwork and sorting that death necessitates. Now she was rigid with tiredness and grief: 'The Olivers are away,' she told Sydney in mid-August, 'but have lent me their house & an old servant who kindly attends to me when I go down to look at the garden. I feel too stiff to move any farther.'[71]

It was while she was sorting through Anne's belongings at the studio that she noticed some black specks clinging to the canvases and stuck to the plaster-cast mask of the nameless girl and other surfaces. She gradually became fixated by the idea that they might have caused Anne's cancer. The level of distress she felt indicates the feverish state of her mind at this time, but the concern itself is not as outlandish as it may at first sound. In and out of the medical community, the theory that some sort of 'cancer germ' existed was widely discussed at the time. Among Charlotte's own friends, for instance, Florence Hardy had wondered if the spores in the trees at Max Gate might be partly responsible for her own cancerous tumour; she had even talked to her doctor about it. That very August of 1927, an article appeared in the press on the findings of new research carried out by the Anglo-Italian doctor Louis Sambon into the geographic distribution of cancer cases. Sambon's research, said the article, pointed definitively 'to the conclusion that the cause [of cancer] is some germ or parasite which for some reason or another particularly infests certain houses and localities'.[72] Charlotte became so terrified by the idea that now she too was contaminated that Dr Cowan sent some of the affected items to the Lister Institute to be analysed; unsurprisingly, the specks were found to be ordinary London soot.

In the last week of September, Charlotte went up to Cambridge to stay with Kate Cockerell for a fortnight while Sydney was away on a Mediterranean cruise with his younger daughter. Katharine, then sixteen, had begged Sydney to let her housebound mother come on the cruise with them, arguing, in a touching letter, that 'It would be such bliss for her not to think of housekeeping and meals, and so nice for her to enter in with us and not feel that she was being left out.'[73] But Sydney wouldn't hear of it: sad as he was about his wife's debilitating condition, he felt the need periodically to have time away from her and escape the sickroom atmosphere of their Shaftesbury Road house. By this time Kate's multiple sclerosis had progressed to a stage where she was no longer able to walk unaided. The arsenic, heat and light treatments she'd been receiving in Harley Street had done nothing to halt the disease, and she was often in considerable pain, confined to the house and garden.

Over the years, Kate's illness had made an outsider of her, and nobody had more time and empathy for outsiders than Charlotte, who had devoted her career to writing about outcasts of one kind or another. During their fortnight together, the two women cooked and shared meals, talked by the fire and pottered in Kate's cherished garden, weeding and tending to the plants. Kate later said of Charlotte that 'She was one of the few people I have known with whom I could be quite intimate without the fear of being laughed at.'[74] Kate, in turn, perfectly understood Charlotte's need for quiet and rest, and provided perhaps, for that brief fortnight, the easy female companionship that Charlotte had lost when Anne died.

Sydney arrived home in time to see Charlotte off at the station on 10 October, and – ever the optimist – noted in his diary that the visit 'seems to have done her good'.[75] Back in London, the stray cat who depended on Charlotte for water was waiting for her on the porch of the studio, 'with a premonition of my return'.[76] Inside, she also found some fresh flowers waiting for her that the Oliver sisters had left, and beside these 'a pile of severely practical letters', which she put aside while she wrote Kate a thank-you note that was full of warmth: 'What a break this last fortnight has made in the dim nightmare,' she told her, 'across which only one valiant lovely figure seems to move – I cannot thank you in words, for the sense of fireside, & home & all the rest. You must understand.'[77] But for all that, the 'dim nightmare' had not gone away. The studio was still in a bad mess – Anne's canvases, paints and brushes in jam jars taking up every available space – 'an infernal problem until I can get someone to move the things & turn it out'.[78]

Friends counselled Charlotte to get out of the empty studio as often as she could manage, and during October and November, she did her best to follow that advice. She went to the Leicester Gallery (in Leicester Square) to see drawings by Henri Fantin-Latour, one of her favourite painters, to hear Chopin with Ethel Oliver ('To me there is no-one like him') and to a Schubert concert that Kate's sister, Joan Kingsford, had asked her to.[79] In the second half of November, she went to stay once again with Ethel and Winifred and spent her time there reading Edward Grey's just-published *The Charm of Birds*, lingering over Robert Gibbings's beautiful wood engravings. By the end of the month, she was writing to Sydney that she was 'pretty well now – thank you – after a quiet time here'.[80]

She stayed on with the Olivers over the Christmas holidays, and they did all they could to make her time as peaceful as possible.[81]

During the 'pure romance' of her childhood Christmases, the festive season had been a time of enchantment for Charlotte, but the joy was always dependent on being in the company of her family.[82] She knew – like the speaker in 'The Farmer's Bride', who poses the question 'What's Christmas-time without there be / Some other in the house than we!' – that the season could also be the loneliest of times. And so it proved to be that bleak December of 1927, notwithstanding the Olivers' usual kindness, as she faced her first Christmas ever without Anne.

She returned from Isleworth early in the New Year, and back in the empty studio she began to be haunted by a new thought. During those '3 terrible days & nights' that preceded Anne's death, there were moments when she'd wondered if Anne had already died, so shallow was her breathing.[83] What if, in fact, she had been alive when they buried her? Charlotte now began to torment herself with the idea that she ought to have asked for a doctor to cut the main artery before the body was taken for burial – a request that, though unusual, was not unheard of at the time: her own publisher, Harold Monro, would ask that one of his veins be opened before his cremation.[84]

On Tuesday 3 January, she made the journey to Layton's Solicitors in Budge Row to draw up a will. Small legacies of money and gifts from her personal effects were to be left to friends – including Ethel and Winifred Oliver, Elsie and James O'Keefe, Sydney and Kate Cockerell, Alida Monro and Katherine Righton. Her estate would amount to £8,608 after tax (a little over £3,500 of that had been inherited from Anne nine months earlier).[85] She instructed that some £2,200 be set apart for investment in trust funds to pay for Freda's 'maintenance, clothing and support', and the remainder was to be divided between two of her Isle of Wight cousins, Ethel and Florence (Gertrude – now 'Sister Mary' – in her convent, was not allowed to inherit) and Katherine Righton, who, like Anne, was a struggling artist and needed the money. The will also included two stipulations, one gruesome and one a final, eloquent comment on a loss that she was still struggling to bear: she asked that her executors, Ethel Oliver and James O'Keefe, should arrange for her main artery to be severed before she was placed in a coffin, and that her remains be buried in the same grave as Anne.[86]

Sydney was with the Hardys at Max Gate when, at nine o'clock on 11 January, Thomas Hardy died of a heart attack. Charlotte, who made it to the funeral service in Westminster Abbey on the 16th, thought the ceremony 'a fine & fitting farewell to a great good man'.[87] While filing out of the Abbey, she bumped into the Cockerells' children and was upset to hear that Kate had suffered a serious relapse.[88] 'I sent you all the love I have for you by the children on Monday,' she wrote to her a few days later, '& this is only to say my thoughts are full of you & to send it again.'[89] Hardy had appointed Sydney Cockerell as his literary executor, and while sorting through the papers on Hardy's desk Sydney made an interesting find. On 23 January, he wrote to Charlotte, 'I think you will be touched to receive the enclosed relic of T. H.'[90] It was a copy of her poem, 'Fin de Fête', which Hardy had copied out in his own hand on a small piece of paper.

A second death occurred that January of 1928 that held less significance for Charlotte. She was staying for a few days with Katherine Righton in Hampstead when, on 31 January, her uncle, Edward Herne Kendall, also suffered a heart attack. Charlotte had been estranged from him for some time and the death would not have been of any consequence to her were it not for the fact that, on paper at least, it may have turned her into a wealthy woman. Edward died intestate, but under the terms of his father's will, all the remaining money and assets accruing from his parents' legacy and that of his sister, Mary Leonora Kendall, now became due to Charlotte.[91] It is an irony entirely in keeping with a life story full of such misfortunes that Charlotte might have become financially solvent at just the point in her life when it no longer mattered to her. A further irony was that sales of *The Farmer's Bride* were at last on the increase. That February of 1928, she sent a note to Harold Monro, on black-bordered notepaper, to thank him for the latest royalty statement, with the comment that she hoped 'the improvement in the sale will continue'.[92]

By the middle of February, Charlotte was sleeping very little and complained that she couldn't see the point of going on with what she called 'the daily round' – let alone making arrangements for the future. 'One can plan & make efforts for other people – it doesn't seem worthwhile for oneself,' she told Kate Cockerell.[93] Most troubling of all, she was still plagued by the thought that, because of her negligence, Anne might have been buried alive. Dr Cowan concluded that the strain of nursing her sister through a long and painful illness had taken its toll on her nerves, and that she was in urgent need of rest and medical supervision. On 15 February, she was admitted to a nursing home at 37 Beaumont Street, near Baker Street, suffering from insomnia and 'neurasthenia'.

The dreary room she was given at the back of the building did nothing to soothe her nerves. Its view was of a thin strip of sky above a high brick wall on which the occasional pigeon perched.[94] When Alida visited a few days later, Charlotte told her 'how very depressed she felt gazing on to the grey bricks where no sun seemed to come'.[95] Of the many studies that have since been carried out on the effect that physical environment has on a person's wellbeing, one of the most famous is based on just such an outlook. It concludes that hospital patients exposed to a view of trees need fewer painkillers and recover faster than those whose rooms look out onto a brick wall.[96] Sydney called at the home on the 24th, and after his visit made an unembellished note in his diary that Charlotte had 'had a breakdown' and was 'in a state of great depression, with nothing & nobody to live for'.[97]

In Anne's final days, Catholicism had been a source of comfort to her.[98] Charlotte had witnessed this and been glad of it. For her own part, she would have dearly liked to believe in God, but the God of her

childhood's *Daily Remembrancer* was too judgemental and too distant
to mean anything to her. The question her 'Madeleine' calls out to
Jesus from the dim corner of a church – 'What can You know, what
can You really see / Of this dark ditch, the soul of me!' – was one for
which Charlotte herself never found an answer. On 20 February, she
wrote to her friend Elsie O'Keefe (whose daughter had died in a traf-
fic accident two years earlier) to thank her for the book she had sent.
It was *The Power of Silence* by the American religious leader Horatio
Dresser, a book which Elsie said had comforted her greatly during her
own grief. Charlotte perfectly understood how, but told Elsie that she
believed 'faith is given us like every other good gift & if we haven't
got it we can but pray for it'.⁹⁹ Fifteen years earlier, in 'Men and Trees
(II)', she had compared religious faith with the ability to apprehend
and be moved by music: 'Religion is like music, one must have an ear
for it,' she wrote; 'some people have none at all; but given the ear it is
all significant and wonderful, from the old plain-song to a rhapsodie
of Brahms. The form changes with our shifting emotions and ideas;
here and there a tune gets lost, or goes out of fashion.'¹⁰⁰ She may have
been unable to tune in to God, but the one faith she did have, she told
Elsie now, was 'in the wonderful everlasting loving kindness of my
friends who have borne so much & done so much for me – & where
that comes from I cannot doubt'.¹⁰¹

Every death interrupts a narrative, but for those who believe in an
afterlife the interruption is a gateway to something greater; earthly
existence pales by comparison. The opposite was true for Charlotte
Mew. For her, the only thing that mattered was the here and now.
It was 'Newlyn Harbour in the sunshine' and the 'throbbing qui-
etness' of an unseen kiss; it was the 'wind-blown space' of a moor,
'lamps hung out along the Seine', the 'palaces and pinnacles and
shining towers' of a loved one's heart, the 'scent from gardens by

some far away blue bay'.[102] It was all life, at its fullest and most blaz-
ing. 'When you are burned quite through you die,' she had written
in 'The Quiet House', and in the same poem, 'Red is the strangest
pain to bear.' By 'red' she meant passion, the eagerness to experience
all that the world had to offer. From her compromised position, she
experienced what she could of it, and when she could not experience
it she poured it into her poems – the 'gold and crimsons you could
almost drink', the 'wild, long rippling call' of a bird in flight, calling
to us through the dusk.[103] In Beaumont Street there was none of
that. On Tuesday 28 February, she sat down at her table and wrote a
short note to Kate Cockerell.

37 Beaumont Street
Marylebone W1
February 28, 1928

Dear Kate

Words can't say how much your good long letter cheered me
or how glad I am to hear from Sydney this afternoon that you
are really making way. Yes one can bear hard things under the
open sky but for weeks now I have seen little of it except through
a window. You do not know how much or with what affection
I have thought of you. What you gave me at Cambridge that
fortnight can't be told this side of silence. – For myself I won't say
much. I just tried my best to keep going & broke down – It was
so lonely – I try still but it is lonelier here.

You understand – and a little I hope – how I think of you. Dear
Kate – my love.

Yours truly, Charlotte

In Mew's 1913 poem 'Péri en Mer', the speaker prefigures her own
death, picturing a bed surrounded by friends:

> One day the friends who stand about my bed
> > Will slowly turn from it to speak of me
> Indulgently, as of the newly dead . . .

The end of Charlotte's own life was to happen very differently. Thursday 22 March would have been Ma's ninety-first birthday; it was also, by painful coincidence, the anniversary of Henry's death. The following day, Charlotte had another visit from Alida, who recalled later that as she was getting ready to leave, Charlotte went over to a 'miserable chest-of-drawers' in the corner of her room, took out the little piece of paper on which Hardy had written her poem and handed it to her, simply saying that she would like her to have it. Alida came away feeling, she said, 'rather sad, but not knowing that I would never see her again'.[104]

As far as the nursing home staff were concerned, Charlotte's condition had improved enough for her to be allowed to leave the premises unaccompanied. On the morning of Saturday 24th, she told Miss Leitch, the proprietor, that she was going out for a short walk. The weather was mild for the time of year but showery, and she had under her arm the horn-handled umbrella she now habitually carried with her − as if it were, Alida later said, 'a weapon against the world'.[105] At a nearby chemist's she bought a bottle of Lysol disinfectant. Its active ingredient in those days was cresol, and the correct dilution was one teaspoon per gallon of water. Charlotte would have read about cases of Lysol poisoning in the papers: in 1927, there had been 361 suicides by Lysol in Britain alone.[106] Back in her room, she poured it neat into a glass, drank it back and lay down on the bed. Miss Leitch found her there soon afterwards and immediately summoned a doctor, who came quickly but was unable to revive her.

A brief report in the *Kensington Post* the following Friday managed to get both Charlotte's name and age wrong, among other errors:

"TIRED OF LIFE"

—◆—

WOMEN WRITER'S SUICIDE

Shortly after returning from a walk, Charlotte Mary New, 53, of 64 Charlotte Street, Marylebone, was found dying from Lysol poisoning in a bedroom at a Beaumont Street nursing home, where she had been staying.

At the inquest on Wednesday, Ethel Louisa New, 14 St. Ann's Villas, Paddington, said the deceased was a writer of verse. She had suffered from her nerves, and since her sister's death last June she frequently had fits of depression, and she had told witness she was tired of life and would take poison, but recently she promised not to do so.

Miss Leitch, matron at the nursing home, said she was found lying on her bed muttering as if in pain. A tumbler and a bottle containing Lysol stood on the washstand. The bottle did not belong to the home.

A verdict of unsound mind was recorded.[107]

One of the features of Lysol suicide that Charlotte would not have read about is that the inside of the mouth – the pharynx and the larynx – is eventually burnt away.[108] For a writer whose poems speak with such unrestrained fluency, there is something particularly bleak about this final, physical silencing. When Alida wrote about the incident in her memoir some years later, she added a further detail that was missing from the newspaper account. As the doctor was attempting to bring Charlotte round (before the Lysol had done its damage), she recovered consciousness just long enough to say, 'Don't keep me, let me go.'[109] The words are an unnerving echo of the final stanza of a poem that would be found and published after her death – called, again with a chilling aptness, 'Absence':

> But call, call, and though Christ stands
> Still with scarred hands
> Over my mouth, I must answer. So,
> I will come – He shall let me go!

When Ethel Oliver came to collect Charlotte's effects from the room, she found an envelope addressed to 'Mrs Inglis' with no letter inside it, beside a large bowl of snowdrops 'that could have come from nowhere else. I knew who had sent them and they did so please her,' Ethel wrote later. The envelope prompted her to compose her own letter to Mrs Inglis; it was a letter in which this quiet, 'Quakerly' and most loyal of friends poured out her own feelings about the woman she had known 'intimately for more than 40 years' – since the days when they had walked home laughing from school together to their lodgings on Haverstock Hill.

> Her life has always been shadowed by tragedy. The gallant fight she made to keep going shames most of us – especially those whose lives have lain along more easy paths. Her sister's illness and death nearly quenched her spirit. These later months have been very sad ones.
>
> The Sister of the nursing home does not think she suffered pain at the last.
>
> All her friends will miss her sorely. She had a unique personality – and was marvellously gifted – deeply affectionate, and oh – so charming.[110]

Postscript

THE SPIRIT AFTERWARDS

A year after Charlotte's death, the Poetry Bookshop released her final, posthumous collection, which they titled *The Rambling Sailor*, after one of the thirty-two poems it contained. Of those poems, found among Charlotte's belongings, there are sixteen that had not been previously published in magazines. A few of these are early attempts, and Alida Monro grouped them together as such in a separate section at the back of the book, but the other pieces suggest that she had in fact gone on producing after she'd been awarded her civil list pension, but hadn't sent the work out – either because her sense of unworthiness in the face of the award had shaken her belief in the poems, or because she simply no longer had the energy or will to do so.

Several of the previously unpublished poems meditate – often in the most matter-of-fact way – on the idea of death. One short lyric titled 'From a Window' shows the speaker engaged in one of Charlotte's favourite pastimes: watching from a high window as life goes on outside. The image brings to mind occasions described in her letters: Charlotte sitting on her trunk at the window of a Dieppe hotel, or standing by the light-flooded windows of the Delancey Street house looking out on the coloured balloons, lemonade stalls and Punch and Judy stands of a Bank Holiday weekend, or watching the birds flying over the trees of Regent's Park. The speaker of 'From a Window' begins in the same enchanted and carefree vein, admiring the dancing leaves of a sycamore, but just three lines in, her delight in the tree triggers a reflection on how much she'll miss it when she's no longer a part of the world. From there it is a short step to her revelation that 'I mean to go through the door without fear'.

It would be wrong to reduce 'From a Window' to the category of a suicide note, but this and other of the later poems intimate that a certain amount of forethought preceded Charlotte's decision to end her life. 'From a Window' is set in June, a month that held special meaning for Charlotte. It was one of her favourite times of year, a time when the flagrantly (and dangerously) beautiful roses that populate her poems were in full bloom, but it was also a month tainted by horror: Henry had been admitted to Bedlam during the June of her fifteenth year, and Anne had died in what turned out to be the last June Charlotte would know. If the poem was written in the immediate aftermath of Anne's death, it might indicate that Charlotte was simply unable to stomach the prospect of a June world devoid of her sister.

In a short introductory note to *The Rambling Sailor*, Alida familiarised readers with the bare facts of Charlotte's life as she knew them: the struggles with poverty, the civil list pension and the poet's final days in a room surrounded by 'grey bricks and greyer life'. She revealed Charlotte's 'dislike of publicity' and 'defiant reserve', talked of Anne's death as 'this last attack of Fate', and ascribed to the author a 'tragic personality' as well as a 'passionate sincerity' and 'deep charm and rare wit'.[1] Alida had known Charlotte for less than a quarter of her lifetime (just twelve of her fifty-eight years) and, however close a friend she felt herself to be, she was never told of Henry or Freda's existence. Yet her early assessment set the tone for a public conception of Mew that persists today. Early reviewers of *The Rambling Sailor* picked up on it immediately, and so began the steady mythologising of her character. Only a year on from her death, Mew's 'deep charm' and 'defiant reserve' were beginning to be forgotten and instead this determined and self-possessed woman was being portrayed in the papers as 'one of the most reserved and shy figures in contemporary literature' and 'one of those retiring souls who hated publicity'.[2] That she disliked publicity is indisputable – but the dislike stemmed from a fierce desire to protect her family's privacy; there is little in any of the first-hand accounts we have of her that bears testimony to claims of shyness.

The tragedies of Charlotte Mew's life are incontrovertible, but they are only part of the story, and perhaps not even the larger part. We know that she was also a woman who loved nothing better than to make people laugh, valued loyalty and stood loyally by her friends, spoke her mind, had an aversion to authoritarianism and peppered her letters with ridiculous, cartoonish drawings. But perhaps her most defining characteristic was her conviction that (as she put it in 'Madeleine in Church') 'we are what we are: the spirit afterwards, but first the touch', alongside her unwavering belief in the importance of honouring that fact.

The Rambling Sailor would go on to bring her further critical acclaim. It is a volume that contains, as *The Sphere* noted, poems 'of an almost unbearable loveliness'.[3] The *Yorkshire Post* included it as one of their 'Books of the Year' and admired its originality ('In poem after poem it is Charlotte Mew who speaks, and not a host of recollections and influences rehashed'), while Humbert Wolfe, writing in the *Observer*, asserted that 'No English poet had less pretension, and few as genuine a claim to be in touch with the source of poetry.'[4] *The Sphere*'s reviewer agreed: 'All her work is beautiful, impassioned, rare,' he wrote, 'and it is impossible to believe that it will not live on.'[5] But already there was some disagreement over the poet's renown, with one paper declaring that 'every lover of modern poetry knows the poet's name and has pondered over and delighted in "The Farmer's Bride", that curious changeling among Georgian Poetry', while another felt sure that 'To the general public she was quite unknown, and even some literary people have never heard her name. Yet she was one of the greatest poets of her time.'[6] Several papers commented on the poems' likely longevity: 'Some of these little songs may remain when more trumpet-like tones of greater poets are forgotten,' one critic opined, with some condescension, in the *Aberdeen Press and Journal*.[7]

The Sphere's reviewer sounded a note of caution in this regard, warning that 'It is still as easy as ever, perhaps easier than ever, for an artist to miss recognition. People are apt to think that in a highly organised civilisation genius is not overlooked. They forget the crowd, the hurry, and the noise, which combine to drown a solo on the pipe.'[8]

Bloomsbury was where Charlotte Mew was born and grew up, where she lived for nine tenths of her life, but it is not where she is buried. Around a dozen people attended her funeral at Hampstead's Fortune Green cemetery, bringing with them bunches of Charlotte's favourite red flowers.[9] Her grave lies in the northern part of the cemetery; in the same section are actor–manager Sir Charles Wyndham, actor Fred Terry (younger brother of Ellen Terry) and virtuoso French horn player Dennis Brain. A clause in her will had stipulated that 'an almond tree or some dwarf tree' be planted in the centre of the shared grave and a headstone erected, bearing a precisely worded inscription. She asked that the date of her own death be inserted when the time came:

TO THE BELOVED MEMORY OF CAROLINE FRANCES ANNE MEW
WHO DEPARTED THIS LIFE ON JUNE 18TH 1927.
'CAST DOWN THE SEED OF WEEPING AND ATTEND.'
HERE LIES ALSO HER SISTER CHARLOTTE MARY MEW
WHO DEPARTED THIS LIFE ON — 19—.

The quotation is Beatrice's merciless response to Dante (from Canto XXXI of the *Purgatorio*) after he has made a tearful confession of his sins. Visitors to the Mew sisters' grave are urged to turn aside from mourning the dead and attend to their own lives; to living them as well and as fully as they can. We might also read it (as Beatrice intends it) as a rebuke; a command to direct our attention to the sort of world that has allowed two talented, courageous and generous women to come to such an end, their final days together spent in scrubbing around for money in an unheated studio for a third sister whose existence they felt unable to acknowledge publicly. The grave has since fallen into disrepair and its headstone lies flat on the grass, mottled with mildew and green algae; so far attempts to have it raised again have been foiled on legal grounds.

As a poet, Charlotte was perhaps more than usually aware of the peculiar power of last words. She knew that the last word in a line carries more weight than the words that precede it; that the final word of a poem is weightier still. The quotation for her own epitaph would have been chosen with great care, and *its* final word merits some attention. 'Cast down the seed of weeping and *attend*.' Charlotte Mew was born attentive – 'there was something piquante about her', as a fellow pupil at her school once put it.[10] She went through life with all her senses open, alert to the 'humming and hammering' of the 'whole world' at her ear.[11] And while the circumstances of her life dictated that she rarely travelled far from home, she absorbed all she could of her surroundings with an almost synaesthetic zeal: her poetry talks of hearing smells, for instance, and of a single moment containing the 'smell of beasts, the smell of dust, the scent of all the roses in the world, the sea, the Spring, / The beat of drums, the pad of hoofs, music, the dream'.

Charlotte's abhorrence of self-promotion, her reluctance to furnish editors with information about her life or working method and her abiding belief that 'the chief, if not the only, value of any work of art is precisely that quality in it which is independent of influences' are impossible for a biographer to ignore.[12] But if she had no interest in fame for herself, there is every indication that she wanted it for her poems. Writing to Edith Sitwell four days after Charlotte's death, Siegfried Sassoon rejoiced in what remained in the world of this rare spirit: 'we have her magnificent poetry,' he wrote, and then continued: 'I am curious to see whether anyone will write about her. [. . .] I have heard Virginia Woolf speak admiringly of her – but – query – is Bloomsbury a generous-minded locality?'[13]

Woolf never did write about Mew's work. Had she done so, she may or may not have been generous-minded in her assessment, but Mew's writing had never depended for its reputation on literary fashion and favour. Her overarching theme – the isolation of the human condition – perhaps speaks more strongly to us today than ever; as does her belief that equanimity can be restored by paying due attention to an earthly stillness that lies just outside the chaos and noise of human life. Beyond that, it is the unique voice at the heart of her poems that has kept the work from fading away, and will continue to do so. In the final analysis it is the words themselves to which we are invited to attend.

Acknowledgements

My interest in Charlotte Mew and her writing, based for a long time on just a handful of poems, smouldered away unexplored until the publication in 2005 of Deryn Rees-Jones's *Modern Women Poets*, an influential anthology that covered a century of women's poetry in English. I was one of the last poets featured in that anthology and Mew was the very first, born exactly one hundred years before me, her placement in the book casting her as the poetic foremother of the many names, famous and less famous, that followed. I began to look for more of her work, hunting out early publications of her poetry and prose in magazines, anthologies and individual volumes, which I've been collecting steadily ever since. Ian Hamilton has remarked that 'Mew's are the kind of poems that force readers to want to know about the author's life and personality', and it was my deep admiration for the poems in particular that led me eventually to Penelope Fitzgerald's *Charlotte Mew and Her Friends*. I shall always be grateful to its author for piquing my curiosity about Mew's life story and for laying questions in my mind about how Mew's work might be discussed in the context of that life. In the end it was the enthusiasm shown by my agent, Georgina Capel, in our first ever meeting, that gave me the impetus – and the courage – I needed to begin this book.

Along the way I have been touched by the ready help offered to me by relatives of Charlotte Mew and her friends. Thank you to Michael and Hilary Barnes for welcoming me into their home and allowing me to view the diaries of Charlotte's cousin, Walter Mew Barnes; also to their son James and to Tim Wheeler, Heather Greetham, Geoffrey Greetham and Mary Blair for helping me locate them in the first place. Thank you to Peter Dickens and other members of the fascinating Chick family for allowing me access to the family's private collection of original papers and artefacts relating to Charlotte Mew, and especially to Tristram Hodgkinson for many interesting exchanges by email, for reading sections relating to the Chick family in draft form, and for meeting with me to share his knowledge and show me the records of his grandmother Margaret Tomlinson, an architectural historian who had the foresight to keep a list of Charlotte Mew's entries in the visitors' book for the family's ancestral home in Branscombe, Hazelwood. Barbara Bender and John Torrance gave me generous help very early on in my research and introduced me to the Chick family's collection; thank you to them for their kind encouragement and for setting me on the right path. Thanks also to Alice and Mark Tremlett for taking time out of their busy family life to show me around Hazelwood. Special thanks to Stephen Oliver (great-nephew of Charlotte's school friend Ethel Oliver) and to his wife, Dawn Oliver, for taking such an interest in my work, for their sustaining friendship during the writing of this book, for their reading of early chapters, their hospitality, and the treasured gift of a manuscript story by Charlotte Mew.

I am hugely grateful to the family of Betty Falkenberg, whose daughter Giselle sent me from the States her mother's collection of papers, including – most helpfully – copies of much of Mew's correspondence. Betty's work on a planned biography of Charlotte Mew was interrupted by illness. I have benefited from her preliminary research and have felt her presence as a guiding spirit during the writing of this book. My profound thanks too for Giselle's precious gift of a piece of Charlotte Mew's embroidery. Thank you also to Andrew Roberts for putting me in touch with the family.

I had useful and instructive conversations with a number of academics and writers about Mew's social and literary connections and aspects of her work. I would like to acknowledge in particular Benjamin Fisher, of the University of Mississippi, for an email correspondence on the friendship between Charlotte Mew and Ella D'Arcy; Nicholas Murray; Suzanne Raitt, biographer of May Sinclair, for a helpful discussion on Sinclair's friendship with Charlotte Mew; Rosemary Ashton; Michèle Roberts; Tim Kendall; John Newton; and Andrew Roberts, author (with Betty Falkenberg) of the website studymore. org.uk, which provides a detailed chronology of Charlotte Mew's life, with links to selected letters, poems and prose extracts. Thank you to all these specialists for advice and help.

I am greatly indebted to Mary C. Davidow, whose pioneering work on the life of Charlotte Mew (in the form of an unpublished PhD dissertation – Brown University, 1960) has provided a cornerstone for all subsequent Mew researchers. More recently, Val Warner's groundbreaking 1981 edition of Mew's poetry and (previously uncollected) prose introduced Mew's writing to a new generation of readers. My deep thanks to her, both for her incisive scholarship and for her personal kindness in supporting my own work on Mew. Thank you too to her publisher, Michael Schmidt, for his generous support and for permission to view items from the Archive of Carcanet Press at the University of Manchester Library.

I am grateful to the following institutions and their staff for assistance: British Architectural Library, Royal Institute of British Architects (Ben Smith); British Museum (Francesca Hillier and Lyn Rees) for information on Charlotte's visits to the museum's Reading Room; Bryn Mawr College Library, Mary C. Davidow Collection (Marianne Hansen); Central Saint Martins Museum (Anna Buruma and Angela Doane) for help with my research into Anne Mew's time at the Royal Female School of Art; Holborn Library, Camden Local Studies and Archives Centre (Tudor Allen); Isle of Wight County Record Office, Heritage Services (Richard Smout and Lesa Davies) for access to Freda Mew's medical records; Kislak Center for Special Collections, Rare Books and Manuscripts, University of Pennsylvania (John Pollack); Museum of the Mind, Bethlem Royal Hospital (Colin Gale) for information and advice on Henry Mew's case notes during his stay at Bethlem; Library of Congress (Jeffrey Flannery and Lewis Wyman); New York Public Library, Berg Collection (Lindsi Barnes, Josh Mckeon and Isaac Gewirtz); Princeton University Library, George Egerton Collection (Sandra Bossert, AnnaLee Pauls, Gabriel Swift and Squirrel Walsh); State University of New York, University at Buffalo, the Poetry Collection (Alison Fraser and James Maynard); Surrey History Centre (Helen F. Keen and Joanna Murtagh) for providing me with Henry Mew's case notes during his stay at Holloway Sanatorium; the National Archives at Kew (Harriet Pilcher) for papers relating to Charlotte Mew's civil list pension; Rosenbach Museum and Library in Philadelphia; Senate House Library, University of London (Richard Temple) for details of student numbers at University College, London during the 1900s; University of Texas at Austin, Harry Ransom Center (Mariah Wahl and Rick Watson); Yale University, Beinecke Rare Book and Manuscript Library, Frederick B. Adams Collection and C. A. Dawson Scott – Marjorie Watts Papers (Ingrid Lennon-Pressey, Adrienne Sharpe and Jessica Tubis).

I could not have completed this book without financial assistance from the Society of Authors (in the form of an Authors' Foundation award in the summer of 2014), from the ever-supportive Royal Literary Fund, and the Hosking Houses Trust, who provided me with a room of my own in which to work on the final chapters of my manuscript. Thank you for the kindness extended to me by Sarah Hosking, Wendy Harrison and Dr Paul Edmondson during my stay in Stratford-on-Avon.

Thank you to my friends and family for their patience and support, especially my mother, Pauline (who did some painstaking detective work for me at the start of my research), Suzannah Dunn, Jo Wheeler (with whom I spent a memorable rainy afternoon in Nunhead Cemetery searching for Henry Mew's grave), and Emily Berry (who, armed with camera, carried out a vital piece of London-based research when I was unable to get there). Thank you, too, to Steve Cook for help with translating the unpublished French poem written by May Sinclair in 1915.

Heartfelt thanks to my editor Matthew Hollis for his passion and expertise and to the rest of the able team at Faber, especially Lavinia Singer, Kate Burton and Kate Ward for skilfully midwifing this book into print under the difficult circumstances of a pandemic lockdown. Many thanks also to my agent Georgina Capel, to Eleo Carson for helpful suggestions on improving the text, Eleanor Rees for copy-editing, Ian Bahrami for proofreading and Sarah Ereira for indexing.

I owe a great deal, as always, to my husband Andrew Stevenson, whose love and companionship has sustained me during the slow evolution of this book, and who has commented in depth on this and various earlier versions. I am grateful too to Rosie Oliver and Auden Witter for suggesting amendments to this paperback edition. Thank you, finally, to Ruffle, my beloved Spanish water dog.

Select Bibliography

The bulk of my research has been drawn from primary sources and contemporary newspapers, magazines and anthologies. I have listed below a selection of titles that informed my understanding of place and period, or from which I have quoted. For readers interested in finding out more about the themes explored in this book, I have also included a brief 'Further Reading' section.

Poem quotations are from *Selected Poetry and Prose*, edited by me and published by Faber (2019). In accordance with that edition, for those poems that were collected in print during Mew's lifetime I have followed the original text of the second, expanded edition of *The Farmer's Bride* (The Poetry Bookshop, 1921) on the basis that Mew appears to have made very slight and occasional modifications to the text of this edition, which was published five years after the first. For poems collected in her posthumous volume *The Rambling Sailor* (The Poetry Bookshop, 1929), I have consulted the original manuscripts and typescripts, alongside the text as it appeared in that volume. When quoting from previously unpublished poems, prose and letters, I have followed the original manuscript or typescript, complete with idiosyncrasies of punctuation and spelling. Quotations from published prose are taken from Val Warner's comprehensive *Collected Poems and Prose* (1981), published by Virago, in association with Carcanet Press.

WORKS BY CHARLOTTE MEW

The Farmer's Bride, London: The Poetry Bookshop, 1916
The Farmer's Bride, London: The Poetry Bookshop, 1921

Saturday Market, New York: Macmillan, 1921

The Rambling Sailor, London: The Poetry Bookshop, 1929

Boland, Eavan (ed.), *Charlotte Mew: Selected Poems*, Manchester: Carcanet, 2008

Hamilton, Ian (ed.), *Charlotte Mew: Selected Poems*, London: Bloomsbury, 1999

Newton, John (ed.), *Charlotte Mew: Complete Poems*, London: Penguin, 2000

Warner, Val, *Charlotte Mew: Collected Poems and Prose*, Manchester and London: Virago, in association with Carcanet, 1981

Warner, Val, *Charlotte Mew: Collected Poems and Selected Prose*, Manchester: Carcanet, 1997

ARCHIVAL SOURCES

Beinecke	Beinecke Rare Book and Manuscript Library, Yale University
Berg	The Henry W. and Albert A. Berg Collection of English and American Literature, the New York Public Library
BL	British Library: Western Collections
BMC	Bryn Mawr College Library Special Collections Department: Mary C. Davidow collection of research materials on the life and career of Charlotte Mew (1869–1928)
Buffalo	Contemporary Manuscripts Collection, the Poetry Collection of the University Libraries, the University at Buffalo, the State University of New York
CSM	Central Saint Martins Museum and Study Collection
Beinecke	Beinecke Rare Book and Manuscript Library, Yale University
GRO	General Register Office
HRC	Harry Ransom Humanities Research Center, the University of Texas at Austin
IWR	Isle of Wight Record Office and Archive
LC	Manuscript Division, Library of Congress, Washington
NA	The National Archives, Kew
Princeton	Rare Books and Special Collections, Princeton University Library

DIARIES, MANUSCRIPTS AND TYPESCRIPTS

Diaries of Sydney Cockerell (BL Add MSS 52655–52666)

Diaries of Walter Mew Barnes for the years 1904–9 (private collection)

Diary of Harriette Chick for 1903 (private collection)

Manuscript of 'Delivered', short story, signed by CMM (private collection)

Manuscript of poem 'Love Love Today' (Charlotte Mary Mew collection of papers, Berg)

Nine typewritten drafts of stories, together with an article about Richard Jefferies; prose, poems, a play and miscellaneous correspondence relating to Charlotte Mew. Poetry Bookshop Papers Vols XXI–XXII (BL Add MS 57754 and 57755)

Works by Charlotte Mew, autograph and typewritten. Supplementary Poetry Bookshop Papers Vol. XXVI (BL Add MS 83382)

Typed and handwritten manuscripts of Mew's poems in the Charles David Abbott collection (Buffalo)

Materials relating to Charlotte Mew's civil list award, Records of the Prime Minister's Office (NA PREM 5/14)

A short story and a group of poems in autograph manuscript and typescript, some signed. Frederick B. Adams Collection of Charlotte Mew (Beinecke-FBA)

Manuscripts of two poems, 'The Forest Road' and 'The Pedlar', by Charlotte Mew. C. A. Dawson Scott – Marjorie Watts Papers (Beinecke-MW)

BIOGRAPHY

Cockerell, Sydney C., 'Miss Charlotte Mew: A Poet of Rare Quality', obituary in *The Times*, 29 March 1928, p. 21a

Davidow, Mary Celine, *Charlotte Mew: Biography and Criticism* (unpublished PhD thesis, Brown University, 1960)

Fitzgerald, Penelope, *Charlotte Mew and Her Friends*, London: Harper Collins, 1984

Holroyd, Michael, 'Said to Be a Writer', in *Unreceived Opinions*, London: Penguin, 1976, pp. 167–74

Monro, Alida, *Collected Poems of Charlotte Mew*, London: Gerald Duckworth, 1953

Watts, Marjorie, 'Memories of Charlotte Mew', PEN Broadsheet 13 (Autumn 1982), pp. 12–13

PLACE AND PERIOD

Streets East of Bloomsbury: A Survey of Streets, Buildings & Former Residents in a Part of Camden, Camden History Society, 2008

Allderidge, Patricia, *Bethlem Hospital 1247–1997: A Pictorial Record*, Sussex: Phillimore & Co., 1997

Ashton, Rosemary, *Victorian Bloomsbury*, New Haven and London: Yale University Press, 2012

Baines, F. E. (ed.), *Records of the Manor Parish and Borough of Hampstead*, London: Whittaker & Co., 1890

Baudelaire, Charles, *The Painter of Modern Life*, London: Penguin Classics, 2010. Originally published in *Le Figaro* in 1863

Bernstein, Susan David, *Roomscape: Women Writers in the British Museum from George Eliot to Virginia Woolf*, Edinburgh: Edinburgh University Press, 2013

Callen, Anthea, *Angel in the Studio: Women in the arts and crafts movement, 1870–1914*, London: Astragal Books, 1979

Chalmers, F. Graeme, *Women in the Nineteenth-Century Art World*, Westport, Connecticut: Greenwood Press, 1998

Clifton, Gloria, *Professionalism, Patronage and Public Service in Victorian London*, London: Bloomsbury Academic, 2015

Collecott, Diana, 'Another Bloomsbury: Women's Networks in Literary London during World War One', in Camboni, Marina (ed.), *Networking Women: Toward a Rewriting of Cultural History, 1890–1939*, Rome: Edizioni di Storia e Letteratura, 2004, pp. 59–77

Colloms, Marianne and Weindling, Dick, *The Good Grave Guide to Hampstead Cemetery, Fortune Green*, London: Camden History Society, 2000

Dale, Antony, *Fashionable Brighton, 1829–1860*, London: Country Life Ltd, 1947

Ditchfield, P. H., *London's West End*, London: Houghton Mifflin/Jonathan Cape, 1925

Dyhouse, Carol, *Girls Growing Up in Late Victorian and Edwardian England*, London: Routledge, 1981

Fullerton, George, *The Family Medical Guide*, London: Chapman & Hall, 1871

Gittings, Clare and Jupp, Peter C. (eds), *Death in England: An Illustrated History*, Manchester: Manchester University Press, 1999

Hardy, Thomas, *Jude the Obscure*, Oxford: Oxford University Press, 2002. First published in book form in 1895

Harte, Negley and North, John, *The World of University College London 1828–1978*, London: University College, London, 1979

Jackson, Holbrook, *The Eighteen Nineties*, London: Grant Richards Ltd, 1922

Jalland, Patricia, *Death in the Victorian Family*, Oxford: Oxford University Press, 1996

Laidlaw, E. E., *A History of the Isle of Wight Hospitals*, Isle of Wight: Cross Publishing, 1994

Maudsley, Henry, *The Pathology of Mind*, London: Macmillan, 1879

May, James Lewis, *John Lane and the '90s*, London: The Bodley Head, 1925

Mitchell, Kevin, *Newport Pubs*, Isle of Wight: Kena Publishing, 1999

Mix, Katherine Lyon, *A Study in Yellow: The Yellow Book and Its Contributors*, Lawrence: University of Kansas Press, 1960

Murray, Nicholas, *Bloomsbury and the Poets*, Presteigne: Rack Press, 2014

Sharp, Evelyn, *Unfinished Adventure: Selected Reminiscences from an Englishwoman's Life*, London: John Lane, The Bodley Head, 1933

Showalter, Elaine, *The Female Malady: Women, Madness and English Culture, 1830–1980*, London: Virago, 1987

Smith, Rev. James, *The Believer's Daily Remembrancer*, London: S. Marshall & Co., 1846

Stead, C. K., *The New Poetic: Yeats to Eliot*, London: Hutchinson University Library, 1975

Swinnerton, Frank, *The Georgian Literary Scene, 1910–1935*, London: Heinemann, 1935

Syrett, Netta, *The Sheltering Tree*, London: Geoffrey Bles, 1939

Tosh, John, *A Man's Place: Masculinity and the Middle-class Home in Victorian England*, New Haven: Yale University Press, 1999

Vicinus, Martha, *Independent Women: Work and Community for Single Women, 1850–1920*, London: Virago, 1985

Walford, Edward, *Old and New London: Volume 6*, London: Cassell, Petter & Galpin, 1878

Woolf, Virginia, 'Mr. Bennett and Mrs. Brown', in *Modernism: An Anthology of Sources and Documents*, eds. Vassiliki Kolocotroni, Jane Goldman and Olga Taxidou, Edinburgh: Edinburgh University Press, 1998

PEOPLE

Archibald, Douglas N. and O'Donnell, William H. (eds), *The Collected Works of W. B. Yeats, Vol. III: Autobiographies*, New York: Scribner, 1999

Ayres, Peter, *Shaping Ecology: The Life of Arthur Tansley*, Chichester: John Wiley & Sons, 2012

Beckson, Karl, *Henry Harland: His Life and Work*, London: The Eighteen Nineties Society, 1978

Belford, Barbara, *Violet: The Story of the Irrepressible Violet Hunt*, New York: Simon & Schuster, 1990

Bell, Anne (ed.), *The Diary of Virginia Woolf, Vol. II: 1920–24*, London: Penguin, 1981

Blunt, Wilfrid, *Cockerell: A Life of Sir Sydney Cockerell*, New York: Alfred Knopf, 1964

Boll, Theophilus E. M., *Miss May Sinclair: Novelist*, New Jersey: Associated University Presses, 1973

Colvin, Howard, *A Biographical Dictionary of British Architects, 1600–1840*: 4th edn, New Haven: Yale University Press, 2008 [1954]

Drake, William, *Sara Teasdale: Woman and Poet*, London: Harper and Row, 1979

Gittings, Robert and Manton, Jo, *The Second Mrs Hardy*, London: Oxford University Press, 1979

Grant, Joy, *Harold Monro and the Poetry Bookshop*, London: Routledge and Kegan Paul, 1967

Graves, Algernon, *The Royal Academy of Arts: A Complete Dictionary of Contributors and their Work from Its Foundation in 1769 to 1904*, Vol. IV, London: Graves and Bell, 1906

Greene, Richard (ed.), *Selected Letters of Edith Sitwell*, London: Little Brown,
    1998

Greener, Amy (ed.), *A Lover of Books: The Life and Literary Papers of Lucy Harrison*,
    London: Dent, 1916

Hassall, Christopher, *Edward Marsh: Patron of the Arts: A Biography*, New York:
    Harcourt, Brace and Company, 1959

Havighurst, Alfred F., *Radical Journalist: H. W. Massingham (1860–1924)*, New York:
    Cambridge University Press, 2009

Hibberd, Dominic, *Harold Monro: Poet of the Age*, Basingstoke: Palgrave, 2001

Hudson, Derek, *Munby, Man of Two Worlds: The Life and Diaries of Arthur J. Munby
    1828–1910*, London: John Murray, 1972

Meynell, Viola (ed.), *Friends of a Lifetime: Letters to S. C. Cockerell*, London:
    Jonathan Cape, 1940

Meynell, Viola (ed.), *The Best of Friends: Further Letters to S. C. Cockerell*, London:
    Rupert Hart-Davis, 1956

Millgate, Michael and Purdy, Richard (eds), *Thomas Hardy: Collected Letters VI*,
    Oxford: Clarendon Press, 1987

Nicolson, Nigel and Trautmann, Joanne (eds), *The Flight of the Mind: The Letters of
    Virginia Woolf, 1888–1912*, Vol. I, London: The Hogarth Press, 1975

Raitt, Suzanne, *May Sinclair: A Modern Victorian*, Oxford: Clarendon Press, 2000

Scott, Bonnie Kime, *Selected Letters of Rebecca West*, New Haven: Yale University
    Press, 2000

Showalter, Elaine (ed.), *Daughters of Decadence: Women Writers of the Fin-de-siècle*,
    London: Virago Press, 1993

Symons, A. J. A., *The Quest for Corvo*, London: The Folio Society, 1952

Tomlinson, Margaret: *Three Generations in the Honiton Lace Trade: A Family History*,
    Seaton: Margaret Tomlinson, 1983

Untermeyer, Louis, *Bygones: The Recollections of Louis Untermeyer*, New York:
    Harcourt, Brace, 1965

Untermeyer, Louis, *From Another World: The Autobiography of Louis Untermeyer*, New
    York: Harcourt, Brace, 1939

Watts, Marjorie, *Mrs Sappho: The Life of C. A. Dawson Scott, Mother of International
    P.E.N.*, London: Gerald Duckworth, 1987

CRITICISM

Bell, Kathleen, 'Charlotte Mew, T. S. Eliot and Modernism', in *Kicking Daffodils:
    Twentieth-century Women Poets*, ed. Vicki Bertram, Edinburgh: Edinburgh
    University Press, 1997, pp. 13–24

Boland, Eavan, 'Charlotte Mew: An Introduction', in *A Journey with Two Maps*, New York and London: Norton & Company, 2012, pp. 143–53

Boll, Theophilus, E. M., 'The Mystery of Charlotte Mew and May Sinclair: An Inquiry', *Bulletin of the New York Public Library*, No. 74 (1970), pp. 445–53

Byron, Glennis, 'Modernism and Its Aftermath', in *Dramatic Monologue*, London: Routledge, 2003, pp. 112–28

Collard, Lorna Reeling, 'Charlotte Mew', in *Contemporary Review*, No. 137 (April 1930), pp. 501–8

Davidow, Mary C., 'The Charlotte Mew–May Sinclair Relationship: A Reply', in *Bulletin of the New York Public Library*, No. 75 (1971), pp. 295–300

Doran, Sabine, 'The Scandal of Yellow Books: From the Yellow Nineties to Modernism' in *The Culture of Yellow*, London: Bloomsbury Academic, 2013, pp. 47–68

Howarth, Peter, 'Fateful Forms: A. E. Housman, Charlotte Mew, Thomas Hardy and Edward Thomas', in *Twentieth-Century English Poetry*, ed. Neil Corcoran, Cambridge: Cambridge University Press, 2007, pp. 59–73

Kendall, Tim, 'The Passion of Charlotte Mew', in *The Oxford Handbook of Victorian Poetry*, ed. Matthew Bevis, Oxford: Oxford University Press, 2013, pp. 640–51

Lees, Edith, 'Olive Schreiner and Her Relation to the Woman Movement', in *Book News Monthly*, Vol. XXXIII (February 1915), New York,

Leighton, Angela, chapter on Charlotte Mew in *Victorian Women Poets: Writing Against the Heart*, Hemel Hempstead: Harvester Wheatsheaf, 1992, pp. 266–98

Leithauser, Brad, 'Small Wonder', *New York Review of Books*, 15 January 1987

Lyon, Janet, 'On the Asylum Road with Woolf and Mew', in *Modernism/Modernity* Vol. XVIII, No. 3, Baltimore: Johns Hopkins University Press, 2012, pp. 551–74

McConeghey Rice, Nelljean, *A New Matrix for Modernism: A Study of the Lives and Poetry of Charlotte Mew and Anna Wickham*, London: Routledge, 2003, pp. 3–77

Merrin, Jeredith, 'The Ballad of Charlotte Mew', in *Modern Philology*, Vol. XCV, No. 2 (November 1997), pp. 200–17

Monro, Harold, 'Charlotte Mew', in *The Bookman*, 8 May 1928, pp. 112–13

Monro, Harold, *Some Contemporary Poets*, London: Leonard Parsons, 1920

Monro, Harold, *Twentieth-Century Poetry*, London: Chatto & Windus, 1929

Moore, Virginia, 'Charlotte Mew', in *Distinguished Women Writers*, Port Washington, New York: Kennikat Press, 1968, pp. 191–202

Newton, John, 'Another Handful of Dust', in *Times Literary Supplement*, 28 April 1995, p. 18

Newton, John, 'Charlotte Mew and the Future of English Poetry', in *New England Review*, Vol. XVIII, No. 2 (Spring 1997), pp. 32–46

Newton, Michael, 'I See Myself Among the Crowd: The Poetry of Charlotte Mew' in *Poetry Review*, Vol. XCIV, No. 1 (Spring 2004), pp. 56–64

Raitt, Suzanne, 'Charlotte Mew and May Sinclair: A Love-Song', in *Critical Quarterly*, Autumn 1995, pp. 3–17

Schmidt, Michael, chapter on Charlotte Mew in *An Introduction to 50 Modern Poets*, London: Pan Books, 1979, pp. 57–63

Swinnerton, Frank, 'The War-Time Afflatus, II: Charlotte Mew', in *The Georgian Literary Scene, 1910–1935*, London: Heinemann, 1935, pp. 237–9

Untermeyer, Louis, chapter on Charlotte Mew in *Lives of the Poets*, New York: Simon and Schuster, 1959, pp. 655–7

Warner, Val, 'Mary Magdalen and the Bride: The Work of Charlotte Mew', in *Poetry Nation* No. 4 (1975), pp. 92–106

Warner, Val, 'New Light on Charlotte Mew', in *PN Review* 117, Vol. XXIV (September 1997), pp. 43–7

ONLINE SOURCES

Roberts, Andrew and Falkenberg, Betty, 'Charlotte Mew Chronology', 2005. Middlesex University resource available at http://studymore.org.uk/ymew.htm

FURTHER READING

For background reading on nineteenth-century Bloomsbury, Rosemary Ashton's *Victorian Bloomsbury* (Yale University Press, 2012) gives an invaluable account of the locale's cultural and institutional past. For a pictorial social context, Christopher Hibbert's *Social History of Victorian Britain* and James Bishop's *Social History of Edwardian Britain* (Angus & Robertson, 1975 and 1977 respectively) feature contemporary photographs and illustrations from the *Illustrated London News* and provide a fascinating record of the period. My understanding of the details of Charlotte Mew's daily life during her childhood was illuminated by Molly Hughes's *A London Child of the 1870s*, republished by Persephone Press in 2005, and Evelyn Sharp's *The London Child* (John Lane/The Bodley Head, 1927). My background reading on eugenics and the history of mental illness includes Angelique Richardson's *Love and Eugenics in the Late Nineteenth Century* (Oxford University Press, 2003), Roy Porter's *A Social History of Madness* (Weidenfeld & Nicolson, 1987) and Francis Galton's *Hereditary Genius*, first published in 1892. For readers interested in discovering more about the group of writers that gathered around *The Yellow Book* periodical in the 1890s, the fullest accounts are given in Katherine Lyon Mix's *A Study in Yellow: The Yellow Book and Its Contributors* (University of Kansas Press, 1960) and James Lewis May's *John Lane and the '90s* (The Bodley Head, 1925).

Appendix: Magazine Publication of Individual Poems and Prose

POEMS

'At the Convent Gate', *Temple Bar* CXXV, 1902

'The Cenotaph', *Westminster Gazette*, 7 September 1919

'The Changeling', *The Englishwoman*, 17 February 1913

'Exspecto Resurrectionem', *Living Age*, 22 March 1913

'Fame', *New Weekly*, 30 May 1914

'The Farmer's Bride', *The Nation*, 3 February 1912

'The Fête', *The Egoist*, 1 May 1914

'Fin de Fête', *The Sphere*, 17 February 1923

'Impossibility', *Pall Mall Gazette*, 23 March 1912

'In the Fields', *The Sphere*, March 1923

'Moorland Night', *Nation and Athenaeum*, 24 January 1925

'Old Shepherd's Prayer', *The New Leader*, 6 October 1922

'Pécheresse', *New Weekly*, 25 July 1914

'The Pedlar', *The Englishwoman* XXI, February 1914

'Péri en Mer', *The Englishwoman* XX, November 1913

'The Rambling Sailor', *The Chapbook*, February 1922

'Sea Love', *The Chapbook*, July 1919

'Song: Love, Love to-day', *The Athenaeum* 24 October 1919

'Song: Oh! Sorrow, Sorrow', *Temple Bar* CXXVI, 1902

'The Sunlit House', *The Bookman* LXXIV, May 1928

'To a Child in Death', *Temple Bar* LV, April 1922

'To a Little Child in Death', *Temple Bar* CXXIV, September 1901

'The Trees are Down', *The Chapbook*, January 1923

'The Voice', *The Englishwoman*, March 1912

'V. R. I', *Temple Bar* CXXVII, March 1901

PROSE

'The China Bowl', *Temple Bar* CXVIII, September 1899

'The Country Sunday', *Temple Bar* CXXXII, November 1905

'A Fatal Fidelity', *Cornhill Magazine* CLXVII, Autumn 1953

'The Governess in Fiction', *The Academy*, 12 August 1899

'The Hay-Market', *New Statesman*, 14 February 1914

'In the Curé's Garden', *Temple Bar* CXXV, June 1902

'The London Sunday', *Temple Bar* CXXXII, December 1905

'Mademoiselle', *Temple Bar* CXXIX, January 1904

'Mark Stafford's Wife', *Temple Bar* CXXXI, January 1905

'Mary Stuart in Fiction', *The Englishwoman* XIV, April 1912

'Men and Trees (I)', *The Englishwoman* XVII, February 1913

'Men and Trees (II)', *The Englishwoman* XVII, March 1913

'Miss Bolt', *Temple Bar* CXXII, April 1901

'Notes in a Brittany Convent', *Temple Bar* CXXIV, October 1901

'An Old Servant', *New Statesman*, October 1913

'An Open Door', *Temple Bar* CXXVII, January 1903

'Passed', *The Yellow Book*, Vol. II, July 1894

'A Permitted Prayer', *The Woman at Home*, July 1897 (uncollected)

'The Poems of Emily Brontë', *Temple Bar* CXXX, August 1904

'The Smile', *Theosophist* XXXV, 8 May 1914

'Some Ways of Love', *Pall Mall Magazine*, September 1901

'The Wheat', *Time and Tide*, 20 February 1954

'A White Night', *Temple Bar* CXXVII, May 1903

Notes and References

ABBREVIATIONS FOR TEXTS

CPP   *Charlotte Mew: Collected Poems and Prose*, edited by Val Warner,
       Manchester and London: Carcanet in association with Virago, 1981
MM   'Charlotte Mew – a Memoir', from *Charlotte Mew: Collected Poems*,
       edited by Alida Monro, London: Gerald Duckworth, 1953
SPP   *Charlotte Mew: Selected Poetry and Prose*, edited by Julia Copus, London:
       Faber & Faber, 2019

ABBREVIATIONS FOR PEOPLE

CADS   Catherine Amy Dawson Scott
CMM   Charlotte Mary Mew
MS   May Sinclair
SCC   Sydney Carlyle Cockerell

NOTES

Introduction

1 MM, p. x.
2 Cockerell, Sydney, 'Obituary. Miss Charlotte Mew. A Poet of Rare Quality', *The Times*, 29 March 1928, p. 21.
3 CPP, p. 358.
4 Anonymous review of the second edition of *The Farmer's Bride* in the *Daily Aberdeen Journal*, 18 March 1921.
5 Cockerell, 'Obituary'.
6 MM, p. xx.
7 CMM to CADS, 12 March 1914. Beinecke-MW.
8 Davidow, Mary Celine, *Charlotte Mew: Biography and Criticism* (unpublished PhD thesis, Brown University, 1960), pp. 47, 41.
9 Mew, Charlotte, 'The Poems of Emily Brontë', CPP, p. 363; originally published in *Temple Bar*, August 1904.

10 Review of *The Farmer's Bride* in *The Herald*, 5 August 1916.

11 Thomas Hardy to J. C. Squire, 27 January 1922, quoted in *Thomas Hardy: Collected Letters VI*, eds. Richard Little Purdy and Michael Millgate (Oxford: Clarendon Press, 1987), p. 113.

12 Siegfried Sassoon to SCC, 8 September 1953, collected in Meynell, Viola (ed.), *The Best of Friends* (London: Rupert Hart-Davis, 1956), pp. 224–5.

13 H.D. writing in *The Egoist*, Vol. III, No. 9 (September 1916), p. 135.

14 Thomas Hardy to J. C. Squire, 27 January 1922, quoted in *Collected Letters VI*, p. 113.

15 Edith Sitwell to Robert Nichols, 26 February 1919, quoted in Greene, Richard (ed.), *Selected Letters of Edith Sitwell* (London: Virago, 1998), p. 29.

16 CMM to Harold Monro, 29 July 1916. Buffalo.

17 Booth, James, *Philip Larkin: Life, Art and Love* (London: Bloomsbury, 2014), p. 297.

18 Philip Larkin to Dan Davin, 20 January 1966, quoted in Thwaite, Anthony (ed.), *Philip Larkin: Selected Letters* (London: Faber & Faber, 1992), p. 380.

19 CMM to Edith Hill, 4 January 1917. Buffalo.

20 Quotations from T. S. Eliot in this paragraph are from 'Tradition and the Individual Talent', first published in *The Egoist* in 1919 and reprinted in *The Sacred Wood* (London: Methuen, 1920).

21 Hamilton, Ian, *Charlotte Mew: Selected Poems* (London: Bloomsbury, 1999); Boland, Eavan, *A Journey with Two Maps* (New York: Norton, 2012), pp. 149–50.

22 Newton, John (ed.), *Charlotte Mew: Complete Poems* (London: Penguin, 2000); Newton, John, 'Charlotte Mew's Place in the Future of English Poetry', *New England Review*, 182 (1997), p. 46.

23 Showalter, Elaine (ed.), *Daughters of Decadence: Women Writers of the Fin-de-siècle* (New Brunswick, New Jersey: Rutgers University Press, 1993), p. xvii.

24 Mew, 'The Poems of Emily Brontë', CPP, p. 357.

25 MM, p. xvi.

Prologue

1 SPP, p. 21.

2 The tribute would appear in Charlotte Mew's essay 'An Old Servant', first published in the *New Statesman* on 18 October 1913.

3 Mew, Charlotte, 'An Old Servant', CPP, p. 401; a 'Lincolnshire woman': Mew knew only that Elizabeth Goodman was from a 'North-county village'; her birth certificate and census records reveal she was born and brought up in Barton-upon-Humber in the north of Lincolnshire, eastern England.

4 Mew, 'An Old Servant', CPP, p. 401.

5 Ibid.

6 CMM to Dorothy Hawksley, 30 November 1925; Felicia Hemans (1793–1835); Thomas Hood (1799–1845).

7 Mew, Charlotte, 'The Country Sunday', CPP, p. 370.

8 Smith, Rev. James, *The Believer's Daily Remembrancer* (London: S. Marshall & Co., 1846), p. 33.

9 Macdonald, Greville, *George Macdonald and His Wife* (New York: Lincoln Macveagh, 1924), p. 305, quoted in Davidow, p. 29.

10 Baby Daniel – later renamed Christopher Barnes – is buried with his brother Richard Cobham and their parents in the Mew family grave in Kensal Green Cemetery. The birth date laid out in raised lead lettering on the grave is 19 November 1875. Curiously, his birth certificate gives 15 November – the same date as Charlotte's birthday. Either the date on the grave is correct (and the '9' was copied out wrongly as '5' when the certificate was drawn up) or the mistake was made by the stonemason, in which case the baby arrived on the very day Charlotte turned six.

11 Mew, 'An Old Servant', CPP, p. 401.

12 Ibid.

13 Mew, 'The Country Sunday', CPP, p. 370: 'God and His angels (those I thought the stars) were certain to be looking down.'

14 Mew, 'An Old Servant', CPP, p. 403.

15 The details about the nursery and daily routine are taken from Mary Davidow (p. 23) and from Mew's own account in three essays: 'An Old Servant', 'Miss Bolt' and 'The Country Sunday'.

16 Smith, p. 348.

17 Edith Sitwell to Robert Nichols, 26 February 1919, quoted in Greene (ed.), p. 29.

18 MM, p. viii.

19 These three descriptions of Mew's nature are taken from MM, p. xii; Ethel Oliver to Ethel Inglis, 28 March 1928 (Berg); and Catherine Dawson Scott, quoted in Watts, Marjorie, *Mrs Sappho* (London: Duckworth, 1987), p. 56.

1 Good Five-O'Clock People

Chapter title: from Mew's poem 'Afternoon Tea'.

1 Davidow, p. 21.

2 Ibid.

3 Mitchell, Kevin, *Newport Pubs* (Isle of Wight: Kena Publishing, 1999), p. 103.

4 *Hampshire Advertiser*, 31 March 1832.

5 *Hampshire Advertiser*, 4 April 1835; *Morning Post*, 3 September 1832.

6 *Harrod & Co.'s Directory of Hampshire & Isle of Wight, 1865* shows 'Newfairlee Farm' in detail, complete with tracks into the farmyard.

7 Davidow, p. 5. The information was apparently taken from letters and papers in the possession of the family of Richard Percy Mew, Charlotte Mew's first cousin.

8 *Isle of Wight Observer*, 18 February 1865.

9 Graves, Algernon, *The Royal Academy of Arts: A Complete Dictionary of Contributors and their Work from Its Foundation in 1769 to 1904* (London: Graves and Bell, 1906), Vol. IV, p. 312.

10 *The Builder*, 20 June 1885, p. 883.

11 Colvin, Howard, *A Biographical Dictionary of British Architects, 1600–1840*, 4th edn (New Haven: Yale University Press, 2008 [1954]), p. 487. In fact, Henry Kendall senior had three sons and four daughters.

12 Kendall senior's first wife, Anne Lyon, was only eleven years old at the time of Kendall junior's birth, and seems therefore an unlikely candidate for his mother; there is no mention anywhere of who else his mother might have been. The second wife, Matilda Alice Clowser, was in her early thirties when she married the ninety-four-year-old Kendall, three years after Anne Lyon's death. If Matilda had been hoping for a long future of financial security, then she was to be disappointed. Kendall died in 1875, at the age of ninety-eight; only a year later, Matilda followed him, after an unpleasant dose of viral hepatitis.

13 MM, p. viii.

14 Sara Teasdale to Ernst Filsinger, 1923, quoted in Drake, William D., *Sara Teasdale: Woman & Poet* (San Francisco: Harper & Row, 1979), pp. 218–19.

15 CMM to SCC, 30 May 1923. Berg.

16 *Pall Mall Gazette*, 1 June 1871.

17 Ibid.

18 Mrs Mew is described as such by two of Charlotte's classmates in Davidow, pp. 20–1.

19 Watts, *Mrs Sappho*, pp. 55 and 59.

20 MM, p. viii.

2 Bad Milk

Chapter title: from *Cassell's Household Guide* (London: Cassell, Petter and Galpin, 1869), p. 83.

1 Information on the occupations of the Mews' neighbours in Doughty Street is from the London Post Office Directories for 1876.

2 *Hampstead and Highgate Express*, 13 July 1878.

3 Ibid.

4 MM, p. ix.

5 Jalland, Patricia, *Death in the Victorian Family* (Oxford: Oxford University Press, 1996), p. 120.

6 *Childhood, Infant and Perinatal Mortality in England and Wales, 2013: Statistical Bulletin* (Office for National Statistics), 10 March 2015, states 3.8 deaths per 1,000 live births in 2013.

7 Jalland, pp. 130 and 119.

8 Smith, p. 85.

9 Two Queen's Nurses, L. C. & A. E. H., *Simple Instructions for the Laying Out of the Dead* (Richmond, 1910), pp. 1–8, quoted in Jalland, p. 212.

10 *Cassell's Household Guide*, p. 83.

11 *Building News*, 7 April 1876.

12 The vestry meeting at which this decision was made was held on Monday 10 April 1876, and reported in the subsequent edition of the *Hampstead and Highgate Express* (on 15 April).

13 Ethel Louisa would serve as a witness at Mew's inquest in 1928.

14 Mew describes her as such in a letter to Sydney Cockerell, 20 September 1919.

15 Davidow, p. 30. The anecdote was related in person by Gertrude Mary Mew to Mary Davidow.

16 Mew, 'The Country Sunday', CPP, p. 370.

17 Mew, 'The Poems of Emily Brontë', CPP, p. 357.

18 Mew, 'The Country Sunday', CPP, p. 371.

19 Smith, p. 296.

20 Mew, 'An Old Servant', CPP, p. 404.

21 Jalland, p. 124.

22 Fullerton, George, *The Family Medical Guide* (London: Chapman & Hall, 1871), p. 241.

23 Mew, Charlotte, 'Miss Bolt', CPP, pp. 338ff. The memoir was first published in *Temple Bar* in 1901.

24 Ibid., p. 338.

25 Ibid., pp. 345–6.

26 Mew, 'An Old Servant', CPP, p. 402.

27 *Hampstead and Highgate Express*, 9 March 1878.

28 *Hampstead and Highgate Express*, 8 November 1878.

29 Penelope Fitzgerald reports that residents complained that the brightness of the brickwork made them dizzy, but no source is given. (Fitzgerald, Penelope, *Charlotte Mew and Her Friends*, London: Harper Collins, 1984, p. 34). If the

complaint was indeed made, then it is an odd one: the red Bracknell bricks used in the build can be found in a number of celebrated London buildings – the Royal Albert Hall and Westminster Cathedral among them. At any rate, the general reaction to the new vestry hall was positive.

30 Extract from a police report on a suffragette meeting at Hampstead Town Hall on 14 February 1913, National Archives, Catalogue ref: HO 45/10695/231366.

31 Alida Monro records this description of Freda by a 'close friend' of Charlotte and Anne Mew: 'The friend who spoke of them, told me that the third sister, Freda, was as remarkable as the other two and was "like a flame"' (MM, p. ix). Monro does not name the friend, but it is likely to have been Ethel Oliver.

32 Ibid.

33 Mew, 'Miss Bolt', CPP, p. 338.

34 Ibid., p. 341.

35 Ibid., p. 346.

3 A Rosebud Set with Little Wilful Thorns

Chapter title: from Tennyson, Alfred, 'The Princess', Part One, line 153.

1 Greener, Amy (ed.), *A Lover of Books: The Life and Literary Papers of Lucy Harrison* (London: Dent, 1916), pp. 22–3.

2 Quoted in Dyhouse, Carol, *Girls Growing Up in Late Victorian and Edwardian England* (London: Routledge, 1981), p. 44.

3 Lord Hatherley, speech delivered at the opening of Leeds High School for Girls, 1876, quoted in *Journal of the Women's Education Union*, 15 April 1876, p. 142.

4 Greener (ed.), p. 48.

5 Ibid., p. 10. The quotation comes from a description given by a relative of Lucy Harrison's English teacher at Bedford College, Dr George Macdonald.

6 Ibid., p. 24.

7 Ibid., pp. 10, 14, 23 and 24.

8 Dyhouse, p. 72.

9 Hudson, Derek, *Munby, Man of Two Worlds: The Life and Diaries of Arthur J. Munby 1828–1910* (London: John Murray, 1972); diary entry for 9 March 1866 quoted in Ashton, Rosemary, *Victorian Bloomsbury* (New Haven and London: Yale University Press, 2012), p. 236.

10 Sharp, Evelyn, *Unfinished Adventure: Selected Reminiscences from an Englishwoman's Life* (London: The Bodley Head, 1933), pp. 32–3.

11 McLaughlin, Colleen, and Clarke, Barbie, 'Relational Matters: A Review of the Impact of School Experience on Mental Health in Early Adolescence', *Educational & Child Psychology*, Vol. 27, No. 1 (British Psychological Society, 2010), pp. 91–103.

12 Harrison, Lucy: 'Three of Shakespeare's Women', quoted in Greener (ed.), p. 143.

13 Greener (ed.), p. 21.

14 Ibid., pp. 56, 59 and 162.

15 Ibid., p. 295.

16 Ibid., p. 63.

17 John Keats to Benjamin Bailey, 22 November 1817, quoted in Warren, Andrew, *The Orient and the Young Romantics* (Cambridge: Cambridge University Press, 2014), p. 250.

18 Mew, 'An Old Servant', CPP, p. 402.

19 Davidow, p. 39.

20 Information on Mew's alleged romance with Sam Chick was communicated to Mary Davidow in August 1958 and reported in Davidow, p. 40.

21 Davidow, p. 41.

22 Information about Ethel Oliver is from a note titled 'Something about EO' written by Stephen Oliver and sent to the author by email, 25 February 2015.

23 Oliver, Stephen, *Professor Daniel Oliver: Botanist, Artist and Quaker*, published by the author, 2016.

24 Amice Lee Macdonell to Mary Davidow, 6 February 1959, quoted in Davidow, p. 357.

25 CMM to Ethel Oliver, 27 June 1911. Buffalo.

26 Frank started at University College, London in 1881 and the following year was awarded an Exhibition at Trinity College, Cambridge.

27 Winifred Oliver attended the Slade as an auditor, rather than as a full student; the work of auditors was not submitted for examination and no degree was awarded at the end of the course.

28 From the introduction to the catalogue for *By-Products of a Botanist*, a 1930 exhibition of Daniel Oliver's drawings, held at Kew Gardens; quoted in Oliver, *Daniel Oliver*. The *Liber Studiorum* ('Book of Studies') was a series of Turner's landscape and seascape compositions published as prints between 1807 and 1819. Turner produced the preliminary etchings for the prints, which were worked in mezzotint by himself and collaborating engravers.

29 Daniel Oliver advised Ruskin on botanical matters. In April 1876, for instance, Ruskin consulted him about the material for his treatise on wild flowers, *Proserpina*.

30 Amice Macdonell Lee to Mary Davidow, 13 February 1958, quoted in Davidow, p. 358.

31 Oliver, *Daniel Oliver*. By the time Ethel and Winifred were living at 2 The Grove in Isleworth, the Oliver family had come to own Christina Rossetti's inlaid Broadwood piano, which Mew played when she stayed at the house.

32 Hannah's grandson, Geoff, is quoted as describing her as such in Stephen Oliver's 'Something about EO'.

33 Amice Lee Macdonell to Mary Davidow, 6 February 1959, quoted in Davidow, p. 357.

34 Stephen Oliver to the author, email, 10 January 2016.

35 Barnard, Amy B., *The Girl's Book About Herself* (London: Cassell, 1912), p. 2, quoted in Dyhouse, p. 132. The line is itself a quotation from Alfred Tennyson's 'The Princess', Part One, line 153.

4 What You're Made, That You'll Be

Chapter title: from Mew's essay 'Miss Bolt'.

1 Mew, 'Miss Bolt', CPP, p. 342.

2 Amice Lee Macdonell to Mary Davidow, 13 February 1959, quoted in Davidow, p. 359.

3 The information on school fees is from an advert in *The Times*, 24 August 1883, p. 12.

4 The figure of £89 for the average annual salary of a clerical worker in 1880 is quoted in *London Clerical Workers 1880–1914: The Search for Stability* by Michael Heller (unpublished PhD thesis, UCL, 2003).

5 Lawrence, D. H., *Aaron's Rod*, ed. Mara Kalnins (Cambridge: Cambridge University Press, 1988), p. 70.

6 Mew, 'An Old Servant', CPP, p. 402.

7 Yates, Edmund, *His Recollections and Experiences* (London: Richard Bentley and Son, 1885), p. 183.

8 Matthew 24:36 (King James Version).

9 Early details of Henry's illness are taken from his admission notes to Bethlem Hospital, dated 14 June 1884, now kept at the Bethlem Museum of the Mind.

10 Amice Macdonell Lee to Mary Davidow, 6 February 1959, quoted in Davidow, p. 357. She describes Edith Scull as 'dark with deep-set brown eyes and rather stout'.

11 The 1881 census shows Ellen Mathews (aged twenty-five) boarding with Lucy Harrison at 80 Gower Street, before the move to Haverstock Hill.

12 Amice Macdonell Lee to Mary Davidow, 13 February 1959, quoted in Davidow, p. 359.

13 Mew, 'The London Sunday', CPP, p. 376. A 'lady's tormenter' was a tot of spirit, usually served in a small metal cup.

14 The deaths of Fred's sons took place in 1867 (Frederick George Webb) and 1876 (Daniel Kendall, renamed Christopher Barnes, and Richard Cobham).

15 Henry's medical notes state that his earliest symptoms had started nine months previously.

16 Acton, William, *The Functions and Disorders of the Reproductive Organs* (London: J. & A. Churchill, 1875), pp. 62 and 64.

17 Quoted in Acton, p. 66.

18 Although Galton's thoughts on eugenics are generally regarded as repellent today, his influence in other areas is widely felt. He formulated the first psychometric tests, for evaluating mental faculties. He also devised a model for identifying and classifying fingerprints, calculating that the odds of finding a 'false positive' (two individuals having identical fingerprints) were around one in 64 billion.

19 Showalter, Elaine, *The Female Malady: Women, Madness and English Culture, 1830–1980* (London: Virago, 1987), p. 105.

20 Maudsley, Henry, *The Pathology of Mind* (London: Macmillan, 1879), p. 88.

21 Allderidge, Patricia, *Bethlem Hospital, 1247–1997: A Pictorial Record* (Chichester: Phillimore & Co., 1997), p. 66.

22 Ibid., pp. 67–73.

23 Walford, Edward, *Old and New London: Volume 6* (London: Cassell, Petter & Galpin, 1878), p. 357.

24 Jeremiah 13:27 (King James Version).

25 'Henry Herne Mew Case Notes', from *Bethlem Hospital Patient Admission Registers and Casebooks 1683–1932*, held at Bethlem Museum of the Mind.

26 Quotations are from Henry Kendall junior's will. The medals cited in the will were for architectural drawings. At a prize-giving event held at the Royal Academy of Arts centre in Somerset House in honour of their sixty-fifth anniversary, Kendall was awarded the silver medal for the best drawing of the front of St Bride's Church and steeple in Fleet Street (*The Court Journal and Fashionable Gazette*, Vol. V, 1833, p. 838).

27 Fitzgerald further suggests that Edward Herne had at one point been articled to his father and was unable to finish his training, but she provides no source (Fitzgerald, pp. 5 and 37).

28 *Illustrated London News*, 20 June 1885, p. 621.

29 *The Graphic*, 22 October 1881, p. 8.

30 Lucy Harrison to Amy Greener, 23 May 1886, quoted in Greener (ed.), p. 26.

31 Amice Lee Macdonell to Mary Davidow, 6 February 1959, quoted in Davidow, p. 358.

5 Marks Upon the Snow

Chapter title: from Mew's poem 'The Call'.

1 Mew, 'Miss Bolt', CPP, p. 346.
2 Fitzgerald, Percy, *London City Suburbs* (London: The Leadenhall Press, 1893), p. 54.
3 Ashton, p. 283.
4 Ellison Powell to his solicitor, 24 February 1890, quoted in Davidow, p. 270.
5 Three servants are listed as resident at the Mews' house in Gordon Street in the 1891 census: Emma Barker (then aged twenty), Emily Sayer (seventeen) and, of course, Elizabeth Goodman (sixty-five).
6 Details of furniture are taken from the will of Charlotte Mary Mew, made on 3 January 1928 at Layton's Solicitors, 29 Budge Row, London EC4. GRO.
7 Margaret Jarman to Mary Davidow, 19 January 1959, quoted in Davidow, p. 356.
8 MM, p. viii.
9 *Whitstable Times and Herne Bay Herald*, 30 July 1887.
10 Dickens, Charles, 'Our Watering-Place', first published in *Household Words*, Vol. III, No. 71 (2 August 1851); reprinted in *Charles Dickens: Selected Journalism 1850–1870*, ed. David Pascoe (London: Penguin Classics, 1997), pp. 129 and 133–4.
11 The cause of death noted on Frederick Mew junior's death certificate is 'Diarrhoea. 48 hours'. GRO.
12 Tomlinson, Margaret, *Three Generations in the Honiton Lace Trade: A Family History* (Margaret Tomlinson, 1983), pp. 66–7.
13 Ibid., p. 62.
14 *Ealing Illustrated* (London: G. Tyer & Co., 1893), quoted in Oates, Jonathan, and Hounsell, Peter, *Ealing: A Concise History* (Stroud: Amberley Publishing, 2014), p. 50.
15 1901 census; Tomlinson, p. 80.
16 Davidow, p. 41.
17 Greener (ed.), pp. 24–5.
18 Meteorological Office, 'Summary of Observations, December 1891' (London: Eyre and Spottiswood, 1891), single-page broadsheet.
19 MM, p. viii.
20 Levy, Amy, 'Readers at the British Museum', *Atalanta: Every Girl's Magazine*, Vol. II (April 1889), pp. 449–54 (accessed online at MyHeritage.com).
21 *Saturday Review*, 14 August 1886, p. 213.
22 Hardy, Thomas, diary entry for 9 March 1888, quoted in Wilson, Keith, *A Companion to Thomas Hardy* (Oxford: Wiley-Blackwell, 2009), p. 97.
23 Anna Maria registered her mother's death and is the named informant on the death certificate.

24 The total of Anna Maria's legacy is given in James & James Solicitors to Walter Mew Barnes, 17 October 1893, quoted in Davidow, p. 274.

25 See James & James Solicitors to Walter Mew Barnes, 15 December 1892, quoted in Davidow, p. 270.

26 Frederick Mew to Walter Mew Barnes, 20 December 1892. BMC.

27 Mew, 'An Old Servant', CPP, p. 401. Mew adds that with her wages, Elizabeth Goodman routinely bought 'a large bag of tarts [. . .] from a grubby little shop near Covent Garden [. . .] and there was a fairing for everyone in the house except the too exalted head'.

28 National Archives: 'Average wages of female domestic servants according to class of work. Figures collected by the Board of Trade in the 1890s based on actual returns from 2,000 households'.

29 Printed rules for the admission, visiting and discharge of patients at Holloway Sanatorium [late nineteenth century], Surrey History Centre (SHC ref. 2620/6/11); the annual cost of Henry's care is calculated from the sanatorium's fees listed in this document.

30 The figure of £225 is the mean average of all the wages listed for the year 1891 for a wide range of occupations (from agricultural labourer to barrister) in Williamson, Jeffrey G., 'The Structure of Pay in Britain, 1710–1911', *Research in Economic History*, Vol. VII (1982), pp. 1–54.

31 'Henry Herne Mew Case Notes', from *Bethlem Hospital Patient Admission Registers and Casebooks 1683–1932*, held at Bethlem Museum of the Mind. Quotations are taken from entries for 30 September, 9 November and 26 November 1884.

32 Details of Henry's illness are taken from his case notes at Holloway Sanatorium, held at the Surrey History Centre in Woking (ref: 2620/4/2, p. 13).

33 Fennell, Phil, *Treatment without Consent: Law, Psychiatry and the Treatment of Mentally Disordered People since 1845* (London: Routledge, 1996), p. 57.

34 Mew, 'An Old Servant', CPP, p. 405.

35 Haweis, Mary Eliza, *The Art of Housekeeping: A Bridal Garland* (London: Sampson Low, Marston, Searle & Rivington, 1889), p. 43.

36 James Sant (1820–1916), British portrait painter who is best known for his images of children and childhood.

37 Mew, 'An Old Servant', CPP, p. 405.

38 MM, p. xiii.

39 Ireland, Mrs Alexander (ed.), *Selections from the Letters of Geraldine Endsor Jewbury to Jane Welsh Carlyle* (London: Longmans, Green, 1892), pp. 347–8, quoted in Vicinus, Martha, *Independent Women* (London: Virago, 1985), p. 9.

40 *Pall Mall Gazette*, 8 June 1889, p. 2.

41 Lees, Edith, 'Olive Schreiner and Her Relation to the Woman Movement', *Book News Monthly*, New York, Vol. XXXIII (February 1915), quoted in Showalter (ed.), *Daughters of Decadence*, p. vii.

42 George Eliot to Edward Burne-Jones, 20 March 1873, quoted in *Selections from George Eliot's Letters*, ed. Gordon Haight (New Haven: Yale University Press, 1985), p. 414.

6 *A* Yellow Book *Discovery*

Chapter title: from a letter from Henry Harland to John Lane, 29 April 1894, quoted in Beckson, Karl, and Samuels Lasner, Mark, '*The Yellow Book* and Beyond: Selected Letters of Henry Harland to John Lane', *English Literature in Transition, 1880–1920*, Vol. XLII, No. 4 (1999), pp. 407–8.

1 Quoted in Syrett, Netta, *The Sheltering Tree* (London: Geoffrey Bles, 1939), p. 80.

2 Davidow, pp. 92–3.

3 Quoted in May, James Lewis, *John Lane and the Nineties* (London: The Bodley Head, 1936), p. 78.

4 Syrett, Netta, p. 80.

5 Quoted in Davidow, p. 51.

6 Sharp, pp. 60–1.

7 Quoted in Mix, Katherine Lyon, *A Study in Yellow:* The Yellow Book *and Its Contributors* (Lawrence: University of Kansas Press, 1960), p. 68.

8 Symons, A. J. A., *The Quest for Corvo* (London: The Folio Society, 1952), p. 96.

9 May, p. 71. The meeting at the Hogarth Club is also reported in an interview with John Lane himself in the *Pall Mall Gazette*, 11 April 1894.

10 May, pp. 31–3.

11 Prospectus, *The Yellow Book* I (April 1894). Mark Samuels Lasner Collection, on loan to the University of Delaware Library, Newark. 'The Yellow Nineties Online', eds. Dennis Denisoff and Lorraine Janzen Kooistra, Ryerson University, 2011, http://www.1890s.ca/HTML.aspx?s=YBV1_prospectus.html.

12 May, pp. 75–6.

13 *St James's Gazette*, 18 April 1894.

14 *The Speaker*, 28 April 1894.

15 Jackson, Holbrook, *The Eighteen Nineties* (London: Grant Richards Ltd, 1922; first edn 1913), p. 46.

16 Henry Harland to John Lane, 29 April 1894, quoted in Beckson and Samuels Lasner, pp. 407–8.

17 Henry Harland to CMM, 29 April 1894, quoted in Davidow, p. 275.

18 Henry Harland to CMM, 3 May 1894, quoted in Davidow, p. 276.

19 Case notes of Henry Herne Mew, patient at Holloway Sanatorium. The case notes are now held by the Surrey History Centre in Woking (ref: 2620/4/2, p. 13).

20 Mew, 'The Poems of Emily Brontë', CPP, p. 362.

21 Henry Harland to John Lane, 12 and 15 June 1894, quoted in Beckson and Samuels Lasner, pp. 410–12.

22 D'Arcy, Ella, '*Yellow Book* Celebrities', reprinted in *English Literature in Transition 1880–1920*, Vol. XXXVII, No. 1 (1994), p. 36.

23 All quotations from this story: Mew, Charlotte, 'Passed', CPP, pp. 69–70.

24 Roberts, Andrew, and Falkenberg, Betty, 'Charlotte Mew Chronology', 2005. Middlesex University resource, available at http://studymore.org.uk/ymew. htm.

25 Almost all of the perimeter wall and the entire underground level remain intact today.

26 Cunningham, Peter, *Handbook of London* (London: John Murray, 1850), p. 436.

27 William Woodward writing in *The Building News and Engineering Journal*, 25 December 1891, p. 923.

28 Baudelaire, Charles, *The Painter of Modern Life* (London: Penguin Classics, 2010), p. 12. Originally published in *Le Figaro* in 1863.

29 Stanley, Maude, 'Clubs for Working Girls', *The Nineteenth Century*, Vol. XXV, No. 143 (January 1889), p. 76.

30 MM, p. xii.

31 Mew, 'Passed', CPP, p. 69.

32 Baudelaire, p. 13.

33 Henry Harland to CMM, 3 May 1894, quoted in Davidow, p. 278.

34 *Glasgow Herald*, 19 July 1894, p. 9.

35 Mew, 'Miss Bolt', CPP, p. 346.

7 *Some Glimpses of the New Woman*

Chapter title: from a feature in the *Pall Mall Gazette* of the same name, 22 September 1894.

1 Ella D'Arcy quoted in May, p. 78.

2 Sharp, p. 58.

3 Sharp, p. 59. Details of the Harlands' drawing room are from *Nicholas Crabbe* by Baron Corvo [Frederick Rolfe] (London: Chatto & Windus, 1958), p. 27.

4 May, p. 78.

5 Sharp, p. 62.

6 Ibid., pp. 61–2.

7 May, p. 76; *St James's Gazette*, 18 April 1894; *The Speaker*, 28 April 1894.

8 May, p. 81.

9 Sharp, p. 57.

10 *Manchester Guardian*, 19 January 1924, quoted in May, pp. 81–2.

11 Sharp, pp. 58 and 61.

12 MM, p. xiv.

13 *Pall Mall Gazette*, 22 September 1894, p. 8.

14 MM, p. xiv.

15 Mew, Charlotte, 'The China Bowl', CPP, p. 87.

16 Henry Harland to CMM, 3 January 1895.

17 Ibid. It was perhaps disingenuous of Harland to claim he was unable to publish Mew's story in *The Yellow Book* because of its length: in the second issue of the magazine, he had published Henry James's far longer 'The Coxon Fund', which took up seventy pages.

18 A typescript of 'A Wedding Day' held at the British Library is dated February 1895 (BL Add MS 57754).

19 All quotations from this story: Mew, Charlotte, 'A Wedding Day', CPP, pp. 219, 217–18, 223, 225.

20 It was first collected by Val Warner in *Charlotte Mew: Collected Poems and Prose* (Manchester: Carcanet in association with Virago, 1981).

21 Wilde brought his libel case against the Marquess after the latter left a calling card at Wilde's hotel accusing him of being a 'Somdomite [*sic*]'.

22 May, p. 80. The mix-up over *The Yellow Book* probably sprang from the fact that the hero in Wilde's only novel, *The Picture of Dorian Gray*, is obsessed with 'the yellow book' gifted to him by the hedonistic Lord Henry, but Wilde's novel was published four years before Harland's magazine appeared.

23 Quoted in Beckson, Karl, *The Oscar Wilde Encyclopedia* (New York: AMS Press, 1998), p. 22.

24 Sharp, p. 58.

25 Greener (ed.), p. 52.

26 Ibid., p. 32.

27 Moore, Virginia, *The Life and Eager Death of Emily Brontë* (London: Rich & Cowan Ltd, 1936), p. 190.

28 Ibid., pp. 189–90.

29 Ibid., pp. 190 and 189.

30 Davidow, p. 42.

31 MM, p. viii.

32 MM, p. xiv.

33 Will of Charlotte Mary Mew, 3 January 1928. GRO.

34 The photograph first appeared in the public domain in 1929, at the front of Mew's posthumous collection, *The Rambling Sailor*.

35 *The Times*, 2 October 1922, p. 7.

36 *Northern Whig*, 28 February 1923, p. 1.

37 *Daily Express*, 25 March 1924, p. 7.

38 *Daily Express*, 8 April 1924, p. 5.

39 Miss Riborg Fagelund to Philip Oliver (son of Frank Oliver; nephew of Ethel and Winifred), 19 August 1958. BMC.

40 Sayers, Dorothy L., 'Are Women Human?: Address Given to a Women's Society, 1938', in *Logos: A Journal of Catholic Thought and Culture*, Vol. VIII, No. 4 (2005), pp. 165–78.

41 Mew, 'The Poems of Emily Brontë', CPP, p. 363.

42 Coleridge, Samuel Taylor, 1 September 1832, *Specimens of the Table Talk of Samuel Taylor Coleridge*, Vol. II (London: John Murray, 1835), p. 96.

43 The handwritten draft of 'Delivered' is dated, in Charlotte's hand, July 1895. A photocopy (sent by Stephen Oliver to Penelope Fitzgerald) is held in the Harry Ransom Humanities Research Center archives, in Box 3.5 of the Penelope Fitzgerald papers.

44 MM, p. xiii.

8 *The World Goes on the Same Outside*

Chapter title: from Mew's poem 'The Quiet House'.

1 Chalmers, F. Graeme, *Women in the Nineteenth-century Art World* (Westport, CT: Greenwood Press, 1998), pp. 51–2.

2 Callen, Anthea, *Angel in the Studio: Women in the Arts and Crafts Movement, 1870–1914* (London: Astragal Books, 1979), p. 40. Newspaper advertisements tell us that day classes at the Royal Female School of Art were charged at fifteen guineas (or just under £16) per year, and evening classes were around five guineas (just over £5), while the government-run South Kensington art schools charged £10 for day and evening classes combined.

3 *Royal Female School of Art reports, 1863–1906* (bound collection), Statement Session 1896–7, pp. 11–14. CSM.

4 *London Evening Standard*, 18 June 1862, p. 3.

5 Greenaway also studied at the Slade and in the women's section of the National Art Training School, which became the Royal College of Art in 1896. She is buried in the same cemetery as Charlotte and Anne.

6 MM, pp. ix–x.

7 *The Spectator*, 9 December 1843, p. 1,172.

8 Miller, Fred, 'Women Workers in the Art Crafts', *The Art Journal*, April 1896, pp. 116–18.

9 *Royal Female School of Art reports, 1863–1906* (bound collection), Statement Session 1894–5, p. 8. CSM.

10 *The Studio: An Illustrated Magazine of Fine and Applied Art*, Vol. XIV, No. 65 (August 1898), p. 216.

11 Mew, 'The China Bowl', CPP, p. 82.

12 The remaining Chick sister, Mary, had her education interrupted by ill health, and eventually it was she who joined her father in the family's lace business. She turned out to be no less remarkable than her sisters and she eventually became the secretary of the Women's International League for Peace and Freedom.

13 Women were not admitted to degree courses at the Slade at this time, but in 1928, Winifred would finally take her degree and be awarded the Gilchrist Medal for her examination result in the Diploma in History of Art.

14 CMM to CADS, 28 September 1913. Beinecke-MW.

15 See, for instance, Edith Chick to Arthur Tansley, 18 October 1900 (Chick family private collection), in which Edith enthuses about having 'famous friends' like Charlotte.

16 *The Spectator*, 13 January 1894, p. 25.

17 *St James's Gazette*, 4 October 1893, p. 16.

18 *Shoreditch Observer*, 25 September, 2 and 9 October 1897.

19 At any rate, no records of further commissions have survived.

20 Death certificate of Frederick Mew. GRO.

21 *Journal of the Royal Institute of British Architects*, 25 March 1899, p. 328.

22 Richard Mew to James Bull, 4 October 1843. IWR.

23 Hayter, p. 31.

24 Davidow, p. 28.

25 Frederick Mew to Walter Mew Barnes, 20 December 1892, quoted in Davidow, p. 272.

26 MM, p. ix.

27 Ibid.

28 For more on the influence of organised religion on London society, see Jerry White's *London in the Nineteenth Century* (Vintage, 2008), pp. 415–44.

29 Henry Herne Mew: case note for 12 June 1898, Holloway Sanatorium (ref: 2620/4/2, p. 13).

30 *England & Wales National Probate Calendar (Index of Wills and Administrations), 1858–1966*.

9 City of White Days

Chapter title: from Mew's poem 'Not for that City'.

1 CMM to Walter Mew Barnes, 24 September 1898, quoted in Davidow, p. 280.

2 *Cassell's Household Guide*, p. 2.

3 MM, p. ix.

4 Davidow, p. 43.

5 Advert for Peckham House Asylum in the *British Medical Journal*, 28 December 1912, p. 48.

6 *Lloyd's Weekly Newspaper*, 17 March 1895, p. 2.

7 *Pall Mall Gazette*, 13 March 1895, p. 7.

8 *Lloyd's Weekly Newspaper*, 17 March 1895, p. 2.

9 Warner, Val (ed.), *Charlotte Mew: Collected Poems and Selected Prose* (Carcanet Press, 1997), p. x.

10 Amice Macdonell Lee to Mary Davidow, 13 February 1958, quoted in Davidow, p. 358.

11 MM, p. ix. See also Chapter 2. As noted previously, the friend in question is very likely Ethel Oliver.

12 In the 1891 census, Col. Webb is listed as retired and living at Walton House with his wife Florence, his father-in-law, his son, three daughters (aged twelve, eleven and six) and six servants.

13 HO4/E2 Case book of admissions (female – indexed) 1898–1902, Whitecroft Hospital, Newport. The document is held at the Isle of Wight Record Office.

14 Penelope Fitzgerald says that Freda began to show signs of schizophrenia 'early in the 1890s' (which appears to be an error as Freda was ten in 1890), and that Frederick Mew 'asserted himself for almost the last time and insisted that she must not be kept in London, but sent back to the Island' – that is, the Isle of Wight, where he was born and raised (Fitzgerald, p. 38). Freda's medical notes tell a different story: they record that the first signs of her mental illness appeared at the start of 1899, when she was aged nineteen, and that she was committed to the Isle of Wight asylum that same year. Frederick Mew died the previous year, in September 1898, without knowing of his daughter's illness.

15 Layton's Solicitors to the Bedford Estate, quoted in Davidow, p. 343.

16 Mew's 'The China Bowl' appeared in *Temple Bar*, Vol. CXVIII (September 1899), pp. 64–90.

17 Mew, 'The China Bowl', CPP, p. 79.

18 Edith Chick to Arthur Tansley, 18 October 1900 (Chick family private collection).

19 Flora Annie Steel (1847–1929) was an English writer whose husband was a

member of the Indian Civil Service and who lived in British India for twenty-two years. She was deeply interested in native Indian life. *Voices in the Night* was hot off the press when this letter was written: it was published in 1900.

20 Edith Chick to Arthur Tansley, 18 October 1900 (Chick family private collection).

21 Ayres, Peter, *Shaping Ecology: The Life of Arthur Tansley* (John Wiley & Sons, 2012), p. 54.

22 At one time this letter was among the records in the office of the Bedford Estate. The estate's early records have since been lost or destroyed.

23 *London Daily News*, 23 January 1901, p. 5.

24 *London Daily News*, 27 February 1901, p. 6.

25 *Pall Mall Gazette*, 18 January 1894.

26 Mew, 'Miss Bolt', CPP, p. 338.

27 The visitors' book kept by the Chicks to record visits to Hazelwood has been lost, but Edith Chick's daughter, Margaret Tomlinson (née Tansley), was judicious enough to copy down a list of Charlotte and Anne Mew's visits before the book went missing. There are no precise dates; only months or seasons (such as 'Summer 1901' or 'April 1908').

28 The details of Hazelwood are from reminiscences of the house told to the author by Dorothy Lumb (daughter of Gillian Chick and a direct descendant of Samuel Chick senior), sent by email on 15 November 2013.

29 *Morning Post*, 3 July 1901. Tickets cost 53s 8d first class or 41s 2d second.

30 Edith Chick to Arthur Tansley, 18 October 1900 (Chick family private collection).

31 Mary Davidow says that the Vocalist was identified as Florence Hughes (later Florence Alsop), but she doesn't say by whom (Davidow, p. 67). No such person appears in Mew's correspondence. Penelope Fitzgerald repeats the suggestion and adds that Florence Hughes was the daughter of painter Arthur Hughes (Fitzgerald, p. 74). This appears to be incorrect: Arthur's daughters were Amy, Agnes and Emily.

32 Margaret Chick, quoted in Davidow, p. 40.

33 Penelope Fitzgerald suggests that the 'Dilettante' was Anne, but that seems unlikely to me. Charlotte viewed her sister as a talented artist (rather than a dabbler), and she was always careful of her feelings. She felt bad that Anne's paintings weren't better known, as would become increasingly clear as the years went by. In addition, Ma was unhappy about being left alone; it's likely that Anne had stayed behind to keep her company.

34 Holroyd, Michael, *Unreceived Opinions* (London: Penguin Books, 1976), p. 170.

35 Fitzgerald, p. 74.

36 Mew, Charlotte, 'Notes in a Brittany Convent', CPP, p. 348.

37 Mew, 'Passed', CPP, p. 69.

38 According to Charlotte Mew's index card, kept at the British Museum's Central Archive, she renewed her Reading Room ticket on Thursday 3 October 1901.

39 *St James's Gazette*, 23 June 1898, p. 11: 'Literary Life in London – as seen from an American point of view'.

40 *Leeds Mercury*, 16 September 1904, p. 4, and *London Evening Standard*, 21 November 1904, p. 5.

41 CMM to Harold Monro, 29 July 1916. Buffalo.

10 *The Whole Gay, Unbearable, Amazing Show*

Chapter title: from Mew's poem 'Ne Me Tangito'.

1 MM, p. xiii.

2 Case note on Freda Kendall Mew for 26 November 1900, from HO4/E2 Case book, Whitecroft County Hospital, Newport.

3 Case note on Freda Kendall Mew for 25 August 1901, from HO4/E2 Case book, Whitecroft County Hospital, Newport.

4 Macphail, S. Rutherford, and Bruce, Lewis C., *Thyroid Feeding in Insanity: a Summary of Thirty Cases Treated by Thyroid Extract in the Derby Borough Asylum* (Glasgow: Alex Macdougall, 1894), p. 7.

5 CMM to Ethel Oliver, 18 April 1902. Buffalo. This and all following quotations from Charlotte's time in Paris are taken from the 18 April letter.

6 Debussy's *Pelléas et Mélisande* premiered at the Opéra-Comique on 30 April 1902.

7 MM, p. x.

8 Ibid.

9 CMM to Walter Mew Barnes, 24 September 1898, quoted in Davidow, p. 280.

10 *Pall Mall Gazette*, 2 April 1900, p. 1. The exhibition was staged at the RBA Galleries in Suffolk Street, London.

11 Diaries of Walter Mew Barnes (Fanny Mew's son) from this period contain fairly regular mentions of Anne and of Mrs Mew, but hardly any of Charlotte.

12 The baby born shortly after Charlotte's sixth birthday had originally been named 'Daniel Kendall Mew', but he was rechristened 'Christopher Barnes' at the age of four months and died soon afterwards.

13 In 1900, University College, London was reconstituted into a federation. The change brought with it a formal renaming of the institution, but 'University College, London' continued to be used informally, as it will be here.

14 Chick, Harriette, diary entry for Sunday 27 July 1903.

15 Stopes, Marie Carmichael, *Radiant Motherhood: A Book for Those Who Are Creating the Future* (London: G. P. Putnam's Sons, 1920), pp. 218–19 and 212.

16 MM, p. xiii.

17 *Devon and Exeter Gazette*, 7 August 1903, p. 12.

18 *Hampshire Advertiser*, 2 January 1904, p. 8.

19 Case note on Freda Kendall Mew for 16 June 1902, from HO4/E2 Case book, Whitecroft County Hospital, Newport.

20 MM, pp. ix–x.

21 Barnes, Walter Mew, diary entry for Friday 29 January 1904 (Barnes family private collection).

22 Barnes, Walter Mew, diary entry for Tuesday 16 February 1904 (Barnes family private collection).

23 'Pam' to Edith Chick, 7 February 1904. Shown to the author by Barbara Bender and quoted here by kind permission of the Chick family.

24 Barnes, Walter Mew, diary entry for Saturday 18 June 1904 (Barnes family private collection).

25 Mew, 'The Poems of Emily Brontë', CPP, p. 365.

26 Ibid., pp. 359–60.

27 Ibid., pp. 361–2.

28 46 Gordon Square was the home of Virginia, Vanessa, Adrian and Thoby Stephen from 1904 to 1907 and is where the Bloomsbury Group began.

29 Woolf, Virginia, 'Old Bloomsbury', written in 1921/2 for the Memoir Club; republished in *Moments of Being: Autobiographical Writings*, ed. Jeanne Schulkind, with an introduction by Hermione Lee (London: Pimlico, 2002), p. 47.

30 Ibid., p. 46.

31 Ibid.

11 Waking and Worried Days

Chapter title: from a letter from Charlotte Mew to Ethel Oliver, 24 July 1909. Buffalo.

1 CMM to Edith Hill, 24 July 1913. Buffalo; Gerald Gould writing in *The Herald*, 8 August 1916, p. 22.

2 CMM to Walter Mew Barnes, 24 September 1898, quoted in Davidow, p. 280.

3 Penelope Fitzgerald calls this maid 'Jane Elnswick', following a draft manuscript of Alida Monro's 1953 introduction to her *Charlotte Mew: Collected Poems* (BL Add MS 57755), but the censuses have 'Elsain'.

4 National Archives: 'Average wages of female domestic servants according to class of work. Figures collected by the Board of Trade in the 1890s based on actual returns from 2,000 households'.

5 MM, pp. xviii–xx.

6 Woolf, Virginia, 'Professions for Women', *Selected Essays* (Oxford: Oxford University Press, 2009), p. 141.

7 MS to CMM, 22 April 1915. Berg.

8 Mew, Charlotte, 'Mark Stafford's Wife', CPP, pp. 181 and 177.

9 Hardy, Thomas, *Jude the Obscure* (Oxford: Oxford University Press, 2002), p. 341.

10 Mew, 'Mark Stafford's Wife', CPP, p. 182.

11 Barnes, Walter Mew, diary entry for Saturday 1 December 1906 (Barnes family private collection).

12 Details of the concert are from the *Isle of Wight County Press and South of England Reporter*, 26 January 1907, p. 8, and the comment on Kate Fielder from the *Wiltshire and Gloucestershire Standard*, 5 November 1904, p. 8.

13 Barnes, Walter Mew, diary entry for 25 January 1907 (Barnes family private collection).

14 Case note on Freda Kendall Mew, 25 January 1907, from HO4/E2 Case book, Whitecroft County Hospital, Newport.

15 Barnes, Walter Mew, diary entry for Sunday 27 January 1907 (Barnes family private collection).

16 *The Autobiography of Lord Alfred Douglas* (London: Martin Secker, 1929), p. 220.

17 MM, p. xii.

18 Mew refers to Elsie only by her first name. Penelope Fitzgerald surmised that she meant Elsie O'Keefe (née Millard), who had been at art school with Anne Mew, but it seems unlikely: Elsie had married in 1902 and had two children by this time, including a sixteen-month-old baby. Elsie Chick, on the other hand, was a student at University College, London, free for the summer vacation.

19 Information on the date of Elsie Chick's entry into University College, London, and of her various prizes, is taken from scans of original records emailed to me on 7 August 2018 by Colin Penman, Head of Records at the university's Special Collections department.

20 CMM to CADS, 1 April 1914, in which Mew mentions that she is 'helping a friend to clear up an MA thesis on old English poetry – about which I know nothing whatever'. Elsie Chick was one of the few people to attend Mew's funeral. Beinecke-MW.

21 CMM to Ethel Oliver, 18 April 1902. Buffalo.

22 CMM to Ethel Oliver, 14 July 1909. Buffalo.

23 CMM to Ethel Oliver, 6 July 1909. Buffalo.

24 Ibid.

25 CMM to Ethel Oliver, 14 July 1909. Buffalo.

26 CMM to Ethel Oliver, 6 July 1909. Buffalo.

27 CMM to Ethel Oliver, 14 July 1909. Buffalo.

28 Ibid.

29 Ibid.

30 Ibid.

31 Mew, 'The Quiet House'.

32 Poem quotations, with composition dates in brackets, are from 'The Quiet House' (before 24 July 1913), 'The Forest Road' (before 8 April 1914), 'In Nunhead Cemetery' (before 24 July 1913), and 'Madeleine in Church' (1914–15), respectively.

33 CMM to Ethel Oliver, 14 July 1909. Buffalo.

34 CMM to Ethel Oliver, 24 July 1909. Buffalo.

35 *Cassell's Household Guide*, III (1869–71), p. 344, quoted in Jalland, p. 221.

36 Henry Massingham interviewed by Jane T. Stoddart on 21 February 1907, quoted in Alfred F. Havighurst's *Radical Journalist: H. W. Massingham (1860–1924)* (New York: Cambridge University Press, 2009), p. 144.

37 Ella D'Arcy quoted in CMM to CADS, 12 March 1914. Beinecke-MW.

38 Ella D'Arcy quoted in ibid.

39 Ibid.

40 Ibid.

41 CMM to Ethel Oliver, 27 June 1911. Buffalo.

42 Ibid.

43 Ibid.

44 Ibid.

45 Ibid.

46 Ibid.

47 Ianthe Jerrold (1897–1977) was thirteen when Mew wrote about her in her letter to Ethel Oliver of 27 June 1911. She lived with her family in Hampton on Thames and was the eldest of five daughters of the biographer and newspaper editor Walter Jerrold and author Clara Bridgeman, who wrote under the name of Clare Jerrold. After publishing two books of poetry by the age of twenty, Ianthe would also go on to become a popular author of detective stories, romances and psychological thrillers.

48 CMM to Ethel Oliver, 27 June 1911. Buffalo.

49 Noyes, Alfred, *Poems* (London: Macmillan, 1906), p. 117.

50 The quotation is from Mew's poem 'On the Road to the Sea', from the second edition of *The Farmer's Bride* (1921).

51 *Shepton Mallet Journal*, 14 July 1911, p. 3.

52 Woolf, Virginia, 'Mr. Bennett and Mrs Brown', quoted in *Modernism: An Anthology of Sources and Documents*, ed. Vassiliki Kolocotroni, Jane Goldman and Olga Taxidou (Edinburgh: Edinburgh University Press, 1988), p. 396.

12 A Voice on the Sharp Air

Chapter title: from Mew's poem 'The Call'.

1 'Many years ago, buying, as was my custom, a copy of *The Nation* one Saturday morning, I opened it eagerly to see if there might be a poem, and was electrified to find printed there "The Farmer's Bride". This poem I immediately committed to memory, and a year or two later repeated it with enthusiasm to Harold Monro, who had recently opened the Poetry Bookshop . . .' (MM, p. vii).

2 *Sheffield Daily Telegraph*, 20 January 1912, p. 9. The quotation is from the letters pages, from a person who signed him or herself 'A. W.'

3 The detail about the boots is from MM, p. xiv.

4 Davidow, p. 42.

5 H.D. in *The Egoist*, Vol. III, No. 9 (September 1916), p. 135.

6 CMM to Lewis Chase, 16 September 1918. LC.

7 Edith Chick to Arthur Tansley, March 1901 (Chick family private collection). Details about the Chicks' servants are from Margaret Tomlinson's self-published *Three Generations in the Honiton Lace Trade: A Family History* (2009 reprint), p. 76.

8 Mew, Charlotte, 'Delivered', short story in manuscript, dated July 1895.

9 Hardy, *Jude the Obscure*, pp. 210 and 341.

10 CMM to SCC, 27 November 1923. Berg.

11 Hardy, *Jude the Obscure*, p. 206.

12 Mew had a personal link with the Commission. Among the writers she'd mixed with at Henry Harland's *Yellow Book* soirées during her twenties was Hubert Crackanthorpe, a story writer of her own age. In 1896, not long after Charlotte had met him, Hubert's body was pulled from the Seine, after his wife had left him for the second time; he was twenty-six. Since Hubert's death, his barrister father, Montague Crackanthorpe, had become President of the Eugenics Education Society and was an expert witness for the Royal Commission. Charlotte, meanwhile, had kept in touch with the family and exchanged occasional letters with Hubert's mother, Blanche.

13 *Report of the Royal Commission on Divorce and Matrimonial Causes* (His Majesty's Stationery Office, 1912), pp. 83 and 89.

14 Ibid., p. 113.

15 'The New Wife' in the 'Life and Letters' section of *The Nation*, Vol. X, No. 16 (20 January 1912), p. 651.

16 *The Nation*, Vol. X, No. 17 (27 January 1912), p. 696.

17 D. H. Lawrence to Edward Garnett, 2[?] May 1913, quoted in *The Selected Letters of D. H. Lawrence*, ed. James T. Boulton (Cambridge: Cambridge University Press, 1997), p. 58. Lawrence made the remark in relation to his new

novel in progress; provisionally titled *The Sisters*, it was an early iteration of what would become in fact two novels, *The Rainbow* and *Women in Love*.

18 CMM to Lewis Chase, 16 September 1918. LC.

19 CMM to Edith Hill, 4 January 1915. Buffalo.

20 *Yorkshire Evening Post*, 5 March 1912, p. 4; *Pall Mall Gazette*, 5 March 1912, p. 2.

21 Mew's poem 'The Voice' was first published in *The Englishwoman*, Vol. XIII (March 1912), p. 304. With a few minor alterations, it would later be retitled 'The Call', by which name it was eventually included in Mew's posthumous collection, *The Rambling Sailor*. It isn't clear whether the alterations were made by Mew or by an editor, since no draft versions of this poem have been found.

22 *Collected Works of W. B. Yeats Vol. III: Autobiographies*, eds. Douglas N. Archibald and William H. O'Donnell (New York: Scribner, 1999), p. 104.

23 CPP, p. 260.

24 *The Englishwoman*, Vol. XIV (April 1912).

25 'On the Asylum Road' was first published in *The Farmer's Bride* (1916).

26 CMM to SCC, 26 April 1923. Berg.

27 *Hampshire Advertiser*, 2 January 1904, p. 8.

28 *Pall Mall Gazette*, 13 May 1912, p. 1.

29 G. B. Stern quoted in Watts, *Mrs Sappho*, p. 77.

30 Horatio Francis Ninian Scott MD (1855–1922).

31 Watts, *Mrs Sappho*, p. 3; Watts, Marjorie, 'Memories of Charlotte Mew', in the PEN Broadsheet, no. 13 (1982), p. 13; Watts, Marjorie, *P.E.N.: The Early Years, 1921–1926* (London: Archive Press, 1971), p. 4.

32 Christopher Scott, quoted in Watts, *Mrs Sappho*, p. 24.

33 Watts, *Mrs Sappho*, p. 4.

34 Monro, Harold, *Some Contemporary Poets: 1920* (London: Leonard Parsons, 1920), p. 21.

35 T. S. Eliot quoted in C. K. Stead's *The New Poetic* (London: Hutchinson, 1975), p. 45.

36 Stanley Braithwaite quoted in *The Sphere*, 6 January 1917, p. 20.

37 *The Globe*, 29 November 1912, p. 8.

38 Masefield, John, 'The Everlasting Mercy', *English Review*, October 1911.

39 Grant, Joy, *Harold Monro & the Poetry Bookshop* (London: Routledge and Kegan Paul, 1967), pp. 92–3.

40 Edward Marsh in his 'Prefatory Note' to *Georgian Poetry 1911–1912* (London: The Poetry Bookshop, 1912).

41 CMM to Ethel Oliver, 27 June 1911. Buffalo.

42 CPP, p. 268.

13 The Din, the Scuffle, the Long Stare

Chapter title: from Mew's poem 'Fame'.

1 Raitt, Suzanne, *May Sinclair: A Modern Victorian* (Oxford: Clarendon Press, 2000), p. 185. Evelyn Underhill was then in her late thirties and had already published her most widely read work, *Mysticism* (1911).

2 CADS letter journal to her daughter, May 1912, quoted in Watts, *Mrs Sappho*, p. 56.

3 CMM to CADS, 13 February 1913. Beinecke-MW.

4 CADS letter journal, quoted in Watts, *Mrs Sappho*, p. 55.

5 Watts, 'Memories of Charlotte Mew', p. 12.

6 Syrett, p. 103.

7 Belford, Barbara, *Violet: The Story of the Irrepressible Violet Hunt* (New York: Simon & Schuster, 1990), p. 205.

8 Virginia Woolf to Lady Cecil, 12 April 1909, in *The Flight of the Mind: The Letters of Virginia Woolf, 1888–1912*, Vol. I, eds. Nigel Nicolson and Joanne Trautmann (London: The Hogarth Press, 1975), p. 390.

9 MS to CADS, 28 October 1919, quoted in Raitt, p. 85.

10 CMM to CADS, 28 March 1913. Beinecke-MW. *The Combined Maze* would one day become a favourite of Agatha Christie's.

11 MS to CMM, dated simply 'Sunday'. Berg.

12 CMM to CADS, 13 February 1913. Beinecke-MW.

13 Ibid.

14 CMM to Edith Hill, 12 March 1913. Buffalo. *The Englishwoman* provided a regular outlet for Charlotte's writing at this time: in February of this year, it had published her poem 'The Changeling', along with an essay entitled 'Men and Trees (I)'. 'Men and Trees (II)' appeared in the same journal in March.

15 Penelope Fitzgerald (Fitzgerald, p. 95) and other sources have located Anne Mew's studio at No. 6 Hogarth Studios, but a letter from Charlotte Mew (CMM to SCC, 7 September 1918. Berg) reveals that it was in fact at No. 7.

16 Detail of the studio is from 'Men and Trees (I)', CPP, p. 388.

17 CMM to CADS, 26 June 1913. Beinecke-MW.

18 Ibid.

19 Ibid.

20 CMM to Edith Hill, 12 March 1913. Buffalo.

21 See CMM to CADS, 2 September 1913; CMM to CADS, 19 December 1913; and CMM to CADS, 1 March 1914, in which CMM asks to take the children to the Coliseum, the Zoo, and a University College, London musical, respectively. Beinecke-MW.

22 Elsie Millard had first come into contact with the Mews when she and Charlotte's sister Anne were students together at the Female School of Art in Queens Square, Bloomsbury. She married James O'Keefe, an Irish civil servant, in 1902, and the couple had two children, Maeve and Manus. James O'Keefe was to be one of Mew's two executors. Elsie's elder sister, Evelyn Millard, was a famous actor.

23 Penelope Fitzgerald describes Maggie Browne as remaining unmarried and 'a professor's daughter' (Fitzgerald, p. 26), but 'Browne' was in fact Maggie's married name. It was her husband who was a professor; her father, according to his death certificate, was a draper and silk merchant.

24 CMM to Edith Hill, 24 July 1913. Buffalo. The details of 'Anglefield', the Brownes' house in Berkhamsted, are from the obituary of Edward Thomas Browne (1866–1937) in the *Journal of the Marine Biological Association*, Vol. XXII (1938), p. 407.

25 CMM to CADS, 26 June 1913. Beinecke-MW.

26 Ibid.

27 MS to CMM, 4 July 1913. Berg.

28 Ibid.

29 The other three poems Charlotte sent to May Sinclair in the summer of 1913 were 'Pécheresse', 'The Sunlit House' and 'Beside the Bed'.

30 MS to CMM, 17 July 1913. Berg.

31 CMM to CADS, 18 July 1913. Beinecke-MW.

32 MS to CMM, 17 July 1913. Berg.

33 CMM to CADS, 18 July 1913. Beinecke-MW.

34 MS to CMM, 17 July 1913. Berg.

35 CMM to CADS, 18 July 1913. Beinecke-MW.

36 See MS to CMM, 17 July 1913. Berg.

37 CMM to Edith Hill, 12 March 1913. Buffalo. The 'little human praise' that Charlotte cites is a quotation from Robert Browning's 1844 poem 'The Boy and the Angel', about the Greek poet Theocritus – once again giving the lie to her comment about not reading much poetry. 'The Boy and the Angel' was first published (in an early form) in *Hood's Magazine* in August 1844. A revised version was later included in Browning's *Poetical Works* (1868).

38 CMM to Edith Hill, 24 March 1913. Buffalo.

39 CPP, p. 388; 'Men and Trees (I)' was first published in *The Englishwoman*, Vol. XVII, No. 50 (February 1913), pp. 121–8; 'The Changeling' appeared in the same volume, pp. 134–6.

40 Mew's essay 'Men and Trees (II)' was first published in *The Englishwoman*, Vol. XVII, No. 51 (March 1913), pp. 311–19. Quotations from this essay: 'Culte du Moi', CPP, p. 395; 'When I leaned against . . .' CPP, p. 396.

41 'Exspecto Resurrectionem' was first published in *Living Age*, 22 March 1913, p. 706.

42 CMM to Edith Hill, 12 March 1913. Buffalo.

43 MM, p. xiv.

44 Ibid.

45 Davidow, p. 36.

46 In 1914, Mew wrote from Dieppe: 'And I should never have done "The Fête" verse if I hadn't been here last year.' CMM to CADS, 8 April 1914. BeineckeMW.

47 For more details on the *Yellow Book* crowd in Dieppe, see Sharp, p. 65.

48 CMM to Ethel Oliver, 27 June 1911. Buffalo.

49 CMM to CADS, 1 April 1914. Beinecke-MW.

50 Ibid.

51 MS to CMM, 29 July 1913. Berg.

52 *Fifeshire Advertiser*, 12 October 1912.

53 Case notes on Freda Kendall Mew for 17 April 1906, 18 February 1899, 29 February 1900 and 25 February 1901.

54 CMM to Edith Hill, 24 July 1913. Buffalo.

55 MS to CMM; not dated, but written in August 1913, on or before the 12th. Berg.

56 Ibid.

57 MS to CMM, 13 August 1913. Berg.

58 Ibid.

59 CMM to CADS, 26 August 1913. Beinecke-MW.

60 MS to CMM, 18 September 1913. Berg.

61 Ibid.

62 CMM to CADS, 26 June 1913. Beinecke-MW.

63 CMM to CADS, 18 July 1913. Beinecke-MW.

64 CMM to Edith Hill, 24 July 1913. Buffalo. 'Little Tich' was the stage name of Harry Relph (1867–1928), a hugely popular English music-hall comedian and dancer, four foot six inches tall; the words 'titch' and 'titchy' were derived from the performer's stage name, rather than the other way round. A fortnight before this letter was written, Little Tich had entertained a large audience at the Victoria Palace with his comic banter, his singing and his Big Boot Dance, for which he was 'called before the curtain again and again' (*The Stage*, 10 July 1913, p. 14). Margaret Cooper was an English pianist, singer and entertainer; an article in the *Sydney Herald* in 1912 called her 'the principal lady entertainer of the day in London'.

65 CMM to CADS , 18 September 1913. Beinecke-MW.

66 CMM to CADS, 28 September 1913. Beinecke-MW.

67 Ibid.

68 CMM to CADS, 7 November 1913. Beinecke-MW.

69 MS to CMM, 5 November 1913. Berg.

70 CMM to CADS, 18 September 1913. Beinecke-MW.

71 Molière, *Dom Juan*, Acte I, Scène 1. The words are spoken by the character Sganarelle, whom Molière insisted on playing himself when performing in the play.

72 'An Old Servant' appeared in the *New Statesman*, 18 October 1913. The first-ever issue of the paper was published on 12 April 1913.

73 MS to CMM, 5 November 1913. Berg.

74 'Péri en Mer' was first published in *The Englishwoman* on 13 November 1913.

75 CMM to Edith Hill, 12 March 1913. Buffalo.

76 *The Spectator*, 31 March 1860.

77 CMM to CADS, 19 December 1913. Beinecke-MW.

78 CMM to CADS, 26 December 1913. Beinecke-MW.

79 Ibid.

80 Ibid.

14: Our Little Wind-blown Hearts

Chapter title: from Mew's poem 'The Forest Road'.

1 CMM to CADS, 26 December 1913. Beinecke-MW.

2 MS to CMM, 1 January 1914. Berg.

3 Davidow, p. 169.

4 Mew, 'Men and Trees (I)', CPP, p. 391.

5 Mew, 'Miss Bolt', CPP, pp. 345–6.

6 CMM to CADS, 5 February 1914. Beinecke-MW.

7 Ibid.

8 Ibid.

9 MS to CADS, 18 February 1914. Beinecke-MW.

10 MS to CMM, 4 March 1914. Berg.

11 MS to CMM, 8 March 1914. Berg.

12 CMM to CADS, 12 March 1914. Beinecke-MW.

13 Ibid.

14 CMM to CADS, 12 March 1914. Beinecke-MW.

15 Ibid.

16 Ibid.

17 CMM to CADS, 10 March 1914. Beinecke-MW.

18 Ibid.

19 CMM to CADS, 28 September 1913. Beinecke-MW.

20 CMM to CADS, 26 June 1913. Beinecke-MW.

21 Details of the reading are quoted from Catherine Dawson Scott's diary, in Watts, *Mrs Sappho*, pp. 56–7; those of Charlotte's dress are from Davidow, p. 42. Penelope Fitzgerald augments the scene with a description of Mew's intonations as she read, and a question-and-answer session that Charlotte 'seemed hardly conscious of', having been 'carried away' by the experience of reading, but no source is provided (Fitzgerald, p. 111).

22 Quoted in Watts, 'Memories of Charlotte Mew', p. 12.

23 Ibid.

24 MS to CMM, 6 January 1915. Berg.

25 MS to CMM, 4 March 1914. Berg.

26 MS to CMM, 8 March 1914. Berg.

27 Ibid.

28 MS to CMM, 17 March 1914. Berg.

29 CMM to CADS, 1 April 1914. Beinecke-MW. Charlotte reported Evelyn's reaction to the poem in this letter to Mrs Sappho, written two days after Evelyn had visited.

30 Ibid.

31 CMM to Ethel Oliver, 8 April 1914. Buffalo.

32 CMM to CADS, 1 April 1914. Beinecke-MW.

33 Ibid.

34 CMM to Ethel Oliver, 8 April 1914. Buffalo.

35 Ibid.

36 Ibid.

37 Ibid.

38 CMM to CADS, 7 April 1914. Beinecke-MW.

39 CMM to Ethel Oliver, 8 April 1914. Buffalo.

40 Ibid.

41 CMM to CADS, 1 April 1914. Beinecke-MW.

42 CMM to Ethel Oliver, 8 April 1914. Buffalo.

43 CMM to CADS, 7 April 1914. Beinecke-MW.

44 CMM to Marjorie, Christopher and Walter ('Toby') Dawson Scott, 24 April 1914. Beinecke-MW.

45 Ibid.

46 MS to CMM, 6 May 1914. Berg.

47 Ibid.

48 Ibid.

49 MS to CMM, 14 May 1914. Berg.

50 Fitzgerald makes the assertion in *Charlotte Mew and Her Friends* (p. 138). It seems to have originated in an article by May Sinclair's first biographer,

Theophilus Boll, entitled 'The Mystery of Charlotte Mew and May Sinclair: An Inquiry' (*Bulletin of the New York Public Library*, no. 74 (1970)). Boll proposed there that Mew declared her love to May Sinclair when she visited her on 9 May. His suggestion is based in turn on two pieces of circumstantial evidence: the ambiguities contained in Sinclair's 14 May letter that I have quoted here, and an account related to him in a letter from the novelist Gladys B. Stern. While preparing his full-length biography, Boll had written to many of Sinclair's acquaintances in search of some salacious detail that might improve the sales of his book; he was hoping, as he put it, that 'If I should find something awful enough, I might produce a best seller, instead of an academic "doubtsell".' Among the replies he received, only one of them – an enclosure in a letter from the novelist Rebecca West – contained a detail that 'baited and hooked' his interest. It was a note from Stern, recalling an occasion when May Sinclair had described to her and West 'how a Lesbian poetess named Charlotte M. had once in a wild fit of passion chased her upstairs into her bedroom'. Stern concluded the note by quoting Sinclair's words, as she remembered them: "'I assure you, Rebecca, I had to leap the bed five times!'" (Boll, 'The Mystery of Charlotte Mew and May Sinclair', p. 453). Mew's first biographer, Mary Davidow, responded that the story 'flies in the face of the general impression one gets of the poet after speaking or corresponding with those who knew her for many years', and pointed out that the date 'forces one to accept a ludicrously out-of-focus sequence of events: two women, one forty-four years old, the other fifty, quietly enjoy supper one Saturday evening in May 1914. Suddenly, the younger one, seized by a wild fit of passion, gives chase to the older woman who makes a dash for the bedroom, of all places, and, amid moving-crates and cartons and displaced furnishings, leaps the bed five times. Five days later, May 14, the victim of this passionate attack writes to ask the attacker to "try her luck again on Tuesday, 19th, 4.30" when the Aldingtons and Evelyn Stuart-Moore [née Underhill] will be present' (Davidow, Mary C., 'The Charlotte Mew–May Sinclair Relationship: A Reply', *Bulletin of the New York Public Library*, no. 75 (1971), p. 299). A more recent biographer of May Sinclair, Suzanne Raitt, makes the further point that 'Stern's recollections were recorded several decades after the event, and are not entirely convincing: it is hard to imagine the tight-lipped Sinclair gossiping about such a delicate matter' (Raitt, p. 190). Interestingly, Boll omitted any mention of the incident in his biography of Sinclair (published three years after his article appeared). In *Charlotte Mew and Her Friends*, Penelope Fitzgerald discounts the story of the bedroom chase, as retold by Boll, but pursues the idea of Mew's barely suppressed passion, based only on the awkward exchange of letters between Mew and Sinclair.

51 CMM to Edith Hill, 24 July 1913. Buffalo.

52 MM, p. xx.

53 CPP, p. 363.

54 CMM to CADS, 13 May 1914. Beinecke-MW.

55 CMM to CADS, 26 June 1914. Beinecke-MW.

56 MS to CMM, 13 June 1914. Berg.

57 Details from the dinner are taken from a write-up in *The Globe*, 23 June 1914, p. 8.

58 The 'diary' is in fact a series of letters sent to Mrs Scott's daughter, Marjorie Watts, that contain dated, diary-type entries. Many of these letters form part of a collection called 'C. A. Dawson Scott – Marjorie Watts papers, 1913–1980', from the Yale Collection of American Literature at the Beinecke Rare Book and Manuscript Library, but none of the entries in that collection dates from earlier than 1920. In 1987, Marjorie Watts wrote her own biography of Mrs Scott, in which she quotes extensively from her mother's diary entries for 1913, including the description of Charlotte as a 'pervert'. Similar quotations for corresponding dates had previously appeared in Fitzgerald's 1984 biography, but there they are differently worded. I have been unable to find any archived diary entries for the period preceding 1920.

59 Quoted in Watts, 'Memories of Charlotte Mew', p. 13.

60 Quoted in ibid., pp. 58–9.

61 Quoted in ibid., p. 13.

15 This Dark Ditch, the Soul of Me!

Chapter title: from Mew's poem 'Madeleine in Church'.

1 *Daily Mail*, 5 August 1914, p. 3.

2 *Pall Mall Gazette*, 7 August 1914, p. 5.

3 Information on James Chick's role in the war is from the *Middlesex County Times*, 22 June 1918.

4 Details of Dorothy Chick's war service are from the *Ealing Gazette*, 8 March 1919, p. 3.

5 Boll, Theophilus E. M., *Miss May Sinclair: Novelist* (New Jersey: Associated University Presses, 1973), p. 107.

6 MS to CMM, 24 December 1914. Berg.

7 Mrs Crackanthorpe quoted in Mew's letter to Edith Hill, 4 January 1915. Buffalo.

8 CMM to Edith Hill, 4 January 1915. Buffalo.

9 CMM to CADS, 13 February 1913. Beinecke-MW.

10 CMM to Edith Hill, 4 January 1915. Buffalo.

11 Ibid.

12 Poem enclosed in an undated note from May Sinclair to Charlotte Mew that is headed 'Monday'. By deduction it must have been written in January 1915, after the 6th. Berg.

13 My thanks to Steve Cook for his help with translating these lines.

14 This revised draft of May Sinclair's poem is written in Sinclair's handwriting on notepaper, undated but headed '9, Gordon Street', which suggests it was done while she was at the house with Charlotte Mew, probably in January 1915. Berg.

15 MS to CMM, 6 January 1915. Berg.

16 Ibid.

17 Ibid.

18 CMM to Edith Hill, 24 July 1913. Buffalo.

19 Angela Leighton points out the similarity between Mew's disdain for the parson urging his congregation back to the fold 'like any flock of baa-ing sheep' and Augusta Webster's mockery, in 'The Castaway', of parsons who would 'teach all us wandering sheep . . . to stand in rows / And baa them hymns and moral songs'. *Victorian Women Poets: Writing Against the Heart* (Charlottesville: University of Virginia Press, 1992), p. 285.

20 Florence Hardy to CMM, 2 October 1921, quoted in Davidow, p. 341.

21 *The Bystander*, 31 March 1915, p. 446.

22 MS to CMM, 22 April 1915. Berg.

23 MS to CMM, 16 June 1915. Berg.

24 A plaque in Queen Square announces that 'Although nearly one thousand people slept in the surrounding buildings no person was injured'. Citizens in areas to the east of the city where further bombs fell that night were less fortunate.

25 Hibberd, Dominic, *Harold Monro: Poet of the Age* (Basingstoke: Palgrave, 2001), pp. 162–3.

26 H.D. to Norman Holmes Pearson, 1937, quoted in Tate, Trudi, *Modernism, History and the First World War* (Manchester: Manchester University Press, 1998), p. 25.

27 Pound, Ezra, 'I Gather the Limbs of Osiris', *New Age*, Vol. X, No. 6 (7 December 1911), p. 130.

28 Monro, Harold, 'The Imagists Discussed', *The Egoist*, 1 May 1915, pp. 77–80.

29 MS to CMM, 9 June 1915. Berg.

30 MS to CMM, 16 June 1915. Berg.

31 MS to CMM, 4 July 1915. Berg.

32 MM, p. vii.

33 Ibid.

34 Ibid., p. viii.

16: The New and True Note of Genius

Chapter title: from a review of *The Farmer's Bride* by Gerald Gould in the *Herald*, 5 August 1916.

1 Hibberd, pp. 122–3.

2 From Harold Monro's entries on the first page of the Poetry Bookshop's readings register, January 1913, reproduced in Hibberd, p. 121.

3 Grant, p. 83.

4 Harold Monro writing in the September issue of *Poetry and Drama*, quoted in Grant, p. 108.

5 CMM to Harold Monro, 14 December 1915. Buffalo.

6 MS to CMM, 27 December 1915. Berg.

7 CMM to Harold Monro, 9 February 1916. Buffalo.

8 CPP, p. xiv.

9 *Liverpool Daily Post*, 15 November 1915, p. 8.

10 CMM to Harold Monro, 9 February 1916.

11 CMM to Harold Monro, 4 March 1916. Buffalo.

12 Ibid.

13 CMM to Harold Monro, 9 March 1916. Buffalo.

14 CMM to Harold Monro, 27 April 1916. Buffalo.

15 *The Globe*, 11 May 1916, p. 3.

16 CMM to Paul Lemperly (an American book collector), 31 August 1921. Beinecke-FBA.

17 MM, p. viii.

18 Alida Klemantaski to Harold Monro (no date supplied), quoted in Hibberd, p. 168.

19 Virginia Woolf quoted in Hibberd, p. 130.

20 Arundel Del Re quoted in Grant, p. 91.

21 For more on the utopian colony at Monte Verità in Ascona, see Hibberd, pp. 71–4.

22 Harold Monro to Alida Klemantaski (no date supplied), quoted in Hibberd, p. 132.

23 Harold's days at the Handel Street training barracks did not last long; as soon as he'd passed his gunnery exam he was posted to a gun station at Newton Heath in Manchester.

24 Hassall, Christopher, *Edward Marsh, Patron of the Arts: A Biography* (New York: Harcourt, Brace and Company, 1959), p. 493.

25 'going dead': Mew quotes Monro in her letter to him of 29 July 1916. Buffalo.

26 CMM to Harold Monro, 29 July 1916. Buffalo.

27 Ibid.

28 Ibid.

29 Gerald Gould writing in the *Herald*, 5 August 1916, p. 11.

30 Ibid.

31 MS to CMM, 25 August 1916. Berg.

32 MS to CMM, 4 August 1916. Berg.

33 Ibid.

34 MS to CMM, 25 August 1916. Berg.

35 Richard Aldington to Amy Lowell, 20 November 1917 (Harvard), quoted in
   Vivien Whelpton's *Richard Aldington: Poet, Soldier and Lover 1911–1929*
   (Cambridge: James Clarke and Co. Ltd, 2014), p. 148.

36 MS to CMM, 25 August 1916. Berg.

37 Ibid.

38 H.D. writing in *The Egoist*, Vol. III, No. 9 (September 1916), p. 135.

39 CMM to CADS, 26 February 1917. Beinecke-MW.

40 CMM to CADS, 24 June 1917. Beinecke-MW.

41 MM, p. xiv.

42 CMM to Alida Klemantaski, 29 May 1918. Buffalo.

43 *The Graphic*, 15 December 1923, p. 34.

44 SCC diary entry for Tuesday 11 June 1918. BL Add MS 52655.

45 Blunt, Wilfrid, *Cockerell* (New York: Alfred Knopf, 1964), p. 31.

46 Commenting on a photograph she had received from Sydney Cockerell, Charlotte
   asked, 'Has anyone remarked that, were the centre figure in Tudor dress, – Behold!
   Shakespeare? I saw it at once.' CMM to SCC, 28 December 1921. Berg.

17 Witnesses to the 'Real Thing'

Chapter title: from a letter from Charlotte Mew to Sydney Cockerell, 10 July 1918.
   Berg.

1 Blunt, p. 135.

2 From the published reminiscences of Henry Wood Nevinson, quoted in CMM
   to SCC, 10 November 1923. Berg.

3 From SCC's diary entry for Monday 24 June 1918. BL Add MS 52655.

4 CMM to SCC, 10 July 1918. Berg.

5 Ibid.

6 Ibid.

7 SCC to CMM, 11 July 1918. Berg.

8 CMM to SCC, 14 July 1918. Berg.

9 SCC to CMM, 17 July 1918. Berg.

10 CMM to SCC, 20 July 1918. Berg.

11 An extract copied out in Charlotte Mew's hand from a letter dated 17 July 1918,
   from Wilfrid Blunt to SCC. Berg.

12 Ibid.

13 Wilfrid Blunt went on to write *Cockerell: A Life of Sir Sydney Cockerell* (New York: Alfred Knopf, 1964).

14 From a letter sent from W. S. Blunt to Sydney Cockerell, dated 17 July 1918 and reprinted in Meynell, Viola (ed.), *Friends of a Lifetime: Letters to S. C. Cockerell* (London: Jonathan Cape, 1940), pp. 202ff.

15 A. E. Housman to SCC, 9 September 1918. Beinecke-FBA.

16 Lewis Chase to CMM, 24 August 1918. Berg.

17 CMM to Lewis Chase, 16 September 1918. LC.

18 CMM to Edith Hill, 4 January 1915. Buffalo.

19 'Drilling in Russell Square' by Edward Shanks from *The Oxford Book of Modern Verse 1892–1935*, ed. W. B. Yeats (Oxford: Oxford University Press, 1935), p. 331.

20 CMM to SCC, 15 September 1918. Berg.

21 Florence Hardy to CMM, 24 September 1918. Berg.

22 Ibid.

23 SCC to CMM, 1 October 1918. Berg.

24 From SCC's diary entry for 12 October 1918. BL Add MS 52655.

25 CMM to SCC, 19 May 1919. Berg.

26 Florence Hardy to CMM, 13 October 1918. Berg.

27 Florence Hardy to SCC, 25 October 1918, quoted in *Letters of Emma and Florence Hardy*, ed. Michael Millgate (Oxford: Clarendon Press, 1996), p. 146.

28 *Western Morning News*, 30 November 1918, p. 4.

29 CMM to Florence Hardy, 2 December 1918, quoted in Davidow, pp. 328–9.

30 Florence Hardy to CMM, 3 December 1918, quoted in Davidow, p. 329.

31 Florence Hardy to SCC, 6 December 1918, collected in Meynell, *The Best of Friends*, p. 300.

32 Ibid.

33 CMM to Florence Hardy, 19 December 1918. BMC.

34 CMM to Florence Hardy, 22 December 1918. Berg.

18 I Have Been Through the Gates

Chapter title: from Mew's poem 'I Have Been Through the Gates'.

1 SCC, diary entry for 22 January 1919. BL Add MS 52656.

2 Edith Sitwell to Robert Nichols, 26 February 1919, quoted in Greener (ed.), p. 29.

3 Ibid.

4 Sitwell, Edith, 'Recent Poetry', *The Sackbut*, Vol. II, No. 4 (October 1921), p. 38.

5 Florence Hardy to CMM, 13 April 1919. Berg.

6 Ibid.

7 CMM to Florence Hardy, 14 April 1919. BMC.

8 *Ealing Gazette*, 8 March 1919, p. 3.

9 CMM to Alida Klemantaski, 7 November 1918. Buffalo.

10 Ibid; CMM to Alida (now Monro), 14 December 1920. Buffalo.

11 Alida Klemantaski to Harold Monro, March 1919, quoted in Hibberd, p. 199.

12 SCC to CMM, 8 May 1919. Berg.

13 CMM to SCC, 10 May 1919; it's possible Anne was going to stay in Branscombe with the Chicks, who were still reeling from the sudden death of the youngest sister, thirty-five-year-old Dorothy. Berg.

14 CMM to Edith Hill, 24 July 1913. Buffalo.

15 Quoted in Blunt, pp. 163–4.

16 CMM to SCC, 20 September 1919. Berg.

17 CMM to SCC, 28 August 1919. Berg.

18 CMM to SCC, 2 November 1919. Berg.

19 CMM to SCC, 28 August 1919. Berg.

20 CMM to SCC, 5 December 1920. Berg.

21 CMM to SCC, 28 August 1919. Berg.

22 CMM to SCC, 20 September 1919. Berg.

23 SCC to CMM, 30 August 1919. Berg.

24 CMM to SCC, 28 August 1919. Berg.

25 CMM to CADS, 13 February 1913. Beinecke-MW.

26 CMM to SCC, 1 September 1919. Berg.

27 SCC to CMM, 2 February 1920. Berg.

28 SCC to CMM, 12 April 1920. Berg.

29 CMM to SCC, 14 [or 18?] April 1920. Berg.

30 CMM to CADS, 28 September 1913. Beinecke-MW; CMM to SCC, 23 November 1919. Berg.

31 CMM to SCC, 20 September 1919. Berg.

32 CMM to SCC, 23 November 1919. Berg.

33 CMM to Florence Hardy, 31 October 1919. BMC.

34 *The Globe*, 13 October 1919, p. 2.

35 *Daily Mirror*, 17 September 1918, p. 6.

36 *Western Times*, 7 March 1919, p. 2.

37 The image appeared in the *Illustrated London News* on 19 July 1919, and in *The Graphic* on 9 August 1919.

38 CMM to SCC, 9 November 1919. Berg.

39 CMM to SCC, 2 November 1919. Berg.

40 Mew, 'The Country Sunday', CPP, p. 371.

41 Ibid.

42 Harold Monro to CMM, 20 December 1919. BL Add MS 57755.

43 CMM to Harold Monro, 30 December 1919. Buffalo.

44 Ibid.

45 Ibid. Mew quotes from a letter sent to her from Edward C. Marsh at Macmillan's on 6 May 1919, which states their reasons for turning the book down. Buffalo.

46 Ibid.

47 CMM to Harold Monro, 27 March 1920. Buffalo.

48 CMM to Alida Monro, 28 March 1920. Berg.

49 Hibberd, p. 210.

50 CMM to Harold Monro, 20 July 1920. Buffalo.

51 SCC diary entry for 26 August 1920. BL Add MS 52657.

52 CMM to SCC, 26 September 1920. Berg.

53 CMM to Kate Cockerell, 28 [or 24?] February 1928. Berg.

19 Minuit Sonné and Not Half the Day's Work Done!

Chapter title: from a letter from Charlotte Mew to Sydney Cockerell, 28 December 1921. Berg.

1 CMM to Harold Monro, 27 April 1916. Buffalo.

2 CMM to SCC, 6 February 1921. Berg. (The lines, spoken by Lady Macbeth in an attempt to stop her husband obsessing about the murder of Duncan, are from *Macbeth*, Act 3, Scene 2: 'Things without all remedy / Should be without regard. What's done is done.')

3 CMM to Alida Monro, 24 February 1921. Buffalo.

4 Florence Hardy to CMM, 2 March 1921. Berg.

5 Ibid.

6 CMM to Alida Monro, 24 February 1921. Buffalo.

7 *The Sphere,* 16 April 1921, p. 74.

8 *The Spectator*, 26 March 1921, p. 23.

9 Edith Sitwell in the *Daily Herald*, 4 April 1921.

10 *New York Times*, 19 June 1921.

11 Louis Untermeyer to CMM, 22 July 1921. Berg.

12 Ibid.

13 Louis Untermeyer to CMM, 1 September 1921. Berg.

14 Ibid.

15 Louis Untermeyer to CMM, 19 November 1922. Berg.

16 The poem never did appear in *Broom*. When Mew wrote two years later to ask

for its return, she was unaware that Kreymborg had clashed with the founder over financial and editing issues and was no longer working for the magazine. Mew never placed it elsewhere and it remained unpublished until after her death.

17 CMM to SCC, 8 March 1922. Berg.

18 Louis Untermeyer to CMM, 9 April 1922. Berg.

19 E. V. Knox, 'The Circus Clown', *Punch*, 24 August 1921, p. 146.

20 CMM to SCC, 15 September 1921. Berg.

21 Thomas Hardy to J. C. Squire, 27 January 1922. Quoted in *Thomas Hardy: Collected Letters VI*, p. 113.

22 Swinnerton, Frank, *The Georgian Literary Scene, 1910–1935* (London: J. M. Dent, 1938), p. 207.

23 Quoted in Grant, p. 131.

24 CMM to Ethel Oliver, 8 April 1914. Buffalo.

25 CMM to SCC, 15 September 1921. Berg.

26 CMM to Florence Hardy, 5 October 1921. BMC.

27 CMM to SCC, 18 December 1921. Berg.

28 CMM to SCC, 28 December 1921. Berg.

29 CMM to SCC, 8 March 1922. Berg.

30 CMM to Florence Hardy, 13 October 1921. BMC.

31 Ibid.

32 CMM to SCC, 6 February 1921. Berg.

33 CMM to Kate Cockerell, 3 January 1922. Rosenbach Museum and Library, Philadelphia.

34 Col. Evelyn Gordon to Anna Maria Mew, 24 November 1921, quoted in Davidow (from the records of the Bedford Estate), p. 342.

35 Ibid.

36 Layton's Solicitors to Col. E. B. Gordon, the Bedford Estate, 8 December 1921, quoted in Davidow (from the records of the Bedford Estate), p. 343.

37 CMM to SCC, 18 December 1921. Berg.

38 MM, pp. x–xi.

39 Riborg Fagelund to Philip Oliver, 19 August 1958. Riborg Fagelund was a neighbour of Ethel Oliver when they lived in Isleworth. The letter is owned by Philip's son, Sir Stephen Oliver; in it, Fagelund notes, 'Miss Mew used to visit Ethel when they lived in Isleworth, and there Miss Mew's parrot was buried.'

40 CMM to SCC, 8 March 1922. Berg.

41 Ibid.

42 Ibid.

43 SCC diary entry for Thursday 30 March 1922. BL Add MS 52659.

44 CMM to Kate Cockerell, 9 May 1922. Berg.

45 CMM to SCC, 5 June 1922. Berg.

46 CMM to SCC, 24 May 1922. Berg.

47 CMM to Kate Cockerell, 9 May 1922. Berg.

48 CMM to Alida Monro, 24 February 1921. Buffalo.

49 CMM to Alida Monro, 7 March 1921. Buffalo.

50 CMM to Harold Monro, 31 January 1922. Buffalo.

51 *Literary Digest*, Vol. LXXIII (April–June 1922), p. 38.

52 CMM to SCC, 15 July 1919. Berg.

53 CMM to Kate Cockerell, 14 August 1922. Berg.

54 CMM to SCC, 15 August 1922. Berg.

55 CMM to SCC, 31 October 1922. Berg.

56 CMM to SCC, 9 December 1922. Berg.

57 CMM to Ethel Inglis, 30 November 1922. Berg.

58 A letter to the editor, published in *The Spectator* on 29 September 1922.

59 SCC, diary entry for 14 February 1923. BL Add MS 52660.

60 CMM to SCC, 1 April 1923. Berg.

61 Cockerell, Sydney, 'Testimony and Appeal' from the will of Sydney Cockerell, addressed to Mrs V. Surtees and posted the day after his death, 2 May 1962. (Collected in the Personal and Literary Papers of Virginia Surtees, in the archives of the Durham County Record Office.)

62 CMM to SCC, 1 April 1923. Berg.

63 SCC to CMM, 5 April 1923. Berg.

64 CMM to SCC, 26 April 1923. Berg.

65 CMM to SCC, 10 May 1923. Berg.

66 Anne Mew to SCC, 14 May 1923. Berg.

67 CMM to SCC, 6 February 1921. Berg.

68 Mew's poem appeared on 6 October 1922, in the very first issue of the *New Leader*, which had emerged from the ashes of its debt-ridden predecessor *Labour Leader*, published since 1909. Its editor, H. N. Brailsford, modelled the new journal on *The Nation*, in which Mew's 'The Farmer's Bride' had appeared in 1912. His aim was that, alongside political issues, the paper should also pay attention to developments in the arts and sciences.

20 *This Rare Spirit*

Chapter title: from a letter written to recommend Charlotte Mew for a civil list pension and signed by Walter de la Mare, Thomas Hardy and John Masefield, 13 July 1923. National Archives NA (PREM 5/14).

1   CMM to Kate Cockerell, 24 May 1923. Beinecke-FBA.

2   CMM to Florence Hardy, 26 May 1923. BMC.

3   CMM to SCC, 30 May 1923. Berg.

4   Mew, 'The Poems of Emily Brontë', CPP, pp. 356–69.

5   Florence Hardy to CMM, 18 May 1923. Berg.

6   CMM to SCC, 30 May 1923. Berg.

7   CMM to SCC, 18 June 1923. Berg.

8   CMM to SCC, 2 March 1924. Berg.

9   Sassoon, Siegfried, diary entry for 6 July 1923, quoted in *Siegfried Sassoon Diaries 1923–1925*, ed. Rupert Hart-Davis (London: Faber, 1985), p. 46.

10 John Masefield to SCC, 19 June 1923. NA (PREM 5/14).

11 Walter de la Mare to SCC, 6 July 1923. NA (PREM 5/14).

12 Siegfried Sassoon to SCC, 7 July 1923, collected in Meynell (ed.), *The Best of Friends*, p. 31.

13 The original letter, written in John Masefield's hand and dated, in Sydney Cockerell's hand, 13 July 1923, is held at the National Archives among the papers concerning a civil list application for Mew. NA (PREM 5/14).

14 SCC to CMM, 15 July 1923. Berg.

15 CMM to SCC, 29 July 1923. Berg.

16 From SCC's diary entry for 21 July 1923. BL Add MS 52660.

17 Patrick Gower to H. J. C. Marshall, 25 July 1923. NA (PREM 5/14).

18 CMM to Mrs Filsinger (Sara Teasdale), 5 August 1923. Princeton.

19 Drake, pp. 218–19. (Quotation of a letter from Sara Teasdale to Ernst Filsinger.)

20 *Nottingham Evening Post*, 15 April 1925, p. 3.

21 Anne Mew to SCC, 7 November 1923. NA (PREM 5/14).

22 SCC to CMM, 8 November 1923. Berg.

23 CMM to SCC, 10 November 1923. Berg.

24 *Pall Mall Gazette*, 18 October 1923, p. 3; details of the show itself are from *The Stage*, 11 October 1923, p. 16.

25 SCC to CMM, 12 November 1923. Berg.

26 Ibid.

27 CMM to SCC, 6 December 1923. Berg.

28 From SCC's diary entry for 5 December 1923. BL Add MS 52660.

29 Walter de la Mare to SCC, 11 December 1923, collected in Meynell (ed.), *The Best of Friends*, p. 33.

30 Patrick Gower to CMM, 28 December 1923. NA (PREM 5/14).

31 Siegfried Sassoon to SCC, 3 January 1924, collected in Meynell (ed.), *The Best of Friends*, p. 33.

32 CMM to SCC, 31 December 1923. Berg.

33 Ibid.

34 CMM to Thomas Hardy, 1 January 1924. Dorset County Museum.

35 John Masefield to CMM, undated. Beinecke-FBA.

36 Siegfried Sassoon to CMM, 3 January 1924. Beinecke-FBA.

37 Ibid.

38 CMM to Siegfried Sassoon, 7 January 1924. Beinecke-FBA.

39 Mew, 'Miss Bolt', CPP, p. 346.

40 CMM to SCC, 2 March 1924. Berg.

41 Davidow, pp. 38–9.

42 CMM to SCC, 1 September 1919. Berg.

43 From SCC's diary entry for 4 April 1924. BL Add MS 52661.

44 CMM to Florence Hardy, 6 May 1924. BMC.

45 Ibid.

46 Hibberd, pp. 220 and 228–9.

47 CMM to SCC, 13 July 1924. Berg.

48 CMM to SCC, 1 June 1924. Berg.

49 CMM to SCC, 13 July 1924. Berg.

50 Eliot, T. S., 'A Commentary', *The Criterion*, Vol. III, pp. 1–5.

51 CMM to SCC, 13 July 1924. Berg.

52 CMM to Florence Hardy, 26 May 1923. BMC.

53 Layton's Solicitors to Col. E. B. Gordon, the Bedford Estate, 8 December 1921, quoted in Davidow, p. 343: 'Our client also has to support two other daughters [in addition to Freda] one of whom is very delicate and is a great expense to her.'

54 CMM to CADS, 26 December 1913. Beinecke-MW.

55 From SCC's diary entry for 12 August 1924. BL Add MS 52661.

56 CMM to SCC, 13 August 1924. Berg.

57 Mew, 'Elinor', CPP, p. 284.

58 SCC, diary entry for 7 October 1924. BL Add MS 52661.

59 See Virginia Woolf's diary entry for 17 October 1924: 'Which reminds me I ought to dash in [i.e. put into the diary] Mrs Hardy in a nursing home, having had her tumour cut out, with Miss Charlotte Mew.' *The Diary of Virginia Woolf, Vol. II, 1920–24*, ed. Anne Bell (London: Penguin, 1981), p. 319.

60 Florence Hardy to CMM, undated (sent in the first week of October 1924). Berg.

61 Ibid.

62 CMM to SCC, 5 December 1924 and 1 June 1922. Berg.

63 CMM to SCC, 18 July 1922. Berg.

64 Ibid.

65 Anne Mew to SCC, 7 November 1923. NA (PREM 5/14).

66 CMM to Kate Cockerell, 11 December 1924. Berg.

67 Ibid.

68 Ibid.

69 CMM to Florence Hardy, 2 December 1924. BMC.

70 CMM to Kate Cockerell, 11 December 1924. Berg.

71 Ibid.

72 CMM to SCC, 14 December 1924. Berg.

73 Untermeyer, Louis, *Bygones: The Recollections of Louis Untermeyer* (New York: Harcourt, Brace, 1965), pp. 91–2; although Untermeyer refers to the Charlotte Street studio as 'a dingy room in Bloomsbury', Hogarth Studios were in fact in the Fitzrovia area of London.

74 Untermeyer, Jean Starr, *Private Collection* (New York: Knopf, 1965), pp. 113–14.

21 The Thing Is Found

Chapter title: from Mew's poem 'Moorland Night'.

1 CMM to Florence Hardy, 31 December 1924. BMC.

2 Ibid.

3 Ibid.

4 SCC diary entry for 15 January 1925. BL Add MS 52662.

5 Ibid.

6 See 'Requiescat' and 'The Changeling'.

7 CMM to Florence Hardy, 16 May 1925. BMC.

8 Florence Hardy to CMM, 27 May 1925. Berg.

9 SCC diary entry for 15 June 1925. BL Add MS 52662.

10 Ibid.

11 CMM to Siegfried Sassoon, 4 April 1925. Beinecke-FBA.

12 CMM to Siegfried Sassoon, 29 April 1925. Beinecke-FBA.

13 Siegfried Sassoon to SCC, 8 September 1953, collected in Meynell (ed.), *The Best of Friends*, pp. 224–5.

14 Virginia Woolf to Ottoline Morrell, February 1924, quoted in *Virginia Woolf: Complete Works* (Oregan Publishing, 2018), p. 1,448.

15 CMM to Ottoline Morrell, 8 September 1925. HRC.

16 CMM to SCC, 18 December 1925. Berg.

17 'In Nunhead Cemetery', lines 36–7.

18 CMM to SCC, 22 December 1925. Berg.

19 CMM to Ottoline Morrell, 29 December 1925. HRC.

20 Dorothy Hawksley, *Charlotte Mary Mew* (1926), held at the National Portrait Gallery, London (NPG 3550).

21 CMM to Dorothy Hawksley, 28 April 1926. Beinecke-FBA.

22 *The Sketch*, 5 May 1926, p. 32.

23 *Modern British Poetry*, ed. Louis Untermeyer (New York: Harcourt, Brace, 1925), p. 220.

24 CMM to Professor Sharon Brown, 19 March 1926. Berg.

25 *Western Daily Press*, 27 August 1926, p. 9.

26 Mew, Charlotte, 'Agläe', CPP, p. 308.

27 ibid, p. 323.

28 ibid, pp. 308–9 and 318.

29 ibid, p. 317.

30 ibid, p. 327.

31 CMM to SCC, 22 June 1926. Berg.

32 CMM to Alida Monro, 1 October 1926. Buffalo.

33 CMM to SCC, 8 October 1926. Berg.

34 CMM to Alida Monro, 3 November 1926. Berg.

35 CMM to SCC, 27 November 1926. Berg.

36 Ibid. The 'friend' was Maggie Browne, who lived with her husband Edward in Berkhamsted – actually in Hertfordshire, though close to the Buckinghamshire border.

37 CMM to Alida Monro, 17 December 1926. Berg.

38 See CMM to Alida Monro, 27 April 1927. Berg.

39 SCC to CMM, 28 December 1926. Berg.

40 CMM to SCC, 30 December 1926. Berg.

41 SCC to CMM, 2 January 1927. Berg.

42 CMM to SCC, 3 January 1927. Berg.

43 CMM to SCC, 5 January 1927. Berg.

44 SCC diary entry for 7 January 1927. BL Add MS 52665.

45 SCC diary entry for 19 January 1927. BL Add MS 52665.

46 SCC diary entry for 2 February 1927. BL Add MS 52665.

47 CMM to SCC, 22 February 1927. Berg.

48 Ibid.

49 *The Tatler*, 22 December 1926, p. 31.

50 CMM to SCC, 22 February 1927. Berg.

51 Garnett, David, *Go She Must!* (London: Chatto & Windus, 1927), p. 34.

52 CMM to SCC, 14 April 1927. Berg.

53 CMM to SCC, 14 and 25 April 1927. Berg.

54 CMM to SCC, 8 May 1927. Berg.

55 CMM to Alida Monro, 27 April 1927. Berg.

56 CMM to Alida Monro, 27 May 1927. BL Add MS 83366.

57 Ibid.

58 CMM to Lady Ottoline Morrell, 12 June 1927. HRC.

59 CMM to Lady Ottoline Morrell, 20 June 1927. HRC.

60 Death certificate of Caroline Frances Anne Mew. GRO.

61 SCC to CMM, 22 June 1927. Berg.

62 CMM to SCC, 25 June 1927. Berg.

63 Ibid.

64 Mew, 'The Poems of Emily Brontë', CPP, pp. 359–60.

65 Mew, *The Rambling Sailor*, p. 29.

66 CMM to Kate Cockerell, 24 May 1923. Beinecke-FBA.

67 The quotation is taken from a letter from George Eliot to the Hon. Mrs Robert Lytton (later Lady Lytton) upon the death of Lord Clarendon. It was written on 25 July 1871.

68 Riborg Fagelund to Philip Oliver, 19 August 1958. Davidow collection.

69 CMM to Ottoline Morrell, 4 August 1927. HRC.

70 CMM to SCC, 16 August 1927. Berg.

71 Ibid.

72 *Todmorden Advertiser and Hebden Bridge Newsletter*, 19 August 1927.

73 Blunt, p. 167.

74 Ibid., p. 168.

75 SCC diary entry for 10 October 1927. BL Add MS 52665.

76 CMM to Kate Cockerell, 11 October 1927. Berg.

77 Ibid.

78 CMM to Kate Cockerell, 27 October 1927. Berg.

79 CMM to Kate Cockerell, 21 November 1927. Beinecke-FBA.

80 CMM to SCC, 25 November 1927. Berg.

81 See Davidow, p. 104.

82 Mew, 'An Old Servant', CPP, p. 402.

83 CMM to Lady Ottoline Morrell, 20 June 1927. HRC.

84 Hibberd, p. 259.

85 Information on probates is taken from the entries for Charlotte Mary Mew and Caroline Frances Anne Mew in the *England & Wales National Probate Calendar (Index of Wills and Administrations), 1858–1995*.

86 Will of Charlotte Mary Mew, 3 January 1928. Principal Probate Registry.

87 CMM to SCC, 17 January 1928. Berg.

88 Ibid.

89 CMM to Kate Cockerell, 19 January 1928. Beinecke-FBA.

90 SCC to CMM, 23 January 1928. Berg.

91 Penelope Fitzgerald states that Edward Herne left Charlotte £8,000 but she provides no source. No probate record for Edward Herne Kendall is listed in the *England & Wales National Probate Calendar (Index of Wills and Administrations), 1858–1995*.

92 CMM to Harold Monro, 20 February 1928. Buffalo.

93 CMM to Kate Cockerell, 27 October 1927. Berg.

94 See MM, pp. xi–xii.

95 Ibid., p. xii.

96 Ulrich, R. S., 'View Through a Window May Influence Recovery from Surgery', *Science*, 224 (4647) (1984), pp. 420–1.

97 SCC diary entry for 24 February 1928. BL Add MS 52666.

98 'she died an Anglo-Catholic . . .': Davidow, p. 109.

99 CMM to Elsie Millard, 20 February 1928. Buffalo.

100 CPP, p. 396.

101 CMM to Elsie Millard, 20 February 1928. Buffalo.

102 Quotations in this and the previous sentence are taken from the following letter and poems, listed in order of appearance: CMM to Edith Hill, 24 July 1913 (Buffalo); 'Madeleine in Church'; 'Smile, Death'; 'The Fête'; 'I Have Been Through the Gates' and (again) 'The Fête'.

103 Quotations are from 'Madeleine in Church' and 'Moorland Night', respectively.

104 MM, p. xii.

105 Ibid., p. viii.

106 *Illustrated Police News*, 26 July 1928, p. 8.

107 *Kensington Post*, 30 March 1928, p. 7.

108 Knight, Bernard, *Forensic Pathology*, 2nd edn (London: Hodder Headline, 1996), p. 577.

109 MM, p. xii.

110 Ethel Oliver to Ethel Inglis, 28 March 1928. Berg.

Postscript

1 *The Rambling Sailor*, pp. 7 and 8.

2 *Aberdeen Press and Journal*, 5 August 1929; *Dundee Courier*, 31 May 1929.

3 Arnold Palmer in *The Sphere*, 1 June 1929.

4 *Yorkshire Post*, 12 June 1929; Humbert Wolfe reviewing *The Rambling Sailor* in the *Observer*, 5 September 1929.

5 *The Sphere*, 1 June 1929.

6 Ibid. *Aberdeen Press and Journal*, 5 August 1929; *Yorkshire Post*, 11 December 1929.

7 *Aberdeen Press and Journal*, 5 August 1929.

8 *The Sphere*, 1 June 1929.

9 Details of Mew's funeral are from a letter sent by Elsie Blackman to Sydney Cockerell, 29 March 1928. Buffalo.

10 Amice Lee Macdonell to Mary Davidow, 13 February 1959, quoted in Davidow, p. 359.

11 SPP, p. 21.

12 CMM to Lewis Chase, 16 September 1918. LC.

13 Siegfried Sassoon to Edith Sitwell, 28 March 1928. Berg.

Text Permissions

Index